Table I. Population Statistics for Martinique, 1802–1847

	Whites	Gens de couleur	Slaves	Total
1802(a)	7,000	12,000	90,000	109,000
1803 (b)	10,078	6,254	89,864	106,196
1805 (c)	9,826	6,578	79,754	96,158
1806 (d)	9,877	6,555	80,473	96,905
1807 (e)	9,953	8,616	81,746	100,315
1810 (f)	8,985	7,100	78,528	94,613
1811(f)	9,206	8,630	78,577	96,413
1816(g)	9,298	9,364	80,800	99,462
1821/2(d)	9,867	11,073	77,412	98,279
1826 (g)	9,937	10,786	81,142	101,865
1831 (g)	9,362	14,055	86,499	109,916
1835 (g)	9,000	29,995	78,076	116,031
1839(h)	10,105	30,718	74,333	115,066
1840(h)	9,904 m=5,104 w=4,890	31,742 m=14,373 w=17,369	76,503	118,149
1841(h)	10,362 m=5,296 w=5,066	32,319 m=13,664 w=18,665	75,225	117,906
1843(h)	8,887 m=4,278 w=4,609	35,706 m=15,570 w=20,136	75,736	120,329
1844(h)	9139 m=4,476 w=4,663	36,626 m=16,050 w=20,576	76,117	121,882
1845(h)	9,219 m=4,488 w=4,731	37,213 m=16,249 w=20,964	76,042	122,474
1846(h)	9,606 m=4,674 w=4,932	37,746 m=16,787 w=20,959	75,339	122,691
1847(h)	9,542 m=4,451 w=5,091	38,729 m=17,071 w=21,658	72,859	121,130

Sources: (a) ADM, CG, C8A105, 1802, Grand Judge Lefessier-Grandpré, November 21, 1802 correspondence; (b) CAOM, C8B25, *Decisions et Rapports, 1804, Aperçu général de la situation de la Martinique pendant l'administration de M. Bertin*; (c) Liliane Chauleau, *Dans les îles du vent: La Martinique (XVII–XIXe siècle)* (Paris: L'Harmattan, 1993), 213; (d) Abbé Bernard David, "La Population d'un quartier de la Martinique au début du XIXe siècle d'après les registres paroissiaux: Rivière-Pilote, 1802-1829," *Revue française d'histoire d'outre-mer* 60, 220 (3rd trimester 1973): 337, 340, 347; (e) CAOM, C8B25, 1807 Census; (f) PRO WO 1:42, 1811, part 2, December 19, 1811, "Report upon the State of the Island of Martinique"; (g) Léo Elisabeth, "The French Antilles," in *Neither Slave Nor Free: The Freedman of African Descent in the Slave Societies of the New World*, ed. David W. Cohen and Jack P. Greene (Baltimore: Johns Hopkins University Press, 1972), 151; (h) *Tableaux et relevés de population, de cultures, de commerce, de navigation, etc. formant la suite des tableaux et relevés insérés dans les notices statistiques sur les colonies françaises* (Paris: Imprimerie Royale, 1840, 1841, 1842, 1843, 1844, 1845, 1846, 1847, 1848).

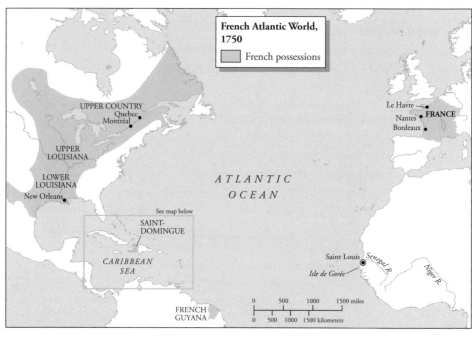

French Atlantic World, 1750

◻ French possessions

UPPER COUNTRY
Québec
Montréal

UPPER LOUISIANA

LOWER LOUISIANA
New Orleans

See map below

SAINT-DOMINGUE

CARIBBEAN SEA

FRENCH GUYANA

ATLANTIC OCEAN

Le Havre
Nantes **FRANCE**
Bordeaux

Saint Louis *Senegal R.*
Isle de Gorée

Niger R.

0   500   1000   1500 miles
0   500   1000 1500 kilometers

French Caribbean Sea, 1750

◻ French possessions

Gulf of Mexico

ATLANTIC OCEAN

CUBA

SAINT-DOMINGUE
Le Cap
SANTO DOMINGO
PUERTO RICO
ST. THOMAS
ST. MARTIN
ST. BARTHÉLEMY

JAMAICA
Port-au-Prince

ST. CHRISTOPHER
GUADELOUPE
MARIE-GALANTE
DOMINICA

CARIBBEAN SEA

MARTINIQUE
ST. LUCIA
ST. VINCENT
BARBADOS

CURAÇAO
GRENADA
TOBAGO
TRINIDAD

VENEZUELA

0   150   300 miles
0   150   300 kilometers

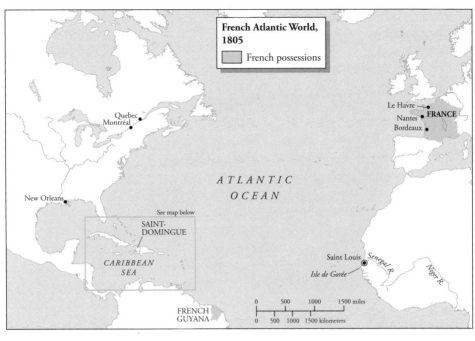

French Atlantic World, 1805

French possessions

Quebec
Montréal

Le Havre
Nantes FRANCE
Bordeaux

New Orleans

See map below

SAINT-
DOMINGUE

ATLANTIC OCEAN

CARIBBEAN SEA

Saint Louis Senegal R.
Isle de Gorée   Niger R.

FRENCH
GUYANA

0   500   1000   1500 miles
0   500 1000 1500 kilometers

French Caribbean Sea, 1805

French possessions

*Gulf
of
Mexico*

ATLANTIC OCEAN

CUBA

Le Cap
SAINT-DOMINGUE SANTO
DOMINGO

ST. THOMAS

PUERTO
RICO

ST. MARTIN
ST. BARTHÉLEMY

JAMAICA Port-au-Prince

ST. CHRISTOPHER
GUADELOUPE

MARIE-
GALANTE

DOMINICA

CARIBBEAN SEA

MARTINIQUE
ST. LUCIA
ST. VINCENT

BARBADOS

CURAÇAO

GRENADA

TOBAGO

TRINIDAD

0   150   300 miles
0   150   300 kilometers

VENEZUELA

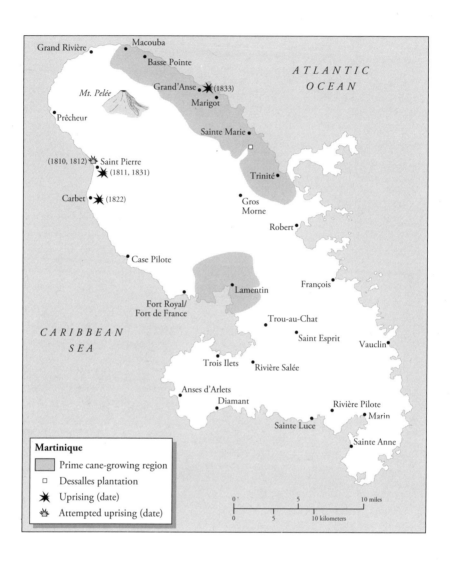

Grand Rivière

Macouba

Basse Pointe

Mt. Pelée

Grand'Anse ✹ (1833)

Marigot

Prêcheur

Sainte Marie

□

(1810, 1812) ✹ Saint Pierre

(1811, 1831) ✹

Trinité

Carbet ✹ (1822)

Gros
Morne

Robert

*ATLANTIC
OCEAN*

Case Pilote

François

Fort Royal/
Fort de France

Lamentin

*CARIBBEAN
SEA*

Trou-au-Chat

Saint Esprit

Vauclin

Trois Ilets

Rivière Salée

Anses d'Arlets

Diamant

Rivière Pilote

Marin

Sainte Luce

Sainte Anne

Martinique

▨ Prime cane-growing region

□ Dessalles plantation

✹ Uprising (date)

✹ Attempted uprising (date)

0 · · · · · 5 · · · · · 10 miles

0 · · · · · 5 · · · · · 10 kilometers

Sweet Liberty:

The Final Days of Slavery in Martinique

EVERY DAY THE Boeings and Airbuses land at Martinique's Lamentin International Airport near Fort-de-France.[1] From the planes descend the tourists, most of them French, who provide the lifeblood of Martinique's economy; for this island, which for so long pumped the bounty of the "white gold" sugar into France's coffers, now depends almost entirely on tourists to sustain it. Once an island peopled by a multitude of enslaved Africans and the cadre of elites who battened on them, Martinique still houses hundreds of thousands of descendants of those enslaved workers. The once mighty elite families have largely gone, succeeded by the expatriates—hoteliers, chefs, shopkeepers, the ambitious, and the simply restless—that scatter themselves across the islands of France's once global empire.

All this stands in stark contrast to the times that began almost 400 years ago, when the Frenchmen came in ships to seek their fortunes, not in planes to share them. In 1635 Pierre Belan d'Esnambuc, a nobleman from Normandy, and approximately one hundred other French Europeans established a settlement on the northwestern coast of Martinique for the Company of the American Islands, the commercial firm holding rights to the French West Indies. With its rich volcanic soil, tropical climate, varied topography, and easy access to the sailing winds of the Lesser Antilles, the island seemed an ideal location for growing a variety of cash crops. D'Esnambuc and his contingent hoped to capitalize on the island's fertility.[2]

Over the next several years, white *engagés* (European indentured servants) of both sexes who contracted for three years in exchange for passage to the

West Indies cleared the dense forests and planted cotton and tobacco in the northern part of the 22 by 50 mile island.[3] By the early 1640s, however, Dutch success in sugarcane cultivation in Brazil, and a Dutch trader's willingness to share his knowledge with Martinique's planters, impelled settlers to invest in the remarkably lucrative crop. Soon thereafter planters brought in enslaved male and female Africans to work the growing number of sugarcane fields. In 1664, encouraged by the potential for profit, Louis XIV issued a royal edict establishing the French West India Company and placing all France's North American and Caribbean territories under royal control. By that time Martinique had grown to approximately 5,400 inhabitants, more than half of them enslaved Africans.[4]

Martinique's economic viability, along with that of Guadeloupe and Saint Domingue (France's other West Indian holdings), became increasingly linked to sugar production for metropolitan consumption in the early eighteenth century. In response Martinican planters converted the vast majority of the island's roughly 425 cultivable square miles to cane cultivation. The nature of sugar as a crop—labor intensive; year-round; best suited to large fields; requiring a mix of field labor and industrial processing that called for onsite supervision, not absentee landlords—henceforth dictated the pyramidal nature of Martinican society. Planters replaced *engagés* with enslaved Africans.[5] Consequently as a general rule only the tens of thousands of *nègres*—enslaved Africans—worked the fields of the few thousand *colons*—rich Creole planters—who in turn aligned themselves with the colonial officials sent from continental France to run the island.[6] *Petits blancs*—former indentured servants and other poor whites who made up the majority of the white population—and the growing number of *gens de couleur*—mixed-race individuals manumitted or born free—took over the island's artisanal jobs.

By midcentury Martinique, like many of the neighboring British and Spanish islands, became a pawn in the endless chess game of European powers. It passed briefly into British hands during the Seven Years War (1762–1763), then back into French hands (1764–1794), and then again to the British during the French Revolution (1794–1802). For the island's inhabitants shifts to British rule meant new administrators empowered to change existing laws and potentially Martinique's social hierarchy. Unlike in nearby Guadeloupe and Saint Domingue where the French Republic abolished slavery during the Revolution, the British maintained the system in Martinique. As a result, despite initial disputes between the island's *petits blancs* and Creoles, Martinique remained relatively stable. In Saint Domingue, on the other hand, enslaved Africans, whites, and *gens de couleur* battled one another for control of the island, and in Guadeloupe formerly enslaved people fought royalists to earn their rights as *nouveaux citoyens* (new citizens). In 1802 Napoleon Bonaparte ordered slavery reestablished throughout the French Caribbean and, in the same year, Martinique passed back into French hands and the control of three French metropolitan officials. Although France finally returned Guadeloupe's formerly enslaved population to the fields through brute force in May 1803, Saint Domingue's inhabitants won their legal and political freedom by establishing the new nation of Hayti in January 1804.[7]

The loss of Saint Domingue left Martinique as France's largest and most productive sugar-producing island in the Caribbean, a treasure almost beyond price with the largest enslaved and free population in the region. This book, a history of Martinique from French reacquisition of the island in 1802 to the abolition of slavery in 1848, chronicles the complicated social relationships on the island during those years and argues the ways race, slavery, class, and gender intersected in Martinique shaped what it meant to be French in the early nineteenth century, not just in Martinique and the Caribbean but in continental France as well.

Martinique's continued status as a slave-holding colony in the first half of the nineteenth century offers a good opportunity to examine the complex interplay between rhetoric and lived experience during the last fifty years of slavery in the French Empire. This book draws on a variety of public sources (court records, official correspondence, colonial budgets, administrative decrees, civil records, newspapers), and private papers (diaries, letters, and inventories) to reconstruct the complicated social and cultural terrain in which the plantation system and the abolitionist movement developed on both sides of the French Atlantic.[8] Martinicans and their fellow citizens in metropolitan France used a complex language (Creoles, *petits blancs*, *gens de couleur*, and *nègres*) to identify differences in racial, economic, gender, and national status. But to contemporaries such terms not only described categories of people but also referenced the intricate and multiple interweavings of such categories. This study deals with how people around the French Atlantic defined, challenged, and policed the legal, social, political, and cultural meanings of labels like "Creole," "French," or "*gens de couleur*." Their confrontations over those meanings ultimately shaped not only their own individual lives but also the contours of the French Empire in the Atlantic.

Over four decades individual and group efforts in Martinique and continental France changed what it meant to be black, white, or mixed-race, rich or poor, male or female, French or not. Those shifting configurations often made for strange bedfellows in the early nineteenth-century French Atlantic, alternately aligning groups across racial, economic, and sometimes even legal (free versus enslaved) boundaries depending on the needs of the moment. To get at this complex story requires combining approaches from the histories of racial, gender, and colonial studies. Because the processes I describe were transatlantic, I engage the very different historical literatures of Martinique, the broader Caribbean, nineteenth-century France, and the Atlantic World.[9] Using such an approach shows that events in Martinique and the relationship between Martinique and metropolitan France changed the way individuals in both places used race to understand themselves, one another, and what it meant to be French.[10] In addition, it reveals that scholars must look closely at the similarities and differences among the region's many islands to gain a better understanding of the broader Caribbean during this period.[11] The history of early nineteenth-century France, and particularly the connection between the French empire and national identity, also requires serious consideration of the impact of tensions in the French West Indies during the last decades of slavery.[12] What it meant to be French between 1802 and 1848 resulted in part from the persistence of race-based slavery in places like Martinique and also the presence of Creoles as well as enslaved and free people of African descent in metropolitan France.[13] As the period progressed, and especially after the French crown granted political rights to the realm's *gens de couleur* in the early 1830s, debates over French national identity increasingly intersected with those about racial identity, and especially those concerning what it meant to be white.[14] Furthermore, because literal freedom ultimately remained linked to white women's sexuality in plantation societies like Martinique, debates about race and nation also combined with discussions about appropriate behavior for France's men and women.[15]

The book that follows examines the final decades of slavery in the French Empire by exploring how Martinican individuals and groups (Creole and metropolitan elites, *petits blancs*, *gens de couleur*, and enslaved Africans) interacted with one another in a constantly shifting political environment and by tracing how these interactions influenced the colony's relationships with, and debates about identity and citizenship in, the broader French Atlantic. During this nearly fifty-year period, Martinique and its inhabitants frequently changed national hands—moving from the French to the British and back again to the French. They also experienced a variety of political regimes—changing from a republic to an empire to a conservative and then a more liberal monarchy. With each shift came new colonial administrators and new policies, all of which provided individuals and groups with an opportunity to redefine racial, class, gender, and national identities. Such fluidity placed Martinicans of all backgrounds on unstable ground, compelling those in positions of power to push harder to maintain the status quo and encouraging others to better their individual and collective positions. In practice this meant all inhabitants helped to shape the island's social, racial, and economic hierarchy, in small ways on a daily basis and in significant ways at particular moments, be it the arrival of a new governor, a local uprising of enslaved workers, or implementation of a new law concerning the plantation system.

I have organized the six chapters that follow chronologically rather than thematically to best show how French on both sides of the Atlantic responded to and helped facilitate these specific historical moments. I also have chosen a chronology that emphasizes the most important moments for my argument rather than one that directly corresponds with more traditional breaks in nineteenth-century French political history. In doing so, I intend to highlight how the history of the French colonies and French imperial policy intersects with that of continental France and how it might make us re-think more conventional periodizations. By focusing my narrative around issues common in the broader Caribbean (like shifts in national sovereignty, fights between colonial administrators on both sides of the Atlantic and island inhabitants, and laws concerning citizens' civil and political rights), I also work to underscore the Atlantic World dimensions of this project.

From the moment that France regained control of Martinique from Great Britain in 1802, the island's elites struggled to unite a white population that found itself severely outnumbered and plagued by internal dissensions. Of the roughly 10,000 whites living in Martinique throughout this period, at most 3,000 large-scale planters and high-placed officials ranked among the island's elite. However they also divided between Creoles born in the West Indies and colonial officials sent from Paris (or London during the British occupation) to administer the island. These two groups constantly negotiated with each other, at times aligning, at other moments at odds. Their contestations revealed neither skin color alone nor elite social standing sufficed to build consensus. Debates *between* Creoles and colonial administrators also illuminate the fragility of the colonial state in nineteenth-century Martinique.[16] The fact that France could maintain slavery until 1848, of course, demonstrates a certain minimal strength; nonetheless, conflicts between Creole officials and colonial officials on both sides of the Atlantic show the limits authorities faced when trying to implement metropolitan policies and the persistent power of local Creoles.[17]

Divisions *among* those officials sent from continental France to run the island further underscore the incoherence of the French colonial state and the ad-hoc nature of colonial policymaking. Administrators often disagreed on how closely they should align themselves, both personally and politically, with the island's white plantocracy and frequently fought over the appropriate boundaries of their respective positions. Throughout the Napoleonic (1802–1815) and Restoration (1815–1830) periods, elite Creoles usually joined with colonial administrators in policing the behavior of elite white women and nonelite whites in general. During the July Monarchy (1830–1848), however, Martinique's Creoles increasingly voiced their dissatisfaction with merchants and shopkeepers originally from the continent who called the island home and with colonial officials sent from metropolitan France to implement new reforms on the island. Although these administrators arrived with explicit instructions to change the status quo, many appeared just as skeptical of the reforms as Martinique's Creoles and often refused to effectively enforce new measures. With the increased turnover in officials beginning in the mid-1830s, such inconsistency created even more strife among these administrators and between them and Creoles who hoped each governor would take their side but feared he might not.

Elite Creoles also struggled between, on the one hand, more closely aligning themselves with the nation in charge at the moment, often to reap the economic benefits of that alliance, and, on the other hand, arguing that the ruling power should recognize the island as exceptional and thus exempt Creoles from laws that disadvantaged them. This argument went hand in hand with their desire to maintain white hegemony on the island and to dictate appropriate behavior for the island's white inhabitants. Race-based slavery of the kind that flourished in the Caribbean and the southern United States up to the mid-nineteenth century shaped gender identities and gender ideology.[18] For Martinique's *colons* using their positions on the island's administrative and judicial councils to craft and uphold ideals of white behavior for men and women seemed the surest way to strengthen white social status. In practice this meant, despite the shifting political and social terrain and their eroding power and control, Creoles repeatedly turned to private schools, charity bureaus, and the courts to reaffirm white superiority, often working within the letter, if not the spirit, of the law to hold onto their former racial and social power.

From the time of Martinique's establishment in the seventeenth century, the island's *colons* had struggled to convince themselves, and others, that all of the island's white inhabitants came from "good stock." As part of that effort, they crafted an ideal of white masculinity that presumed plantocrat status; it posited all white men as loving fathers and faithful spouses within stable white households, men who unquestioningly provided for their families' comfortable lifestyle and had an appropriate level of education. To delimit the boundaries of whiteness and shore up elite identity, elite whites also created and trumpeted an ideal of white womanhood that cast them as the physical guardians of white purity and as custodians of the cultural markers of white identity.[19] Elite Creoles, male and female, especially promoted a racialized ideal of female sexual honor and economic leisure. In practice this meant that white women should have only marital sex and then only with white men. It also required that white women eschew work in favor of a life of relative financial ease, focused on mothering.

Despite such prescriptions, the survival of the plantation system required white Martinican women to take an active role in many aspects of colonial life. As a result elite Creoles here, as in other colonial contexts, simultaneously had to argue that elite white women did not and should not work while in fact counting on these women to manage enslaved workers, negotiate with local creditors of all racial backgrounds, and otherwise assist in family business affairs. Consequently, elite white Martinican women played important practical as well as symbolic roles in the structure and daily operation of Martinican society. Portraying these women as autonomous actors produces a more complex account of nineteenth-century French colonialism and reveals the various ways they both maintained and undermined proslavery values and institutions.

Despite this reality, because in Martinique, as in most slave societies, children inherited the legal status of their mothers (legally free women had free children, enslaved women bore enslaved offspring), elites focused particularly on controlling white women's sexual behavior. Those white Martinican women, and especially elites, who participated in interracial sexual affairs or bore children out of wedlock presented a significant threat to white hegemony by contributing to the growth of Martinique's *gens de couleur* population and raising questions about the purity of Creole blood. In the eyes of many metropolitan French in Martinique and on the continent, even elite Creoles bore *la tâche de sang mêlé*, the stain of mixed blood, that marked them as somehow less civilized, and therefore less French, than their metropolitan counterparts. As Creoles' formal power waned in the July Monarchy maintaining the myth that white women only had sex with their white husbands became increasingly important as a marker of Creole status. By the same token questioning an elite white woman's sexual virtue became a way to discredit possible marriage partners, political opponents, and even economic competitors.

The elite ideals of white masculinity and femininity set up many Martinicans for inevitable failure. Because of its economic imperatives, it specifically en-sured that those known as *petits blancs* could not possibly qualify as truly white based on the elite criteria. Yet the vast majority of Martinique's white inhabitants, the *petits blancs*, numbered somewhere between 4,000 and 7,000 and belonged to strata elsewhere known as the popular and middle classes. The colonial context, however, obscured such distinctions. Because elite white colonial planters created the category to exclude anyone they felt unsuited to their group, it numbered not only male and female physical laborers—farmers, carpenters, blacksmiths, cooks, bakers, masons, laundresses—but also small businessmen and -women—boutique owners, hatmakers, dressmakers, sta-tioners, clerks, petty shopkeepers, and even pharmacists. These *petits blancs* played an essential role in the business of tropical cash-crop agriculture be-cause, along with many *gens de couleur*, this group formed the backbone of the island's service industries. Consequently elite prototyping could not wish these worthies away.

Through their mere existence, however, Martinique's poorer whites threatened elite ideals of white masculinity and femininity and challenged elite ideologies about how plantation society should function. For this reason elites tried to use charitable, educational, and judicial institutions to control Martinique's *petit blancs*, and especially those seeking financial help or openly consorting with the island's *gens de couleur*. While they ultimately looked to uplift all whites to make the myth of ideal white behavior a reality, elite Creoles also used *petits blancs* as convenient scapegoats, blaming these per-ceived male and female inferiors, common color or no, for the downfall of white colonial society. Of course not only *petits blancs* struggled financially or participated in interracial relationships. Elite white planters, despite living evidence to the contrary, nonetheless publicly blamed the island's mixed race population on Martinique's *petits blancs*, all the while maintaining a veil of silence about their own relationships. Denial absolved elites from responsibil-ity for the growing mixed-race population or the degeneration of the island's colonial whites, thus preserving elites' sense of self and their class-specific definition of whiteness.

Although faced with almost constant efforts to constrain them, Mart-inique's *petits blancs* developed personal and professional relationships with a variety of individuals elites deemed inappropriate. And they did so, often repeatedly, despite institutions that denied them economic help and judicial bodies that punished them for such behavior. As Martinique's elites felt more under siege from metropolitan authorities during the July Monarchy, other *petits blancs* also used the same institutions to gain footing against free mixed-race people whom they thought received unfair privileges. The varied actions of these whites illustrate that different actors had different understandings of just what constituted whiteness in Martinique and often defied prescribed ideals. Such behavior also reinforces Cooper and Stoler's claim that "we can certainly not understand the construction of whiteness . . . without exploring its class dimensions."[20]

In a further effort to solidify white hegemony on the island, Martinique's elites also tried to thwart any social, legal, or economic advancement by the island's *gens de couleur*. By the time France regained control of Martinique in 1802, nearly 150 years of racial mixing had made it more and more difficult to distinguish the approximately 10,000 *gens de couleur* on the island solely on the basis of skin color. Many administrators and elite *colons* feared that without skin color as a viable visual demarcation, the supposedly impermeable boundaries between races and classes would disintegrate, heralding the downfall of the colony. Consequently elite Creoles and officials worked hard to thwart any such melding. Despite their efforts, the island's mixed race population grew steadily throughout the Napoleonic and Restoration periods and then mushroomed during the July Monarchy. By 1848 approximately 36,000 free mixed-race individuals called the island home and their ranks included day laborers, members of the artisanal classes, merchants, and even some small plantation owners. As with the island's *petits blancs*, their different economic positions created divergent interests and meant they had competing goals.

Nonetheless Martinique's white plantocracy in general preferred to ignore such differences and focused instead on the *gens de couleur*'s shared African background. Not surprisingly, the inability to determine an individual's racial status, and the dire speculations that stemmed from that uncertainty, dated back to the early eighteenth century. As a result, as in many other slaveholding societies, Martinicans developed a complex system of classification over the years to identify individuals based on skin color. At least seven different categories prevailed during the final days of slavery. The *blanc*, or white, sat at the top of the racial hierarchy and supposedly descended from "pure" whites. The *noir*, or black, anchored the ladder and had only other blacks as ancestors. In between at least five different categories distinguished one's proximity to the presumed racial purity of the white on top: the *quarteron*, the descendant of a *mestive* and a white; the *mestif*, the offspring of a *mulâtresse* and a white; the *mulâtre*, the descendant of a white and a black; the *câpre*, the offspring of a *mulâtresse* and a *nègre*; and the *grife*, a descendant of a *câpresse* and a *nègre*.[21] During the eighteenth century, those manumitted through military service, self-purchase, or by their owners became known as the *gens de couleur.*

Although the island's legally manumitted *gens de couleur* technically qualified as free citizens, their growing numbers, status, and opportunity to pass as whites nevertheless drove members of the powerful Creole-controlled courts, advisory councils, and even Creole-influenced governors to deny them civil and social rights.[22] A series of decrees and ordinances ensued that in 1764 forbade free mixed-race people from practicing surgery, pharmacy, or medicine; in 1765 prohibited them from working as or serving the island's bailiffs, notaries, or clerks of court, and further banned them from gathering in large crowds;[23] in 1773 barred them from taking the names of any whites on the island;[24] and in 1774 directed all *gens de couleur* bearing the names of white Martinicans to inform local authorities of both their current name, which they had to abandon, and the name they would use in the future.[25] In 1779 "the decrease in distance between the general appearances" of free mixed-race people and white Martinicans prompted a law prohibiting *gens de couleur* from wearing clothing, hairstyles, or other finery worn by whites[26] and a 1781 decree enjoined island officials from using the term "Monsieur" or "Madame" when referring to *gens de couleur* in official documents.[27] Such measures combined with other informal pressures significantly limited the opportunities of this population.

In 1791 free mixed-race individuals who met the requirements, and then in 1792 all *gens de couleur* throughout the French realm, theoretically gained political rights.[28] Technically, Martinique's *gens de couleur* also enjoyed such liberties. When the British took control of the island in 1794, however, they abolished such privileges. On regaining the island in 1802 the French vigorously sought to return Martinique's free mixed-race population to its pre-revolutionary status. As the *gens de couleur* grew in numerical strength throughout the first half of the nineteenth century, however, elites became increasingly concerned about the white community's precarious demographic and economic position. They further worried about the close physical proximity between Martinique's *petits blancs* and *gens de couleur* in the artisanal trades and also about the concentration of free mixed-race individuals in the island's commercial center, Saint Pierre, and administrative capital, Fort Royal. To maintain white control, Creole and metropolitan elites thus used Martinique's administrative and judicial bodies to stymie any social or legal advancements for free mixed-race individuals. During the 1830s, however, and especially after the French government officially extended full civil rights to France's *gens de couleur* in 1833, Creoles and metropolitan administrators increasingly parted ways over treatment of these new citizens.

Martinique's *gens de couleur*, for their part, struggled to participate in the limited openings available to them. When possible they took advantage of economic opportunities, securing charitable assistance and new professional opportunities. When legislation made it available, they also fought for access to private and public education and eventually the right to vote and hold office. Through letters, pamphlets, petitions, and the courts, both in Martinique and continental France, they sought to ensure their rights as full French citizens and reap the benefits afforded to members of the French nation. Although many worked within legal boundaries to gain their rights, others participated in secret conspiracies or took violently to the streets. That they did so at times with other free mixed-race Martinicans, at other moments with members of Martinique's enslaved community, and even on occasion with *colons* and *petits blancs* simply underscores the shifting salience of racial, class, and national identities throughout the period.

Enslaved African laborers comprised the majority of Martinique's population and, not surprisingly, debates about their status and their actions factored prominently during the final fifty years of slavery. In 1696 they numbered 13,126 of a total population of 20,066[29] and immediately preceding emancipation in 1848 they still accounted for 67,447 of Martinique's 120,357 inhabitants.[30] Like elsewhere in the Caribbean, the vast majority of these enslaved individuals toiled on coffee, indigo, or sugar plantations in the island's rural areas. By the early nineteenth century others worked primarily as day laborers in Fort Royal or Saint Pierre and, in exchange for a fee paid to their masters, they experienced a degree of mobility. These *negrès de journée* (day negroes) or *nègres à loyer* (negroes for hire), as many urban enslaved workers were called, also included an indeterminate number of people of African descent known as *libres de fait* or *patronés*. This group occupied a particularly complicated position on the island. In practice many of these workers had achieved a level of personal freedom and independence from their masters; however, because their masters often refused to pay the steep manumission tax that accompanied the freeing of an enslaved person, legally they remained property.

Island officials had relied on this manumission tax to stem what they perceived as an unacceptable increase in the number of legal manumissions since the early eighteenth century. The Edict of 1685, also known as the Code Noir, had provided few legal paths to obtaining freedom from slavery. Article 9 stipulated when an enslaved woman married her master, she and any children from the union would become free. However, Article 13, designed to protect a master's rights, declared marriage insufficient to gain freedom. These articles came into conflict time and again throughout the course of the eighteenth century; consequently local administrators individually interpreted how marriage related to manumission. Article 55 of the Code Noir also provided for manumission. It officially decreed that masters could manumit any enslaved individual over the age of twenty without the consent of the government and without offering a reason for manumission, although owners still had to pay a steep manumission tax. Nevertheless, as early as 1713 the king forbade manumission without the express consent of the governor of the island.[31]

In response to such difficulties, by mid-century a number of planters sent their enslaved workers abroad to be freed or obtained foreign freedom certificates for them.[32] Many others simply granted their slaves de facto freedom and ignored the manumission tax. As a result, by the early nineteenth century Martinique's *patroné* population came to play an important role in the social dynamics on the island. And, as in many plantation societies, the freed included women, a number of whom had established personal, and often intimate, relationships with their white male owners.[33] These women increasingly worried the island's elite, who saw in them tangible evidence of the reality and dangers of racial mixing in Martinique.

In order to maintain white dominance on the island, Martinique's elites worked to control this diverse enslaved population at all costs. They continued to deny enslaved Africans basic necessities like food, clothing, religious and educational training, even during the July Monarchy when direct laws demanded such changes. They also created extrajudicial councils to try those accused of poisoning people and animals, meting out horrific punishments to any found guilty and deporting those deemed too troublesome. Repeatedly elite whites argued that any ameliorations to the plantation system would mean the downfall of their community both in the Caribbean and in continental France. To the bitter end many frequently insisted enslaved Africans were nothing more than property while simultaneously participating in intimate relationships with enslaved men and women.

Despite such brutal measures, Martinique's enslaved community nonetheless strove individually and in groups to resist exploitation and take advantage of any social and political openings. When the French or British granted amnesty, many took it. Many also worked outside of legal channels to better their positions. Some ran away. Some participated in organized rebellions with other enslaved individuals or *gens de couleur* or joined in illegal business ventures. Some poisoned animals and humans. Others managed to gain their freedom whether through commitment to their owners, their own industriousness, the dictates of the courts, or changing legislation.

Because many in France's Atlantic port cities and Paris had extensive personal and professional links with the island, Martinicans' daily struggles to shape the island's social and racial hierarchy also reverberated nearly 3,000 miles across the Atlantic in continental France. After the loss of Saint Domingue in 1804, Martinique became France's most important Caribbean holding and, consequently, a decline in the price of sugar, an uprising of enslaved workers in the commercial center of Saint Pierre, or a revolt by *gens de couleur* near Grand'Anse affected those on the island as well as business associates, family members, and political leaders in metropolitan France. As the plantation system came to an end, Martinicans and their supporters on the continent joined a growing chorus of voices questioning the parameters of the French Empire and of French national identity.

The physical presence of colonists visiting and resident in metropolitan France further called into question what role the colony and colonists of all backgrounds played in the French nation and highlighted two separate but interconnected issues: the colony's future economic relationship with metropolitan France and the role race would play in the definition of French national identity. Elite Creole men and women frequently traveled back and forth between the French West Indies and continental France on personal and business matters. Elite white women played especially important roles during these trips, often staying in the metropole for extended periods to guarantee educational and professional opportunities for their children and to negotiate with creditors in places like Bordeaux, Nantes, and Paris. While there they also helped to establish a network of Creoles that provided essential social, economic, and political support as the century progressed.[34] From its beginnings in the Napoleonic period as an informal group of Creole families, largely connected by blood and money, and throughout the Restoration, elite Creoles grew into an organized cohort of proslavery advocates who mobilized the press to defend against attacks on the supposed "barbarism" of French colonials and their status as French nationals. By the late Restoration and early July Monarchy, the network had expanded into a well-financed French West Indian colonial lobby that played a significant role in French politics. In the early 1830s the lobby argued against extending rights to the realm's *gens de couleur* and, after losing that fight, in the late 1830s they increasingly turned their attention to thwarting the abolitionist movement, which they framed as an assault against the property rights of French (colonial) citizens. At a moment when the July Monarchy struggled to affirm the sanctity of property and the virtues of a laissez faire economy, such claims, combined with the government's increased oversight of the plantation system in general, called into question the regime's sincerity.

The presence of enslaved and free people of African descent in France's capital and Atlantic port cities made these debates even more contentious. Both enslaved Africans and *gens de couleur* had called continental France home since the eighteenth century, a fact that had long troubled metropolitan officials. To better monitor this population of African descent, on August 9, 1777, metropolitan officials enacted the Declaration pour la police des Noirs (Police des Noirs), which attempted to prevent the future entry of all "blacks, mulattoes, and other people of color," into metropolitan French territory.[35] In order to let colonists bring their enslaved domestic servants with them, supposedly only for use on the trip across the ocean, the law did allow one *noir* or *mulâtre*, male or female, to accompany a free person to metropolitan France; however that free person had to provide the treasurer of the colony with 1,000 livres to guarantee the return of the *noir* or *mulâtre*.[36] In 1778 an *arrêt du conseil* required those of African descent in the metropole to carry *cartouches*, or identity cards, and another banned interracial marriages to help prevent the "stain of mixed blood" on French metropolitan soil.[37]

By the nineteenth century, enslaved people in Paris and Atlantic port cities called into question France's supposed "free soil" policy forbidding slavery on French soil. Likewise denying *gens de couleur* civil, social, and political rights because of their racial background flew in the face of the ideals of the French Revolution and underscored how much had changed between 1792 and 1802 for all French citizens. Official bans at times forbade any travel between metropolitan France and the colonies and at other times allowed people of African descent to make the voyage but only under very limited conditions. Nonetheless many enslaved and free mixed-race servants accompanied elite Creoles from places like Martinique on their trips and other *gens de couleur* made the trip as individuals or in groups. Whether they stayed in port cities, made their way to rural villages, or traveled to Paris, enslaved and free people of African descent appeared in a variety of venues attending the theater with their masters, running errands, and even publishing daily newspapers.

Although the numbers of people of African descent in metropolitan France probably never exceeded 5,000, a small number in comparison to the 25 million continental French, their highly visible presence in the nineteenth century created significant controversy.[38] For local, regional, and national officials, as well as ordinary French citizens, the presence of enslaved and free people of African descent in the streets, in the shops, and in the courtrooms underscored how seemingly colonial issues, like slavery and racial mixing, also surfaced as metropolitan issues. As successive regimes extended rights to a broader segment of the continental population and worked to unite all of the French Empire under one coherent set of policies, enslaved and free people of color served as a tangible reminder that race, class, and location, among other things, influenced an individual's access to the fruits of liberty, equality, and brotherhood.

"That Your Hearts Will Blossom and Again Become French": The Early Napoleonic Period

ON THEIR ARRIVAL in Martinique following nearly six years of British occupation, Martinique's three new administrators—the captain general, the colonial prefect, and the chief judge—set about realigning the island and its inhabitants with metropolitan France to solidify French power in the region. As captain general, contre amiral Louis Thomas Villaret-Joyeuse wielded complete military power as well as the right to name the candidates for all of the island's administrative and judicial posts, after the recommendation of the colonial prefect or the chief judge. Charles Henry Bertin, the colonial prefect, administered finances, oversaw general accounting, and introduced candidates for administrative offices in the colonies. For his part, Lefessier-Grandpré assumed the post of chief judge and alone had the right to make provisional rules on procedural matters, as well as to register and prepare laws appropriate to the future civil and criminal code of the colony.[1]

When the trio arrived, they found a highly stratified population riven by racial, economic, and social differences. Approximately 110,000 people called Martinique home in late 1802; and although Lefessier-Grandpré neatly categorized them as 7,000 *européens ou creole blancs*, 12,000 *gens de couleur*, and 90,000 *esclaves*, not surprisingly the boundaries between these groups were by no means stable and differences within each group prevented them from acting as cohesive units.[2] Despite their shared racial background, colonial administrators and the island's white population by no means functioned as a united whole. The colonial administrators' European origin, and the fact that they ultimately had to answer to metropolitan French authority, often set them

apart from Martinique's Creoles and *colons* who historically had wielded political and economic control. As a result Martinique's colonial administrators
frequently encountered resistance from the island's white planters who had a
vested interest in maintaining the island's racial and social hierarchy and, as
a result, these officials sometimes found themselves limited in implementing
colonial policies.

Divisions within Martinique's white community also meant that although
administrators worried about the small number of whites living on the island,
they remained wary of just anyone joining the white ranks. As a result they
kept an especially close eye on new arrivals. Although few and incomplete,
passenger lists from the period provide a detailed account of some who made
the trip between metropolitan France and the Caribbean and underscore the
important connections between the two regions. From Marseille alone 456
white men, women, and children made the voyage between late 1802 and mid-
1803; 211 headed for Martinique, including large-scale merchants, landowners,
bakers, masons, and a cook.[3] Many others, for whom no record survives, also
came, however, for by the end of the year the island's white population had
grown by roughly 3,000 to 10,078.[4] Demographic surges like these made unity
based on shared race even more difficult to achieve.

It also made disagreements among Creole elites and colonial administrators of potentially greater concern. On a number of occasions Martinique's
colons took colonial officials on both sides of the Atlantic to task for what they
perceived as the Ministry of the Marine's failure to learn the lessons of Saint
Domingue. Because of Guadeloupe's, Saint Domingue's, and Martinique's
close physical proximity, Creoles feared Martinique might fall victim to the
violence that had engulfed France's other Caribbean holdings since 1791. After
1802 the "specter of Saint Domingue" haunted the island's white population
and planters repeatedly complained that metropolitan France had abandoned
its citizens in the French Atlantic, calling into question the boundaries of the
French nation and citizenship. Guadeloupe had returned to French control
in December 1794 after a seven-month struggle with the British.[5] As a result,
unlike in Martinique where the British occupation had retained slavery intact,
the French National Convention's 1794 decree of emancipation had taken effect in Guadeloupe. Martinique's elite Creoles had long feared an uprising
sparked by this emancipated population a short sail away in Guadeloupe. The
campaign of General Richepance and 3,400 troops that reimposed slavery in
Guadeloupe in mid-1802, however, soon showed the ferocious determination of French metropolitan administrators to keep slavery at all costs.[6] While
concerns about Guadeloupe proved short-lived, fears about an uprising from

Saint Domingue nonetheless continued to plague the colony. The island's chief judge Lefessier-Grandpré believed that Martinicans constantly worried about the inevitability of "the fruits of death, like those in Saint Domingue," but predicted that ultimately "fear will kill the colonies sooner."[7]

French colonial officials' explicit reference to the separation between the colony and metropolitan France, and the initial implication that Martinique's inhabitants might include less than completely loyal French subjects, also heightened tensions between Martinique's white planters and the island's officials. Even though colonial administrators well knew of the many differences separating members of Martinican society, and even though they at times worked hard to sustain those differences, administrators consistently juxtaposed a unified "colony" with a united "European" France. Not surprisingly they found the colony inferior when compared to the continent. Mere residence in the French West Indies—location—thus became an important mark against full membership in the French citizenry.

Motivated by their desire to reestablish French control and gain Creole loyalty, however, colonial administrators struggled both to acknowledge and to efface the colony's differences. In his proclamation after reclaiming the island, Villaret-Joyeuse indicated although the colonists' hearts once may have belonged to the motherland, he doubted their loyalty had survived the years of British rule and claimed "the nature of the population, their cultures, and their existence differs quite essentially from the organization of European societies."[8] Nonetheless Villaret-Joyeuse addressed the populace as members of the French nation: "Frenchmen, war and dissensions have separated you from the mother country, peace will bring you back to the metropole." Only by vigilantly policing those "who dare to trouble the social order," he continued, could they secure the island's good fortune and then could the inhabitants' "hearts blossom and again become French."[9]

Beyond rhetorical inclusion, Martinique's colonial administrators saw restoring commerce as the best way to solidify the island's links with the continent and assure Martinicans' loyalty to the French nation. Toward that end, when signatories from Fort Royal asked that foreign vessels, and particularly American ones, be allowed to dock in the port, Captain General Villaret-Joyeuse and Colonial Prefect Bertin provided provisional authorization.[10] The links between Martinique and the United States throughout the early Napoleonic period centered on commerce and, in particular, around Martinican efforts to ensure good relations between the island and American vessels in a period when European wars frequently interrupted traffic to and from the continent.[11] When France, and therefore Martinique, once again declared war on Great Britain in June 1803 the island's need for supplies made commercial links with the United States increasingly important and motivated the island's merchants, claiming status as French citizens, to clamor for even more assistance from French officials who quickly responded. Colonial Prefect Bertin announced his intention to try and procure funds, arms, and munitions from the United States and opened all of the island's ports to neutral vessels.[12] The British blockade of the island, however, virtually isolated it from all outside contact, ensuring that Creoles would continue to complain about their abandonment by colonial officials on both sides of the Atlantic.[13]

The island's *petits blancs* and colonial officials also failed to make common cause. Economic differences between Martinique's elite Creoles and *petits blancs*, however, united white elites in an attempt to enforce a class-specific definition of white male behavior. Both officials and *colons* railed at what they saw as misguided *petits blancs* attempting to secure the civil and political rights promised to the broader white French populace at the height of the Revolutionary Terror (1793–1794). By promising a right to food, a job, and the vote, among other things, colonial administrators argued, the Revolution had wrongly encouraged Martinique's *petits blancs* to push for social justice. Villaret-Joyeuse voiced his concern about their "often misguided hopes," which in his mind "naturally dispose them towards revolution."[14] Like the captain general, Lefessier-Grandpré also suspected the *petits blancs*. Although he believed the island's property owners and merchants "sincerely attached to France, by familial sentiments, and by unity of origin, language, and mores," he noted the presence of "four or five thousand white wage earners who, like those in France, are less discontent with their sort than eager for change."[15] Even if not discontent, he argued, they often failed to cooperate with either local or metropolitan authorities and believed "themselves to be below their *niche* and only obey the government when they want to."[16] Such disregard for French authority threatened not only metropolitan control but also attempts to create a unified French empire.

To stamp out the possibility of revolution from this poor white population, Villaret-Joyeuse took a number of steps, ordering the island's battalion commanders and parish superintendents to detain all individuals, "without distinction of color," if they lacked a passport and also instructing the new colonial police force to keep an eye on the "*petits blancs* who can be counted among the crowd."[17] To eradicate the visible presence of any white men who failed to function as self-sufficient husbands and fathers, Lefessier-Grandpré suggested that, as in continental France, all indigents be incorporated into the military.[18]

Just as elite whites grappled with strictly defining and enforcing white male behavior in Martinique, during the early years of the Napoleonic period elite Creoles, aided by colonial administrators, also worked to prescribe the behavior of the island's white women. The assumption that white women would live in relative comfort, with no need to earn a living, undergirded the ideal of appropriate white female behavior throughout the first half of the nineteenth century. The existence of *poor white* women in Martinique, and especially white women living on the margins, significantly complicated the situation. As a result, soon after their return to the island, colonial administrators labored to keep Martinique's white women from falling into an unseemly poverty seen as degrading to the broader white community.[19] These efforts included supplying food and safe passage to the widows and children of deceased military and administrative officers so they did not fall into an "unfortunate situation." The presence of these women so bothered Villaret-Joyeuse he insisted they leave the island as quickly as possible and at government expense provided, of course, the male head of household had died after France repossessed the island in 1802.[20]

The island's colonial officials also supported charities specifically designated for the island's poor white children and women. Since 1741, the *dames dominicaines*, a continental religious order well known for their charitable work, had administered a foundling home for white male and female abandoned infants and also a home for female orphans.[21] A 1784 order mandated that all white abandoned children be placed in the *dames dominicaines'* foundling home, but only after a royal physician had confirmed their color and inscribed it on their baptismal or birth record. All abandoned children of color, on the other hand, the ordinance ordered sold for the profit of the king.[22] Rumors at the time suggested the mothers of the *mulâtres-blancs*, or "mulatto whites," as they were called, who peopled the island's foundling hospital included several daughters of the island's wealthy plantation owners, the *beautés princières* of the Antilles.[23] Such rumors undoubtedly further compelled elites to financially support those in the foundling home (*enfants trouvés*) and found-children placed with other families (*enfants trouvés externes*). Public funds also provided for an orphanage for young girls (*orphelines*), and a hospice for poor white women (*femmes indigentes*).[24] The plight of these white girls and women on the edge of poverty so concerned colonial administrators that they raised the government's allotment for each charitable endeavor and further stipulated using the proceeds from former ecclesiastic, now national, holdings to support the institutions.[25]

In addition to sharing an ideal of appropriate white behavior, colonial administrators and Martinique's *colons* also united in their concerns about the island's *gens de couleur* and enslaved populations. Eight years of British occupation left French authorities uncertain whether the previous legal and social measures designed to constrain these groups continued to be enforced, and they worked to reassert their own authority over both free and enslaved people of African descent whom they viewed with suspicion and fear. Villaret-Joyeuse took a number of steps to ensure the clear subordination of both populations to the island's white inhabitants and thwart any potential realignment of the island's racial and social hierarchy.

Insisting that a "new ambition" motivated the island's mixed race population and that the island's enslaved inhabitants needed "discipline," just two weeks after taking control Villaret-Joyeuse reinstated all pre-1789 laws relating to the policing of Martinique's *gens de couleur* and enslaved population.[26] Because of the "extreme increase" in the number of *gens de couleur*, that "dangerous caste which sees the colonies as their patrimony that has been usurped by the whites," and because of the "heavy fermentation that reigns among these men, equally deprived of fortune, consideration, and liberty," he also closed public schools for enslaved Martinicans and mixed race people.[27] Although schools for the island's *gens de couleur* had existed long before 1802, after 1789 colonial administrators increasingly viewed them as incubators for revolution and Villaret-Joyeuse concluded the government could "not allow the tinderbox of a false light, one that will sooner or later rekindle the fire of revolution, to survive." In response to any who opposed the measure based on the gains of the 1789 Revolution, he further denounced the "philosophical systems" advocating education as "simply . . . incompatible" with "existence in our colonies, which depends on slavery and the distinction of colors," and indicated "recent experience," undoubtedly the uprisings in Saint Domingue, had demonstrated "a misapplication of the spirit of enlightenment can be used to dangerous ends."[28] Most practically, he argued, because the island's *gens de couleur* were "destined to the mechanical trades, they have no need for any other sort of talent," and thus had no need for education in the first place. By closing the schools, he concluded, the government could "snuff out the germ of this dangerous instruction which [is] corrupted by false maxims and contagious examples."[29]

Rumors of a plot between Martinique's and Saint Domingue's free mixed-race inhabitants appeared to create just the upheaval that Villaret-Joyeuse feared and underscored ongoing fears about Saint Domingue and the potential lesson it provided to other enslaved and free laborers in the Caribbean. In response to the news, Chief Judge Lefessier-Grandpré argued the recent actions of Martinique's *gens de couleur* indicated they had "drunk from the cup of pride and power," and "more or less participated in the crimes produced by this double war" between France and Great Britain and the war between loyalists and revolutionaries in Martinique.[30] To prevent a crisis and ensure only those loyal to France remained on the island, Villaret-Joyeuse instructed the new colonial police force to monitor the mixed race population, and made further plans to ship all *gens de couleur* found guilty of assassination, arson, or poisoning to Venezuela.[31] Officials also intensified their surveillance of the mixed-race population by requiring all *gens de couleur* to verify their manumissions with the government and the captain general created a special tribunal to judge any enslaved and free mixed-race Martinicans accused of poisoning.[32] By the end of the year these combined measures apparently had succeeded; the number of *gens de couleur* on the island had officially dropped from the 1802 estimate of 12,000 to 6,254.[33]

Although colonial administrators appeared to have restored order on the island, some metropolitan French would have preferred the dangers inherent in racial slavery remain confined to colonial places like Martinique. Since the mid-eighteenth century, however, the transfer of people, things, and ideas between metropolitan France and the islands meant those issues intricately connected to broader discussions about what territory and which people belonged to the French nation. During the early Napoleonic period, the physical presence of colonial inhabitants provided perhaps the most visible evidence of the links connecting the various parts of France's Atlantic empire. Nearly two-thirds of France's departments (administrative units) had colonists in permanent residence in 1801 and at least 6,989 white colonists lived in metropolitan France. Because they served as arrival and departure points for metropolitan French territory, port cities in particular experienced daily reminders of France's overseas possessions through the influx of people traveling to and from the Caribbean. Of the known white colonists spread throughout the realm, 1,800 had located in or near Paris. Nearly 5,800 colonists, however, congregated in those departments bordering on port cities: near Marseille, the Bouches-du-Rhone claimed 494 colonists; near Bordeaux, the Charente-inférieure (Charente-maritime) had 493 and the Gironde had 946 colonists; near Nantes, the Loire-inférieure (Loire-Atlantique) had 206 and the Morbihan housed 169 colonists, and; near Le Havre, approximately 200 colonists resided in the Seine-inférieure (Seine-maritime).[34]

Given the changing situation in the French West Indies and the fluid nature of this population, these numbers probably indicate only a portion of the colonial community in continental France. Nonetheless these nearly 7,000 white colonists had significance beyond their numbers. A number asked for aid from the Bureau of Hospitals and Assistance because of their economic troubles and their requests intersected with discussions about the role of the French West Indian colonies and colonists in the French family. The recent uprisings in Saint Domingue and Guadeloupe had placed the property and livelihood of French colonists, and those who depended on them on the continent, in direct jeopardy and further raised the question of what responsibility the metropolitan government had to its citizens around the Atlantic. A 1799 law dictated French West Indian refugees residing in the metropole could receive monthly support, but not indemnity, for lost property in any of France's Caribbean holdings.[35] This assistance depended, however, on a colonist's ability to prove he or she had held land as property in the colonies. Only if the refugee could establish ownership would the government grant a certificate confirming a right to governmental assistance. How long such assistance would last remained unclear and extended only to white individuals.

Enslaved and free individuals of African descent also made the trip across the Atlantic, however, and made continental France home. A series of measures in the early Napoleonic period, however, indicate metropolitan officials had no intention of upholding earlier gains for *gens de couleur* (civil and political rights) and enslaved Africans (legal freedom) granted during the Revolution. On the contrary, the presence of these individuals on the continent sparked concerns about racial mixing and further underscored the Napoleonic Consulate and Empire was anything but color blind. Although the Police des Noirs regulating people of African descent was suspended during the Revolution, in February 1802 Napoleon renewed it as well as earlier royal legislation requiring blacks to carry *cartouches* (identity cards) while on the continent.[36] He also implemented another decree completely banning mixed-race people from entering metropolitan territory.[37] Official concerns about racial mixing further manifested themselves in early 1803, when the minister of justice again informed the prefects of France's departments "acts of marriage between whites and negresses, or between negroes and whites will not be accepted."[38] Such a decree suggests that, regardless of the numbers, metropolitan officials, like their colonial counterparts, worried about those of African descent in their midst and especially feared the results of racial mixing on the French nation.

* * *

Even among the three colonial officials who administered the newly retaken colony, different degrees of alliance with Creoles and fissures in colonial policy prevented any kind of united front. The arrival of the new colonial prefect,

Pierre Clément Laussat, simply exacerbated those divisions. On a foggy evening in April 1804 Laussat stepped off an American merchant ship near Saint Pierre, Martinique, and waded to shore.[39] In his pocket he carried false papers identifying him as Peter Lanthois, a naturalized American citizen, in case the British overtook him before completing his journey between New Orleans and the island. Thanks in part to military gains on the continent and a new relationship between the United States and France following the Louisiana Purchase in 1803, his voyage had been uneventful and he was eager to begin his duties as the island's new colonial prefect. Born in 1756 to an influential noble family living near Bordeaux, Laussat was ideally positioned to join France's colonial service. He trained in the law in the 1770s, gained a government position in the 1780s, and then, like many other nobles, in 1789 he renounced his noble rank, publicly embraced the new democratic principles sweeping the land, and rode out the Revolution in a series of administrative posts. In 1799 he supported Napoleon Bonaparte's coup d'état and eventually came to the First Consul's attention through a family friend. In a series of meetings, Laussat so distinguished himself to Napoleon that in August 1802 the First Consul granted Laussat's request to serve as colonial prefect in the French colony of Louisiana.[40]

After overseeing the transfer of that property to the United States of America, Laussat made his way to Martinique. He soon found, however, that Louisiana and Martinique, though both French colonies, were not administered the same way and over the next eighteen months he found himself in a series of disputes with not only Captain General Villaret-Joyeuse but also a number of Creole officials. These disputes prevented the administration from articulating a homogeneous, coherent colonial policy and again demonstrated it was unclear just how Martinique and its inhabitants figured into the broader French nation.

Initially the conflicts between Villaret-Joyeuse and Colonial Prefect Laussat revolved around the boundaries between their respective offices and related specifically to questions about how closely metropolitan magistrates should align with the island's Creole elite. Within months of Laussat's arrival he and Villaret-Joyeuse fought over nominations for the island's judicial positions.[41] In his role as colonial prefect Laussat was supposed to suggest the names for the administrative and judicial posts and Villaret-Joyeuse to make the final selection. According to Laussat, however, by ignoring Laussat's list Villaret-Joyeuse had refused to follow these regulations and, in the process, had "denatured the dignity, the character, [and] the powers of the colonial prefect."[42] Their feud over this issue only intensified when Villaret-Joyeuse further refused to consult Laussat for nominations for several new vacant administrative posts.[43]

The promulgation of the Napoleonic Civil Code also revealed the different ways Villaret-Joyeuse and Laussat approached their relationship with Martinique's plantocracy and the island's relationship to continental France. To the great relief of the island's Creoles, by the time of Laussat's arrival, Villaret-Joyeuse looked to realign the two places but now appeared to recognize the special needs of the island. Laussat, on the other hand, preferred encouraging the island's inhabitants to adopt metropolitan laws, customs, and mores rather than claim special privileges. Like other administrators in France's more rural areas, Villaret-Joyeuse and Laussat served as quasi field observers in Martinique, charged with identifying and delineating the island's most dramatic differences in order to supplant them with standardized French mores.[44] The promulgation of the Civil Code in the French West Indies was intended to do just that. Instead, however, Villaret-Joyeuse, with the approval of the island's Creole-controlled Sovereign Council, modified Article 3 to the Code dealing with issues like marriage and inheritance. The modification not only maintained Creole particularity and highlighted the fractured nature of the French Empire but also underscored how the need to sustain the social and economic order by subjugating people of color modified law in the colonial context and led to limitations on applying the metropole's legal standards.

According to Villaret-Joyeuse applying the Napoleonic Code would "assure the happiness of France" in Martinique and bring the island into "precious conformity with the laws of the metropole;" nonetheless he deemed it "wise and necessary to adapt them to the land, the habits, the type of property, and the diverse class of men who compose the island."[45] Article 3, he pointed out, contained clauses that might weaken "the distinction of colors in the colonies [which] has been understood [as] indispensable in slave countries."[46] To help "maintain . . . the line of demarcation that always has existed between the white class and the class of *gens de couleur* and their descendants," he thus suggested a modification that would explicitly forbid interracial mixing by making all laws related to family, like marriage, "valid in the colony only between whites and whites and between *affranchis* and their descendants."[47] Such a modification, he concluded, was in keeping with the French government's understanding "the *Code* could, in some ways, be contrary to the interests of the colony," and its stipulation that the three magistrates of the colony "suspend the execution of any measures that could harm local conventions." Essentially Villaret-Joyeuse argued if the Code threatened island stability and especially economic output, then officials had the power to selectively implement its provisions. The loss of Saint Domingue and its sugar meant the French Empire depended more than ever on Martinique's cash crop exports. As a result, in practice, the Napoleonic regime was not interested in sacrificing economic profit for legal consistency.

Colonial prefect Laussat, like Villaret-Joyeuse, also spoke of the links between the colonies and metropolitan France and his desire to strengthen them. He too emphasized the fundamental differences between the two places. Unlike Villaret-Joyeuse, however, he did not suggest that Martinique should receive special consideration. Instead, he argued that the promulgation of the Code would allow "Frenchmen from one river to the next . . . to embrace one another as brothers, despite the vast seas, and frequent enemies, who separate them."[48] Furthermore he noted the Civil Code would enable Martinican colonists truly to share what it meant to be French by strengthening "more and more the indissoluble ties of sentiment and conformity that unite you to the metropole."[49] Laussat saw conformity, and not adaptation, as crucial to the island's future and he believed that the Code would, and should, replace Creole ways with continental France's "pure opinions, her fundamental maxims, her customs, her affections."[50] Unlike Villaret-Joyeuse, who looked to modify continental law to fit Martinique's mores, Laussat looked to modify the mores of the colony to fit continental law.

Villaret-Joyeuse and Laussat also disagreed about whether to create a Court of Appeal peopled with the island's wealthiest white planters, and Martinique's *colons* took advantage of this disagreement to reestablish their judicial power. Prior to the Revolution the Sovereign Council, comprised of administrators and notable Creoles, had held jurisdiction in civil, administrative, and judicial matters. During the British occupation of Martinique from 1794–1802, this council had continued to sit. After the French reacquired the island, however, and after the implementation of Napoleonic justice, its status changed.[51] Villaret-Joyeuse looked to reestablish a similar council in personnel but limit it to judicial functions only, defending the court as always comprised of the richest and most distinguished inhabitants, unpaid for their efforts but feeling "the esteem of their *concitoyens* was adequate recompense."[52] Laussat, however, opposed the new body, viewing it as yet another modification to metropolitan laws and institutions. He also saw it as too close an alliance between Martinican Creoles and metropolitan officials and therefore informed the minister of the marine he felt it "important to secretly undermine" this new tribunal.[53] Despite his objections the Court of Appeal was created and stacked with elite white planters loyal to Villaret-Joyeuse.

At least some of Martinique's *colons* used these positions, and other close ties to the captain general, to criticize Laussat and his measures to ensure the island's economic security. For the island's wealthy colonists and colonial administrators order meant increased trade and profit. In light of the economic stagnation brought on by Great Britain's blockade of Martinique in 1803 and the loss of Saint Domingue and establishment of Haiti in January 1804, Creoles and colonial administrators looked to renew economic contacts with the United States and strengthen those with metropolitan France if at all possible. Napoleon Bonaparte himself tried to make increased trade a reality, ordering three frigates, including the *Ville-de-Milan* and the *Président*, to leave France's Atlantic port cities and travel to Martinique to "revitalize this precious colony" with 600 men, 4,500 guns, and powder.[54] By fall 1804 the *Ville-de-Milan* arrived at the northeastern port of Trinité with 220 men and a supply of arms, and then moved to the southwestern administrative port of Fort Royal where, according to Villaret-Joyeuse, its presence served as an important deterrent to British attacks.[55] It also clearly facilitated trade for at the same time, the *Président* left Guadeloupe, where it had initially landed, and headed for the United States returning to Martinique at year's end loaded with merchandise.[56]

This increase in commerce greatly relieved the island's notables who rejoiced to see twenty-four American ships in port, as well as a French squadron, three frigates, two corvettes, two ships, and one brig weigh anchor in the island's ports between January and July 1805.[57] While the presence of these vessels did help keep trade alive, the island nevertheless suffered significant economic losses and by the end of the year, Martinique's economic situation had so soured that Creoles increasingly called on colonial administrators to enact measures that would stimulate trade and remove those that hindered it. Laussat refused to bow to Creole pressure, however, and, in the interests of French commerce, closed all but four ports to foreign commerce, setting off a wave of protest and renewed fights between the captain general and colonial prefect.[58] One hundred-thirty of the island's elites had signed a petition protesting the closing of the ports and, when Villaret-Joyeuse demanded that the colonial prefect reconsider the measure, Laussat accused him of "showing too much kindness for certain eminent members of the anglophile party" and stubbornly declined the request.[59] Shortly thereafter someone posted a series of caricatures of Laussat in Saint Pierre, where he resided, and also in Fort Royal. Laussat speculated that his decisions regarding the ports had provoked the insults and in a letter to the minister of the marine he faulted Villaret-Joyeuse for failing to identify and punish the culprits and subsequently demanded Villaret-Joyeuse reprimand two of the island's Creole elite, one of whom served as the head of the national guard in Saint Pierre and the other as police captain in nearby Mouillage.[60] According to Laussat, both men had neglected to visit him on the first day of the New Year, as required by law, and thus needed reprimanding. As it turns out both also had helped sponsor a banquet for Villaret-Joyeuse on his mid-December trip to Saint Pierre, a banquet attended by a number of *colons* where the entertainment included a song with what the excluded Laussat termed "anglophile" lyrics.[61] Villaret-Joyeuse had refused to chastise the banquet attendees and rejected as "impossible" Laussat's demand that he discipline the men in question.[62]

To Laussat's relief, he did, however, authorize the arrest and deportation of two men accused of posting insulting caricatures and poems of Laussat.[63] Despite this brief reconciliation, elite Creoles took advantage of Villaret-Joyeuse's and Laussat's ongoing feud to gain even more economic concessions. In one instance, they secured Villaret-Joyeuse's help to overturn a charge of contrabanding against an American vessel, *Commerce of New York*.[64] They also convinced him to reverse Laussat's decision about the ports, reopening those in question as well as three others. Villaret-Joyeuse further agreed to abolish the fees for the inscription and transcription of mortgages primarily at the insistence of, Laussat contended, one of the island's wealthiest white planters and interim *procureur général*, Pierre Nicolas François Bence de Sainte-Catherine. Bence, as he was known, had been born in Lamentin, near Fort Royal, in 1764 and like many other young *colons* he had been educated in continental France at the Collège du Juilly near Paris. Prior to his 1805 appointment, he had served on Martinique's Superior Council and as a judge on the island's Court of Appeal.[65] Despite such stellar credentials, due to his mounting concerns about the influence Martinique's Creoles had on Villaret-Joyeuse, Laussat found Bence's new position yet another indicator that the captain general lacked "the firmness necessary for governor" and that he worried too much about his popularity.[66]

In addition to fueling conflicts over administrators' duties, Villaret-Joyeuse and Laussat's disagreement over which of the island's ports would remain open to trade also exacerbated tensions between the island's *colons* and *petits blancs*. In response, each group—the island's port city merchants and Martinique's rich white planters—tried to rally government support by defaming the other group in the eyes of administrators and turning the officials against one another. The island's merchants called the planters "rich anglophile colonists" and the planters labeled the merchants "patriots . . . [who] have no property, [and] have come from France to make their fortunes."[67] At a moment when the upper echelons of *petits blancs* might gain financial ground, Martinique's *colons* wanted to assure Villaret-Joyeuse saw them as a threat to the island. One of the island's notables therefore told the captain general a party "contrary to public tranquility" and hostile to the captain general had formed in Saint Pierre and looked to Laussat, who appeared to support them, for leadership.[68] This strategy proved successful when Villaret-Joyeuse demanded Laussat leave Saint Pierre and relocate to Fort Royal, where Villaret-Joyeuse and the island's wealthiest white planters congregated.[69] Undoubtedly, Laussat contended, Villaret-Joyeuse insisted on the move so he could gather more personal power and turn elite planters, "the anglophile party," against Laussat and force his return to France.[70]

Although Martinique's *colons* managed to successfully take advantage of the captain general's and colonial prefect's disputes, the island's poorest *petits blancs* were less fortunate. Since 1803 the number of whites on the island had actually decreased by about 200 to approximately 9,800.[71] Ever concerned about colonial finances, Laussat nonetheless worried that residents might take advantage of government assistance and, in an attempt to rationalize distribution, he reorganized the process by which inhabitants could gain indigence certificates exempting them from taxes and authorizing them to receive limited monetary support. He instructed the police captain, the priest, and three property-holding residents "among the most heavily taxed in the area" in each parish henceforth to gather, discuss, and award certificates.[72] Such a system made it harder to obtain aid and by doing so, Laussat hoped, would prevent those unworthy of help from depleting the island's coffers.

While such a distinction between worthy and unworthy poor undoubtedly denied assistance to some, others like the island's poorest white women and children, benefited from Laussat's stereotype of white French femininity. Even though the ministerial budget had no official allocation for the foundling home (internal/external), the orphanage, or hospice for indigent women, and their expenses had "no analogue in those of the other colonies," Laussat nonetheless found them "useful in themselves and recommendable in their goal."[73] Consequently he flouted official rules and recommended approximately 36,000 francs for supporting 52 people.[74] In his mind, political authority would be undermined by the presence of poor whites obviously ignoring official racial ideology, so Laussat found discretionary money in the budget to increase the allotment for these longstanding charitable institutions.

Martinique's *gens de couleur* also benefited, though in limited ways, from assumptions about their behavior. Despite continental fears, in the immediate aftermath of Haiti's founding, the island's free mixed-race inhabitants had not revolted but rather, as Villaret-Joyeuse observed, showed "laudable service" in the face of potential Caribbean-wide unrest.[75] In exchange for the relative stability, Villaret-Joyeuse therefore ordered the island's postal service reorganized and required each parish to designate a free mixed-race man to head its service and to recruit a permanent corps of mail carriers from the *gens de couleur* population.[76] For free mixed-race individuals, such positions not only expanded their professional options but also importantly exempted them from military service.

Changes to the postal service benefited only a limited number of the island's free mixed-race population. More significant were the new constraints on the upward social mobility of Martinique's *gens de couleur*. The Civil Code's new proscription against members of Martinique's white population bequeathing money or other valuables to freed men and women or their descendants blocked *gens de couleur* advancement. Its inclusion in the Civil Code nonetheless serves as an important reminder that these island populations had important connections, be they personal or economic or both, to whites whose bequests could potentially upset Martinique's social and racial hierarchy. That Martinique's *gens de couleur* could make donations to white people, even though this conflicted with the directives of the Civil Code, also demonstrates those intimate links as well as Creole beliefs that the island's free mixed-race inhabitants owed all to Martinique's white plantocrats. Villaret-Joyeuse called the measure "one of those modifications in the disposition of the *Code* that colonial interests require," further underscoring the point that colonial interests were white interests.[77]

Following the loss of Saint Domingue, Martinique's enslaved population encountered increasingly punitive measures. Villaret-Joyeuse's attempts to return enslaved workers "to discipline" in 1802 clearly had not completely succeeded, as evidenced by his creation in 1803 of a special tribunal to judge enslaved Martinicans accused of poisoning. By Laussat's arrival an increase in the number of and concerns about islandwide poisonings prompted Villaret-Joyeuse to expand the tribunal's power and present a new list of crimes committed by enslaved Martinicans that it could consider.[78] Repeated rumors that Jean-Jacques Dessalines, the ruler of Haiti, had sent boatloads of people "to introduce his doctrines, apostles, and principles" in the islands and that he looked specifically to foment rebellion among Guadeloupe's and Martinique's enslaved inhabitants also prompted officials to monitor the island's enslaved laborers even more closely.[79]

Despite such measures some of the island's enslaved people nonetheless viewed this period as one of potential change. The significant decline in the island's enslaved population between 1803 and 1805, which fell from

approximately 90,000 to 80,000, indicated that a number of enslaved individuals potentially benefited from Laussat's desire to regularize the island's
finances.[80] While this shift in numbers may have reflected a more accurate accounting of the enslaved community, it also may have stemmed from planters
unofficially freeing enslaved Africans to avoid paying the manumission fee or
property taxes on them during trying economic times. Laussat's position on
manumissions suggests the latter. After establishment of the three-magistrate
system in the French West Indies, only the colonial prefect held the power
to manumit an enslaved African and collect the manumission fee. Prior to
Laussat's arrival, Martinique's Creoles had requested administrators create a
commission to revise the manumission process. The resulting loss in revenue that would ensue with more official manumissions, however, prompted
Laussat to recommend suppressing the commission in 1805.[81] If owners did
grant some enslaved laborers de facto freedom, those individuals would have
joined the ranks of the island's *patronés*, and with that status perhaps a bit
more flexibility in their daily lives.

As an incident in early spring 1806 indicated, however, for some Creoles
and their enslaved workers, manumission laws did not necessarily apply. In
preparation for a trip to the continent, the Misses Hurault, members of an
elite Creole family, sought permission to emancipate Rosalie, a forty-year-old
mulâtresse, and her eight-year-old son before transporting them to the metropole.[82] Initially, Laussat refused to grant the two enslaved Martinicans their
freedom, arguing "the great number of emancipations on this abandoned island has always appeared to me a dangerous wound for the colonial system."[83]
The Creole Madame Tascher de La Pagerie, a friend of the Hurault family and
Empress Josephine's mother, had other priorities, however. She had planned to
travel to metropolitan France with the Misses Hurault, Rosalie, and Rosalie's
son and expressed her frustration to Villaret-Joyeuse about Laussat's decision.[84] Not surprisingly the will of the prefect proved no match for the wishes
of Napoleon's mother-in-law and, at the urging of the captain general, Laussat
eventually granted not only the two liberties sought for Rosalie and her son
but also a decree of emancipation for one of Madame La Pagerie's own enslaved domestics.[85]

Madame La Pagerie's position as an elite on the island with intimate
links to Napoleon Bonaparte clearly helped her obtain freedom for her own
enslaved domestics and for those traveling with her. After the loss of Saint
Domingue, Napoleon Bonaparte had strategic interests in the island, which
was France's most valuable asset in the region. The increased number of warships that Napoleon sent to the French West Indies and dispersed throughout

the western Atlantic Ocean brought closer oversight between the Minister of the Marine , Denis Decrès, in Paris and colonial administrators in Martinique. Bonaparte, however, also involved himself in the colony's matters and found conflicts between Captain General Villaret-Joyeuse and Colonial Prefect Laussat particularly disturbing. After reading a dispatch from Laussat regarding the questionable song offered at the 1805 banquet for Villaret-Joyeuse, for example, Napoleon informed Decrès that he found the song in question "quite truly anglophile," and instructed the minister to immediately provide three things: a list of all officers on the island who had not fought for France on the continent; a list of all of the members of the Creole-controlled Court of Appeal established by Villaret-Joyeuse in 1804; and a list of all individuals who "behaved badly." With the information provided, Napoleon planned to replace all officers who had not fought on the continent with "better ones," to restock the Court of Appeal so that the great majority consisted of "men from France, enemies of the English," and to deport any troublemakers to the continent.[86]

Napoleon also instructed Decrès to inform Villaret-Joyeuse of the emperor's surprise that the island police had not quashed abuses like the song and to confirm the impropriety of "French officers" dining to the "elegies of anglophilia." Stressing that he well knew Villaret-Joyeuse had "too much indulgence" for some who abused the emperor's name, Napoleon insisted Villaret-Joyeuse create order. To stiffen his officials' resolve, he further ordered the minister to send three vessels to the island, each carrying letters urging Laussat to "stand firm," and missives designed to "give [Villaret-Joyeuse] more character and exhort him to reprimand the English partisans."[87] In response Minister Decrès suggested replacing Captain General Villaret-Joyeuse and Chief Judge Lefessier-Grandpré, who had earlier requested a transfer due to poor health.[88] Napoleon agreed to both measures, adding that he eventually wanted "only devoted military men and English enemies," in charge of the island.[89] In the meantime, however, he instructed Decrès to deal with Villaret-Joyeuse, which Decrès did by detailing what sanctions the captain general should apply to the perpetrators of the "caricatures and songs offending colonial authorities."[90]

Because he wanted to strengthen French authority and limit British loyalty on the island, Napoleon frowned on disputes among Martinique's colonial administrators. But clearly Bonaparte also had personal interests in the island; not only did Madame Tascher de La Pagerie live in Martinique, Empress Josephine also spent time there visiting the hot springs near Saint-Pierre, for example, in 1805.[91] As owners of a sugar plantation near Les Trois-Îlets on the southwestern edge of the island, the Tascher de La Pagerie family was particularly invested in solidifying Creole power in Martinique and in placing Creoles in continental France in advantageous positions. To that end, Madame Tascher de La Pagerie as well as her sister, Rose, frequently contacted Josephine in Paris to relay their concerns on the island and to ask for her help to secure the futures of other Martinicans living in or traveling to Paris.[92] Through their letters, and Empress Josephine's connections, they provided members of Martinique's wealthiest white families access to unique economic and political opportunities.

For other Martinican colonists living in metropolitan France, the loss of Saint Domingue also brought new complications. For those looking to continue or secure government assistance, a new measure requiring them to obtain a certificate confirming they had owned property in the colonies made it increasingly difficult to gain aid.[93] Men like Pierre François Delisle La Chasserie also found the supposed stability in Martinique when compared to the chaos in France's former colony of Saint Domingue actually impeded their efforts to obtain a certificate. Delisle La Chasserie and his family had lived in Paris since well before the Revolution and had managed to exist on revenues from their property in Martinique until 1792. After the loss of this income like others they sought government assistance when granted to colonists in 1799; without such support, Delisle La Chasserie noted, colonists "surely would have succumbed . . . under the weight of misery and need."[94] After France renewed its war with Britain, however, Delisle La Chasserie argued his family had "plunged anew into the most frightful indigence," and like many others in 1804 they fell victim to the provisions of a new law requiring proof of property ownership.[95] The Delisle La Chasserie family still needed governmental assistance and felt frustrated that Saint Domingue colonists continued to receive aid, regardless of their current situation.[96] Surely colonists from Martinique also merited continued help, Delisle La Chasserie believed. Consequently he and seven other Martinican colonists sent the minister of the general police a petition declaring themselves no "less unfortunate than their compatriots from Saint Domingue," and underscoring their "horrors of misery and need."[97] They further argued that, since they could not bear the immense expenses required to return to their homes, they should enjoy the same support as "their compatriots from Saint Domingue" noting they, too, had lost their "means of existence."[98] Metropolitan administrators, however, remained unconvinced that Martinican colonists could not return to the island and, faced with the burden of supporting refugees from Saint Domingue who clearly had lost all property in the islands, held fast to the dictates of the new law, further straining the relationship between the mainland and France's allegedly stable colony of Martinique.

The loss of Saint Domingue also complicated life for *gens de couleur* living in metropolitan France. With the boundaries of the French nation at stake, it seems, even the existence of a small number of *gens de couleur* on the continent posed a threat. Metropolitan administrators increasingly saw them as a population that needed to be controlled and enacted a series of measures to monitor them. Keeping the continent safe from potential harm, however, required the coordination of local, regional, and national authorities, all on the look out for dangerous behavior. Because of recent events in Saint Domingue in metropolitan France being of African descent became reason enough to warrant suspicion. Officials worried especially that a network of *gens de couleur* roaming the Atlantic would incite rebellion and bring the downfall of France's remaining West Indian colonies. When a number of free mixed-race individuals in France's Atlantic and Mediterranean port cities applied for passports for the United States but instead returned to Martinique, for example, France's minister of justice feared that "several had taken up . . . with enemies of the Republic." As a result, he refused any future passports to "this class" of people.[99]

To better monitor *gens de couleur* who remained on the continent, the minister of war also asked the prefects of each maritime department for an accounting of all indigent people of African descent in the area under their control.[100] Lamenting the existence in France of "a certain quantity of men of color, disreputable and without profession, that laziness, vagabondage, or the lack of a mode of existence, make dangerous for the public tranquility,"[101] he looked for a way to have "those blacks or men of color who have no fixed profession, who have no recognizable method of existence, or who can not offer any guarantee for their conduct," serve the Empire.[102] This prompted officials from throughout each department to update the prefect on the number and status of any *gens de couleur* in their cities or communes. The mayor of Montpellier on the Mediterranean coast noted no *gens de couleur* in his area met the minister of war's criteria but suggested any throughout the country who did might reinforce a French battalion completely comprised of mixed-race men then fighting in Italy.[103]

While officials intended this heightened scrutiny to police those *gens de couleur* living permanently in metropolitan France, metropolitan officials also worried that free mixed-race men traveling on ships to the continent might spread rebellion. As a result administrators issued alerts about traveling mixed-race people and interviewed mixed-race sailors on their arrival in French ports.

As fears about a possible *gens de couleur* conspiracy in Tours, in the department of the Indre and Loire and upriver from the Atlantic port of Nantes, also indicate, authorities further believed a mixed-race rebellion might find its way beyond the edges of the Atlantic and into the continent's interior. Officials at the local, regional, and national level thus again mobilized to prevent unrest.

In early 1806, the general police in Paris informed the prefect of the Hérault that a group of French *mulâtres* and *mulâtresses* seeking refuge in Cuba had collected money to aid a French *mulâtre* under surveillance in Tours. To what end this money might be used remained a mystery, however, and therefore officials in the capital directed departmental and local officials to watch for a *mulâtresse* tasked to deliver money and intelligence to the man in question. They also warned authorities in the Hérault and Tours to look for "all other *gens de couleur* of either sex" who might be in the area in order "to learn with certainty their future destination and clarify their movements."[104] After establishment of Haiti, a number of mixed-race individuals had fled to Cuba and undoubtedly officials worried the *mulâtresse* making her way to the continent brought the seeds of rebellion along with financial assistance. For officials, preventing another possible Saint Domingue, and this time on the continent, certainly justified close supervision of all mixed-race individuals in metropolitan France.

*   *   *

After years of working to solidify their formal power on the island, in May 1806 Creoles greeted Captain General Villaret-Joyeuse's new choice for interim chief judge, the Creole *procureur général* Bence, with delight. When the previous head, Lefessier-Grandpré, left the island, Villaret-Joyeuse ignored Colonial Prefect Laussat's advice and independently named Bence to the post.[105] Because Laussat had asked Minister of the Marine Decrès to name "a magistrate from the metropole" as the next chief judge long before Lefessier-Grandpré's departure, he saw Bence's appointment as an ominous sign and further proof that Villaret-Joyeuse hoped to make himself the "sole master" of policing the island and enforcing government order.[106] Creoles, on the other hand, saw Bence's appointment as strengthening local white control and offered it as evidence that Creoles knew best and could and should proceed as they saw fit in colonial matters.

Not surprisingly, Bence's appointment set off a new round of conflicts, this time between Bence and Laussat, over island administration. Now that a Creole (Bence) and a seemingly ardent Creole supporter (Villaret-Joyeuse) held two of the three top administrative positions on the island, Laussat worried Creole particularity and influence in Martinique would increase. Within a month of his appointment Bence and Laussat embroiled themselves in a conflict over the Napoleonic Code with Bence demanding a modification that would favor Creole over metropolitan interests in vacant property on the island.[107] The two also fought extensively over how justice was applied in Martinique, with Laussat seeing the island as deviating further from rather than converging with metropolitan judicial standards.

The most glaring example came in the special tribunal's increasingly brutal treatment of enslaved Africans suspected of poisoning animals and people. The number of enslaved Africans in Martinique had burgeoned from 75,584 in 1805 to 80,473 in 1806 and 81,746 in 1807.[108] This increase in numbers and a spate of poisonings convinced administrators and Creoles alike that the enslaved population waxed increasingly dangerous and were in need of discipline. The case that brought the most attention on the island and in metropolitan France took place in June 1806, when the special tribunal heard charges against a mixed-race woman, Émilie, accused of trying to poison Madame Tascher de La Pagerie at her plantation in Trois-Îlets.[109] After a lengthy interrogation, at which the enslaved woman finally admitted to putting glass in her mistress's food, the Creole tribunal sentenced Émilie to be boiled alive.[110] Creoles no doubt hoped that such a horrific death would serve as a warning to other possible poisoners, but their methods and punishment also came to the attention of colonial administrators in metropolitan France and raised doubts about Creole abilities to adhere to metropolitan judicial standards.

Less than a year later officials in continental France unveiled a plan to reform Martinique's judicial system. Believing a metropolitan education necessary to properly administer justice, colonial officials in Paris reestablished the pre-1789 stipulation that only men educated in metropolitan France could serve as members of the colonial tribunals. Fortunately, Minister of the Marine Decrès noted, "even the maritime war has not interrupted the travels of our colonial inhabitants and nothing prevents them from sending their children to France for instruction and to earn the necessary degree" prerequisite for the bench.[111] He hoped this requirement would "strengthen more and more the links that unite the metropole and her colonies," and "maintain among the young creoles, who are destined for a juridical career, a love for quality studies and an understanding of the laws from their source."[112] The island's Creole families did not see the measure as creating a united France, however, but rather as a condemnation of Creole ability. In response Bence and Creoles fought back, using the special tribunal in November 1807, to condemn enslaved Africans who were accused of a plot to poison ten of

Martinique's wealthiest planters and assassinate a number of white plantation managers.[113]

When the chance arose, Martinique's white planters also sent their sons to be educated in America. Since 1790 a number of young Creoles, out of necessity, had gone to Baltimore and even Great Britain to study.[114] Colonial administrators in the metropole, however, saw an education anywhere other than in continental France as a threat and thus tried to appease Creoles by granting passage on French warships to young Martinicans bound for metropolitan France to study law.[115] The new requirements for a seat on the island's tribunals simply strengthened Creole resolve to provide the education they thought best for a Creole man, however, and few took advantage of the offer.

Martinique's *colons*, through Bence, also tried to block any other changes to the judicial system, like establishing justices of the peace, which might dilute Creole power. Since Bence's appointment, Laussat claimed, the civil procedure of the Code had fallen into desuetude and he described the state of justice practiced on the island in 1807 as reminiscent of the ancien régime.[116] Justice failed to function in Martinique, he claimed, precisely because Bence allied with the Court of Appeal, composed of "fourteen of the principal planters," and they all desired the poor application of the Napoleonic Code and the creation of more positions that might take power out of the hands of the Creole elite.[117]

Laussat also blamed Bence and Martinique's *colons* for the island's heightened economic woes. Bence's inability to effectively mediate the numerous conflicts among the island's planters and local and metropolitan merchants, he insisted, meant even efforts like the continental warships sent to Martinique to secure the island proved ineffective because Creoles demanded unreasonable trading terms. By trying to block those parts of the Napoleonic Code they found economically disadvantageous, Laussat also contended, the Creole-controlled Court of Appeal further alienated some metropolitan merchants on the island and on the continent. As a result of their claims to Creole exceptionalism, he concluded, the island had suffered "complete stagnation" of commerce and even the Americans "left the sugar and took the money."[118]

Martinique's strained commercial transactions with their Atlantic World trading partners became even more complicated when the United States Congress issued an embargo against French products and the French retaliated with an embargo against American products in 1808.[119] And yet, despite such interference, the possibility of mutual trade inspired both Martinican and American merchants and justified continued risky business ventures. In the spring of 1808 five different American vessels arrived in Martinique's ports and by fall the *Pylade* arrived from Philadelphia with flour and at least eighty other American vessels anchored in port carrying foodstuffs and other cargo.[120] Despite renewed American efforts to enforce their embargo, Martinique also renewed economic contacts with the European continent. The *Hyène* arrived from Bordeaux in late summer armed with weapons and merchandise and the brig *Oreste* from Bayonne also made dock with 300 barrels of flour; along with a number of other commercial ships in mid-fall it headed back to a French Atlantic port with a cargo of colonial products.[121]

While increased trade ultimately helped ease economic tensions, much to the dismay of Martinique's Creoles it also facilitated easier transport of *gens de couleur* around the Atlantic basin. Because they still feared a Caribbean-wide revolt colonial administrators and elite Creoles thus enacted measures to confirm the official count of 6,555 *gens de couleur* on the island.[122] One decree ruled any titles of emancipation obtained in other colonies, even French colonies, invalid in Martinique until recognized and renewed by public officials.[123] Another rendered individuals legitimately free only in three circumstances: if they had received a title of liberty after repossession of the island in 1802, if they had an existing title of liberty verified after 1803, or if they had a provisional authorization granted by Colonial Prefect Laussat.[124] These stipulations guaranteed that only those *gens de couleur* on the island after the initial wave of immigration, or known personally by Laussat, would have legitimate status in Martinique. By the end of 1807, as officials and elite Creoles feared, however, the official count of *gens de couleur* had increased by 2,100 to 8,616, nearly equaling that of the white population.[125]

For Martinique's Creoles such an increase in the free mixed-race population potentially meant two things: either more contact between *gens de couleur* and the island's poorer whites working in similar trades or more mixed-race people living on the margins because they could not find work. Both possibilities troubled elites for they believed more contact between *petits blancs* and *gens de couleur* would result either in common interests between the groups or conflicts over work, or in unemployment of mixed-race people that would bring increased indigence and ultimately rebellion. Regardless of the result, trouble seemed inevitable.

The increase in Martinique's *gens de couleur* population further concerned officials like Laussat because, he believed, the competition between the island's poor whites and free mixed-race inhabitants put whites at "quite a disadvantage." The majority of *petits blancs*, he contended, found it difficult "to save themselves from misery when reduced to such levels," and many were.[126] If the island's free mixed-race inhabitants took over all of the artisanal jobs available in Martinique, elites worried that would push the island's poorer whites even closer to the edge of poverty and further diminish all of Martinique's white community in the eyes of those abroad. To prevent that from happening they therefore monetarily supported the neediest of Martinique's 9,953 white inhabitants.[127] This included providing more aid for those white women and abandoned and orphaned white children who could not support themselves, increasing the allotment for the foundling home and charity hospice by approximately 1,000 francs to 31,000 francs in 1806, and, due to economic difficulties, projecting a decreased but still substantial allotment of 24,500 francs for the same aid one year later.[128]

Martinique's elite whites also continued to offer assistance to an increasing number of whites and *gens de couleur* who took advantage of this aid intended for the island's neediest members. A growth in the number of people on the indigence lists worried colonial administrators on the continent, however, since indigent status still exempted one from paying taxes or making public contributions to the treasury. The ongoing conflict with Great Britain meant that the Empire needed more funds than ever and could not afford to have any solvent citizens avoid their obligations. When an investigation revealed that some Martinican Creoles who had more than five enslaved workers and some *gens de couleur* who had more than two had gained an exemption, the Ministry of the Marine in Paris called for closer oversight of the rolls. The lists continued to swell, however, and Laussat chided Martinicans for failing to pay their fair share when "even in the middle of war, the emperor has not for a second lost sight of Martinique," and sent much needed aid to the island.[129]

Other *petits blancs* and *gens de couleur* took advantage of fights between, on the one hand, Villaret-Joyeuse and the island's *colons*, and, on the other hand, Laussat, to formalize intimate interracial relationships that Creoles saw as detrimental to the island's racial and social hierarchy. The Arisy case, as it became known, revealed the difficulty of applying metropolitan law in the colonies, highlighted divisions among colonial administrators in Martinique, and underscored the continued influence of Martinique's elite Creoles despite metropolitan efforts to curtail their power. Sieur Arisy, a poor white dockworker arrived at Laussat's office in late July 1807. As required by French law, Arisy had come to inform the colonial prefect of his upcoming marriage and after a brief exchange, he departed. Shortly thereafter, however, Laussat received a letter from Martinique's interim *procureur général*, Georges Cacqueray de Valmenier, a wealthy white owner of a profitable sugar plantation who had arrived on the island nearly fifteen years earlier and closely aligned with the island's Creoles.[130] As chance would have it, Valmenier's letter informed Laussat that Arisy planned to marry a free *métisse*—a person with a white and mulatto parent—living in nearby Rivière-Pilote. Based on the previous modification to Article 3 of the Civil Code that had caused such tension between Laussat and Villaret-Joyeuse, Arisy's pending interracial marriage seemed illegal. By 1807, however, that modification seemed in doubt for in his letter Valmenier explicitly reminded Laussat that even though no metropolitan law actually prohibited such marriages he believed them "infinitely repugnant to good order," which, he noted, "has not been present since the reestablishment of the French government." Valmenier further stated "in his opinion the government had the right to oppose such alliances as necessary modifications to the *Code Civil* . . . at the least, it could force a white who degraded himself in this way to leave the colony with his wife."[131] For Valmenier such relationships not only degraded those whites immediately involved but also presented such a threat to the social order that they needed to be removed from public view.

Although Laussat, too, opposed locals practicing this *tâche de sang mêlé*, or "stain of mixed blood" as he put it, he claimed he could do little to prevent a union between Arisy and his *métisse* intended, not because the modification of Article 3 might impede their marriage, but rather because Villaret-Joyeuse had declared a state of siege, thus suspending all laws and taking over almost all powers himself. This situation, Laussat asserted, meant only the governor could intervene in the case if he saw fit. In the meantime, he thus issued the authorization for the wedding. Ten days later, however, Arisy returned to Laussat with a petition from a local priest who claimed he could not accept the colonial prefect's authorization and marry the couple because Villaret-Joyeuse had prohibited all marriages between whites and mixed-race individuals unless he personally sanctioned them.[132]

As Laussat admitted in a letter to the minister of the marine, certainly Villaret-Joyeuse had the right to issue such a directive but Laussat worried that the captain general would answer such a contentious question "militarily and with the stroke of a pen." Laussat's concern deepened when he learned Villaret-Joyeuse had acted at the Creole Valmenier's urging and that Valmenier had himself informed the priest of the ban. Certainly colonial officials should "listen attentively to the Creoles," Laussat contended, but one need not believe everything they said or do everything they asked. By forbidding interracial unions, Laussat continued, Villaret-Joyeuse had acted "like a *colon*." But given no alternative, Laussat revoked his previous authorization.

Ultimately he did not have to do so for Arisy soon visited Laussat one last time, withdrew his original petition, and in its place initiated a new one. In this one Arisy again asked for permission to marry but not as a white. Rather, seeing that he would find nothing but obstacles as a *petit blanc*, Arisy returned and said, "I am a *mulâtre* and I demand to be married as a *mulâtre*."[133] Villaret Joyeuse's ban on interracial unions thus had the opposite effect of its goal; when Arisy declared himself a *mulâtre* rather than a white, he turned the racial hierarchy on its head and tried to overcome official attempts to control his future. By renouncing his status as a white in favor of that of a mixed-race man, Arisy also demonstrated the flexibility of the theoretically rigid racial divisions between Martinique's inhabitants. In fact, at least in the white dockworker's eyes, these divisions clearly existed as purely social, not natural, constructions. Through his claim, "I am a *mulâtre* and I demand to be married as a *mulâtre*," Arisy affirmed his belief that he could change his racial status at will.

In the minds of elites, such a disavowal of this supposed marker of racial privilege fundamentally threatened white social superiority. If whites like Arisy might forego the social and legal benefits that came with the designation white, then how could elites contend such benefits needed safeguarding? And how could whites make cross-class alliances? Certainly if white men could define or redefine their status, the system could not still function. Arisy's claim also tapped into the fear that racial mixing among the island's poor white and free mixed-race populations now had made it impossible to tell a person's racial classification by sight alone. What if, in reality, Arisy *was* a mixed-race man who had passed as a white man all along? That he was not native to Martinique only strengthened this possibility because there existed no island record of his birth and therefore no official memory of his racial status. One had only his word, and the official paperwork based on it. In such a fragile structure, Martinique's elite Creoles saw the potential for destruction of the society in which they had so much invested.

Ironically enough, just two days before Arisy submitted his request to marry his mixed-race beloved, the Minister of the Marine in continental France distributed a circular designed to forestall "the impolitic and scandalous mixing of French blood and other grave inconveniences that could result" from relationships between whites and people of African descent in the metropole. In an effort to stem "the increase . . . in the number of *noirs* and *gens de couleur* of both sexes that have been and daily are introduced to the continental territory of the Empire," the circular reaffirmed earlier laws banning the introduction of mixed-race people to metropolitan France. It further instructed the captain general and colonial prefect of each colony to send him a list of people of African descent who had received permission to travel to metropolitan France, and instructed port authorities to return any unauthorized mixed-race individuals to the colonies. To dissuade ship owners from illegally transporting mixed-race people, the circular also indicated that ship owners would bear the cost of guarding any unauthorized persons during their stay on the docks.[134]

Clearly the 1802 measure banning individuals of African descent from the mainland had failed and the stipulation that administrators in each colony provide a list of travelers underscored metropolitan fears that *gens de couleur* continued to arrive on the continent, whether or not they had permission. At least one of the mixed-race people in question was actually an enslaved domestic servant for Colonial Prefect Laussat's family. In 1806 Madame Laussat had accompanied her three daughters from Martinique to Paris to enroll them in schools in the French capital. Although Laussat looked on the separation from his wife and daughters as a sacrifice, he thought it among his "most sacred" responsibilities as a father to ensure his daughters' education.[135] This "sacrifice" served more than one purpose, however, for in addition to the assumption that white women would marry and bear children, the elite ideal for white Martinican women also required a visible life of financial ease, often manifested in trips back and forth to metropolitan France inspired by a desire to secure the best education for both sons and daughters.

Madame Laussat admirably fulfilled this ideal for elite Creole women and in so doing gained the respect of Creole women like Rose Tascher de La Pagerie, Empress Josephine's aunt. Like many other elite Creole women making the trip, she also solidified networks between Creoles on the island and those in metropolitan France.[136] Rose Tascher de La Pagerie took advantage of Madame Laussat's visit to metropolitan France to send letters to her niece the empress and in them praised Madame Laussat as a "virtuous mother" and one of "few women capable of making such a sacrifice" as to leave her home and her friends. She further reminded Empress Josephine that the two women had met during one of the empress's visits to the island and thus asked Josephine to assist Madame Laussat if possible and to "grant her your special protection."[137] Creole connections, and certainly those that closely tied the Laussat family to Empress Josephine, were vital to maintaining family, business, and political connections around the French Atlantic.

While in metropolitan France Creole women of means like Madame Laussat communicated their privilege by attending their enslaved domestics. Bringing along an enslaved domestic on one's trip across the Atlantic was a perquisite of this elite white female privilege and bringing along more than one thus indicated access to people of influence who could make exceptions to the law. At the time of the Laussat women's departure, the 1777 law that allowed only one enslaved person to accompany a free person to metropolitan France had forced Madame Laussat to leave behind Solitude, a twenty-two-year-old enslaved *câpresse* whom Laùssat claimed, "has served my wife with great devotion."[138] As a result Madame Laussat had made her husband promise he would send Solitude along to metropolitan France when possible, even though it violated the law in spirit if not in letter. Laussat did just this nearly a year later when he asked two other Creole women bound for the continent to conduct Solitude to Paris and to deliver her to Madame Laussat.[139]

Although Laussat may not have thought Solitude endangered life on the continent, a number of measures indicate metropolitan administrators in Paris increasingly saw people of African descent in their midst as a threat. In addition to the circular banning the immigration of mixed-race people in 1807, officials also expanded their surveillance and called for an accounting of all people of African descent, regardless of status, then residing in the metropole.[140] Each mayor had to provide a list of all mixed-race individuals under his jurisdiction and include color, sex, age, profession, place of residence, and arrival date in France for each.[141] As before, people of mixed-race descent appeared most prominently in France's port cities—the Hérault reported sixteen individuals of color[142] and the department of the Gironde reported 180 people of color in Bordeaux alone.[143] At the final accounting, the minister of war determined that no more than 2,000 people of African descent lived in France's continental territory, a small number in comparison with the nearly 26 million inhabitants of metropolitan France.[144]

The administration's response to them seems quite out of proportion to the amount of practical danger they might have presented. However French authorities believed preventing the introduction of the so-called "African race" into continental France no small matter. On the contrary, according to the circular, the presence of individuals of African descent threatened the very foundations of the French family, namely, the purity of French blood. To the Ministry of the Marine, at least, the mixing of French blood (presumed to be "white") with that of the "African race" loomed as a menace to avoid in continental as well as colonial France because officials feared the inability to identify individuals by skin color. If visible racial markers disappeared on the continent as they threatened to in Martinique, then continental French would lose an important source of identity and power—the belief in a metropolitan France with laws and population inherently superior to that in the French colonies.

* * *

In 1808 Napoleon Bonaparte and his forces continued their march across Europe, gathering more territory for the French Empire. In the French West Indies, however, a different picture emerged. In November, the British secured their stranglehold on communication of all sorts and by mid-month at least twenty British warships blockaded the island, leaving Martinicans in a state of misery.[145] When Villaret-Joyeuse attempted to leave the island the British captured his ship and escort and detained him in the name of Great Britian.[146] By early February 1809 they had control of Martinique, too.

CHAPTER TWO

"Happy to Consider Itself an Ancient British Possession": The British Occupation of Martinique

ON FEBRUARY 26, 1809, as part of the ongoing battle between Great Britain and Napoleon, approximately 15,000 British forces descended on the island of Martinique in two columns ultimately forcing the surrender of Martinique's Captain General Villaret-Joyeuse.[1] For the next five years, the British administered the island under the leadership of three different governors and provided the possibility for a complete restructuring of the island's social dynamics.[2] Immediately following their conquest of the island Governor George Beckwith set out to establish control over the island's 8,985 whites, 7,100 *gens de couleur*, and 78,528 enslaved Africans.[3] In many ways British concerns about the island's stability and their initial efforts to administer it closely paralleled those of the previous French administration. They faced the additional burden, however, of demanding allegiance from a foreign population, including some who sought changes under British rule and others who wanted to maintain the status quo.

British administrators turned first to securing the support of Martinique's white elites. Men like the wealthy planter Pierre Dieudonné Dessalles potentially offered much to British officials. A staunch supporter of the Bourbon royal family, to the point of annually mourning the anniversary of Louis XVI's execution, Dessalles came from a family that had numbered among the island's wealthiest inhabitants since the mid-eighteenth century. Although born in metropolitan France, following the death of his father in 1808 Dessalles

spent the majority of his time in Martinique tending the family sugar plantation, La Nouvelle Cité, and a small coffee plantation, La Caféière, just outside
of Sainte-Marie on the island's northeastern coast. The plantations' location
in the middle of the island's most fertile land made them among the most
profitable in Martinique.[4] Dessalles was also well placed politically so much
so that when he married Anna de Bence de Sainte-Catherine, the daughter of
Martinique's interim chief judge, Captain General Villaret-Joyeuse and Colonial Prefect Laussat had served as his witnesses.[5]

   The wealth and family pedigree of men like Dessalles made them elite
among the elite, and thus particularly attractive to Martinique's new British
administrators. But Creoles also saw opportunity in the shift in power and
looked, in particular, to enhance their administrative and judicial hold on
the island. They convinced Governor George Beckwith to maintain the Privy
Council, an advisory body comprised of seven of the island's most noteworthy
inhabitants, and also the judicial power of the Court of Appeal.[6] Under Governor John Brodrick they worked to restore the court "to its former consideration
and dignity," namely the pre-1789 civil and judicial functions that the British
had maintained between 1794 and 1802 when they controlled the island.[7] Based
on who sat on the Court, and what they requested, Brodrick recommended
the British Colonial Office agree, noting, "the Court of Appeal is composed of
men of the oldest established families and of the most considerable property in
this island." Measures like allowing the Court to regain their right to remonstrance, in particular, should go forward, he argued, especially because "should
the objections of the Council appear unfounded," the governor had the right to
overrule them. Brodrick felt "assured that the result can only be to strengthen
the attachment of this colony to his majesty's person," and at the urging of
Martinique's white plantocrats he thus asked the Colonial Office to solicit the
king for "his most gracious consent to their reinstatement."[8] Such a measure,
he believed, could only solidify the support of Martinqiue's *colons* for British
rule, an important consideration in volatile times.

   In exchange for supporting British administrators, Martinique's elite Creoles also requested help securing their family members' return to Martinique.
Through the economic networks of the eighteenth-and nineteenth-century
Atlantic World, Martinique had long had extensive financial links with Great
Britain and when the island fell into British hands many Martinican Creoles
found themselves stuck in Britain, unable to return home. At least twenty
well-positioned white Martinicans appealed to the British Crown for passports to legally return to the island in 1809 and at least forty did the same
in 1810.[9] To aid them in their efforts, Creoles also enlisted the paid services

of a supporter in London, Robert Thore Milnes, naming him deputy agent for the colony of Martinique and instructing him to communicate with the British Colonial Office at Whitehall about cases that involved the interests of British merchants, Creole families, and British administrators in London and Martinique. Within six months of the British occupation, Milnes, aided by a London merchant, made a case for four Martinican colonists as assets (or at least not threats) to British rule in the colonies. Though French, and members of families once loyal to the French king, they all regarded Bonaparte as a usurper, not their object of allegiance, he contended. Thinking, perhaps, that the plantocracy would serve a foreign king more loyally than a French pretender, and hoping to bind the Creole elite to the British cause, the Colonial Office granted passage to all four.[10]

Milnes also took up the case of those like François Michel and his son, both of whom had shown what some interpreted as hostility to the British presence in Martinique.[11] Michel had served in the French navy under the monarchy and then engaged in some maritime adventuring in his own vessel until taken by the British on his way back to Martinique in 1809.[12] After François Michel's arrest the British also took his son, already in England, into custody and for almost a year, despite Governor Brodrick's request for their release, both languished in prison without receiving passports.[13] Although the senior Michel had been captured on vessels hostile to the British, Brodrick noted at the time that he had assurances of both men's character from "many of the most respectable inhabitants of this island," and thus he could safely recommend their return to Martinique. To Brodrick's entreaty Milnes added his own tribute to the power of class, writing the Colonial Office that he hoped "the respectability of their connections in the colony, as certified by Gen. Brodrick, who ventures to be himself responsible for their good conduct," would suffice to end the incarceration of the men.[14] Although it took time after almost two years the Messieurs Michel finally received word of their impending release.[15] Ultimately British administrators determined the affront further delay might cause Martinique's *colons*, many of whom vouched for the Michels, would cause more harm than either father or son might.

In addition to securing the return of loved ones, elite planters also asked British officials to help them maintain the myth of appropriate white behavior Creoles had so carefully crafted. Although British officials did not always personally support Creole requests, they helped when they could to further cement the relationship between the new national sovereign and Martinique's plantocrats. Nicolas de Percin, a member of the Privy Council and of one of Martinique's most prestigious families, for example, "urgently requested" that

Governor Brodrick solicit a dispensation of marriage for his relative, Bernard Barran de Percin, and the prospective groom's niece. Prior to the 1789 French Revolution, the pope had frequently accorded permission for marital unions between closely related family members. Since the promulgation of the Code Civil, however, only the king could grant such a dispensation. Brodrick acknowledged that he made the request "with considerable diffidence," and then only to restore "the honor of one of the first families in the island, many members of which have given conspicuous proofs of their attachment to His Majesty's government." Despite an ideal of elite white behavior that explicitly proscribed such acts for white men and women, the uncle and niece in question had already consummated their relationship, outside the bonds of matrimony, not to mention propriety, and had produced a child. Although he personally deplored such unseemly behavior, Brodrick asked the king to rescue "an infant already born from the stain of bastardy."[16] By permitting the marriage and thus making the child legitimate, the British would also allow the Percin family to restore their family honor and hopefully secure them as important allies.

Solidifying such friendships gained importance as Martinicans repeatedly called for the economic benefits of British rule and financial assistance from their new king. Because trade with the other British islands was sporadic and Martinicans found themselves almost cut-off from their traditional trading networks, distinguished *colons* on the Privy Council increasingly complained about what they perceived as their unequal status vis-à-vis other British subjects.[17] They expressed particular dismay that when the British took over the island only those ships then in Martinique's harbors could acquire legal registration to navigate freely; ships at sea could get no registration at all.[18] This meant that a significant number of the island's proprietors, regardless of their national status, had lost all ability to conduct business and were forced to sell their vessels. Ship owners who had come to the island legally after the British conquest also encountered hardships, as they were forced to take out a register and to pay the usual Customs House fees but received a simple coasting pass in return. Because the coasting pass only allowed vessels to trade in Martinique's ports and banned any commerce with neighboring colonies proprietors bearing the pass felt denied a right that all other inhabitants of the British colonies enjoyed. They further complained that those who had French charters for their docked vessels when the British arrived had privileges that those who had sworn allegiance to Great Britain, or who had acquired ships since the conquest, did not. Such a situation, which benefited those loyal to France and punished those now loyal to Great Britain, benefited the wrong people, they argued, and ran counter to British interests.

Governor Brodrick agreed and to remedy this inconsistency he urged the Colonial Office to take up this matter directly with the king.[19] At the request of Martinique's Creoles he also undertook a number of other steps to facilitate trade. In response to a petition from "respectable planters" on the windward side of the island Brodrick opened the port of Trinité to trade.[20] Following a Court of Appeal session at which Martinique's *procureur du roi* lamented the British king's failure to bestow on "his new subjects all the benefits which the people under his power enjoyed," Brodrick also implemented selective duties on certain items imported from the United States and premiums on British staple goods.[21] While the island certainly had flourished under British rule, Brodrick contended, he believed it still had "need of that protection and attentive care of its interest" that only the king could provide. He thus concluded that until British merchants agreed to trade more consistently with Martinique, the economic well-being of the island dictated such tactics.[22]

The British, of course, had their own sugar colonies, whose planters did not welcome the sudden addition of potential competitors in islands long, and perhaps soon again, in the hands of the French. This British plantocracy also had its own lobby in London, which managed to exclude Martinique's sugar from British markets through trade bans, taxes, and eventually regulations barring Martinican ships from British ports. These policies, together with prohibitions against Martinicans engaging in "foreign" trade, brought Martinique's economy to a near standstill in 1811 and produced a split between British administrators in Martinique and their superiors in London not unlike those past and future among their French counterparts. To administrators in London, favoring the "old" British colonies made sense; to those in Martinique, it constituted a folly that might well eventuate in a rebellion, which in the worst possible case might unite some segments of the island's population across racial and economic lines.

In the spring of 1811, a petition expressing Martinicans' ongoing frustration at their exclusion from free trade provided just such an example. Although Brodrick noted, "no body in this island . . . can be considered as representing the whole community," his letter to the Colonial Office accompanying the petition pointed out that the signatures came from every parish and included clergy, planters, and large and small merchants, underscoring the breadth of the concern. He added "the present state of the commercial relations of this island seem fully to justify the alarms which have been conceived in regard to its future prospects." So as not to suggest outright rebellion, however, he re-iterated "the sentiments of veneration and attachment of the great majority of the inhabitants to His Majesty's person and government."[23] In their petition, Martinique's inhabitants explicitly argued their current status as British subjects entitled them to all the benefits and protections that implied and to more effectively plead their case they used familial language indicating they had always remained British subjects, regardless of who actually controlled the island. The petition's signatories, including Pierre Dessalles and a number of the island's most important inhabitants, decried the "daily increase in danger that threatened them with total destruction," and expressed a desire to deposit their worries "on His Majesty's paternal chest."[24] During the previous British occupation, they noted, they had sought his assistance and thought of themselves as his children; now, they wondered, would the king allow the destruction of "this colony, which by one of the sweetest fictions of memory, and despite all of its various titles, is happy to consider itself an ancient British possession"?[25]

A parliamentary bill designed to reserve Martinican products for foreign export threatened just such an outcome. With continental European ports closed to England and all its possessions, Martinique's products rotted in warehouses waiting for re-export while sugar from other British islands like Jamaica and Barbados sold in Liverpool and Edinburgh. Such an arrangement, Martinique's inhabitants argued, absolutely ran counter to a colony's purpose "to consume the excess crops and manufactures of the metropole and to give them their products in return." This arrangement, the petitioners continued, formed "a family pact between the mother country and her colonies," an understanding that the current trade restrictions on Martinican products violated, further suggesting "the metropole appears to have forgotten her maternal cares. If Martinique can not obtain the entrance of her products into England, she is therefore not considered as a colony."[26] Although a reply from London was weeks, if not months, away, in immediate response to their pleas Brodrick ordered that no American vessel offload its cargo in Martinique unless it reburdened its hull with Martinican products of equivalent value, or to its capacity.[27]

This measure, Brodrick hoped, would stimulate trade even though Martinicans had little money with which to buy products. No doubt he also hoped to risk any outright rebellion by Martinique's Creole planters. In 1794 the general shift in France against property owners, and certainly against aristocrats, had helped to push many wealthy ennobled Martinicans into the arms of the British who had upheld slavery on the island when the revolutionaries had banned it throughout the French realm. By 1809, however, the situation had changed. For some of Martinique's plantocracy, loyalty to their property, which in their minds included their enslaved workers, meant loyalty to those who could protect it and trumped any theoretical attachment to a specific monarch, whatever the nationality. Although they had not openly protested British rule, rumors of Creole plots to oust the British from the island had plagued officials since the early days of the occupation and consequently they constantly looked for any sign of intrigue.

A report from DuBuc de Marintille, a former resident of Guadeloupe who had left the islands during the 1789 Revolution and was then residing in New York, contended that British survival in the French West Indies ultimately depended on the ability to discern friend from foe.[28] Based on their previous successes against the British at Guadeloupe in 1794,[29] DuBuc de Marintille warned, France would no doubt launch an attack against Martinique with a view to "subverting the whole island." For this reason he recommended deporting some inhabitants and threatening those who remained with confiscation of their property if they proved disloyal. Such a tactic, he indicated, would undoubtedly create more allies. To unite all of the inhabitants of the island, he further argued, administrators might also consider submitting a general petition "freely subscribed by them," to the king "supplicating his majesty never to give up Martinique to the government of Bonaparte."[30] Drawing on planter hatred of the "usurper" Bonaparte, DuBuc de Marintille concluded, would unite elite white planters like Dessalles in support of the British.

When a clandestine correspondence between Decrès, the French minister of the marine, and several wealthy Martinican colonists came to light, DuBuc de Marintille's prediction appeared to come true. Upon learning the news then-governor Beckwith proclaimed the administration would consider anyone who received a letter from Decrès, or knew of someone who had received a letter, as having violated the oath of allegiance required by the British government shortly after occupying the island. He also threatened severe sanctions, including deportation, for any betrayals.[31] A Creole plot just a year later that involved communication between someone well known to the British government (who had received official permission to travel to and from the island) and parties in metropolitan France only heightened administrators' anxieties about enemies in their midst and further indicated French Atlantic commercial networks continued to function despite ongoing hostilities. In November 1810 a Martinican merchant, LeCamus, sailed for London with a valid passport from Brodrick, who had issued it due to "the respectability of the branches of [LeCamus's] family residing in the island." Ten days later, however, "well disposed inhabitants" of LeCamus's neighborhood convinced the governor that LeCamus carried subversive clandestine correspondence which prompted him to contact the Colonial Office and recommend authorities detain LeCamus on his arrival in Portsmouth.[32] As feared, when Portsmouth's mayor and local officials took LeCamus into custody, he carried sixty-five letters and packets to a number of different people in France and in London. Some of those letters, officials claimed, also revealed LeCamus's extensive, and dangerous, connections on the continent.[33] One letter from Vernier in Martinique to an important Creole merchant, Henri Petit, then residing in London suggested, for example, that for a price LeCamus could tell Petit how to secure clandestine passage to continental France.[34] If elite French sympathizers could move freely between the islands, London, and continental France, administrators worried, they could seed chaos as they went. Consequently British officials around the Atlantic, and certainly in Martinique, had to remain ever vigilant of a possible uprising from all of the island's inhabitants and also from abroad.

This meant keeping a watchful eye on the island's *petits blancs* who also looked for new opportunities with the transfer of Martinique from French to British control. Upon taking control of the island British administrators had granted residence permits both to French soldiers who deserted before the occupation and to other individuals who provided important services. In general, however, British officials believed "strangers to the colony and without property," would endanger public security if they escaped police surveillance and consequently ordered masters of passenger boats to present the passports of white passengers on arrival and also required white nonresident passengers to petition for temporary residence.[35]

After a failed rebellion apparently masterminded by Martinique's *petits blancs* and including *gens de couleur* British administrators worried even more about the island's poorer whites. In an attempt to reclaim nearby French possessions, barely a year after securing Martinique the British sent forces stationed on the island to Guadeloupe, leaving Martinique temporarily in the hands of Major General Carmichael. According to a "respectable authority," just days later French prisoners of war held at the local fort planned to overpower their guards and, with the help of "some disaffected inhabitants,"—*petits blancs*—and also "inconsiderate and unprincipled persons from the great population in the commercial town of Saint Pierre,"—*gens de couleur*—the interracial group planned to take the local fort and oust the British.[36] Thanks to the advanced warning, apparently from a loyal Creole elite, the plot failed. It nonetheless signaled that a rebellion that crossed lines of race and class presented a serious threat.

In response to the thwarted coup British administrators tried a number of punitive measures to ensure the island's stability from internal and external threats. For as their continued movement around the Atlantic Basin indicated, some *petits blancs* and free mixed-race individuals in Martinique and

Guadeloupe looked to capitalize on fights over national sovereignty around the region. British officials in Martinique thus limited immigration, and in particular tried to exclude any travelers coming from Guadeloupe. Although the British had also managed to briefly occupy that island in 1810, its proximity fueled worries about the spread of seditious information and the organization of a potential inter-island rebellion. To prevent Guadeloupe and Martinique from continuing to swap "vagabonds and disreputable people," Governor Brodrick also ordered visas for Guadeloupe denied to all suspicious individuals, regardless of their skin color.[37] Despite such precautions *petits blancs* and free mixed-race individuals continued to arrive on the island, prompting one decree that ordered the arrest of all foreigners, white or mixed-race, who lacked a valid permit of residence and another that forbade white individuals from disembarking in Martinique without written permission.[38]

Governor Brodrick blamed the island's judicial (French) rules, among other things, for allowing Martinicans like those traveling between the islands too much liberty and giving them too much license. In Martinique he decried "the inefficacy of the laws of this island for the maintenance of internal tranquility," and lamented in particular "the strong prejudice against the infliction of the punishment of death on white persons," a sentence which *colons* absolutely deplored because they believed it caused familial disgrace and degraded whites in the eyes of Martinique's free and enslaved Africans. According to Brodrick, however, police reports and magistrates' complaints about the behavior of Martinique's *petits blancs* indicated they had a "certainty of impunity" that encouraged rebellions like the one mentioned above. Unfortunately, he concluded, showing the "delinquents" just how narrowly constrained authorities felt in inflicting punishment "drains the law of all of its [effect]," and ultimately acquiesced to illegal and disruptive behavior, sending the message of an island ripe for the picking.[39] As long as the island's elites refused to adequately punish all offenders, he concluded, British officials thus were limited in their ability to rule the island and create stability if their actions potentially upset Martinique's racial and social hierarchy.

To avoid future chaos, and to potentially cement the loyalty of Martinique's seemingly unruly *petits blancs* and free mixed-race individuals, in adition to punitive measures Brodrick tried to provide economic stability for those who lived on the margins by establishing charity bureaus in Fort Royal, Saint Pierre, and Mouillage as institutions "of humanity and at the same time of policing." By including *gens de couleur* and whites in the British government's benevolence, Brodrick provided organized public assistance to all of the colony's free inhabitants. While this was an important indicator the British government wanted to avoid further alienating Martinique's free men, like most public assistance programs individuals had to meet certain criteria to receive aid and the British excluded the "lazy, drunk, or [those who] generally led a bad life." To insure appropriately worthy beneficiaries, the decree also required local civil authorities, parish priests, and four notable inhabitants in each parish to confirm the need of the applicant and his family, further empowering the ruling Creole elite to effectively decide who merited assistance.[40] When the initial three bureaus proved unable to handle the number of Martinicans applying for aid, Brodrick required each of Martinique's rural parishes to build and help support the new charity outposts. Any person who found him/herself unable to pay the appropriate taxes was instructed to report to the local charity bureau and obtain a certificate of indigence either from the bureau or from a "competent assembly."[41]

The creation of rural charity outposts was significant for it greatly facilitated the chance that *gens de couleur* might also apply for and receive aid. This was no small matter for with a shift from French to British rule Martinique's approximately 7,100 *gens de couleur* also hoped for a change for the better. As previously noted, however, British administrators initially viewed this population with just as much suspicion as the island's other inhabitants, requiring, for example, newly arrived mixed-race passengers also to present their passports on arrival and to petition for temporary residence.[42] After evidence of the 1809 elite conspiracy came to light and following the thwarted 1810 interracial rebellion involving *petits blancs* and *gens de couleur*, however, British officials increasingly tried to provide free mixed-race Martinicans with some reason to support Great Britain. In addition to allowing them access to the charity bureaus, they also passed a regulation granting limited civil rights to the island's *gens de couleur*. Their need to keep Martinique's *colons* as friends, however, also prompted British officials to require "the free *gens de couleur* understand they are freed men or the descendants of freed men and whatever distance there is from their origin, nothing can make them equal with whites; nor make them forget the respect they must have for them."[43] They further decreed free individuals of African descent could only own property or participate in the same circumscribed sphere of activities that had existed under the French if the new administrators had recognized their titles of liberty.[44] In practice, although this provided some of Martinique's *gens de couleur* with new opportunities, it also gave British officials another way to deny rights to any *gens de couleur* they, or the island's Creoles, deemed dangerous. Ultimately they hoped for stability.

* * *

Within two months of Lieutenant-General Charles Wale's arrival in Martinique, an attempted rebellion by enslaved and free individuals of African descent shook Saint Pierre and set in motion a series of events that, ironically, ultimately curtailed the power of the Creole elite and improved the lives of the island's enslaved and free mixed-race populations. When Wale took command of Martinique in July 1811 he found an island destabilized by economic stagnation and shifting demographics.[45] Although Martinique's enslaved African population remained relatively constant from the previous year at 78,577, the white population had increased a little over 2 percent from 8,985 to 9,206 people and the *gens de couleur* population had grown by 20 percent from 7,100 to 8,630.[46] Creoles worried about this dramatic shift and feared the British had allowed Martinique's *gens de couleur* too many freedoms thus encouraging them to take matters into their own hands. This seemed the case on September 18, 1811, when a domestic of one of Martinique's Creole planters in Saint Pierre exposed a terrifying plot to his master. Apparently, that very night, a group of enslaved and free mixed-race individuals planned to set fire to Saint Pierre and then, in the words of the planter Pierre Dessalles, cry "fire" and "indiscriminately slit the throats of all whites—women, children, and old."[47] From Saint Pierre, the domestic noted, the group planned to spread out and eliminate all of Martinique's other whites.

This plot intended to, in the words of Dessalles, "found a second Haitian empire" in Martinique nonetheless proved short-lived when the Creole, alerted by his domestic, immediately informed Governor Wale of the planned uprising who called out the troops and militias in Saint Pierre. While both white and free mixed-race militiamen searched for those slated to participate in the rebellion, Wale described "the partial insurrection of some negroes of this town" and the ringleaders' arrest in a letter to the Colonial Office. He confirmed "no bloodshed had ensued," and promised any who had fled to the colony's interior would quickly be "exterminated." In the meantime, however, he believed it "necessary to make an example" of those already arrested.[48]

By the following day the militias had captured or killed all of the principal actors in the planned uprising and rounded up a number of other conspirators; shortly after Wale convoked a special session of the Creole-controlled Court of Appeal to try the "villains."[49] Many of those involved in the attempt, however, had escaped to the rugged terrain surrounding Saint Pierre and, despite Wale's earlier promises, eluded capture. Nonetheless the British eventually arrested twenty-eight people and the Court of Appeal tried them at

the end of September and beginning of October, ultimately condemning sixteen men—seven free mixed-race individuals and nine enslaved laborers—for
their part in the failed rebellion.[50] Believing that a pardon might help the
British keep order on the island by encouraging other "misguided persons to
abandon like wicked and deplorable plots," Wale granted one defendant, an
eighteen year-old enslaved domestic, a respite from execution, pending the
king's judgment.[51]

Before his execution, one of the leaders of the rebellion also indicated
that pardons might produce more informants and prevent massive disruptions
with Atlantic World dimensions that he knew were already in progress. In his
testimony Thétis claimed he had left Saint Domingue in 1803 for the express
purpose of inciting rebellion among Martinique's enslaved laborers and, at the
same time, "four boats of negroes, mulattos, and whites" had also set out for
the islands to promise liberty to enslaved people.[52] Fomentors of rebellion thus
crossed racial and class lines, he indicated, which made anyone in Martinique,
or on any other island, a potential enemy of the British. Thétis also claimed,
"every month, Bonaparte sends a number of emissaries from France who go
to New England and then to Saint Domingue . . . to cause chaos in the other
colonies that [Bonaparte] wants to see destroyed if he can not have them." If
Thétis's claims were true, British administrators and Martinicans had every
reason to fear, or welcome, a complete reversal of the island's social and racial
hierarchy.

Creoles, for their parts, feared such a change and Pierre Dessalles, who
served as a judge in the October trial, worried repeatedly about renewed troubles but informed his father-in-law, one-time chief judge Bence, that he hoped
the island would "have peace for a long time."[53] Wale also appeared uneasy
about the future, feeling "still more confirmed in my opinion that the enemy
has his partisans who would . . . sacrifice this colony to the horrors of a revolutionary insurrection like that of St. Domingo."[54] To prevent such a calamity he
recommended deporting from the colony "all those who having no property at
stake cannot produce the most unequivocal proof of good conduct and attachment to the British government." To help police that suspect population, and
to provide security against an enemy attack, Wale also created the "Corps of
Royal Martinicans," which included only "British-born subjects," aged sixteen
to fifty-five.[55] To convince any enslaved laborers or *gens de couleur* they would
gain more by exposing a plot than they could hope to win by participating
in it, he also offered rewards to those who had warned of the September 1811
rebellion. "To impress upon the minds of that class of people, who were unfortunately implicated in the conspiracy, that rewards as well as punishments

are the result of justice," he presented the rewards in a ceremony in the middle of Fort Royal and immediately before the Court of Appeal session so the event would be as public as possible.[56]

Wale undoubtedly hoped his actions might unearth another conspiracy of enslaved and free people of African descent, and, indeed, shortly after the presentation he learned of a fresh plot involving some of Martinique's Creoles acting in concert with *gens de couleur*. If members of these two groups formed an alliance, British officials worried, then surely the island would fall. Wale thus turned to those Creoles he believed unquestionably loyal to the British to determine the seriousness of the purported coup. His investigation unearthed even more divisions among the island's *colons*, however, which made solidifying that group's allegiance nearly impossible and further suggested even his supposed allies were suspect. According to an informant, the plot in question intended to "wrest the island from the British and to hold it for Buonaparte" and included Creoles as well as free mixed-race individuals like Gourard Fauvel, a land surveyor and local *mulâtre* who had approached the informant to join the conspiracy.[57] Hoping to learn more, Wale urged the informant and two other Martinicans to play along with Fauvel. When the counterconspiracy surfaced inadvertently, however, British authorities arrested the *mulâtre* Fauvel and promised to spare him a charge of treason only if he divulged full details of the plot.[58] In response to Fauvel's disclosures, Wale then ordered the arrest of five Creoles, "three of them planters of considerable prosperity and two others of less note."[59] After a series of personal interviews with each of the accused, four of the five admitted to complicity, and Wale believed the fifth guilty as well.[60]

According to Fauvel, he first learned of the conspiracy through a series of anonymous letters and understood that seven people in Saint Pierre had organized it, that sixty more had sworn secrecy, and that 700 people around the island stood ready to join the rebellion. The conspirators intended to take over the government in Bonaparte's name, he claimed, by first surprising and overwhelming the garrison in Saint Pierre. Then Fauvel and fifteen others would seize the governor and poison the fort's cisterns, leading eventually to the fall of the entire island. Fauvel's first task, however, involved discerning the opinions and garnering the support of several people near Fort Royal, including the five Creoles eventually arrested by the British.[61] Wale's description of each accused man, and their subsequent punishments, show how money and family connections among white Martinicans influenced the definition of loyal behavior in Wale's eyes.

One of the accused, Fontanne de l'Isle, Wale painted as a "man of good family, dependent upon his mother, a lady of property in the island;" another accused, Fontanne de l'Isle's cousin de Mascaras, was "a man without property dependent on Madame de l'Isle." Both men, Wale insisted, only refused to take an active part in the plot because they "fear[ed] the consequences," and not because they thought it treasonous. Despite their knowledge of the conspiracy and their failure to disclose it, Wale ultimately judged them "insignificant characters, dangerous only in the colony" and consequently deported the two to America where they had family and business connections.[62]

Unlike de l'Isle and de Mascaras, who had family connections but no independent property of their own, the third man accused, Louis Michel de Luppé, had both and they afforded him special treatment. Wale called de Luppé "a planter of good family and considerable property in the island," and noted he served as captain of dragoons in the Trinité militia and a planter in the bountiful area of Robert.[63] De Luppé also knew of the plot but claimed he thought it "absurd and chimerical" and had therefore refused to join it. De Luppé further insisted he also had warned Fauvel against participating. In his correspondence with the Colonial Office Wale noted de Luppé's culpability in failing to expose the plot, but "hoping to get further information out of him," he promised that if de Luppé revealed all, he could return to his plantation. After testifying, in English, de Luppé, this man of "timid character . . . not to be feared as an enemy," therefore went back to his home unpunished. Although his involvement closely mirrored that of de l'Isle and de Mascaras—he knew of the plot but did not reveal it—he suffered no further consequences.[64]

The fourth accused, Catalogne, a man of property in the island and "connected with many of the most respectable families," repeatedly denied any knowledge of the plot and Fauvel's original accusation against him constituted the only bit of evidence tying him to the conspiracy. Based on the word of the former president of the Privy Council, Du Buc St. Olympe, however, Wale believed Catalogne probably did know about the plans.[65] According to St. Olympe, Catalogne also had served as an officer in Trinité's militia and commanded the battalion when the British captured the island. He explicitly resigned that position to avoid taking the oath of allegiance to the British while serving as a French soldier, however. St. Olympe further doubted Catalogne had ever taken the oath; in fact, he labeled Catalogne a "Bonapartist," and thus suspected him of taking part in this interracial conspiracy to rid the island of British power.[66]

Wale had intended to send Catalogne to England but, "lest His Royal Highness should think the evidence insufficient for the adoption of such a measure," he instead informed the Colonial Office that he had allowed Catalogne, like de Luppé, to return to his island plantation. His family connections, rather than a lack of evidence, undoubtedly also saved him from a charge of treason. Catalogne's brother-in-law, Gallet, a member of the Privy Council and "a man of the first respectability," promised Wale an indemnity of 1,000 pounds sterling if Catalogne left his estate or had "any conversation inimical to the government."[67] Such influence no doubt helped Wale decide he could safely return Catalogne to his family's oversight.

Jean Baptiste Marie Chansel de Fonrose (Fonrose), the fifth Creole accused in the conspiracy, presented the most difficulty for Wale and other British administrators. A man linked to "the first families in the island," he too had "large possessions in the colony."[68] Unlike de Luppé and Catalogne, however, Fonrose's property and connections appear to have worked against him in the minds of other Creoles and ultimately in Wale's. Fonrose initially denied knowing about the plot. After arriving in Martinique in 1801, Fonrose had married his first cousin, who owned a *sucrerie* in Vauclin, Martinique, and had served as captain in the local militia and taken the oath of allegiance under Du Buc St. Olympe.[69] St. Olympe, however, had less than flattering things to say about Fonrose, insisting that the man had long craved an appointment to the Court of Appeal but, "based on his private conduct," the other members had blocked his admission. Although St. Olympe did not specify what Fonrose had done to make himself ineligible for the post, he also denounced Fonrose as "a Bonapartist."[70] After Wale told Fonrose that others had placed him at a meeting where Fauvel talked about the alleged plot, Fonrose finally admitted he did know about the conspiracy but claimed he, too, had taken it for a "joke" and tried to dissuade Fauvel from participating.[71]

To Wale's surprise Fonrose further insisted the plot included Creoles who held some of the most important political and judicial positions on the island, which smacked of something more than an isolated episode of discontent "confined to the heated imaginations of a few restless partisans of Buonaparte" as Wale had earlier believed.[72] Rather, according to Fonrose, the conspirators counted heavily on Messieurs Nicolas de Percin and Dugué, both members of the Privy Council, and also on Catalogne, whose brother-in-law Gallet also served on the advisory board.[73] When pressed Fonrose admitted Fauvel did not confirm any of the men as members of the conspiracy but Fonrose claimed to have personal experience implicating Nicolas de Percin and Dugué as suspects. On a visit to a wealthy relative, Fonrose claimed, he had overheard the man call de Percin "the most dangerous man in the colony" because he publicly blamed General Wale for all the colony's woes and also said Martinique's troubles would only end when Wale was "chased away."[74] As for Dugué, Joseph

Maillet—a young man whom Governor Brodrick had granted permission to return to the island—told Fonrose "many people mistrusted Dugué" because of the "caresses they saw him give to the *gens de couleur*." For that reason, Fonrose continued, many supposed "like . . . his father," Dugué would take up the *gens de couleur* cause. Whether literal or metaphoric, Dugué's "caresses" and his alliances with the island's free mixed-race population made him suspect in Fonrose's mind.

The potential involvement of Privy Council members de Percin and Dugué ultimately convinced Wale not to bring the affair to a public trial since French law required public disclosure of anyone mentioned in a case of treason. The confusion that might arise from "the implication of so many families," Wale informed the Colonial Office, especially if insufficient evidence precluded convictions, would no doubt create the "worst of circumstances." Continued secrecy, he therefore concluded, would let him determine if all the culpable had indeed been identified or if he needed to probe for additional suspects.[75]

Although Wale tried to keep the conspiracy a secret, many around the island sensed something amiss and this again opened the doors for a shift in the relationship between British administrators and Martinique's various populations. It also revealed disagreements between British colonial administrators in England and those in Martinique; like their French counterparts, British officials failed to speak with a united voice and exposed the ad-hoc, situational character of British colonial policy on the island. Of the five Creoles accused, Wale sent only Fonrose to England to be tried for treason, claiming he was "too dangerous" to remain on the island. After weeks of consideration, however, the admiralty office, citing the exorbitant expenses involved in transporting the necessary witnesses from Martinique to London to participate in a trial of treason against Fonrose, indicated they intended to ship him back to Martinique or to some other destination.[76]

The new secretary of state of the Colonial Office, Earl Bathurst, also rejected Wale's characterization of Fonrose as too dangerous to leave in Martinique, or to send to continental France where, "as a martyr to his cause," Wale believed Bonaparte might favor him and encourage more partisans in Martinique to imitate him. The Colonial Office further questioned Wale's assertion that in America Fonrose could "plot against this government" and informed Wale the king disagreed with his handling of the affair and insisted it had produced the "greatest embarrassment."[77] What, precisely, caused such embarrassment for the Colonial Office Wale never learned although he did find out that Fonrose had been sent from England to Gottenburg. The episode concluded, Wale therefore released the free mixed-race Fauvel.[78] Although neither party mentioned the incident again, it marked a turning point in the relationship between Wale and his superiors in Great Britain.

Not surprisingly, after the thwarted Creole/*gens de couleur* conspiracy, Wale proved less willing to offer help to Martinique's *colons*. To maintain control on the island, however, he still had to find ways to appease Martinique's Creole elite. After the United States declared war on Great Britain in 1812, the island's *colons* called even louder for the return of their loved ones, for economic security, and for French justice, and Wale increasingly turned to a select group of Creoles for advice. These white plantocrats, however, took this opportunity to rid themselves of other Martinicans they believed threatened the island's racial or social hierarchy in some way. This was especially clear in the case of Jossie, a Martinican in England who requested permission to return to Martinique. In 1810 Jossie, a merchant on the island who owned no property, and his colleague Thounens had left Martinique with passports for America.[79] Although the two men had authorization only to the United States, they went first to France, intending to continue on to the United States and then back to Martinique. Somehow they ended up in England, however, and from there petitioned the Colonial Office for permission to return to Martinique. Because they had gone unauthorized to France, however, the Colonial Office denied them passage to Martinique instead granting them permission to return to the United States, their original authorized destination.[80]

The war between Great Britain and the United States ultimately made such a return impossible for Jossie and Thounens and the Colonial Office subsequently consulted Wale to ask if anything other than their original misuse of their passports prevented the men's return to the island.[81] Wale initially told the Colonial Office that although he agreed the island's inhabitants should not shuttle between Martinique and France, he believed the Colonial Office's plan to send the two men to America problematic since too many individuals traveled "between this island and France by way of America and St. Bartholomew."[82] After further investigation Wale also indicated the "best authority" on the island claimed Jossie "had principles in direct opposition to the interests of Great Britain," and further denounced Thounens, although an "insignificant character," as a "Bonapartist," and thus best kept out of the colony.[83] After additional consideration in the end the Colonial Office decided that such Creole denunciations, combined with the men's illegal trip to France, which all now found "prejudicial to the safety of His Majesty's colony," warranted denying Jossie and Thounens permission to return to Martinique.[84]

This initial setback did not deter Jossie's family, however, and his niece's actions the following year further illustrate the resilience of French Atlantic networks, and Creole women's important role in them, even in times of war. With Governor Wale's permission Mademoiselle Jossie left Saint Pierre in February 1813 with the express intent of finding her uncle in London. On her departure she carried several letters from local Martinicans to friends, relatives, and business partners throughout metropolitan France. Based on the contents, their writers clearly expected either her or Jossie to deliver the letters, as well as debt payments and rent money for family members throughout continental France. Before those letters reached their recipients, however, the French intercepted a British ship and found the missives in Jossie's bag, indicating that niece and uncle had found one another in England and that Jossie intended to return to Martinique without permission. As a result of the confiscation of the Jossie family belongings, Doulert never received the letter and the substantial sum that a boutique owner in Martinique had collected from one of Doulert's clients.[85] Fonrose Dariste, a son of the wealthy Dariste family who was then pursuing his education in Paris, also had to survive without the 1,528 *francs* his brother had sent with Mademoiselle Jossie.[86]

Mademoiselle Jossie's voyage and the letters she carried are an important reminder of the crucial role Martinican women played in maintaining transatlantic connections. Wale granted Mademoiselle Jossie permission to leave the island, perhaps assuming because she was a woman she posed less of a threat to the island than did her uncle or assuming as a good niece she planned to tend to her uncle during his exile in London. Whatever the reason under the best of circumstances a trip across the ocean represented a significant hardship since the voyage itself, fraught with dangers, could last as long as two months. Even if a traveler arrived safely at her destination, the passage meant approximately 3,000 miles separated the traveler from her family. Although undoubtedly many Creole women who made the voyage had support networks on each shore, the impediments created by the physical and temporal distance between the opposite sides of the Atlantic, especially during a period of international conflict, made their roles as coordinators of such business dealings even more vital.[87]

In addition to carrying letters and payments (like Mademoiselle Jossie) or supervising children (like Colonial Prefect Laussat's wife), during the British occupation of Martinique, Creole women from the island carried out a number of other tasks directly related to family business ventures throughout the French Atlantic World. Mézérenc, for example, represented her family in their running fight with creditors over the family inheritance.[88] Genty of Saint Pierre used her stay in Bordeaux to collect money that metropolitan debtors owed her husband.[89] According to Genty's never delivered letter, she also planned to manage the money her husband expected both from other Martinicans residing in France and also from the anticipated sale of Genty's Martinican sugar, no matter how meager the profits.[90]

Governor Wale well knew of Martinique's failing economy and shortly after taking control he worked to garner white planter support by trying to improve trade. Just one week before the uprising of *gens de couleur* and enslaved Africans in September 1811, he informed Martinique's Privy Council that the British Lords of the Committee of Trade had decided to grant licenses to Martinicans who wanted to trade sugar or coffee, Martinique's principal crops, with continental France; they would even allow the trade to take place in French vessels.[91] In the aftermath of that revolt, Creoles took advantage of Wale's new need to secure *colon* loyalty by trying a new tactic to lobby for what they saw as their economic rights as British subjects. Rather than complain simply to Wale or the Colonial Office, they now asked their representative, Deputy Agent of the Colony Robert Thore Milnes, to intervene on their behalf directly with colonial administrators across the Atlantic. In the shadow of the uprising, Milnes linked the island's economic distress explicitly to Martinique's racial imbalance and suggested continued economic hardship might compel the majority enslaved population, in particular, to increasingly violent ends like those recently displayed around the Atlantic world. Unlike during the first British occupation, in 1812 the enslaved African population outnumbered whites on the island almost eight to one and, according to Milnes, had "begun to show signs of discontent & to enter into secret plots for the destruction of the white inhabitants." Although Wale's diligence had thwarted the rebellion, Milnes invoked the specter of Saint Domingue, warning the "slaves being driven by famine" might sooner or later establish "an independency such as at St. Domingo in the midst of the Leeward Islands."[92] Given the possibility of an Atlantic-wide rebellion, he implied, it would not simply serve the interests of the island's planters, but also the interest of the entire British Empire in the Caribbean, to allow French plantocrats to trade their sugar on the home markets and also with continental France.[93]

When such measures apparently fell on deaf ears, nearly a year later Martinique's Privy Council returned to an earlier strategy to gain assistance—petitioning the king. Once again they employed explicitly familial language to characterize the island's past and present relationship with Great Britain, claiming they did not "dare to look back at those happy times when as adopted children of Great Britain the principles of justice formed the basis of our laws and relationships with the mother country."[94] They further lamented that the relationship had changed and claimed "those memories can only make us feel more strongly the miserable state into which the bill [regarding trade] we ask to be repealed has pushed us."[95] Despite the Creole/*gens de couleur* conspiracy in early 1812, in his letter accompanying the petition Wale underscored the continued deprivation on the island and observed that efforts to send produce to England for reshipment to foreign ports had proven "ruinous" and "almost the whole export trade of this colony has been confined to that of molasses, bought by the Americans."[96] War, in Wale's words, "shut up the only remaining market for the produce of this island; the utmost distress pervades all ranks of inhabitants."[97] Previously he had recommended patience to the island's inhabitants, he claimed, but now he felt unless a foreign market appeared or the legislature soon admitted Martinican produce to British home consumption "ruin must be the inevitable consequence."[98]

The success of Great Britain's allies in northern Europe dramatically raised the demand for, and price of, sugar from the island's planters in 1813.[99] Nonetheless Wale worried that Creole "jealousies of their neighbour's superior prosperity and fears of returning under [sic] the tyranny of their former oppressors, make at present but lukewarm friends to the cause."[100] Great Britain's refusal to allow Martinican ships into British ports, and final clarification denying that Martinicans were British subjects, further rankled Creoles. In practice the island continued to be subject to the random arrivals of British ships, and to extortionate shipping charges, angering Martinican merchants.[101] They also responded poorly to the news that, although they could enjoy the privileges conferred on aliens in any place surrendered to the king, only British subjects who had "never taken the oath of allegiance to any foreign state, except under a capitulation, or a person . . . made denizen by Letters patent, or naturalized by Act of Parliament," could register a ship as a British vessel.[102] Clearly none of Martinique's French inhabitants fit those requirements.

The British superintendent of aliens provided even more depressing news for Martinique's Frenchmen, noting, "in all acts of Parliament, all legal proceedings, and all legal disquisitions, where the personal privilege of a British subject is in question, that phrase always means a 'British born subject;' it is by birth only and not by conquest or cession that such personal privilege arises."[103] Consequently while Martinicans might want to claim rights as British subjects and reap the full benefits of that status, one needed not simply the "national, political character," that came through conquest or cession, but also the "municipal, personal character" available only to those born on British soil; all others remained, in British eyes, simply aliens.[104] With such a ruling, Martinique's *colons* came to believe their requests for an equal playing field in the British markets would always be denied.

Such a clear indication of their subordinate status in the empire angered Creoles, but a natural disaster shortly after the Superintendent's ruling revealed how contingent and ad hoc colonial policy could be. In summer 1813 a devastating hurricane swept through the Caribbean and although it caused minimal loss of life (none in Martinique) it completely destroyed forty-one vessels from England and Sweden in Saint Pierre's commercial port and prompted Wale to take matters into his own hands, regardless of official British mercantile policy.[105] Immediately after the emergency he requested that the Colonial Office allow French inhabitants to register their ships for commerce, that it authorize ships built on the island to provide intra-island transport, and that it let British ships export coffee, sugar, rum, and molasses to ports in Spanish and Portuguese America to purchase necessities.[106] While awaiting further instructions from the home office, he also issued a proclamation allowing British vessels or those of any other nation friendly with Britain to import staples from any port for three months.[107]

Despite his requests and temporary measures Martinique's planters found Wale's response to the worsening economic situation inadequate and contacted Deputy Agent for the Colony Milnes, who in turn wrote to the Colonial Office to "detail the severe losses which the planters have suffered."[108] On their behalf he asked the Colonial Office to request an order temporarily restricting the extra duty placed on their produce sold for home consumption, arguing, "the quantity of sugar that can come to market here is but trifling, the favor solicited cannot be materially injurious to our old West India possessions though it may afford some relief to the planters of Martinique."[109] Despite their ruling one year earlier categorizing Martinicans as aliens in the British Empire, in response to the economic crisis and to the pleas of Wale, Creole planters, and their supports in London, the Committee of Privy Council for Trade decided Martinican sugar could enter the home market without duties and Martinicans could build and register cruising ships and use them for transporting items between the island's ports.[110]

Although they ultimately gained the economic concessions they sought, under Wale's tenure Creoles lost their hold over other traditional strongholds, like the Court of Appeal. As a result they viewed his efforts not just as an infringement on their rights but also as a clear indication that he hoped to secure the allegiance of the island's enslaved and free mixed-race population to the detriment of *colons*. In early 1812, for example, Wale reversed the Court of Appeal's judgment in the cases of five "criminals" they had recently sentenced to hanging: two convicted of "mutinous words," the other three for "running away" (*marronnage*).[111] In a letter to the island's head French judicial figure, procureur général Valmenier, Wale praised the Court, which now included the planter Pierre Dessalles, as "selected from the most respectable part of the community both for education and property in the colony," and indicated he did not, in principle, disagree with their decision.[112] Rather, he informed them, he believed once again showing mercy would help sustain the tranquility that had reigned on the island since the September 1811 uprising. Lest they think he questioned their verdict, however, and to obviate "any jealousy on the part of that respectable body of magistrates," he observed, "the judge's duty is to decide according to law: it is mine to temper justice with mercy, as far as I may consider it safe to the colony."[113] His powers as governor, Wale believed, allowed him such discretion and he deemed it better to tender mercy rather than inflict punishment if it might provide stability.

The elite Creole members of the Court of Appeal, however, disagreed with his reversal of their judgment and also with his claim that it was his "duty to consult the real interests of the colony with as much zeal as I [invoke] the prerogatives of His Majesty's representative for the benefit of every class of its inhabitants."[114] They wanted Wale to work only for their interests and found insulting his suggestion that he, a British governor, and not they, *colons* with deep roots on the island, had the colony's "real interests" at heart. In his response to Wale, the president of the Court of Appeal thus noted while he did not question Wale's authority to commute the executions, clearly Wale and the court had different opinions about how best to maintain order.

Martinique's elites similarly bridled at what they saw as Wale's interference in the post of vendue master, viewing it as another attack on their judicial and economic power. Since its creation shortly after the British took control of Martinique, the position of vendue master had sparked disagreement between Creoles and British administrators over just what privileges and responsibilities this position entailed. In broad terms the vendue master had oversight of sales of immoveable (land and buildings) and moveable (everything else) property on behalf of the British government.[115] Such an oversight directly conflicted with the position of the *huissier*, however, who under the French system oversaw such sales ordered by the courts to ensure the rights of defendants and plaintiffs.[116] Despite their overlapping jurisdictions, in the interests of maintaining as much consistency as possible, the British had allowed both the vendue master and the *huissiers* to exist. Because both positions yielded a profit—the vendue master charged a 5 percent flat commission on the sale, the *huissier* a 2 1/2 percent commission plus additional administrative charges— either the island's one British appointed vendue master or the multiple French *huissiers* stood to lose money depending on the position's definition.[117]

In the fall of 1813 Governor Wale and Martinique's procureur général Valmenier argued over the purview of each office, with Wale insisting the vendue master had to attend all sales, even those ordered by the courts, and Valmenier claiming that a previous governor, Beckwith, had confirmed a *huissier* should preside over all judicial sales and that a vendue master had no jurisdiction there.[118] At the continued insistence of the current British vendue master Governor Wale finally referred the matter to the Colonial Office for clarification. When that clarification arrived, Valmenier and other Creoles viewed it as a significant infringement on their rights. According to the Colonial Office, in the future the vendue master would oversee all sales, whether of immoveables or moveables, voluntarily made by the island's inhabitants and would charge a 5 percent commission. He would also administer all sales of moveables ordered by the Courts of Justice, but at the same rate of 2 1/2 percent commission and administrative fees formerly charged by the *huissier*. Only those sales of immoveables dictated by express order or decree of a Court of Justice's final verdict convoked the *huissier*, they determined, and then at the rates and fees previously charged.[119] Not surprisingly many of Martinique's elite Creoles viewed the articulated responsibilities of the vendue master as an ominous sign of expanding British power.

For those still undecided, the case of the *mûlatresse* Mésdélices confirmed fears that Wale, backed by the British government across the Atlantic, would take what measures he saw fit to curtail the island's Creole-controlled judiciary. Of just as much concern to Creoles, the case further revealed that *gens de couleur* and their supporters saw disputes between Wale and Martinique's white plantocrats as an opportunity to push for a consistent application of justice and more equitable treatment for the island's enslaved and free African populations. In March 1814, Wale received a complaint on behalf of Mésdélices, a *mûlatresse* who had lingered in Saint Pierre's jail since 1813 by virtue of an order to sell her as the enslaved domestic (and thus the legal property) of a Creole, Raymond Chavés.[120] After months of requests French officials had refused to acknowledge her status as a *femme de couleur* or release her, despite the fact that Chavés—her legitimate owner, long-time partner, and father of her children—had taken her to Trinidad on a valid passport from Martinican officials, that he had voluntarily consented to her manumission there, that Trinidad's governor had legally freed her on December 21, 1812 according to the laws of that island, that she had returned a month later to Martinique, the island of her birth, and that there she had registered as a free woman and paid her manumission fee.[121]

The case once again brought Wale and procureur général Valmenier into conflict. As luck would have it, Valmenier happened to be at the government house when Wale received the complaint and when Wale asked him why Mésdélices remained in jail the procureur général responded that even though Chavés had relinquished all rights to Mésdélices she remained subject to seizure as an *épave*, or enslaved person forfeit to the Crown, for having obtained her freedom somewhere other than the island of her birth.[122] The following day, unsatisfied with Valmenier's explanation, Wale contacted Saint Pierre's royal prosecutor, Regnaudin, both to determine why the government still held Mésdélices and to stop any proceedings then in process against the woman. He also personally went to Saint Pierre and discussed the matter with Regnaudin who further informed the governor that a 1768 French law prohibited inhabitants of the colony from sending their enslaved laborers to foreign islands to buy their freedom; this law, Regnaudin claimed, made Mésdélices's manumission invalid.[123]

Wale disagreed with the French official's finding, however, claiming one of Governor Beckwith's decrees shortly after taking control of the island had clearly annulled the 1768 law. He further added that with Martinique in British hands, the British island of Trinidad was not a foreign island but part of the same empire, and consequently the terms of the 1768 law would not apply even if still in effect. Based on this reasoning, and also because Mésdélices was soon to give birth, Wale directed Regnaudin to release her, to clear her of any charges brought against her by the state, and to hold on false imprisonment anyone who attempted to detain her as an enslaved person.[124] To ensure no miscommunication, he also put his verbal instructions in a letter that he posted to Regnaudin.[125] When the royal prosecutor failed to respond to this letter, as the law bound him to do, Wale sent his personal secretary to determine if Regnaudin had received the missive. Regnaudin indicated that he had and had followed the governor's directions. Nearly a month later, however, Wale received a letter from Regnaudin and a copy of the proceedings of the Tribunal of First Instance in Saint Pierre, both of which indicated that contrary to Wale's instructions Mésdélices had remained in jail and Regnaudin had initiated a judgment against her on behalf of the Crown. To add insult to injury, the Court of Appeal had also confirmed the tribunal's decision.

When Wale contacted Regnaudin for an explanation, the royal prosecutor claimed he had mistaken Wale's initial instructions. But a series of letters between Regnaudin and procureur général Valmenier showed that Regnaudin had well understood those directions and that he and Valmenier had secretly conspired to pronounce a judgment against Mésdélices before her actual trial. When confronted with this information, Regnaudin denied ever speaking to Valmenier on the subject and Valmenier refused to produce a letter clearly illustrating their discussions about the case. Valmenier also refused Wale's request to annul the Court of Appeal's confirmation of the verdict against Mésdélices.[126]

In the face of such blatant abuse of the judicial process, and flagrant disregard for his instructions and authority as governor, Wale took two important steps that cemented divisions between the island's elite white planters and British officials and promised to radically alter the island's demography. In response to the controversy surrounding Mésdélices's certificate of manumission, Wale issued a proclamation explicitly abrogating the 1768 ordinance. By doing this, he told the Colonial Office in London, he hoped to speak directly to, by his estimate, the "not less than a thousand persons of colour, who being refused their freedom in this colony, have obtained it in others, returning and living peaceably and quietly here under the benign government of His Majesty." If the 1768 measure stood, he argued, Martinique's *colons* might also subject those *gens de couleur* to suffer seizure for the profit of the [British] Crown and, if that happened, they might "in a state of desperation, [break] out into open Rebellion against a government which so oppresses them . . . inducing their numerous connexions [sic] among the free people of colour and slaves of the colony to join them."[127]

Martinique's elite planters, not surprisingly, responded to this measure with outrage. The abrogation of the 1768 law theoretically created at least several hundred new *gens de couleur*, further threatening Creole power and removing a tool *colons* had long used to restrict the growth of Martinique's free mixed-race population. First Mésdélices, then several hundred, and perhaps in the near future several thousand, new *gens de couleur* meant an unacceptable shift in the island's demographics and a potential collapse of its racial and social hierarchy. When Wale suspended both *procureur général* Valmenier and royal prosecutor Regnaudin over their failure to follow his instructions, Creoles saw their dismissal as yet another unjustified, direct attack on Creole judicial power. Wale characterized the two men's behavior as "caballing conduct," however, and he hoped the prince regent would find the evidence "sufficient to justify my conduct in dispensing with their future services in their same situations under the Crown."[128]

Creoles also responded with anger to Wale's continued efforts to reform what he characterized as "the most horrid abuses of arbitrary power, risen into acts of the greatest cruelty, against an helpless and oppressed People."[129] Wale concluded that under men like Valmenier and Regnaudin the island's arbitrary judicial system had cruelly abused the island's *gens de couleur* and enslaved inhabitants, and he therefore worked to make systemic changes. After viewing the unspeakable conditions in which Mésdélices and other men and women of all classes and colors (and even cattle) lived in the Saint Pierre jail, he authorized construction of a new jail. He also had an insane asylum built, which he described as "a paradise" in comparison with the old jail that had housed the mentally ill. Finally, he oversaw the creation of a poor house that would accommodate thirty poor people, "the first establishment of the kind, excepting that for orphans at St. Pierre, in the colony."[130] All these measures he hoped would better the lives of countless Martinicans.

Wale also focused on more intimate, individual changes. He replaced the dismissed royal prosecutor with a man whose nineteen years of experience as a lawyer in Martinique and whose sizeable estate there gave him a "solid interest in the police and welfare of the colony." He left the position of *procureur général* vacant, however, waiting on further instructions from the prince regent. The Court of Appeal, for their part, registered an official complaint against the dismissal of Valmenier and Regnaudin and the appointment of a new royal prosecutor but Wale moved forward with his campaign of reform and charged the new royal prosecutor with investigating a well-known planter rumored to have kept a runaway enslaved man chained to the floor for three years. According to Wale, "my bringing this man to trial has created a cabal against me by several of the landed proprietors, perhaps with some, fear for themselves may operate, but a Frenchman and a colonist will hold it to be a bad example to prosecute a gentleman for anything that he may do to his slave." Despite such generalized opposition and also a Privy Council member's assertion that, in prosecuting the planter, Wale had set "the whole colony in mourning," Wale forged ahead until leaving for a six-month sabbatical at the end of July 1814.[131] Undoubtedly he intended to continue his crusade after returning to the island the following January. He never had the chance.

* * *

In December 1814 the French officially regained control of Martinique. Although the British would again rule the island during Napoleon's brief return to power, Wale never again had the opportunity to right what he perceived as grievous wrongs. When French colonial administrators returned for good in 1815, they proclaimed the benefits, including the joy of heart, of reunion with France. While hoping to find residual loyalty, and to inspire even more of it, the newly arrived colonial administrators, knowing full well that the Creole elite had twice coexisted peacefully (for the most part) with their British occupiers, that the majority of them had sworn allegiance to the British crown, and that they had found that supplications to "his majesty" from "his loyal subjects" served about as well with one king as another, regarded their Creole brethren with suspicion. And well they might.

CHAPTER THREE

"Your French and Loyal Hearts":
The First Decade of the Restoration

AFTER FIVE YEARS of British rule, the French regained physical control of Martinique in 1815 with the restoration of the Bourbon family and Louis XVIII's ascension to the French throne. On the island, the cycle renewed. Like after previous periods of foreign control, colonial officials focused on re-integrating the island into the French Empire under the guidance of a new governor, Pierre-René-Marie Vaugiraud. On his arrival Vaugiraud congratulated the island's inhabitants for their show of fidelity under British rule, noting, "your French and loyal hearts waited only for the flying of the white flag [the sign of the Bourbons] to give in to exhilaration." Now that a "legitimate King," Louis XVIII, sat on the throne, he continued, Martinicans should "reunite all of your methods, all of your efforts to augmenting your products." This, he assured them, would return them to "the beautiful days of your prosperity."[1]

French around the Atlantic waited eagerly for the island's return to stability, so much so that many took advantage of the new found peace and the favorable late-summer sailing weather to make their way to Martinique and begin a new life. In the six months following Vaugiraud's welcome, some 215 people arrived on the island and over the next two years another 531 departed for Martinique from Marseille alone.[2] Martinique had experienced a similar onslaught of *petits blancs* bound for the colonies following the island's previous return to French rule. This time, however, immigrants from an even broader range of occupations arrived in Martinique as renewed contact with the French West Indies beckoned to those seeking work in trans-Atlantic colonial commerce. Bakers, tailors, cooks, wig and hat makers looked for a fresh start as did dozens of clerks and merchants, most with families.[3] At least one hundred of those whites traveling from continental France to Martinique were white women accompanying husbands or brothers, and some officially declared themselves hatmakers, alcohol vendors, domestics, schoolmistresses, dressmakers, and dress shop owners.[4] Although they provided vital quotidian work for the colony's daily functioning, their visibility nonetheless undermined the ideal of white female leisure.

All of these travelers to Martinique undoubtedly hoped their arrival on the island would open a host of new opportunities to them. Colonial administrators on both sides of the Atlantic, for their part, sought to augment the island's white population and create a better ratio among Martinique's different populations. The island's demographics had markedly shifted during British rule and by 1816 the island's whites numbered 9,298, *gens de couleur* 9,364, and enslaved Africans 80,800.[5] For the first time under French rule, mixed-race peoples outnumbered the white population and this worried whites on both sides of the Atlantic. As before, however, not just any white would do. Vaugiraud voiced his concern that an onslaught of France's least desirables, many of them former supporters of Napoleon, plagued places like Martinique, and "pursued by either public opinion or the tribunal, look to flee French soil and come here to mill about with adventurers and disreputable people."[6] Although Martinique needed more whites, he implied, those who had recently arrived did not fit the bill.

Vaugiraud's concern held particularly true in the case of Tholosan, a free Martinican *mulâtre* deported from the island during the early years of the 1789 French Revolution and his white wife, both of whom returned to Martinique in 1815. Purity of white womanhood persisted as an important symbol of pro-slavery rhetoric during the early years of the Restoration and Tholosan and his wife exposed the fragility of this ideal and served as a reminder of the realities of racial mixing and its threat to the island's social order. Vaugiraud claimed the arrival of this couple created a scandal stemming from "the spectacle of the degradation of a white woman descended to the ranks of the *affranchis*" through interracial marriage. During the Napoleonic period, martial law had outlawed such unions. By 1815, however, a cloud of uncertainty had descended on the legal restrictions regarding interracial marriages in the colonies, although custom still clearly proscribed them. Vaugiraud declared such a union "subversive to the colonial system . . . not only because they have never been permitted in our islands but also because the idea never even occurred to anyone," and insisted that maintaining order in Martinique required "the

distance between the color white and all others." The marriage between Tholosan and "this white woman," as he called Tholosan's wife, threatened that
separation. The potential consequences of such a blurring of boundaries, Vaugiraud further suggested, one could see in the fact "the two had been insulted
by the entire population." Vaugiraud took some solace in his belief that the
enslaved and *gens de couleur* population appeared "themselves offended to see
this *mélange*." Nonetheless, as a precaution, he asked the commander of the
second division in Saint Pierre to carefully watch the man and his family until
they left the island.[7]

Vaugiraud's attention to the couple demonstrates the degree to which
colonial administrators, despite official rhetoric, worried perpetually about
threats to the racial boundaries that underlay Creole privilege and the colonial
system generally. For Vaugiraud, Tholosan's wife fell well short of the model of
white womanhood and her behavior threatened to banish her from the ranks
of whites into that of the *gens de couleur*. This was no small matter. In addition to Tholosan, a number of other free mixed-race inhabitants had seized
on Martinique's reintegration into the French Empire to travel to the island,
much to the chagrin of colonial administrators and Martinique's *colons*. Vaugiraud worried about the increase in Martinique's *gens de couleur* population
and especially about the arrival of those, like Tholosan, who had spent time in
continental France where, due to the very different racial demographics and
social hierarchy, they may have grown to see themselves as equal to whites. In
a letter to the minister of the marine, he argued it would be "a great risk to
let *gens de couleur* who had spent time in France, especially during revolutionary epochs," to return to the colonies.[8] To control the seemingly unchecked
growth of this portion of the population, early in his tenure Vaugiraud called
for the capture of all deserters, indigents, and vagabonds and in particular
free mixed-race people without family ties.[9] He needed metropolitan help,
however, and thus called on the minister of the marine to do all he could to
prevent the transatlantic migration of *gens de couleur* from the metropole.

In the midst of the shifting demographics on the island, colonial administrators like Governor-General Vaugiraud looked once again to cement the loyalty of Martinique's elite white planters, presuming them to be, for the most
part, a stable group on the island. They especially hoped to secure elite white
help in increasing the island's productivity and thus French prosperity. For
their part, Martinique's *colons* saw this return to the French fold as a chance
to solidify their control on the island. They thus welcomed measures that
returned the Sovereign Council to its pre-Revolutionary status and restored
its jurisdiction in administrative, policing, financial, and judicial matters.[10]As

they would repeatedly attempt over the next thirty years, Creoles also looked to secure white dominance in Martinique through educational institutions designed to teach white boys and girls how to be good Creoles. An important opportunity came in 1815 when the governor transferred the island's foundling home and the female charity hospice from the *dames dominicaines* to lay oversight.[11] Both institutions had long served as bulwarks of Creole privilege on the island and by shifting their administration to lay women, who henceforth would be paid by the government, Creoles extended their control over Martinique's neediest white inhabitants and put white Creole women in charge of training them in their ideal of proper white behavior.

Creoles also pressed to create educational institutions for the island's wealthiest white children. This included petitioning Vaugiraud to reestablish the Collège de Saint-Victor, a boys' school initially chartered in 1768 that had closed. There, they hoped, Martinican youth might "receive an education rivaling that of the best French schools." In early 1816 the school re-opened, with government assistance. To guarantee "the instructional methods and *ouvrages* followed for different subjects absolutely paralleled those in France's *lycées*," required a substantial investment and therefore to reach as many students as possible, the institution accepted full-time boarders, who would pay 1,500 francs, as well as part-time boarders at a rate of 1,000 francs, and also day students paying 500 francs.[12]

To ensure that planters' daughters grew to be appropriate Creole wives and mothers, Martinique's plantocrats also petitioned Vaugiraud to create a lay-administered boarding school for white girls. Although some wealthy white families sent their sons and daughters to metropolitan France for their education, this necessitated a prolonged separation that the rocky economic climate made more difficult emotionally and financially. Martinique's Creole director of the interior estimated that a year's education for girls on the continent often cost 1,600 to 1,900 francs and he argued that educating white colonial girls there actually distorted their development and, by extension the future health of the colony, by exposing them to unnamed mores unsuited to the island's plantation system. "The young female destined to live and die in the colonies where she was born," the director noted, should "have a simple education, continually directed towards her future," and "on her soil," he concluded, "she can receive an education that will conform her to her existence."[13]

In response to this petition, colonial administrators used municipal funds to create the Royal School for Girls in Saint Pierre, entrusting its direction to two handpicked laywomen. In their mission statement, the founders declared their hope that this institution, too, would rival those on the continent and charged the directors, assisted by a staff of female instructors and male professors of the arts, with instructing female pupils in good manners, ways "appropriate to their sex," and the principles of the Roman Catholic Church.[14] Unlike the Collège de Saint-Victor, the Royal School for Girls only accepted full-time boarders at a cost of nearly 1,200 francs for fees and tuition, guaranteeing only the daughters of Martinique's wealthiest *colons* could afford it.[15]

Because time on the continent still served as an indicator of elite status for Martinique's Creoles, following their return to the French Empire, many looked to strengthen the island's links with metropolitan France. As a result, even though they sought to create schools on the island, *colons* also petitioned metropolitan administrators to support the education of French colonial citizens in continental France. In August 1816 the government responded, guaranteeing three spots at the prestigious Maison Royale de Saint-Denis for Martinican girls between the ages of six and twelve whose fathers had served as officers in the French military. The Maison Royale de Saint-Denis, the Ministry of the Marine assured Creoles, "occupied the first ranks and was intended for *demoiselles* who, after receiving their education there, would enter equally prestigious ranks in society."[16] Out of a desire to "give testament to our benevolence and an indication of our special protection, in recompense for their attachment to our person and our family," the new Bourbon monarchy also allotted six scholarships for Creole boys to attend continental *collèges royaux*.[17] These spaces, intended for boys between ages nine and fourteen who belonged to "property-holding Creole families living in the colonies," required knowledge of Latin and would be given to petitioners chosen by the minister of marine. In addition to the scholarship, the government also granted recipients free passage on a government vessel to and from the continent. The minister of the marine hoped that Martinicans would happily embrace the metropolitan government's "new act of benevolence" for its French colonial citizens and see the gestures as evidence of colonists' place in the French national family.[18]

To reestablish their economic status in the French Empire, Creoles in Martinique and metropolitan France also worked to highlight the importance of colonial commerce and solidify links with a number of metropolitan businesses. Although a number of Creole women returned to Martinique after 1814, others remained in the French capital and the provinces, continuing to facilitate the transatlantic connections they had maintained during the British occupation of the island. The six-year correspondence of widow Soubiran, a Martinican woman splitting her time between Paris and Morne Rouge, Martinique illustrates the complexity and extent of the Creole network and its dependence on Creole women who grasped and pursued the intricacies of transatlantic commerce despite an ideal that sought to limit their business activities.

Between 1814 and 1820, Soubiran corresponded with Louis Pecoul, a lawyer in Martinique, concerning her significant commercial interests around the Atlantic basin and in particular about her attempts to secure her portion from the sale of a plantation she owned with her brother-in-law, Fournier.[19] After the property was sold and accounts settled in early 1814, Fournier owed his sister-in-law, Soubiran, 21,798 francs. Finding himself unable to pay the full debt, at year's end Fournier suggested transferring an annuity worth approximately 6,000 francs to Soubiran to serve as a partial payment on his debt. Because the annuity was originally in francs *en tiers consolidé*, however, which were worth 72 or 73 francs in continental France at the time, Soubiran worked to secure the payment as quickly as possible to avoid losing any capital. Noting that Fournier held liens on a number of other properties in Martinique, she also encouraged Pecoul to accept them if Fournier offered them as payment.[20]

On the advice of Pecoul, and because she was herself in Paris, Soubiran also enlisted the help of de la Servalle, Fournier's niece, in securing payment on Fournier's debt. By the end of 1814, however, de la Servalle claimed not to have heard any word of the matter from her family and Soubiran was unable to collect any money. She thus wrote Pecoul in Saint Pierre asking him to visit Fournier and to request that Fournier immediately send de la Servalle financial power of attorney so the two women could handle the 6,000 francs transfer in Paris. She also asked Pecoul to urge Fournier to pay the remaining 15,000 francs he owed her as soon as possible.[21]

That Fournier was Soubiran's brother-in-law, and that she was forced to negotiate with his niece in Paris, undoubtedly complicated the widow's position. So, too, did Fournier's connection with other well-placed Creoles who also owed the widow money. Shortly after learning of Fournier's offer to transfer the annuity, Soubiran also heard he had been appointed secretary to Dubuc, an important Creole planter who then served as the island's *intendant*, an important administrative and political post. This news, she informed Pecoul in February 1815, made her happy "at first for him [Fournier] and then because it would assure my accounts." As it turns out, however, her joy was premature. Over the next eighteen months she struggled to gather payments from Fournier, Dubuc, and another influential Creole planter, Grenonville. According to a March 1810 judgment registered in Paris against Dubuc, he owed Soubiran 6,765 francs but had yet to pay her.[22] Grenonville, for his part, owed her 45,800 francs but seemed to question whether or not he needed to pay, in his words, "a creditor who was no longer present" on the island. That he disputed only 12,000 francs of the total sum Soubiran found even more confusing and was surprised "Monsieur Grenonville has made me wait eight months for the payment of these 12,000 francs. It seems I have waited such a long time he would not want to make me endure another delay."[23]

Soubiran had yet to collect on any of these outstanding debts by fall 1815 even after visiting de la Servalle in Paris a second time. This visit further concerned Soubiran for de la Servalle first claimed not to have received the power of attorney from Fournier and then showed her one but said it was useless because the names had been misspelled. Finally she insisted she had written Fournier for a new power of attorney but her uncle had not yet responded. Such subterfuge boded ill for the future, Soubiran believed. Because she had been unable to use this capital over the past fifteen months, she already had lost significant sums of money. To make matters worse, she also feared de la Servalle was about to ask her for a personal loan, something Soubiran could not possibly consider under the circumstances.[24]

Unable to collect on these debts, and perhaps in response to Grenonville's comments about not paying absent creditors, Soubiran returned to her properties in Morne Rouge near Saint Pierre. Even though present on the island, the widow nonetheless continued to conduct her business affairs through Pecoul and expected a much quicker response now that they were both on the same side of the Atlantic. In January 1816 she exhorted him to visit Fournier and force the man to at least authorize another female family member in Martinique, his sister, to pay the widow the interest on the annuity while she waited for the payment. Likewise, while she welcomed the news that Grenonille planned to pay his debt by sending eight barrels of sugar to Papillon, an agent in Le Havre, who would sell it and forward her the proceeds, she also informed Pecoul she impatiently awaited the funds because she needed to make her own payments.[25] One month later, still without payment from Fournier, she urged Pecoul to visit him a third time and insist that he authorize his sister to pay the sum in question.[26]

Soubiran finally received some satisfaction, receiving 5,200 francs from Fournier in April. The money did not come from the annuity, however. Rather another Creole who also had dealings with Fournier, Spitalier, extended her the money from one of Fournier's accounts in a Parisian bank. Soubiran also received payment from Grenonville. Because Grenonville had only sent seven rather than eight barrels of sugar, however, after paying Papillon in Le Havre all appropriate expenses, she ultimately had received a little less than 10,000 francs. Grenonville thus still owed her 2,000 francs. Soubiran also awaited payment from Dubuc and asked Pecoul to hand deliver a letter to the official that insisted he reimburse her immediately. She further asked him to once again turn his attention to her affairs in England. She was "completely dependent" on him to gain access to the unknown sum owed her, she noted, and thanked him for his efforts on her behalf around the Atlantic.[27]

Having heard nothing for several months, Soubiran again contacted Pecoul in the summer of 1816 to express her frustration that after six years Dubuc still owed her money and refused to respond to the three letters she had written to him since her return to Martinique. Worse yet his nephew, who was charged with handling the payments, had recently informed the widow that the money supposedly allocated for the debt was gone and therefore he would be forced to suspend payment indefinitely. She despaired of ever receiving payment from either Dubuc or Fournier. In the case of her brother-in-law, final payment was a long time coming; not until March 1820 did de la Servalle finally pay the remaining 1,000 francs of her uncle's debt during one of her visits to Martinique. After six years, numerous letters and the involvement of Creole men and women on both sides of the Atlantic, Soubiran rejoiced that she could finally send Pecoul a receipt, in triplicate, for Fournier's closed account.[28]

French colonial citizens like Soubiran, de la Servalle, Spitalier, and Papillon who traveled between the continent and the Caribbean played vital economic roles in the French Empire. There were many others. Between 1815 and 1817, 183 white Martinicans—152 men and 31 women—traveled to Marseille, many of them with enslaved domestics.[29] By their presence, the enslaved and free domestics who often accompanied legal travelers from Martinique reminded everyone that French commerce in the Caribbean was founded on chattel slavery and highlighted metropolitan France's intimate, if conflicted, relationship with the institution. With a return to Bourbon rule, it remained to be seen how the new regime would respond to people of African descent in continental France. Initially the 1777 Police des Noirs, which technically banned all "blacks, mulattoes, and other people of color" from continental French territory, still prevailed, as did the provision that allowed one enslaved *noir* or *mulâtre*, male or female, to accompany a free person during her ocean voyage to metropolitan France, provided that person guaranteed the enslaved individual's return with a 1,000 livres surety.[30] The provision requiring enslaved people to stay in France's port cities, however, remained as loosely enforced as ever and some owners took advantage of the opportunity to bring their enslaved and free domestics into France's continental interior. Pierre Dessalles's wife, daughter, and son, for example, brought along their "good old *négresse*," on their trip to Bordeaux in 1815, and Pierre Dessalles took his enslaved domestic, Fortunée, and her two sons, Dieudonné and Saint Fort, when he joined them in 1816.[31]

Other free mixed-race individuals like Louis Montleon also made the transatlantic trip.[32] While officials struggled with how to respond to *gens de couleur* in their midst, conversations at the highest levels of government indicate they also worried about free mixed-race individuals who traveled to the colonies. In early 1817 then Minister of the Marine St. Hilaire explicitly reiterated the concern Governor Vaugiraud had made to him about Martinique's *gens de couleur* population and added his own about the dangers they posed to France's most important sugar colony. Their "disturbing increase," as well as "their increasing pretentions," presented trouble, he reported, and further warned the Council of Ministers that free mixed-race individuals in the colonies looked to outside help, perhaps from Saint Domingue or even continental France, to better their positions and upset the region's racial and social hierarchy.[33] Governor Vaugiraud's concerns, as articulated to the Council of Ministers through the minister of the marine, apparently made an impression. In October 1817, a ministerial dispatch explicitly reiterated earlier bans against *gens de couleur* traveling to and from continental France.[34]

* * *

A political shift in metropolitan France following the Congress of Aix-la-Chapelle in 1818 presented a new opportunity for colonists around the French Atlantic to renegotiate their relationships with one another and the continent. A period of political pragmatism reigned on the continent leading to the appointment of a new governor in Martinique, François-Xavier Donzelot, a military man who had distinguished himself in the Napoleonic campaigns and had most recently served as France's governor in the Ionian islands.[35] After his arrival, Donzelot set out to implement continental reforms and to reorient Martinique's relationship with the continent. Like his predecessors he found himself walking a tightrope between more closely aligning the island with metropolitan French standards and appeasing the Creole elite on whom the prosperity of the island depended. Time and again, however, he sided with the island's *colons.*

A series of initiatives, all with the explicit goal of augmenting Martinique's white population by shipping poor continental whites to the island, signaled a change in how colonial administrators perceived the relationship between island and metropole. Although none of the measures ever transpired, the plans themselves, and Creole resistance to them, reveal both French metropolitan and elite Creole concerns about the shift in Martinique's demographics and their shared desire to increase the island's white population to provide stability. While French metropolitan officials may have looked to Martinique as a place that could absorb the continent's excess (poorest and neediest) people and thus provide increased security in this volatile corner of the French Empire, Creoles adamantly opposed such an influx of continental whites due to their stereotypes about *petits blancs* and their fears that poorer whites could not help but engage in interracial sexual relationships with the island's *gens de couleur* and thus hasten the downfall of colonial society.

One proposal submitted to the minister of the marine suggested sending white artisans to the French West Indies to "increase the numerical and moral force" of the whites currently living there; to return enslaved blacks to cultivation by supplying whites for the artisanal trades, and; to serve as a counter to those *gens de couleur* who might want to follow the example of Saint Domingue and foment rebellion.[36] In addition to helping to prevent a still-feared Atlantic-wide rebellion, just as important, the proposal suggested, sending white workers to the French Caribbean also would "open new and important possibilities for the surplus population of France."[37] Another plan submitted to the Council of Ministers recommended bolstering the number of *petits blancs* by sending white agriculturalists to the French West Indies through a so-called "military colonization" that each year, for five years, would send 5,000 men, artisans or agriculturalists, in battalions. These men would work, either individually or in associations, at their assigned tasks and would provide "an intelligent, robust population capable of defending itself from internal and external [dangers]." The proposal also stipulated that, if possible, only men thirty-five years old or older and, preferably those accompanied by their wives and children, should have a place in the worker battalion.

Donzelot responded favorably to both proposals, noting, "white agriculturalists and workers could be very profitably introduced in Martinique by inserting them into the staff of existing plantations."[38] He felt so strongly about bringing white workers to the island that he even requested fifteen agricultural workers to work in a private sugar refinery that had experienced great losses.[39] Based on their assumptions that these poor white men would establish dangerously close relationships with the island's free mixed-race inhabitants, Martinique's white planters, however, initially refused to endorse any plan to transport white workers.[40]

Colonial administrators in France clearly hoped to make some kind of shipment of continental whites, however, and even suggested sending abandoned and orphaned metropolitan boys who, on their twelfth birthdays, became the responsibility of the Ministry of the Marine.[41] Trained in agricultural work or the mechanical professions, they would work for free until age twenty-five.[42] Because metropolitan administrators believed these unfortunate young men could increase the outnumbered white population and undertake a variety of beneficial tasks by working on private or royal plantations, they urged Martinique's white planters to consider the proposal and instructed Donzelot to seek the support of a number of wealthy planters and influential local officials. The responses Donzelot received from Martinique's Creoles reveal how deeply they feared that poor whites from the continent and free mixed-race Martinicans would mix, whether through interracial sexual relationships or by finding common cause in shared working conditions. For Martinique's *colons* both possibilities threatened a dangerous realignment of the island's racial and social hierarchy that could not be tolerated.

Of the many planters who responded, only one believed the plan to send orphans to the island might work. Fougainville, owner of a profitable plantation located near Rivière-Pilote on the southern part of the island, thought the measure feasible but only if the boys had not yet passed the age of twelve or thirteen and if sent only to private plantations. If these conditions held, the planter claimed, "the tender childhood of these unfortunates, exempt of anticolonial prejudice, could be molded to the ideas of their benefactors [and] the colony would be enriched by their industry and fortified by their spirit and number."[43]

Fougainville's opinion notwithstanding, the majority of Martinique's planters and Creole officials believed the venture foolhardy. Some argued the orphaned boys ultimately would find no way to make a living. Assier de Montrose, a *colon* living near Grand'Anse on the northern tip of the island, argued because the children sent to Martinique would arrive without an education they would only "augment the already considerable number of wretches who vegetated in the colony."[44] Others contended too many white workers already lived on the island. Lamentin's police captain, as well as Soubiran's delinquent debtor, Grenonville, noted since 1814 all the local parishes had seen an increase in the number of immigrating whites who eventually ended up destitute.[45] Several claimed Martinique had enough needy orphaned children of its own and, like LaGrange, the owner of a large sugar plantation on the Atlantic coast, added if colonists wished "to charge themselves with raising illegitimate children, they [could] easily find some in Martinique."[46] DuHaut of Grand'Anse and de Perpignan of Saint Pierre argued the "poor orphaned creoles" of Martinique who received aid from the island's charity bureaus and then set out to earn their own way should receive preference over strangers, especially when their current numbers exceeded the available positions for them.[47]

While many elite Creoles remained silent about their fears the island's *petits blancs* and *gens de couleur* would join ranks, some explicitly objected to the transport of continental male orphans on the grounds that an unhealthy proximity between these boys and free mixed-race individuals could only result in whites that acted like, and ultimately would support, this population. Even if colonists wanted to take on the children, LaGrange noted, they would have to apprentice them to *gens de couleur* and "living constantly and indispensably among negroes or *gens de couleur* [the white orphans], could not help but to contract the vices inherent to this type of man, whether it be laziness, lying, stealing, or other hidden crimes."[48] Just as problematically, he continued, putting children in such close physical and economic proximity with the mixed-race population would mean "these whites will want to help them."[49] In Martinican society, where elites believed that white dominance depended on a separation between the island's races, such an affinity clearly embodied risks much too dangerous to contemplate, let alone facilitate.

In his response, Dugué, commander of Martinique's local militia and one of the men accused in a thwarted conspiracy during the British occupation, reiterated a number of elite white stereotypes about *petits blancs* men, including the sexual taboos poor white men supposedly enjoyed breaking in the colony and the assumption that the orphan boys would follow in their footsteps and contribute to racial mixing on the island. "The frequenting of negroes, and their liaisons with women of this class, which is so easy, would inevitably ruin these children," he argued. "In general, inhabitants already consider the class of white subalterns who frequent their slaves as a necessary, if unfortunate, compromise."[50] Dugué's contention that Martinique's *petits blancs*, rather than *colons*, had interracial sexual relationships and that their close physical proximity to enslaved women through their roles as plantation managers and accountants, for example, reflected elite efforts to absolve themselves of complicity in the island's racial mixing and endorse publicly the elite ideal of appropriate (and exclusively white on white) sexual behavior. For Dugué to make such a claim, however, is especially striking considering that in 1812 others had accused him of precisely the same kinds of affairs (see Chapter 2).

None of the agricultural workers or orphaned metropolitan boys ever found their way to Martinique, at least not as part of an organized government effort. In his final response on the proposals to the minister of the marine, Donzelot asserted that although colonists wanted to increase Martinique's white population, orphaned white boys and single white men would not do. Elite white planters wanted white metropolitan families to swell their ranks, he contended, not unattached individuals who would inevitably increase the size of the mixed-race population. Donzelot did indicate, however, if France ever decided to send a certain number of agricultural families to Martinique then planters would happily accept the orphans and place them with these families.[51]

Ever concerned about the behavior of the island's *petits blancs*, with the arrival of Donzelot Creoles pushed to control not only those who joined their ranks but also to maintain control over the bulwarks of formal Creole indoctrination, the island's charity bureaus and foundling home. The new continental regime's pragmatism also encouraged metropolitan administrators to ensure all worthy white Martinicans received assistance, signifying an attempt to integrate *petits blancs* into the community of French citizens. Because ultimately Martinique's elite Creoles and metropolitan administrators shared the same goal—a more stable white community—if not the same rationale—white hegemony versus a productive colony—many *colons* accepted the changes. Donzelot required improvements to the charity bureaus created under the British, however, stipulating that in the future the colonial budget would allot only 4,550 francs a year to the charity bureaus.[52] To ensure the appropriate use of funds, he further required each bureau to provide Martinique's director of the interior with a full name, position, and other general observations on each applicant and also save the records for the following year. Gathering such extensive information, administrators hoped, would allow the government to provide true indigents with better care and avoid contributing to the "death of a worthy soul."[53] It would also prevent the island's Creoles who oversaw the bureaus from exercising too much liberty in how they determined need and allotted aid.

In addition to overhauling the charity bureaus, to provide more opportunities for Martinique's *petits blancs*, Donzelot also ordered a reorganization of the foundling home. A one-time transfer of 38,574 francs from colonial to municipal funds and a yearly allotment of 3,000 francs from the colonial budget henceforth would support the orphanage and the charity hospice for girls.[54] The institutions also received new instructions: In the future, the orphanage would only admit boys under the age of twelve and after the age of sixteen all boys had to leave. Clearly authorities assumed that after that age young white men would and should earn their own keep. The new rules also only admitted girls under the age of fifteen and required that they leave at the age of twenty-one. So as to encourage the marriage of these unfortunate young white women, at the time of their departure young female orphans also received a *trousseau* and, if funds allowed, the administrative council also could grant them a gift.[55]

In the interest of white social superiority and island stability, the administration also granted the laywomen directors of the orphanage permission to accept non-orphaned white children into the institution for a fee, and instructed them to raise and educate those children in the same manner as the orphans. Because Creoles had long viewed the foundling home's orphans as *mulâtres-blancs*, they had previously frowned on contact between the orphans and even Martinique's poorest legitimate whites. That Martinique's *colons* now tolerated such association, and even helped finance it, represented an important shift in how they viewed the island's poor white population, indicating a shared racial background and improved education now seemed more important than illegitimacy.[56]

To provide the best opportunities for even more of Martinique's white daughters, Donzelot, with the support of Creole elite, also called for a reorganization of Saint Pierre's Royal School for Girls and expanded its mandate.[57] Between its opening and the end of 1818, as many as seventy-five young white women attended the school.[58] Among the reasons for guaranteeing its preservation, Donzelot noted "the girls who receive their education in France and can not marry there have a difficult time adjusting to life when they return here."[59] For this reason, Donzelot asserted the institution had to provide the daughters of Martinique's planters all the continent could offer, but at home. He therefore expanded the curriculum to include geography, mythology, and history. Because many other Creole girls needed its instruction, Donzelot also increased the class size from fifty to 150 students and instructed the school to accept up to six students between the ages of six and thirteen on government scholarships.[60]

In addition to tripling its enrollment capacity and expanding its curriculum, the reorganization also brought new restrictions for the staff that reflected elite Creoles' worries about their personal conduct and their belief that some of the lay instructors needed stricter supervision. The female director, instructors, and assistants found themselves subjected to a dress code, forbidden from leaving the students, and warned against receiving visitors in the parlor, henceforth reserved for fathers, mothers, and other relatives or representatives of the female pupils.[61] Elites, Creole and metropolitan alike, clearly looked to this lay staff of women to train the island's white girls in the mores of plantation society. Unless they themselves behaved circumspectly, however, they could not serve as role models to the island's young girls.

Despite such extensive efforts to train the island's whites in the *elite* ideal of appropriate behavior, a number of *petits blancs* ignored these norms and Martinique's white elites were put in an awkward position of having to reprimand them without degrading them in the eyes of the island's enslaved and free mixed-race inhabitants. Prior to Donzelot's tenure Martinique's judicial system allowed Creoles a tremendous amount of flexibility in charging individuals with crimes and handing out punishments. New metropolitan efforts to create some administrative and judicial consistency in the French realm, however, made it more difficult for Martinique's elite white planters to take matters into their own hands. Shortly after his arrival Donzelot disbanded the Creole-controlled Sovereign Council and in its place created the Governmental and Administrative Council to handle financial and administrative affairs and invested the new Royal Court with policing and juridical authority. Two new Tribunals of First Instance in Fort Royal and Saint Pierre henceforth assumed jurisdiction of most criminal and commercial affairs.[62] Despite these changes Creoles found a way to work within the new organization of the courts to achieve their goals, a strategy they would return to repeatedly over the next thirty years.

To punish those whites who transgressed the modes of acceptable behavior, but who did not actually break the law, for example, Martinique's elite whites used the judicial system to their advantage by invoking a September 1817 decree that allowed the governor to call a special council when he deemed public security in jeopardy.[63] This council—comprised of the island's governor, military commander, *procureur général*, and the head representative of the Ministry of the Marine—had the authority to deport undesirables; and between 1819 and 1821, this extrajudicial special council deported eleven individuals. Seven of those eleven were whites and the charges brought against them illustrate very different interpretations of what constituted appropriate white behavior.

Martinican officials used this extrajudicial special council to deport those whites they saw as a direct threat to the island's social hierarchy by associating with people of African descent. According to Donzelot, the special council was quite adept at policing a community of "young men with passionate heads," who broke taboos about interracial mixing.[64] At least three of the seven whites stood accused of associating with free mixed-race and enslaved Martinicans: Heude St. Vincent, a thirty-four-year-old native of Martinique, was sent to the United States for "drinking and eating with the negroes";[65] François Vandenbrouck was deported to Wilmington, North Carolina for being a "very bad subject " and "eating with negroes";[66] and François Meslé, a thirty-nine year old metal smith living in Saint Pierre, was given six years banishment to the United States for "presiding over an orgy of enslaved women."[67] For these white men simply being in the company of people of African descent—

whether simply eating or supposedly overseeing seemingly deviant sexual behavior—presented enough of a threat to the island's racial and social hierarchy to warrant their removal.

Donzelot claimed the threat of deportation also had proven especially helpful in reestablishing "peace in the bosom of families," wracked by violence.[68] The extrajudicial special council deported four white men for threatening their families: Pierre Marie LeBlanc, a thirty-seven-year-old Parisian and former jail keeper in Trinité, for refusing to pay his debts and running an illegal tavern, all to the "detriment of his family"; Jean-Philippe Egidius, a thirty-six-year-old tailor from Saint Esprit, for being "continually drunk" and for "getting along poorly with his wife, whom he frequently hit"; Jacques Goubert, a twenty-six-year-old from Rouen, for being "without resources" and for threatening his neighbors with a knife; and Silvestre Mésire, a twenty-one-year-old from Trinité, for committing "great excesses of brutality against his family and neighbors" when intoxicated, as well as raping a ten-year-old girl, mistreating her infirm father, and burning the cottage of her mother.[69]

Unless the deportee could pay for the trip himself, the passage came at the king's expense, presumably a small price to pay to maintain public tranquility. While these men left involuntarily, some poor whites appear to have consciously used the elite ideal of appropriate white behavior to leave the island with government assistance. To help sustain the myth of white stability, metropolitan administrators granted Gabriel Dubrutz and Antoine Joseph Pietrucci 200 francs each to leave Martinique and return to continental France because of their poverty.[70] Likewise Egalité Lemercier got assistance to return to Aix-en-Provence and instructions to contact the mayor of the city on his arrival to receive a passport allowing him further aid.[71] Thirty-two-year-old Jean Dominique LeBlanc, along with her four daughters, also received 600 francs and passage on a commercial vessel because of their "state of misery."[72] The "state of indigence" of Femme Labbé, a sixty-five-year-old former inhabitant of Saint Domingue, and of Nancy Meloux gained each of them 200 francs and passage for continental France.[73]

The willingness of elites to pay for the involuntary and voluntary departure of those *petits blancs* who did not meet their expectations illustrates how deeply they worried about whites who fell into poverty or associated with *gens de couleur*. The significant increase in the number of *gens de couleur* who called the island home during the early years of the Restoration undoubtedly contributed to those fears. Since rejoining the French Empire, the island's white population had increased by 569 to 9,867 and the enslaved population had decreased by 3,388 to 77,412. In the same five-year period, however, Martinique's *gens de couleur* population had grown by 1,709 people and by 1822 numbered 11,073.[74] Creoles viewed this significant immigration of free mixed-race individuals with alarm and, not surprisingly, did what they could to monitor and control them. Their efforts included using the extrajudicial special council to deport *gens de couleur* like Jean-Marie Bernard for threatening public safety. Bernard, a forty-four year-old *homme de couleur* from Rivière-Pilote, had been deported by the British to mainland France during the French Revolution due to "his character and his conduct."[75] On his arrival in continental France, he had enlisted in the French army and eventually spent nearly fifteen years in the commune of Saint Just, located in the department of the Charente-Inférieure. Out of a desire to be reunited with her son in her old age, his widowed mother, a Martinican *femme de couleur libre*, obtained his pardon and Bernard returned to the island in 1818.[76] After his return, his mother entrusted him with overseeing her plantation in Saint Esprit but, in an 1820 petition to the Martinican government, she claimed her son had tried to "become master rather than overseer" and had eventually chased her off the property, "treating her like *une esclave*." When she tried to return, she informed authorities, her son had threatened to kill her and, for that reason, she requested his deportation. Eight "principal inhabitants" of the region, including the local police captain, confirmed widow Bernard's account and also recommended he be deported.[77]

Bernard, however, had other plans. He gathered the support of eight local inhabitants and also submitted a petition with the signatures of thirty-five inhabitants from his previous home on the continent, all attesting to his "good conduct and morality," during his stay in Saint Just. The special council ultimately decided these recommendations did not bear on his mistreatment of his mother, however, and unanimously decided to banish him from the island for six years, but only after he secured any property owed to him. After liquidating some of her assets, Bernard's mother gave her son 5,000 colonial livres as well as an enslaved *nègre*, and Bernard, his wife, his young child, and the *nègre* departed the island in November 1820 for St. Thomas and ultimately Trinidad.[78]

The extrajudicial special council also worked to rid the island of Gandou, a *mulâtre libre* living in Sainte-Marie, who had previously been deported from Martinique on two separate occasions before his case came to their attention in 1820. Nearly twelve years before, in 1808, French authorities had deported Gandou after he brandished a gun at two Creole planters from Saint-Marie, Le Sage and his father-in-law. After illegally returning to the island, officials banished Gandou a second time due to "bad conduct," but he returned yet again without authorization. Since that time his behavior, witnesses indicated, had been as disturbing as before his last departure and included spending three days in the middle of the main road in Sainte-Marie sleeping off a drinking binge and threatening to beat the enslaved workers of Madame Gissac Dessalles, the owner of a nearby plantation and a relative of Pierre Dessalles's.[79]

In a complaint she made to officials, Gissac Dessalles also claimed Gandou had threatened to set fire to her plantation if her enslaved laborers did not provide him with a bottle of *tafia* and a knife he claimed they had stolen from him. On December 28, 1820, in response to pleas from local inhabitants, Sainte-Marie's police captain arrested Gandou and later suggested Gandou be placed on a police work gang since deportation did not seem to deter the man. Based on his previous behavior and the likelihood that he would cause continued trouble due to his "constant state of drunkenness," however, the extrajudicial special council ultimately decided to permanently deport him to the United States.[80]

They also deported Louis Maximin, a *mulâtre libre* born in Anse d'Arlet. In March 1820, authorities in Diamant arrested Maximin for first freeing Judith, an enslaved *négresse* held in the *cachot* (prison cell) on the LaTournelle plantation for supposedly poisoning other enslaved workers, and then assisting her to flee. Another enslaved *négresse*, Marie Ursule, told Richer, Diamant's police captain, and Genty, the overseer on the LaTournelle plantation, that Maximin had once helped her escape and flee a *cachot* and further claimed she had seen Maximin help Judith and watched the two flee into the woods. Based on her directions, Richer and Genty thus located Maximin's hiding place. During his questioning back at the LaTournelle plantation Maximin repeatedly denied any knowledge of Judith's escape from the *cachot* or of her whereabouts and only confessed to helping her after LaTournelle threatened to have him jailed for previously assisting Marie Ursule. To avoid any prosecution, Maximin eventually agreed to find and return Judith.[81]

After three days and Judith's continued absence, however, LaTournelle decided Maximin was stalling for time and had him arrested. When Judith was found, LaTournelle returned her to his plantation *cachot*. From her cell she corroborated Marie Ursule's story and indicated she and Maximin, whom she identified as her lover, had worked to free her from the plantation prison. Based on his assistance to both Judith and, perhaps, Marie-Ursule, the extrajudicial special council ultimately decided Maximin presented a danger in Diamant and the colony and permanently deported him to the United States.[82]

By deporting free mixed-race individuals whom they believed an immediate threat to islandwide stability, Martinique's Creoles hoped to prevent the ever-increasing population of *gens de couleur* from destabilizing the island's social and racial hierarchy. But free mixed-race individuals also fought back against what they perceived to be an unacceptable limitation on their rights as French citizens and took advantage of the arrival of Baron Delamardelle, the king's envoy, to voice their grievances. In 1819 King Louis XVIII had sent Baron Delamardelle to fully implement the Napoleonic Codes in Martinique, and between March and July 1820 he found himself battling with Creoles and Donzelot over issues like public testimony in criminal trials, the jury system, and lawyers for defendants.[83] Seeing in Delamardelle a potential advocate, in 1820 a group of *gens de couleur* gave him a petition to help secure greater legal rights they felt Creoles had denied them through institutions like the extrajudicial special council.[84]

Delamardelle viewed this council as an example of the dangers of Creole exceptionalism and communicated as much to the Ministry of the Marine. In yet another attempt to bring the colony in line with metropolitan French standards and more closely control what counted as French justice, in January 1822 the king decreed that extrajudicial punishments, like the deportations handed out by the extrajudicial council, must cease based on his "desire that in the colonies, one adhered as much as possible to common law, especially as it related to individual liberty."[85] Not surprisingly Martinique's Creoles viewed the new measure as yet another assault on Creole power and on their claim that they knew best how to maintain order in this part of the French Atlantic. They also believed it dangerously limited their ability to thwart a new rash of suspected poisonings (of people and animals) by enslaved people that terrified Martinique's plantocracy.[86] Poisoning, or suspicions of it, by enslaved individuals of course was not new; rumors of poisoning conspiracies dated back to the early days of the colony and, as previously indicated, in 1806, the *métisse* Émilie, one of Madame de La Pagerie's house servants, had been boiled alive for attempting to poison the former Empress Josephine's mother.

A significant decrease (by nearly 3,400) in the enslaved population since 1816, however, seemed to lend credence to Creole worries that enslaved people were intent on overturning the plantation system by diminishing the work force. As in the initial years of return to French rule, it is quite possible that the illegal manumission of enslaved laborers accounted for the shift in the number of enslaved and *gens de couleur* Martinicans. Even Donzelot initially voiced his own skepticism as to whether or not as many enslaved laborers could have undertaken the number of poisonings that Creoles suspected.[87] By midsummer 1822, however, Creoles apparently convinced Donzelot of a vast conspiracy of enslaved laborers intent on destroying the colony through poison. In response to the growing concerns of Martinique's *colons*, in August he thus surpassed his designated powers and created a provostial court to try enslaved Africans outside of the newly reorganized judicial system.[88] In the months immediately following its creation, the court tried and then executed hundreds of slaves and sentenced others to harsh punishment, including deportation, often on fairly scant evidence.[89] Seeing the provostial court as yet another example, like the extrajudicial council, of Donzelot's too-close alliance with Martinique's Creoles and with their attempts to bolster white hegemony by circumventing the court system, by September administrators in metropolitan France asked Donzelot to justify his actions.

In his response Donzelot appeared to serve as a Creole mouthpiece, defending both the extrajudicial special council and the provostial court as absolutely necessary to maintaining order because of the island's social and racial hierarchy. In Martinique, he contended, Creoles drew an important distinction between judicial judgments and those passed by extrajudicial entities like the special council and provostial court. Sentences handed out by the extrajudicial special council, he insisted, were seen as less dishonorable than those given by the traditional courts and, for that reason, families and neighbors were more likely to come forward to testify against individuals to that council than they were in Martinique's tribunals. As evidence of this dynamic he noted that in the case of Silvestre Mésire, the last white man deported by the extrajudicial special council, his family and neighbors finally denounced him only out of the hope that the council would sentence him to five years of hard labor somewhere off the island, despite the fact that he raped a ten-year-old girl, set fire to sugar fields, mistreated enslaved workers, and threatened to assassinate a number of Martinicans and set fire to their plantations. When they learned he would be deported, Donzelot contended, a number of witnesses against him pleaded that Mésire be set free, claiming he had been adequately punished by his weeks of detention. Given this response, it seemed quite unlikely to Donzelot that these same people would ever have come forward to testify in a traditional court that might have sentenced Mésire to permanent banishment or even death. If the extrajudicial special council had not existed, he thus concluded, Mésire would still be menacing the island. In the colonies, where "all sorts of dangerous and turbulent adventurers and individuals" arrive daily, the governor insisted, order could only be maintained "through swift and severe policing."[90] Only extrajudicial bodies like the special council and the provostial court could provide such measures.

In his defense of the provostial court created to try accused poisoners,

Donzelot again called for an exception to metropolitan standards in this unique part of the French Empire. Because the island depended on the orderly functioning of the enslaved labor force, he worried "ordinary courts," those arranged on a metropolitan model, could not bring "the wretches who are guilty of this crime," to justice before they endangered the entire plantation system. To further make his point, Donzelot once again raised the specter of Haiti and again claimed only entities like the provostial court, which could act swiftly and serve as a deterrent, could prevent another Saint Domingue.[91]

Despite his own concerns about the status of justice on the island for Martinique's free inhabitants, in the case of the provostial court, Baron Delamardelle also argued, "it is not when our colonies are in danger that [the] governor's authority should be weakened." Rather, he claimed, it would suffice to "regularize and temper arbitrariness."[92] The 1817 royal decision creating the extrajudicial special council had done just that. Although the council had been limited by the January 1822 decree, he believed it could still deport individuals but only after "very serious consideration." In any case, since the measure "clearly applied only to *free* people," he found no conflict in the provostial court deporting enslaved people who potentially threatened the island.[93] For him French justice obviously only applied to legally free French citizens and, even then, given the nature of the plantation system, could be dispensed with if public security required.

As Donzelot and Martinique's *colons* struggled to administer the justice they saw fit, news of the vagaries of Creole control in the Caribbean reached the continent with the increased number of French West Indians traveling across the Atlantic. In 1818, 280 white Martinicans arrived in France's port cities and joined a well-established network of colonists from all walks of life.[94] This included *gens de couleur* who, inspired by the new political climate, saw hopes for a more complete integration into the French citizenry. An important example of their changing status came in August 1818 with a decree that finally granted free mixed-race individuals the right to freely leave the colonies and travel abroad or to continental France.[95] As cases before the extrajudicial special council suggest, some *gens de couleur* took advantage of the opening to travel to Martinique. Others, however, made their way to the continent. In 1818, twenty-five year old Lise Celeste, a free mixed-race Martinican, and twenty-one year old Adrien Bessai, a *femme de couleur* born in Nantes, left Martinique for Nantes, as did Jean Louis, a free mixed-race man who worked as a shoemaker.[96] Yet another example of the changing status of *gens de couleur* in the French Empire came in February 1819 when metropolitan officials formally lifted the 1803 ministerial decree banning marriage between blacks and whites on the continent.[97] Beginning in 1819 deputies in the French Senate like the Duc de Broglie also more frequently called for extending rights to France's *gens de couleur*.[98]

Metropolitan French pamphleteers and newspapers also increasingly brought the evils of slavery and the plantation system to their readers' attention. On his return to continental France Julien, a former quartermaster for the army in Martinique, published *Martinique, 1820*, harshly criticizing the island's Creole elite and their treatment of free mixed-race Martinicans. By 1822 it had appeared in Fort Royal and, according to Donzelot, not only produced "unreasonable pretensions among the *gens de couleur*," but also had frightened the other inhabitants because it closely paralleled the "demagoguery" that had brought the downfall of Saint Domingue. Afraid that such works would "revive passions and cause scandal" in the colonies by revisiting the racial troubles that had wracked the colony during the early years of the French Revolution, Donzelot called for metropolitan officials to prevent the future transport of such brochures.[99]

The 1822 creation of the Société de la Morale Chrétienne commission opposing the slave trade only fueled the fire of those critical of the plantation system. In this new anticolonial environment Creoles like Pierre Dessalles's mother who made the transatlantic trip in 1822 with three enslaved domestics in tow encountered increased criticism from their metropolitan brethren.[100] In March her son wrote her complaining of unfair continental criticism of the colony's social and racial hierarchy and the not so subtle damning of Creoles as barbaric. In particular he rebuked the "severity" of a metropolitan family friend, recently returned to the island, who had decried the planters' cruel treatment of the enslaved population. In his own defense, and in defense of his colleagues, Dessalles characterized white metropolitans "who do not know the infernal race that we have to guide," as actually more cruel than Creoles in their treatment of enslaved people.[101] Fresh from his time on the continent, Dessalles contended, this friend appeared to have been influenced by recent metropolitan discussions that cast the island in a very negative light, which only worsened by year's end.

* * *

On the night of October 12, 1822, barely six weeks after the provostial court's creation and just three months after the Vesey Conspiracy rocked South Carolina, somewhere between thirty and forty enslaved *nègres* revolted while working on a canal bordering several wealthy plantations in the small burg of Carbet, just south of Saint Pierre. After months of worrying that Martinique's

racial and social hierarchy would be undone by a conspiracy of enslaved poisoners, Creoles now confronted an outright attack by enslaved laborers armed
to, in Governor's Donzelot's words, "slit the throats of all whites and *gens
de couleur* on the plantations" of Saint Pierre and in surrounding parishes.[102]
Despite their plans to widen the rebellion, the arrival of Colonel Barré, Martinique's second in military command, as well as four companies of Martinique's second battalion and five companies of Fort Royal's mixed-race militia,
limited the uprising of enslaved workers to the outskirts of Carbet. Nonetheless the following morning found two white male inhabitants dead and five
other whites, including the Creole widow Lévignan, and two *gens de couleur*
seriously wounded.[103]

News of the uprising sent shock waves through the colony and the island's
plantocracy reacted with particular horror to reports that a young enslaved
man, Narcisse, whom Lévignan had nursed after his mother died, had been
among the insurgents and had left the widow for dead "with her head almost
open."[104] Over the next ten days, authorities searched for more insurgents and
their leaders, placing a reward on the head of each suspect to encourage his or
her capture. During the search for those involved, the four leaders of the uprising died and several others also perished from hunger or wounds they received
from the pursuing *gens de couleur* militiamen.[105] In the end, officials arrested
sixty-two enslaved Martinicans and the courts tried them for their participation. The verdict against the defendants pronounced on November 16, 1822,
condemned twenty-one enslaved workers to execution, ten to forced labor for
life, and seventeen to whipping; the court acquitted fourteen others.[106]

Although punishments against those accused in the Carbet uprising fell
swiftly and severely, many elite Martinicans blamed the island's colonial officials for creating an environment that allowed such chaos in the first place.
In the immediate aftermath of the revolt, the planter Dessalles claimed, "the
government wants our ruin," and concluded, "the apathy of the governor and
his entourage is positively dreadful. One would almost be tempted to think
they laugh at our troubles!"[107] Some elite Martinicans also worried that their
fellow citizens on the continent would blame Creoles for the recent violence.
Even though Bellard, a prominent planter from Saint Pierre, believed the uprising sought "fire and the assassination of all the whites," he felt confident
"the philanthropists . . . will no doubt attribute these crimes to the severity of
the master; the assassin will find apologists in France."[108] In the months following the uprising, Martinican Creoles thus launched a metropolitan press
campaign to defend planters against increasing criticism that they held responsibility for the violence of the plantation system. Unlike their previous

attempts to defend themselves against anticolonial attacks, Creoles and their supporters in continental France increasingly used the details of the recent poisonings and the Carbet revolt to suggest that any amelioration to the conditions of enslaved Africans would put the physical safety of the island's white women in danger from what Creoles increasingly characterized as marauding hypersexualized enslaved men.

A mid-December edition of the *Journal de Paris* contained a letter from a colonist in Saint Pierre who specifically noted, for example, that during the October 1822 uprising, twenty-one "*noirs*" had assassinated two white planters and seriously injured a white woman and three or four other whites.[109] Another letter printed on January 12, 1823, reiterated white colonists' fears about the safety of their women. Referring to the recent outbreak of poisonings in the summer and fall of 1822, the writer noted that not only had the number of deaths from poison increased, but also that at that time forty suspected "negroes" had committed "several atrocious crimes against not only white inhabitants, but also against innocent women."[110] Such explicit references to white women in harm's way, Creoles hoped, would underscore the vulnerability of the entire white community.

In response to such claims, slavery opponents tried to counter concerns about white women's safety by instead showing how the institution of slavery degraded them. *Moeurs des trois couleurs*, a pamphlet strongly criticizing the colonial system, appeared in Paris in late 1822 and explicitly linked slavery and metropolitan France.[111] In this essay—which rumors suggested had been written by a Martinican Creole, De Lucy—the author argued the colonial system had ceased to work for metropolitan France, Creoles, or enslaved Africans. The author's reported status made this a particularly controversial claim, for as a Creole he held a potent legitimacy in the eyes of metropolitan French and his pamphlet enraged Creoles who saw in his writing a betrayal by one of their own.

According to the author, slavery degraded all three interested parties. He used as evidence the outbreak of poisonings on the island in the early 1820s, which he claimed ultimately saw the execution of more than 600 and the punishment of more than 1,000 others.[112] In addition to focusing on what he deemed the horrible excesses of colonial masters and enslaved Africans, the anonymous writer also argued that the degradation of white and enslaved women ranked among the system's most pernicious effects.[113] He painted the following picture of life in the colonies: white male colonists took sexual advantage of their enslaved female workers; this drove the white wives of these men "to fury in their jealousy," and, "isolated on their plantations and separated on all occasions," they "became despotic" in their punishment of their husbands' mistresses, ordering whippings that even they could not watch; in return, enslaved women, and others on their behalf, driven to "despair," sought revenge on white women and their children by poisoning human beings and livestock; white masters then resorted to horrible excesses in searching for the culprits, often killing as many as twenty enslaved workers and confining the accused in three-by-four-foot *cachots*; if the accused did not die in captivity, a court stocked with relatives of the accuser often sentenced him or her to death.[114] Despite the horrors committed, the author refused to blame any of the inhabitants and argued instead that such "a situation against nature" necessarily led to "abominable vices;" common sense, he concluded, necessitated a change before "the torrent returned to its source."[115] As it currently functioned, the plantation system, controlled by white men, pitted women of all racial backgrounds against one another and seemed to assure they would meet violent ends.

Although this Creole advocated change, the Carbet uprising convinced white planters like Dessalles that, regardless of any precautions the government might take, the mere proximity of Haiti to the other French possessions would inevitably infect enslaved Martinicans with the fervor for freedom. When that came to pass, it would end in the destruction of the economy and the murder of all whites. Given Martinique's increasingly fragile economy, planters no doubt believed that end could not be far away. Faced with limits on their ability to control the island's enslaved population, *colons* thus turned their sights to shoring up the island's *petits blancs* by again reorganizing the island's charity bureaus. With Donzelot's help, Creoles managed to significantly increase the usual allotment to the charity bureaus from 5,000 francs to 15,000 in Fort Royal; 7,500 in Saint Pierre; and 7,500 in Mouillage. The colony's "desperate" state, he argued, also justified an additional 3,000 francs to support the needy in Fort Royal's seventeen parishes, in Saint Pierre's five parishes and in Mouillage's five parishes throughout the course of the year.[116] Such assistance, Creoles hoped, would stabilize Martinique's poorer white population and thus the island's social hierarchy.

Meeting the economic needs of Martinique's *colons*, however, would prove more difficult. After the Napoleonic wars, the Restoration government tried to deal with the then shortage of sugar by setting uniform duties on French colonial and foreign sugars and, in the process, set the stage for future economic difficulties. The British took advantage of this situation and dumped stockpiled sugar on the market. In practice, this shut down the continental beet sugar industry begun under Napoleon until basically the July Monarchy. In response to British actions, French producers called for protection and between 1814 and 1822 a series of measures helped French colonial sugar producers corner the metropolitan French market. Legislation in 1822 and 1823, combined with an irregular international market, however, threatened the profits of Martinican planters like Dessalles when prices were low and kept them from selling when prices rose.[117] Wholesale sugar trading with France's port cities was one of Martinique's most prosperous and financially risky businesses. Planters' dependence on *commissionaires*, factors who received plantation produce on consignment for continental French commercial companies and supplied local plantations with all of their supplies, complicated the economic crisis.[118] The vagaries of the markets, and the large capital investment in sugar production, meant planters, including Dessalles, often found themselves in debt to these intermediaries.

Between 1822 and 1824 Madame Dupuy, a widowed merchant in Saint Pierre who took over her husband's trading ventures, served as *commissionaire* for the Dessalles family.[119] As one of Martinique's most prosperous colonists, Dessalles's business constituted big business indeed. As a result, the Dupuy trading house likely numbered among the eight to ten large-scale merchants who dominated the commercial center of Saint Pierre during this period.[120] According to Dessalles, Dupuy's son actually headed the trading house following the death of his father. Nonetheless, in his correspondence, Dessalles only speaks of widow Dupuy and appears to have conducted all of his business with her directly even though their relationship was extensive and riddled with controversy.[121]

In addition to Creole women like Dupuy, in the early 1820s *gens de couleur* increasingly served as *commissionaires* on the island. In these roles, they not only supplied Martinique's *gens de couleur* coffee planters but also a greater number of white planters who also found themselves indebted to these free mixed-race merchants and their employers in metropolitan France.[122] When combined with a new metropolitan measure reinstating time limits to repay their debts, many of Martinique's Creoles found themselves increasingly under pressure from, and seemingly beholden to, the island's *gens de couleurs*, a situation that directly threatened the island's racial hierarchy. In response some of Martinique's *colons* fought to maintain their social status by accusing *gens de couleur*, and especially those who had managed to prosper, of any number of crimes. Some accused *gens de couleur* in the rash of poisonings that continued to sweep the island. One case described by Dessalles in a letter to his mother in 1823 involved a number of wealthy *gens de couleur* merchants who were sentenced to death for their crimes. Of free-mixed-race and enslaved

Martinicans in general he concluded, "they have but one thing in mind . . . the destruction of whites and the overthrow of the government." [123] For Dessalles *gens de couleur* now threatened to upset Martinique's social hierarchy not only through their economic dominance but also through poison. Such concerns also prompted other Creoles, like the police captains in the parishes of Macouba, Basse Pointe, and Grand'Anse, to claim the free mixed-race militias who had put down the Carbet rebellion and spent ten days looking for additional insurgents had actually masterminded the uprising.[124]

Dessalles's personal concerns about the disruptions *gens de couleur* might cause on the island were heightened by the return of Honoré, one of his former enslaved domestics who had accompanied Dessalles's mother to continental France in 1822. Shortly after his arrival on the continent, Honoré had apparently begun to take unprecedented "liberties," prompting Dessalles to remark "Paris is a dangerous city for all of our *esclaves*" and to welcome the enslaved man's return to Martinique, and presumably an appropriate environment, at the end of the year.[125] Before Honoré left continental France, however, Dessalles's mother had granted Honoré his freedom and, according to Dessalles, when he arrived in Fort Royal in January 1823 he "astonished everyone with his manners, his looks, his pretensions, and his language," so much so that Dessalles proclaimed, "I would give a great deal not to have had him return to Martinique . . . as soon as I find a favorable opportunity to get him out of this colony, I will seize it."[126] But that did not immediately happen and, much to Dessalles's chagrin, Honoré apparently was glad to be back in Martinique and had even found some business success, as evidenced by the 4,000 livres that Edouard, the concierge of the Court of Appeal, owed him by mid-December.[127]

Continental France, Dessalles believed, had forever changed Honoré, as had freedom. The return of two *gens de couleur*, Monlouis Thébia and Joseph Richer, further fueled Creole worries that a vast transatlantic conspiracy of *gens de couleur* was underway to overthrow Martinique's *colons*. The two *mestif* tailors had come back to the island after spending several years in metropolitan France where they had connections in the capital and in Atlantic port cities. Shortly after their arrival on the island in early to mid-November 1823, an anonymous Creole wrote Saint Pierre's royal prosecutor claiming "a duty for a man to help government officials when the occasion arose." According to him, the recently arrived men had originally left the colony for Paris to "support the intrigues and pernicious ways" of Joseph Litté, the "deputy" of the *gens de couleur*, and to help him "undermine our colonial system." Motivated by news of the establishment of a "new organization" in the colonies, since their return they had actively met with Saint Pierre's *"comité secret"* of mixed-race people to prepare for the kind of change suggested by legislative deputies like Gabriel-Joseph Laisné de Villevêque, whose previous support of *gens de couleur* had already caused a "profusion of scandal" in Martinique. Thébia and Richer's association with Joseph Millet, an *homme de couleur* working as a confectioner in Saint Pierre, indicated they represented a significant threat to islandwide stability, the letter writer concluded, and demanded Martinican officials' immediate action.[128]

So, too, did the appearance of *De la situation des gens de couleur libres aux Antilles Françaises* (The Status of Free Men of Color in the French Antilles), an anonymous pamphlet originally published in Paris that criticized the treatment of free mixed-race Martinicans. According to the same police captains who had blamed *gens de couleur* for the Carbet uprising, Montlouis Thébia and Joseph Richer had distributed "this infamous libel, this seditious tract" on their return to Martinique, inciting a number of mixed-race individuals to flout the island's laws. Such license could not be tolerated, they argued, and demanded Donzelot do something "to return them [*gens de couleur* who had broken the law] to their place," further warning "the whites will never consent to see as their equals men who, like the majority of *gens de couleur*, still have relatives in our *ateliers* [enslaved work gangs]."[129] Only violence, he implied, could follow.

* * *

At the end of December it did. In response to growing Creole anxiety, authorities raided the homes of *gens de couleur* throughout the colony and confiscated seditious material, including copies of the Parisian pamphlet. Days later their arrest of seven free mixed-race merchants—the recently returned Montlouis Thébia and Joseph Richer, their associate Joseph Millet, another *homme de couleur* Laborde and Cyrille-Charles-Auguste Bissette, Louis Fabien, *fils*, and Jean-Baptiste Volny—set in motion a series of events that would come to be known as the Bissette Affair.[130] The varied responses to the affair underscores the important role Martinican events had in shaping colonial policy and in helping to more specifically define which colonial inhabitants could claim rights as French citizens during the Restoration.

Authorities charged the seven *gens de couleur* with conspiracy at the end of December and over the next few weeks Martinique's *colons* worked as quickly as possible to implement their own form of Creole justice. In response to their increasing concerns about the vagaries of colonial justice, in January 1824 colonial officials in metropolitan France chose Girard to serve as the island's first metropolitan *procureur général.*[131] Martinique's Creoles viewed his appointment as an assault against local privilege, and wealthy planters like Dessalles predicted he would be "fairly ineffectual."[132] Because he did not arrive on the island until 1825, the Creole planter Richard De Lucy (the brother of the Creole writer of *Moeurs des trois couleurs*) served as the interim *procureur général* and under his guidance the court tried Bissette, Fabien, *fils*, and Volny as the alleged ringleaders of the alleged plot to overturn Martinique's social hierarchy. The closed-door trial relied mainly on copies of the anonymous tract (which Bissette reportedly had written) imported by Thébia and Richer as well as drafts of petitions to the governor, the king, and the Parisian chambers in Paris, all of which demanded justice for Martinique's *gens de couleur.* All three men were sentenced to exile and had their property confiscated. Searching for an even more severe penalty, however, De Lucy appealed the case, and at a second trial the Creole-controlled court sentenced Bissette, Fabien *fils*, and Volny to be branded and confined to the galleys for life and sent Laborde, Millet, Richer, and Thébia into permanent exile. Although the men immediately tried to appeal the ruling to the Court of Cassation in Paris, the recorder refused to acknowledge the request and thus two years would pass before they would have the chance to contest the Martinican court's ruling. In the meantime, officials sent all the men to the port city of Brest with Bissette, Fabien *fils*, and Volny making their way to Bordeaux.[133]

In the meantime Creoles continued to exact their revenge on the island's *gens de couleur.* Based on the testimony of Modeste, a *câpre* owned by one of Martinique's *colons*, and Régis, a local *homme de couleur*, authorities claimed the conspiracy involved hundreds of Martinique's wealthiest *gens de couleur*, many of them intermediaries in the sugar trade, and that the island's free mixed-race inhabitants had intended to "make the blood of the *colons* run" on December 25, 1823.[134] Shortly after the arrest of the plot's seven purported ringleaders local authorities rounded up hundreds of *gens de couleur* around the island. Based on his contention that the courts could not convict those in question because they had had too much time to destroy any evidence of "their plot," the new interim *procureur général* De Lucy suggested officials deport the men, either to continental France or the Spanish Caribbean. He further recommended they never be allowed to return to the island lest "their appearance . . . re-ignite the flame" of rebellion, and also called for the disarming of Martinique's free mixed-race militias.[135]

Over the next two months, Martinican officials followed De Lucy's recommendations, eventually deporting 260 *gens de couleur* merchants. When called to account for the speed of their departures, De Lucy assured the Ministry of the Marine that the deportees had been allowed to meet with notaries and their families to put their affairs in order before leaving the island.[136] As his explanatory letter to the minister of the marine illustrates, however, De Lucy and Martinique's other Creoles had no particular interest in explaining themselves to the continental French whom they held responsible for inciting free mixed-race individuals to push for equality.[137] Debates in the French senate in 1820, 1821, and 1822, along with the "careless encouragements" of many deputies "on the left" to "an ambitious and proud class [*gens de couleur*]" had created "murderous consequences" for the French colonies, De Lucy contended.[138] The recent troubles, he further warned, were just the beginning and therefore "the existence of the French Antilles . . . the life and fortune of the *colons*," rested with the ministers and the king, "one word could save them, another word could abandon them to the furor of the two inferior classes." "The fate of the entire white population rests in your hands," he boldly told the minister of the marine, clearly hoping for a series of new measures that would reassert Creole control in Martinique.[139]

In the aftermath of the Bissette Affair colonial officials in metropolitan France did take steps to stabilize the island but not the ones Creoles like De Lucy had hoped for. Alarmed by the still waning numbers of enslaved workers, and aware that the end of the Atlantic slave trade in 1818 technically meant any future growth in Martinique's enslaved population could come only from natural reproduction, ministry officials worked to improve conditions for and augment the number of Martinique's enslaved workers. In February 1824 the Ministry of the Marine instructed Martinique's administrators to exercise more vigilance when granting manumissions and, in particular, to refuse any requests to free enslaved women under the age of fifty.[140] Such a measure they believed would help to ensure more children born into slavery; it also, however, would prevent planters from abandoning enslaved women in their old-age. A ministerial dispatch completely banned enslaved individuals from accompanying their masters to metropolitan territory and another measure mandated improved conditions, in general, for enslaved Martinicans belonging to the Crown and working at the local government hospital.[141]

Despite such measures the poisonings that had swept the island for more than four years continued unabated. For planters like Dessalles, whose plantation also suffered a series of poisonings in the summer of 1824, stability demanded that the provostial court continue to function and that planters wield harsh punishment against any, including free mixed-race individuals, who might be involved in the island-wide conspiracy.[142] After the Bissette Affair Martinique's *colons* more and more frequently argued that *gens de couleur* masterminded the islandwide poisonings.[143] In an 1825 letter to his mother in continental France, Dessalles himself claimed, "the current poisonings come from the *gens de couleur*, who direct the slaves toward evil," and he re-iterated a need to remain vigilant.[144]

Because of the increasingly tenuous position of the island's white population, *colons* also dealt harshly with whites who transgressed elite norms of behavior. This was especially true of an undisclosed number of elite white women who, because of their interracial sexual relationships, made a mockery of elites' ideal of white women as the beacons of moral and racial purity.[145] Perhaps not surprisingly, given how completely such affairs undermined Martinique's racial and social hierarchy, the official records of the time say nothing of these relationships or of the women's deportation. Only ten years later, in a footnote, did a justice of the peace in Trinité insist: "since 1822 and 1823, we have no longer had to deport white women of ill repute who, although belonging to the best families, threw themselves entirely into the middle of the slave quarters and could only be made to leave by force."[146] In 1822, at such a turbulent moment, with the white population seemingly under siege by Martinique's enslaved and free mixed-race populations, *colons* clearly found such behavior an absolute threat to the island's social and racial hierarchy.

In the wake of these deportations of wealthy white women, Creoles saw metropolitan attempts to further reform Saint Pierre's Royal School for Girls as yet another criticism of Creole mores and an attack on the colony's status within the French Empire and responded defensively. As early as 1822 the minister of the marine had communicated his desire to send the Sisters of Saint Joseph, a religious congregation well known on the continent for their instruction of young women, to Martinique to teach the island's young Creole girls. Governor Donzelot initially declined their assistance, however, arguing white Martinican women already ran several well-functioning primary schools for young girls.[147] The minister of the marine no longer trusted Donzelot, however, and granted the Sisters of Saint Joseph permission to open two boarding schools on the island despite the governor's opposition.[148] He further accused the female director of the Royal School for Girls of showing hostility toward the boarding school's chaplain and of other "unmentionable abuses" that completely destroyed public confidence in the institution; by then, only four pupils remained at the institution.[149] "General opinion," the ministry concluded, demanded transfer of the establishment from the lay staff to an instructional religious congregation, the Sisters of Saint Joseph, and it called for an immediate report about the allegedly "grave abuses" at the Saint Pierre boarding school.[150]

That the Ministry of the Marine transferred the Royal School for Girls in Saint Pierre to the Sisters of Saint Joseph in the aftermath of the Bissette Affair, and authorized the creation of another boarding school in Fort Royal, further demonstrates their opinion about Creole-led institutions.[151] Both establishments, once operating under the charge of a superior and two nuns of the Order, would still accept only full-time boarders and maintain essentially the same curriculum "directed toward the cares that the mother of a family must know."[152] By taking the institutions out of Creole hands, however, colonial authorities on the continent marked a metropolitan-based education as preferable to a Creole one and indicated they would no longer tolerate a system that allowed Creoles to teach other Creoles how to deviate from continental standards.

Administrators in metropolitan France also demonstrated that while they hoped for an increase in the number of whites from France sent to Martinique "in order to reunite a mass of whites against the colored population," they would not support unworthy whites simply to help them maintain the Creole ideal of racial superiority.[153] In 1824 an order created new commissions in each charity bureau and instructed them to revise the indigence lists to avoid supporting "lazy" inhabitants who "lacked industry" and "lived off treasury resources."[154] Identifying the truly needy demanded a rigorous effort, the order noted, since the number of indigents had continued to grow and that meant a bigger expense for the colonial government. To cull the indigence lists, administrators renewed previous demands and called for reports that commented on each applicant's morality, noted any useful skills that applicants might put to good use, and suggested an appropriate amount in aid. Although these new commissions drew their members from the same group of Martinicans who had previously served, metropolitan officials undoubtedly hoped the increased demand for information would preclude any free rides.

In continental France the Bissette Affair prompted an outpouring of press beginning in the spring of 1824 that, by calling attention to the plight of *gens de couleur* in Martinique, further underscored how the existence of free mixed-race individuals struggling for rights around the French Atlantic complicated ideas about French identity and citizenship. One letter writer to the Paris-based newspaper *Le Pilote* denounced the deportation of Bissette and his colleagues and questioned Martinican officials' extrajudicial efforts to "destroy all men of this [mixed] race." The writer also condemned official efforts to deport men like Precop, a sixty-year-old inhabitant of Carbet who had always served as "the father who fed all of the poor *petits blancs* of his parish." Officials attempted to justify such horrors, the writer concluded, by claiming that

Bissette and the other *gens de couleur* had conspired to "slit the throats" of all whites at the end of 1823. Although not a scrap of evidence supported this conspiracy, the author concluded, such official "horrors" continued nonetheless, and under the reign of a supposedly just king.[155] These attacks on a regime that would tolerate such abuses only added to the increasing calls for changes in Martinique and in metropolitan France.

François-André Isambert, a talented young lawyer, was among those advocating that France's *gens de couleur* be granted the same rights as all other French citizens. As chance would have it, while in Bordeaux visiting Marie-Louise Lambert, a *femme de couleur* client convicted by Martinique's provostial court awaiting an appeal to the Court of Cassation, Isambert met Bissette, Fabien *fils*, and Volny and agreed to take on their case.[156] In an effort to also have their case heard before the Court of Cassation, Isambert implemented his own pamphlet campaign, with the help of anticolonial supporters, publishing two pamphlets in Paris in 1824 that highlighted the inconsistencies of colonial justice.[157]

Publicity about the Bissette affair also attracted the attention and support of other well-placed people like Claude Chauveau-Lagarde, a jurist noted for taking on controversial cases, and legislators like Benjamin Constant, the Duc de Broglie, and Laisné de Villevêque, who Creoles had criticized for his inflammatory statements in the French chambers since 1819. In July 1824 Constant took up the *gens de couleur* cause during a budget debate in the chambers, expressing his concern that deporting 260 merchants from Martinique could not possibly help colonial commerce. To further make his point, he also presented a letter in which the heads of several Parisian firms took issue with the deportation of the *gens de couleur* merchants from Martinique and testified to their fine character.[158]

Ever on the defense, in response to the support voiced for France's *gens de couleur* Creoles countered what they perceived as attacks on their Creole character and colonial status by arguing free mixed-race individuals potentially threatened the very foundations of French identity and thus the entire realm. The Creole Gauvain, for example, argued that, despite claims to the contrary, Martinique's "classes" did resemble those in France, most specifically in their concern over bloodlines. He complained that continental French unjustly blamed white colonists for their desire to maintain racial boundaries and further accused those on the continent of hypocrisy for criticizing Creoles who wanted to avoid racial mixing: "Why do the French, proud to be born on the banks of the Seine, the Loire, or the Saone, as well as on the Danube, why do they blame their brothers in the colonies for not wanting to have relatives in the tribes of Senegal or Gambia?" For Gauvain, it seemed incongruous that metropolitan Frenchmen who worried so about their own familial status should think ill of French in places like Martinique who also worried about their lineage. As his comments suggest, he chafed at the idea that continental French might force colonial families into a "lower caste," defined by literal or supposed racial mixing, that would separate them from the rest of the presumably racially pure French family.[159]

Based on his contention that Creoles in the West Indies were French, Gauvain saw maintaining clear racial boundaries as a pressing national question, but not just in the colonies. He also claimed metropolitan French territory lay vulnerable to "*mulâtres* of a clear color" who might pass as whites in the metropole. Precisely this "prostitution of the French name," in the form of someone other than a white gaining French citizenship, threatened the very foundations of French national identity.[160]

Such a possibility, Creoles hoped to communicate, made the presence of *gens de couleur* in continental France, and certainly men like the four lesser known free mixed-race men originally implicated as leaders in the Bissette Affair, potentially even more dangerous as they extended their commercial and personal networks around the realm. While in metropolitan France, Laborde, Millet, Richer, and Thébia made extensive contact with members of France's wider port communities and their futures involved local and national officials as well as business people throughout continental France. Their own actions, and those taken on their behalf, underscore not only the interracial nature of colonial commerce during the Restoration, but also metropolitan officials' increasingly convoluted justifications for denying free mixed-race individuals their rights as part of the French nation.

After waiting on board ship at the port city of Brest for four months, Laborde, Millet, Richer, and Thébia requested permission to travel to Paris in August 1824. Officials denied their request, however, and informed them they would be given passports and required to leave continental French territory.[161] After arriving in Le Havre a month later, Laborde and Richer left for the Caribbean island of St. Thomas as directed.[162] Millet and Thébia, however, wrote the city's subprefect and requested permission to stay, citing their own interests as well as those of "a great number of French [commercial] houses with which we are in business, and with whom we cannot fulfill our obligations if the government does not allow us to prolong our stay in France."[163] They also asked the subprefect to intervene on their behalf and swore that they would do nothing that would make him regret his efforts. To further convince the subprefect to help them remain on the continent, Millet noted his wife and children were on their way to metropolitan French territory to join him and insisted he could not possibly leave before they arrived.[164]

As additional evidence of their good conduct, Millet and Thébia further enlisted the help of E. Petit, part owner of a very respectable commercial house in Le Havre and, according to the subprefect, a well-known supporter of the Bourbon Monarchy.[165] E. Petit confirmed his commercial house had transacted "numerous commercial operations" with Millet and Thébia "over several years" and indicated they were happy to help the two mixed-race men given their "difficult position."[166] Henri Petit, the other owner of the Petit commercial house and marshal of Le Havre's cavalry honor guard, also wrote on behalf of Millet and Thébia, claiming the entire community had taken on "these unfortunates worthy of interest," and had opened the two men's eyes to law and order. Millet and Thébia had served as correspondents for his commercial house for many years and, according to Henri Petit, even Le Havre's local administrators judged them like all the city's other inhabitants. Like his brother, he consequently asked the two men be allowed to stay, noting in the metropole "their presence would no longer disrupt the colonial system and [would] also reassure the merchants who, like us, have undertaken considerable commercial ventures with them." He concluded by offering his personal guarantee that Millet and Thébia would conduct themselves well, "as devout and loyal subjects."[167]

The subprefect forwarded the letters of the Petit brothers and Millet and Thébia's petition to the minister of the interior and added his own. Under the influence of the Petit brothers, he contended, Millet and Thébia could not possibly disrupt public tranquility; furthermore, based on his observations of them, the two men expressed a "deep regret at having been pulled in by bad council."[168] Based on that evidence he recommended they be allowed to stay in Le Havre and, one month later, received word that the minister of the interior had granted the men's request to stay in metropolitan French territory for an extra six months.[169]

In his reply to the minister of the marine, the subprefect assured the official he would continue his surveillance of the two men, emphasizing "they appear to be men of gentle temperament and stay far away from all political discussion."[170] Though the subprefect undoubtedly believed his surveillance was appropriate, the minister of the marine had a different opinion. Less than two weeks later, in response to a letter from the ministry, the subprefect assured his superiors that his surveillance was "general" and in no way imposed any obligation on Millet or Thébia; rather, he argued, it consisted simply of determining, as with all other inhabitants of the region, if any of the men's actions might threaten public tranquility.[171] Although he did not say so explicitly, the subprefect undoubtedly hoped to convey that his attentions to the two men was not a result of their mixed-race ancestry.

Although Millet and Thébia were supposed to stay in Le Havre only six months, Millet at least managed to extend his stay. More than two years later, Millet and his extended family were still in metropolitan French territory when they again appeared in official documents. In August 1826, the director of police wrote to the minister of the marine to determine if Joseph Millet's wife, her two sisters, and their two children could return to Martinique to attend the widow Millet in her old age. Because nothing legally prevented their travel, the minister instructed the director to issue the passports. Joseph Millet, however, was to remain on the continent.[172]

The year 1826 also proved to be important for the three reported ringleaders of the Bissette Affair and for all others interested in seeing France's *gens de couleur* secure their legal rights as French citizens. In August 1825, the royal ordinance declaring Haitian independence with an indemnity of 150 million francs to be distributed to the island's former proprietors finally appeared in print. When Martinicans and their supporters on the continent learned the news, it evoked rage, fear, as well as, once again, the ghost of Haiti's horrors. Those French merchants directly involved in colonial commerce agonized about not only the potential for racial violence in Martinique but also the economic consequences of liberating Saint Domingue. The planter Dessalles decried the government's actions noting, "the news of the independence of Saint Domingue has been devastating to the entire white population of these colonies." Like many others, he further wondered whether the safeguards put into place to protect Martinique and Guadeloupe would "stand up to the contagion?" If not, he predicted, "we will fall into a true slump," that might mean the end of the plantation system as then constructed.[173]

By the end of 1825 the French cabinet found itself criticized from both ends of the political spectrum leading to a significant realignment in the ministry when the French legislative chambers reconvened in 1826.[174] To counter opposition claims that the administration tolerated the vagaries of the Old Régime, in metropolitan France and on the island, King Charles X replaced Governor Donzelot, believing he had established too close a relationship with the island's Creole planters. In Donzelot's place, he named General François-Marie-Michel, Comte de Bouillé, and looked to him to facilitate reforms on the island. That was easier said than done, however, after Donzelot informed the minister he would not leave his post in disarray and chaos, nor until he had prepared a report on the state of the island for his successor. Finally, at the end of June, he grudgingly departed Martinique and left de Bouillé to administer the island without the benefit of the promised report.[175] The shift in the ministry also forced the minister of the marine to reconsider requests for the Court of Cassation to hear Bissette, Fabien, *fils* and Volny's appeal. Isambert and Chauveau-Lagarde also used their leverage as members of the Court of Cassation to convince the court to consider the appeal and, in March, they succeeded when the court's president requested that Martinican officials send the transcripts from the original trial.

A whirlwind of press followed the Court of Cassation's decision to hear the appeal, a right technically due all French citizens, and more fervently called for equitable treatment for France's *gens de couleur* on both sides of the Atlantic. The Duc de Broglie's anticolonial speeches in the Chamber of Peers in May, as well as the publication of more pamphlets by Isambert and Chauveau-Lagarde, further sparked anticolonial sentiment.[176] The anticolonial movement gained even more publicity after the Court of Cassation overturned the Martinican court's verdict against Bissette, Fabien, *fils* and Volny and sent the case back to the Court of Appeal in Guadeloupe in late September. It also announced the commutation of several other cases, including that of the *femme de couleur* Marie-Louise Lambert whom the Martinican provostial court had found guilty in a poisoning case. Because a provostial court judgment could not be overturned, the Court of Cassation had little choice but to uphold the provostial court's decision in the Lambert case. Just weeks later, however, on November 10, 1826, a ministerial decree abolished the provostial court, referencing the Lambert case as an example of its faulty justice.[177]

***

Creoles viewed the abolition of the provostial court as yet another infringement on their formal and informal power on the island. Although they had managed to secure and even extend their control over institutions after France first regained the island in 1815, under Donzelot's tenure they had increasingly seen their power erode while, in their minds, Martinique's *gens de couleur* gained in economic and political stature and enslaved workers became increasingly violent. As a result they looked on the Comte de Bouillé's appointment with apprehension.

Figure 1. *Le Creole*, in *Les Français peints par eux-mêmes: encyclopédie morale du dix-neuvième siècle*. Paris: L. Curmer, 1841–42, tome 8, Rare Book, Manuscript and Special Collections Library, Duke University.

Figure 2. *La Creole*, in *Les Français peints par eux-mêmes: encyclopédie morale du dix-neuvième siècle*. Paris: L. Curmer, 1841–42, tome 8, Rare Book, Manuscript and Special Collections Library, Duke University.

Figure 3. *Le Mulatre*, in *Les Français peints par eux-mêmes: encyclopédie morale du dix-neuvième siècle*. Paris: L. Curmer, 1841–42, tome 8, Rare Book, Manuscript and Special Collections Library, Duke University.

Figure 4. *Negresse*, in *Les Français peints par eux-mêmes:*
encyclopédie morale du dix-neuvième siècle. Paris: L. Curmer,
1841–42, tome 8, Rare Book, Manuscript and Special
Collections Library, Duke University.

"In the Colonies, It Is Impossible That a White Would Align Himself with Slaves": Shifts in Colonial Policy

ON HIS ARRIVAL in Martinique, Comte de Bouillé set about wresting control from the island's *colons* and permanently aligning Martinique's administrative structure with continental France. His first task was to implement an ordinance replacing the previous three administrator system with a governor—assisted by a Private Council and General Council—a military commander, a colonial treasurer, a director of the interior, and a *procureur général*. The Private Council replaced the Governmental and Administrative Council created under Donzelot and also answered directly to the governor. It included the new director of the interior, the *procureur général*, and two white colonists. The new General Council, composed of twelve elected white colonists, deliberated and gave advice on local affairs, but like the Private Council could only advise, not mandate.[1] The director of the interior had responsibility for economic issues, as well as surveillance of vagabonds and other suspect individuals and the *procureur général* headed the island's judicial organization and directly oversaw its notaries and lawyers.[2]

Officials hoped the ordinance and the new administrative structure would guarantee all of the island's inhabitants more equitable treatment and to that end de Bouillé also reorganized traditional venues of Creole control, consolidating the foundling home and the charity hospice for white women and transferring the combined institution from lay control to the Sisters of Saint Joseph. Henceforth Martinique's poor Creole girls and women, poor white female orphans, and white "found children" of both sexes would be housed in a twelve-room building that ultimately allowed colonial administrators closer oversight of the institutions that Creoles had long used to shore up Martinique's *petits blancs* at government expense. As of the summer of 1827, the foundling home continued to accept only children clearly identified as part of the white community and at the time of its consolidation with the charity hospice housed fifty white children of both sexes.[3] Although the new charity hospice would continue its policy of racial exclusivity under the Sisters of Saint Joseph, from that point forward the administration required, as exactly as possible, a list of all orphans that included age, family, birthplace, and a reason for admitting any new children. In addition to new caregivers, the young girls at the orphanage received new training—sewing, embroidery, washing, and ironing—to sustain themselves later in life. A previous restructuring had forbidden orphaned girls to stay in the home after the age of twenty-one, however that measure had been loosely enforced and consequently the new organization declared that all female orphans who had reached the age of twenty-one would continue to receive financial support only until the following year. If their "conduct was good," twenty-one-year-old female orphans would qualify for one final allotment of money and a trousseau designed to help them in their new life outside the facility.[4] As a consequence, the thirty-eight girls living in the institution in 1829 potentially had access to continued financial support after leaving.[5]

For the poor white women living at the charity hospice at the time of its transfer, the reorganization indicated that, unlike in the past, white women could not simply exist at the government's cost. It also, however, provided a mechanism for white female orphans to continue to receive government care. As long as "they could present sufficient guarantees about their morality," under the new rules of the institution young women past the age of twenty-one could qualify as "poor women" and remain in the facility. The ill or infirm would receive financial care from the hospice; all others, however, had to earn their keep through hard work. For each boarder, the colonial budget provided an annual sum of 500 francs, as well as assistance from doctors and necessary medicines. While the white women living in the charity hospice did not have to undertake any "lucrative work" on the hospice's behalf they did have to submit to a daily regimen designed to "maintain them in regularity and peace." Not surprisingly, those who refused such drudgery got banished from the home.[6] With the shift to the Sisters of Saint Joseph, however, colonial administrators had a better chance to determine who stayed and who went.

The administrative restructuring also officially sanctioned the opening of private primary schools in Martinique for free children of any racial background.[7] Because primary schools could now enroll *gens de couleur*, Creoles worried that education in Martinique would no longer remain the exclusive domain of white inhabitants and they thus fought to ensure the Sisters of Saint Joseph's Saint Pierre Royal School for Girls continued to accept only white girls. In 1827 the institution enrolled eighty-two of the island's wealthiest Creole daughters, and by economizing and selling handiwork sent from the Order in continental France and offering music lessons, the twelve Sisters of Saint Joseph who oversaw the school had managed to accrue nearly 33,000 francs in assets.[8] Prompted by the school's financial success in its three years under the Sisters' control, and desirous of more funds to use as they saw fit, Martinique's *colons* thus suggested the Order should buy their own building, rather than continue on at the island's expense. The school's headmistress, Sister Marie-Thérèse Javouhey, however, told Sister Anne-Marie Javouhey, the Order's head in Paris, that buying a building had never been part of their agreement with the Ministry of the Marine. The headmistress further warned if the Sisters did purchase a new facility the government would not want to continue to pay their food, lodging, and meager salary. Because they could potentially earn nearly 18,000 francs if they had twenty teachers on the island as the administration requested, and they could send back any profits to help the Order in continental France, Sister Marie-Thérèse argued buying their own building would be disastrous for everyone.[9] The head of the Order apparently agreed and convinced the Ministry of the Marine the Sisters of Saint Joseph should continue in their original agreement.

Despite Comte de Bouillé's initial success in creating more metropolitan oversight of some Creole institutions, ultimately the 1827 administrative reorganization simply restructured rather than eliminated Creole power in Martinique's bureaucracy. As one metropolitan official, Joseph-Barthélémy-Honoré-Louis-Amable de Ricard, noted, "the Creoles will find this organization perfect if, as they appear to hope, they obtain the places of Director [of the Interior] and *procureur général*, who, with the three councilors of the Private Council and the General Council, [will] assure them the direction of all affairs."[10] Nothing in the new ordinance prohibited a Creole from serving as director of the interior or *procureur général*, and if both positions went to Creoles, they also would monopolize the Private Council. In the end, even the secretary's position went to "an influential man and anti-metropolitan."[11] As a result, de Ricard warned only by placing "the reins of government . . . in firm and capable hands . . . [in] a man who dares to free himself from the opinion of the Private Council and who little fears to lose the friendship of the *colons* or to expose himself to their hatred and their denunciation" could colonial officials prevent Creoles from further co-opting the new system.[12] Ultimately Comte de Bouillé proved not to be that man, however, and from their positions on the councils and the courts Martinique's Creoles found ways to maintain their traditional power.

Repeated metropolitan attempts to take power out of Creole hands nonetheless made elite planters believe that future white dominance increasingly depended on uniformity within the island's white community and demanded *petits blancs* not fall into desperate poverty. Even de Ricard agreed "whites in misery offer here a dangerous *tableau* which inspires in *negroes* and *hommes de couleur* a hatred that could have disastrous results."[13] To help the island's *petits blancs*, Martinique's elite planters turned again to the charity bureaus as they had many times before. After the 1822 Carbet uprising, however, an increasing number of free mixed-race Martinicans had also taken advantage of this assistance, including taking up residence alongside poor whites in Fort Royal's charity hospital. According to Martinique's Creole director of the interior, Vicomte de Rosily, the hospice building needed extensive repairs to prevent "the unfortunate families whose misery has forced them to find shelter there" from being "covered by its ruins." Although *colons* undoubtedly found such blurring of racial boundaries a threat to the island's racial hierarchy, they also refused to abandon the dozen or so white individuals also seeking refuge in the poor hospital and consequently authorized the colonial government to spend approximately 32,000 francs to make appropriate repairs.[14]

Such tangible reminders of the reality of racial mixing on the island made Martinique's *colons* even more insistent that white social superiority required poor white allegiance to elite ideals of behavior. As a series of cases indicate, however, whites of both sexes and from all economic backgrounds repeatedly ignored elite prescriptions against public violence and racial mixing. By creating public records in public forums, the new administrative reforms made it increasingly difficult for the island's white planters to deny white behavior that they previously had kept hidden through their judicial positions. Rather than fight the new system, however, Martinique's elite Creoles used their positions on the Tribunals of First Instance and on the Royal Court and supplanted supposedly colorblind justice with racial privilege to reprimand those they believed a threat to islandwide stability.[15]

Two cases involving white men engaged in public disputes provided an ideal opportunity for the court to remind Martinique's white community, and *petits blancs* in particular, that in public they needed to maintain the appearance of complete coherence with elite white norms and serve as an example to the island's *gens de couleur*. In the first case a white Martinican and his two sons came before Fort Royal's Tribunal of First Instance accused of beating another white man to death with a whip. Because colonial laws reserved the whip for punishment of enslaved people, its use by a white man to kill another white, under any circumstance, was particularly shocking. The tribunal's Creole members sent a message about how whites should behave, banishing the oldest son, accused of the murder, for ten years and sentencing the youngest son and father each to three months in prison for their actions.[16]

In a second case two white managers, Messieurs Lamotte and Lauziere, from the government-owned plantation Saint Jacques also came before the Tribunal of First Instance in Fort Royal. In the public square of nearby Lamentin, Lamotte had apparently struck his former boss, Lauziere, and drawn blood and then months later again hit Lauziere, this time with a cattle prod, creating "several other scandalous scenes." While Lamotte's violence certainly was cause for concern in and of itself, the court found its *public* display the most egregious transgression. They also noted, however, that "such outbursts, although always reprehensible," could help elites reinforce prescribed norms when they took place "between individuals who, due to their class and their quality, must provide good examples in the colony." The tribunal's Creole magistrates undoubtedly hoped Lamotte's three months imprisonment and his 100 francs fines would serve as lessons to other whites who participated in such unruly behavior and as reminders of the responsibility the white community had to the rest of Martinique's population.[17]

As two other cases indicate, in addition to reprimanding members of Martinique's poor white community who had transgressed prescribed norms, Creoles on the courts also felt compelled to punish elite white men whom they felt provided a bad example to the white population. Joseph Saint Thevenin appeared before Martinique's Royal Court accused of several "attempts against public security, the security of his family and of his neighborhood," as well as the attempted assassination of his brother-in-law. According to Thevenin's victimized brother-in-law, Joseph Saint Thevenin had come to his plantation and menaced him with a machete and a pistol before running away. Thevenin later returned to the plantation, apparently not only bent on killing his brother-in-law but also on burning down one of his mother's quarters for enslaved workers. The court eventually ruled that as "a dangerous man to society and his family" who had several times compromised public tranquility, Joseph Saint Thevenin be banished from the colony for ten years and bear responsibility for the cost of the proceedings.[18] Those on the court clearly believed that it could not allow white men from plantation-owning families to run around wielding machetes and burning property.

Nor, it appears, could they ignore Creole men like Saint Maur Desfontaines-Préfontaines who threatened his widowed mother because she would not facilitate his interracial sexual relationship. Desfontaines-Préfontaines stood before the Tribunal of First Instance in Fort Royal accused of beating his mother, repeatedly threatening her, and troubling public tranquility. The accusations marked the second time his mother had brought suit against him and she did so, she said, "to save her life." According to widow Desfontaines-Préfontaines, her son had threatened to kill her if she did not receive his mistress, a *mulâtresse* named Virginie, on her plantation. In a drunken rage Desfontaines-Préfontaines apparently had forced his mother to flee her plantation and, when she returned, threw a chair at her. Based on his mother's testimony and other witnesses to his threats and menaces, the court decided his behavior toward his mother and other members of his family, as well as his intimate relationships with "perverse people," (Virginie) marked him as a "danger to the quarter and the tranquility of the colony." Consequently they sentenced him to lifelong deportation from the French West Indies.[19] Elite white men who threatened their mothers also could not be tolerated.

In addition to using the courts to send a message to the island's white men, Martinique's Creoles also took advantage of this venue to highlight what they viewed as the ongoing dangers faced by Martinique's white women from the enslaved population. After the abolition of the provostial court in 1826, Martinique's Creole magistrates increasingly deported those individuals they suspected of poisoning animals and individuals.[20] When members of Martinique's enslaved community fought in other violent ways against the island's brutally repressive plantation system, however, as in the case of Théresine, Creoles opted for an open trial accompanied by much publicity because they believed it would help them make their argument about the need for severe punishment of enslaved workers. Théresine, an enslaved domestic of the Creole Dames St. Yves, came before the Royal Court in March 1828 accused of theft and killing her owner with premeditation. After an extensive trial that featured testimony by Dame St. Yves's plantation manager, the autopsy of the royal physician, evidence of Théresine's sole presence in the house at the time of the incident, blood on the bedroom linens, and a money-filled kerchief in Théresine's possession at the time of her arrest, the court convicted Théresine on both counts. They then meted out a gruesome punishment, sentencing her to amputation of her right hand for her theft, and then strangulation and hanging for the murder of Dame St. Yves.[21] Undoubtedly elite Creoles hoped the details of the crime would serve to deter those who called the enslaved labor system unjust and the punishment would hinder similar violence by enslaved workers in the future.

Although elites welcomed the opportunity to let court cases underscore the dangers white women encountered on the island, they tried to mitigate the fall-out when white plantocrat women, like Dame Dubuc de Rivery, came to trial because of their violent behavior. While owning enslaved workers remained an important marker of elite status, the ideal of white femininity made little room for Creole women to personally punish them. When they did, and when those actions became public, Creole women overstepped the boundaries of propriety and Martinican elites did all they could to stifle publicity. This was the case when Dame Dubuc de Rivery appeared before the Fort Royal Tribunal of First Instance charged with excessively punishing several of her 150 enslaved laborers and contributing to the death of her male enslaved domestic, Rémy. Dubuc de Rivery's plantation manager testified that she had previously stabbed an enslaved servant, Firmine, in the stomach with a knife and the former police captain in Robert recommended, for the sake of "public interest" and to prevent further "disorder in the neighborhood," the court prohibit Dame Dubuc de Rivery from personally managing her plantation in the future. Several of her other former managers also swore she frequently ordered "cruel and rigorous punishment without motive and for sheer caprice" and "did not cease to beat the *nègres* until their blood ran."[22]

Based on the testimony of numerous witnesses the court ultimately found Dame Dubuc de Rivery innocent of Rémy's death. They did, however, find her guilty of seriously injuring her enslaved domestic Firmine and of frequently committing "atrocious cruelties" against her other enslaved workers, including depriving them of food and clothing. The court consequently ordered her enslaved laborers be sold, condemned her to pay the expenses of the trial, and banished her from both continental and colonial French territory for twenty years. As for Firmine, they returned her to the plantation where she suffered a severe beating for having involved the authorities in the first place.[23]

Although Martinique's Creole magistrates took Dame Dubuc de Rivery's actions seriously, they also did all they could to protect her and the white community from public scrutiny of her behavior. Before the trial, Dame Dubuc de Rivery's counsel requested, and received, a closed-door hearing.[24] Furthermore, on appeal, the Creole-dominated Royal Court overturned her sentence and reduced her exile from twenty to three years.[25]

Dame Dubuc de Rivery's trial serves as a tangible reminder that for many white Martinican women their lived reality did not coincide with Creoles' ideal of white femininity. A number of other white women who appeared before the island's courts during the spring and summer of 1828 confirmed this discrepancy. While they clearly were not the first white women to participate in the kind of commercial transactions that brought them before the courts, the records generated as a result of the administrative restructuring on the island offer a hitherto unavailable cataloging of the variety and complexity of their business dealings. Many white women came before the court courtesy of their husbands' authorizations or acting on their husbands' behalf.[26] Other white women acted independently, and many, as wives *separées de biens*, no longer legally held property in common with their husbands, and therefore were not held liable for their debts.[27] As dressmakers, bakers, furniture wholesalers and *marchandes publiques* (female merchants) of all sorts, they shouldered legal responsibility for their own business ventures.[28]

With poor white women like widow Schaumbourg, whom authorities believed threatened the reputation of the white community, the courts took public action. The Fort Royal Tribunal of First Instance summoned Schaumbourg ten times to account for her actions over a two-month period in the summer of 1828. Although she never made an appearance, the court ordered her to pay more than 10,000 francs to seven different business partners. After she failed to answer any of the summons issued, the court noted the extent of her troubles: "she is notoriously bankrupt; she is in this state due to her flight; she fled after an accounting of her assets; she clandestinely took merchandise that was the property of her creditors."[29] Such an accounting of her failings did not bode well for her creditors and, ultimately, two merchants from Fort Royal, two from Saint-Pierre, another from the nearby island of Saint-Lucie, and three ship captains failed to recover what Schaumbourg owed.

Although Schaumbourg struggled in her dealings with primarily white male merchants, other court records show many white Martinican widows succeeded in public commerce and frequently counted mixed-race women among their business partners.[30] Some Creole widows, like Pisant de la Rifaudière and le Tavernier, contracted with free mixed-race women like Rosette and Marguerite, who worked as petty merchants in Saint Pierre.[31] Other white Martinican widows, like Puilhery and Gaschel Saint-Helene, a proprietor residing in metropolitan France, rented space to free mixed-race women like Anastasie and Laurette.[32]

Creole women like the widows who appeared before Martinique's tribunals and the free mixed-race women who worked as their business partners helped to make the island's economy run. By crossing economic and racial boundaries, however, their business relationships also raised troubling questions about the continued limits France's *gens de couleur* faced around the French Atlantic. Metropolitan attention to the conclusion of the Bissette Affair also underscored the myriad ways that France's free mixed-race individuals were denied their civil and legal rights. In March 1827 Guadeloupe's Royal Court finally re-tried the case against Bissette and the other *gens de couleur* implicated in the purported 1823 conspiracy as directed by the Parisian Court of Cassation. The Royal Court ultimately suspended Fabien, *fils* and Volny's sentences and reduced Bissette's punishment to ten years in exile and the cost of the proceedings. But the men's lawyer, Isambert, took issue with the form of the proceedings—they took place in closed session—and also with the basis for the court's decision—a law that banned possession of recognized seditious works. According to Isambert, not only did justice require a public trial but also the law against seditious works used to convict the men had not been promulgated in Guadeloupe and, even if it had been, it only applied to writings already deemed seditious, which "The Status of Free Men of Color in the French Antilles" had not been. Based on his objections Bissette, Fabien, *fils*, and Volny once again appealed their case to the Parisian Court of Cassation.[33] In the meantime, anticolonial proponents in the metropolitan press continued to make their case public, publishing, for example, an account of the proceedings before Guadeloupe's Royal Court and an analysis of the case.[34]

The Court of Cassation finally considered the men's second appeal in December 1827 but this time rejected their request. Colonial authorities had the right to hold the proceedings behind closed doors, the court decided, but did determine they did not have the authority to evaluate whether or not the pamphlet in question met the criteria established for seditious materials.[35] As in the days following the Court of Cassation's original review of the Bissette Affair, the metropolitan French press immediately responded to the Court's verdict. The following day the *Moniteur* and the *Gazette des Tribunaux*, for example, both carried stories that once again outlined the injustices endured by those involved in the Bissette Affair.[36] Shortly after the verdict, Bissette also delivered a petition to the Chamber of Deputies and the Chamber of Peers, insisting *gens de couleur* be granted the rights due all free French citizens, and subsequently had the petition printed.[37]

Although the Bissette Affair was officially closed, the matter of just what place free mixed-race individuals had in the French national family was far from decided. When Baron Guillaume Hyde de Neuville took over as the new minister of the marine in early March 1828, he made it clear the new ministry intended to seriously address the long debated question, informing the Chamber of Deputies "the security of the colonies" as well as "the rights of humanity," required *gens de couleurs* be afforded equitable treatment. While change clearly was on the horizon, his insistence that France's *colons* first be consulted about what measures would help ensure "the interests of white families," in the colonies indicated he had not forgotten Martinique's Creoles.[38] The continued importance of white Martinicans in France's capital and port cities—at least 267 passengers made the transatlantic trip from Martinique to continental France in 1828—as well as his former position as a representative from the Nièvre (near Lyons) had made him quite aware of the long complicated tentacles of colonial commerce and its importance to French citizens around the realm.[39]

The appearance of several short stories openly supporting interracial relationships in the French West Indies and metropolitan France also reminded continental France that seemingly colonial issues were also metropolitan issues. Two stories in 1828 by a woman calling herself "femme" Sophie Doin addressed colonial fears of rebellion and the ensuing reversal of the colonial social structure as well as the possibility of racial mixing in metropolitan France.[40] *Blanche et noir* tells the story of Domingo, an enslaved man, and Hauteville, the "douce" white wife of a rich *colon* who saves Domingo from life as an orphan on an unidentified French West Indian island. Upon the birth of their daughter, Pauline, Hauteville convinces her husband to appoint six-year-old Domingo as the girl's servant and the two children grow up together, a star-crossed couple. At the end of the tale, following a bloody revolt by the island's enslaved workers, Pauline and Domingo flee to the woods to escape society's wrath. Twelve years later they still live there and the story concludes with the "negroes" voicing their sorrow for Pauline and arguing that she merits being a *noire* (black woman). *Noire et blanc* tells the tale of a *nègresse* who saves her master from fighting in Cap Français, Saint Domingue. The *nègresse*, who remains nameless, escapes the island with her master and goes with him to America, then on to France. In the metropole, a series of misadventures ensues ending happily with a reunion at which the master vows to love the *nègresse* for all time.[41]

Such explicit discussions of interracial relationships in the French West Indies no doubt deeply unsettled Creole planters and their supporters in metropolitan France. Time and again they had argued that such racial mixing would undermine the plantation system. As a result, Doin's suggestion that such relationships could root in true feelings and could benefit men and women both in the colonies and in metropolitan France potentially undermined their claims. Most specifically, the idea that a white woman could love an enslaved or free man of African descent, and cast aside a white man in his favor, flew in the face of elite ideals of white femininity and masculinity, not to mention concerns about racial purity and discussions of beauty as white. As a result, the stories touched a deeply felt, if never spoken, fear that indeed white women might choose such relationships if given the opportunity. The idea that a white woman, even on the continent, might facilitate such a union, even if she did not personally participate, further violated standards and called into question the relationship that Creole women in Martinique and continental France had with enslaved and free African men who often accompanied them on their journeys. That these same *hommes de couleur* were slowly securing civil and political rights in the French Empire only heightened Creole anxiety.

* * *

In September 1828, just six months after Hyde de Neuville took over as minister of the marine, the reform-minded Martignac ministry that had come to power in France in 1827 ordered a thorough reorganization of the colonial judicial system in yet another attempt to strip Martinique's Creole magistrates of their power. A new ordinance restructured the judiciary by creating justices of the peace in each of the island's communes and encouraged the inclusion of metropolitan magistrates for the Tribunals of First Instance in Fort Royal and Saint Pierre to help facilitate their new function as courts of last resort on verdicts rendered by the justices of the peace. The restructuring also created an Assize Court, comprised of three councilors from the Royal Court and four members from the College of Assessors, a pool of eligible magistrates who did not hold other permanent judicial positions. This new Assize Court would have authority in criminal matters leaving the Private Council with final judgment on their verdicts. Although the judicial restructuring gave sovereign justice to the Royal Court, it diminished its powers of final authority in administrative and financial matters and ultimately subjected its ruling to metropolitan review.[42] And, in a final affront to Creoles, the legislation diminished the role of the court's chief justice, limiting him to a three-year term, while augmenting that of the king's representative, the *procureur général.* To prevent the close bonds between the *procureur général* and the island's local elites that had previously stood in the way of metropolitan reforms, the decree also required that a lawyer from metropolitan France fill this position in the future and further forbade him from acquiring property or marrying in the colony.[43]

Martinique's Creoles and their supporters initially viewed this reworking of colonial justice as yet another assault on Creole power but hesitated to respond too quickly. As the planter Pierre Dessalles told his mother, "[I] must ride the waves if I am not to make enemies of my colleagues," on Martinique's new judicial benches.[44] Despite his anxiety Dessalles opted for cooperation at this point and when he received a letter from Hyde de Neuville appointing him as a provisional councilor on the Royal Court in October 1828, he accepted.[45] Five months later, however, he and his fellow members of the court responded swiftly and definitively to a new assault on their power. When Hyde de Neuville suggested metropolitan French, not Creoles, should fill all vacant judicial positions in the future and that the magistrates henceforth should be paid, Dessalles and all the other councilors resigned. On a visit to Paris, the president of the Royal Court, the Creole Comte de Grenonville, also managed to secure a personal audience with King Charles X to discuss the issue, "humbly beseeching" the king to consider Creole requests to maintain the posts as unpaid positions "for the sake of honor."[46] The resignations and the Comte de Grenonville's personal visit with Charles X apparently worked for the councilors resumed their offices in August 1829, and when the ordinance finally took effect in Martinique four months later the stipulation regarding paid metropolitan magistrates had disappeared.[47]

By introducing the criminal procedures, as well as the penal, commercial, and criminal instructions of the Civil Code in Martinique, colonial administrators in metropolitan France hoped to dramatically reform existing colonial legislation relative to the island's *gens de couleur* and finally wrest juridical control from those elite whites who had long exerted it. Just as the 1827 administrative reorganization had simply rerouted Creole power through the Private and General Councils, however, the 1828 judicial reorganization left primarily the same Creoles in powerful positions in the courtroom and introduced new planters, like Pierre Dessalles, who found metropolitan oversight on the island even more of an affront to colonists' status among the community of French citizens.

Increased metropolitan oversight deeply worried *colons* like Dessalles and significantly heightened tensions between Creole and metropolitan French on the island. Although previously Martinique's *colons* had focused their animosity for French from the continent on colonial administrators, an incident between a Creole and a continental French merchant and its aftermath illustrates increasingly strained relations between whites born on opposite sides of the Atlantic. According to Cardini, the head of Martinique's police force, one of Martinique's Creole merchants, Pavillo, had charge of organizing a ball in Fort Royal to honor the arrival of Martinique's new governor, Louis Henri de Saulces de Freycinet.[48] Because of his supposedly "hot head" and "poor comportment" at a previous event in Saint Pierre, however, metropolitan merchants sponsoring the event objected to Pavillo's appointment. Nonetheless he retained the position and the ball began without incident. By the end of the evening, however, Pavillo's behavior had provoked five separate challenges to duel with metropolitan merchants, including one from a merchant who killed Pavillo the following morning. After Pavillo's death, his witnesses allegedly took the fatal bullet to a member of former Empress Josephine's Creole family, who declared the slug should be sent to a "European" as a symbol of what their violence had accomplished. This, Cardini concluded in his report, "is what comes of the animosity that exists between the Creoles and the Europeans."[49]

Cardini contended the incident had long lasting repercussions not just for the white community but also for the safety of the entire island, eventually sparking a September confrontation between a Creole lieutenant colonel of the militia and a metropolitan judge auditor. Their dispute, Cardini argued, resulted from "the animosity that reigns here between Creoles and Europeans. Since the Pavillo affair, the Creoles search for an occasion to revenge his death and the Europeans want to be respected."[50] That Creoles felt compelled to duel with their metropolitan counterparts in order to restore Creole honor reveals their heightened concerns about how French citizens on the continent perceived the colonies and their inhabitants.[51]

According to Cardini, the divisions within the island's white community, "the shameful conduct of the whites and . . . the distinction between Creoles and Europeans," also led to a "very bad effect on the class of *gens de couleur*," increasing their "air of satisfaction and watchfulness."[52] Since the judicial reorganization Martinique's free mixed-race population had taken men like Minister of the Marine Hyde de Neuville seriously when they promised equitable treatment for France's *gens de couleur*. As a result free mixed-race Martinicans had increasingly availed themselves of, and demanded the administration guarantee, their right to adequate education. This included possibly integrating the Saint Pierre Royal Schools for Girls. The mere suggestion of racial integration at the Sisters of Saint Joseph's boarding school made Creoles even more insistent that the colony stop paying the expenses for an institution they could no longer completely control. In 1829 the school taught eighty students and since taking control five years earlier the Sisters of Saint Joseph had sent 30,500 francs back to metropolitan France. For this reason, while Creoles remained irritated that the government had transferred control of the school out of lay hands, they also realized if it remained under government control it ultimately would have to admit *femmes de couleur* and thus pushed again for the Sisters of Saint Joseph to assume control of the school. They also, however, wanted them to assume all expenses whereas the Order believed the nuns on the island should receive some form of government assistance. To avoid what appeared to be a standoff between the two groups, the minister of the marine informed the nuns he wanted the colony to give them what they asked for, including ownership of the building and the 600 francs stipends for each nun, and further insisted "the Sisters of Saint Joseph have done so much good in the colonies that one could not do enough for them."[53]

As a result of the ministry's intervention by June the Sisters of Saint Joseph and Martinique's Private Council and governor finally had reached an agreement. The government transferred the school to the benefit of the Order and also allocated an annual subvention of 12,000 francs from Martinique's colonial budget; the Sisters of Saint Joseph, for their part, would henceforth be responsible for the school and staff upkeep and provisioning, as well as for six scholarships for Creole girls.[54] From that time forward, however, the Order could spend their funds as they saw fit, much to the dismay of Martinique's *colons*. In the first six months of 1829 the Order had collected just over 33,000 francs and spent a little more than 27,000 francs, leaving them with a surplus of nearly 6,000 francs.[55] While this angered some Creoles, to the joy of others, the Sisters also had more leeway over who enrolled in the institution and for the time being they maintained its racial exclusivity.

Some Creole parents nonetheless worried the quality of education at the institution had deteriorated since 1827. Unsatisfied with the "great inferiority" of the religious instructors then assigned to the institution, and undoubtedly irritated that the minister of the marine had taken the institution out of lay hands and given such generous terms to the Order when they took it over completely, many Martinican planters had removed their daughters from the school. Members of the General Council, including its president, the Creole De Lucy, had entrusted their own daughters to the institution and argued that the Royal School for Girls had floundered. They thus found it imperative to "take the greatest care to revive an institution which, for some time, has declined from the prosperous state it enjoyed under the previous administration."[56] To remedy the situation, Martinique's metropolitan *procureur général* suggested six new nuns be sent from metropolitan France to replace those "judged to be insufficient to their obligations."[57] Such a change, he hoped, would restore confidence among the island's Creole parents. Concerns about the institution also made their way to Paris and to the minister of the marine, who indicated his continued desire to have the Sisters of Saint Joseph, rather than laywomen, run the school. As a result he personally communicated with head of the Order, urging her to "remedy the problems" identified and return the institution to its standing.[58]

According to the head of the Sisters of Saint Joseph, Anne-Marie Javouhey, however, the quality of education had not diminished at the Royal School for Girls. But many Creoles still worried that because the school received an annual subvention the government would require it to admit free mixed-race girls thus reducing its appeal and prestige. "If the *mulâtres* obtain what they desire," she told the institution's headmistress, Marie-Thérèse Javouhey, "it is feared we will be obliged to receive *mulâtresses* in our boarding school." If that happened elite Creoles would lose even more confidence in the establishment and thus Anne-Marie Javouhey instructed Marie-Thérèse Javouhey to "speak nothing" of the news and instead to use "prudence and wisdom" and to seek council from the priest and the colonial administration as events unfolded.[59] Although the Order would accept free mixed-race girls if forced, Anne-Marie Javouhey clearly worried such integration would encourage Martinique's *colons* to withdraw their daughters from the school thus robbing the Order of much needed income that they used to support their other missions around the Atlantic.

As they worked to integrate this bastion of Creole power, the island's *gens de couleur* also pushed to open even more private schools for Martinique's free mixed-race inhabitants. By the summer of 1830 Fort Royal had three private institutions for whites that taught a total of fifty-eight students and ten institutions for *gens de couleur* that taught 154 students. Saint Pierre hosted eighteen private institutions for whites and twelve for mixed-race children.[60] Threatened by the growing reality that they were losing education as a marker of white social superiority, Martinique's Private Council tried to curtail the creation of new institutions and control those that already existed by regulating the opening of private schools. As Martinique's *procureur général* from metropolitan France noted, however, the council did not have the power to deny a petition based solely on reputation, and therefore could not outright deny a petition from a free mixed-race individual solely on his or her racial background.[61] But this did not deter Creoles on the council, who declared it consequently would fall to the director of the interior, wealthy white planter Vicomte de Rosily, to ensure that free mixed-race children received instruction that would foster white social privilege. Through his surveillance, the Creole council insisted, the director of the interior should assure "in the primary schools where *gens de couleur* children are accepted, one will not teach anything contrary to . . . the principals according to which this part of the colonial population must be strictly maintained in its respect towards whites."[62]

In addition to securing education, Martinique's *gens de couleur* also called for an end to the use of racial markers in official documents and asked to be accorded titles of respect like "Monsieur" and "Madame" and to wear what they pleased.[63] For their part, Martinique's white community balked at any changes they thought might upset the island's social hierarchy and tried to reinforce white superiority wherever possible, and especially in the courts. Despite the intentions of the September 1828 ordinance, Martinique's Creoles managed to use their positions on the island's courts to maintain white superiority with the support of Saint Pierre's new metropolitan royal prosecutor, Champvallier, further raising concerns about the too-close alliance between *colons* and metropolitan officials. After his arrival in Martinique, Champvallier had established close links with a number of Creole families and aspired to wed a young Creole woman.[64] Encouraged by his new Creole supporters, under his tenure he "established two different weights and measures in the administration of justice," in Martinique, one for whites and one for *gens de couleur*.[65] These different standards most clearly played themselves out in instances where *petits blancs* violently responded to both so-called "Europeans," whom they accused of supporting an overturn of the island's racial and social hierarchy, and free mixed-race Martinicans. That Creoles now tolerated such public displays of seemingly inappropriate behavior by the island's poorer whites indicates just how intent they were to uphold white superiority.

During a play performed by a traveling company at Saint Pierre's theater in April 1830 one of the actors, Richer, repeatedly denigrated the titles "Sieur" and "Madame," mocking *gens de couleur* who had laid claim to these formerly white titles. Immediately after the performance, Martinique's director of the interior, at the urging of colonial officials, thus ordered his arrest. As news of Richer's detention made its way around the still crowded theater, however, a riot ensued where the actor's followers chanted "Richer, Richer," in support of his puns, and a number of *petits blancs* tore up chairs, threw stones, charged the official box, and defended the whites-only seating area in the racially segregated theater, the *Spectacle*. By the time calm returned, officials had charged eight white men with rebellion.[66]

When the case came before Martinique's Royal Court, the Creole judges, guided by Saint Pierre's Creole-aligned royal prosecutor, Champvallier, ultimately decided none of the eight men's actions constituted violence toward the island's police and therefore did not meet the requirements necessary for a charge of rebellion. They also cleared five of the men of all other charges and released them: Messieurs Fasia, a general shopkeeper, and Lange, a jeweler, who had shouted "calumnies against the authorities and vociferations against

Boitel," the metropolitan *procureur général*; Lesage, a merchant's assistant, who had "uttered protests"; Rebuffaud, unemployed, who had participated in the riot and lived "in a state of vagabondage"; and Turbé, another merchant's assistant, who had thrown punches during the skirmish.[67]

Only three accused whites—Bonifaye, an unemployed Martinican living with his father; Saint Yves, the assistant clerk of courts for the Saint Pierre Justice of the Peace; and Grosjean, another unemployed Martinican—received any substantial punishment. Although the court determined that Bonifaye had broken seats in the arena, they eventually decided "his extreme youth leads us to believe he was carried away by the effervescence of the moment and the long detention he has already endured will suffice to make him more cautious" in the future; as a result, they released him without further punishment. The court also found even though Saint Yves had "uttered protests," broken into the authorities' *loge*, and thrown debris into the Saint Pierre arena, like Bonifaye "his youth, the long detention he has already endured, and the Saint Pierre police captain's belief he had been agitated by the effervescence of the moment and not criminal intention," required only a 100 francs fine as punishment. For his threats to push a local official down the stairs and hit him with a stone, the court sentenced Grosjean to a 200 francs fine.[68]

To protect Creole privilege against both free mixed-race pretentions and "European" support of that community, Martinique's judges clearly decided that young white men who threatened colonial administrators, and publicly taunted the island's *gens de couleur*, "in the effervescence of the moment," warranted only moderate punishment. Colonial authorities in France, however, disagreed. Just a month after the trial they instructed Martinique's governor to use the title "Sieur" and "Madame" for free mixed-race individuals in all official documents and further indicated henceforth *gens de couleur* could sit anywhere they wanted at Saint Pierre's public theater.[69]

Creole magistrates also worked to protect Creole social superiority by meting out lighter sentences to *petits blancs* involved in altercations with free mixed-race women and men. A number of domestic violence cases involving white men and *femmes de couleur* appeared before Martinique's Royal Court in the spring of 1830, reinforcing elite assumptions about poor white men's sexual behavior. To discourage racial mixing, Creole magistrates handed out jail time and monetary fines, but their desire to maintain all of the island's whites in a position above Martinique's *gens de couleur*, especially as free mixed-race individuals gained in status, also compelled Creoles on the bench to shield the white men involved from severe punishment. As a result the Royal Court ultimately acquitted Antoine Dancy, a white sailor, of all charges claiming he had assaulted the mixed-race woman Alexandrine, asserting it "not proven" that Dancy had actually struck her and that, on the contrary, Alexandrine had "touched Dancy on the shoulder first, prompting him to repulse her."[70] The court did sentence Alexandre Auguetil, a white petty merchant, to a 50-franc fine and the cost of the proceedings for having beaten and injured a *femme de couleur*, Rose, though they noted "extenuating circumstances" in the case.[71] The court also found Charles Guinel, a white tailor, guilty of beating and administering "grave violence" against Anne Marie, a free *câpresse*, and condemned him to three months imprisonment, a 300-franc fine, and the cost of the proceedings.[72] The tailor, however, must not have served out his jail time for barely a month later he once again faced charges of beating Anne Marie. In this case, recidivism seems to have paid: this second time the court issued only a 39-franc fine.[73]

Several trials involving disputes between *petits blancs* and *hommes de couleur* also came before Martinique's courts and once again the whites involved received light sentences. According to Cardini, the confrontations "have their source only in the hatred of the whites towards the colored class, and since that class has acquired a certain social equality, and some civil rights, this hatred of the whites has accrued to the point that it now erupts under any absurd pretext."[74] Regardless of what motivated the fights, the trials indicate that both poor whites and free mixed-race individuals increasingly took matters into their own hands to secure their places in the island's shifting social hierarchy. Likewise the courts' verdicts illustrate Martinique's plantocracy saw the incidents as an opportunity to maintain the social status of the island's *petits blancs* above that of Martinique's mixed-race inhabitants.

On four different occasions the Royal Court heard cases where white men stood accused of "poor treatment" of *gens de couleur* and each time the court dismissed the case without any proceedings based on a supposed lack of evidence.[75] In cases when sentences did follow, white men clearly fared better than their *gens de couleur* co-defendants. In one instance, Thuret, a white employee with Martinique's customs office, and Alfred, an *homme de couleur*, appeared before the Royal Court, charged with exchanging blows. On the afternoon of December 19, 1829, Alfred apparently had struck Thuret on the left ear and had drawn blood. A fight then ensued and both threw punches. Based on the witnesses' reports and the findings of the proceeding, the court sentenced the *homme de couleur* Alfred to two months in prison, a 100-franc fine, and three-quarters of the total court expenses. The white Thuret, on the other hand, had to pay only 50 francs and one-quarter of the total court expenses because the court determined he "had only [attacked] Alfred because of the blows he had received."[76]

While the court basically absolved Thuret for his involvement in this al-tercation, a subsequent case indicates the fight between Thuret and Alfred led to a larger, more violent, fracas later that same night, one that involved a num-ber of *petits blancs* and *gens de couleur*. On the day after the Royal Court ren-dered its verdict in the case between Thuret and Alfred, four white men—the Ancinall brothers, Delonge, and, once again, Thuret—came before the Royal Court charged with having conspired to hit and injure an *homme de couleur*, François Barthelemy. Several witnesses testified that Barthelemy was "suddenly and without provocation attacked by a group of young men, some of whom were armed with batons and rock-laden handkerchiefs." The attack "seriously compromised" public order and seriously injured Barthelemy. Although all four white men initially stood accused as part of the "assailing group," the court failed to implicate Delonge or Thuret, citing lack of evidence. They did sentence the Ancinall brothers to three months in prison each and a fine of 200 francs, as well as the total cost of the proceedings. Considering that the *homme de couleur* Alfred had received two months in prison, a 100-franc fine, and three-quarters of the total court expenses for merely"exchanging blows" with Thuret, the Ancinall brothers received a mild punishment.[77]

Although they repeatedly failed to receive equitable treatment from the island's courts, Martinique's *gens de couleur* nonetheless continued to take their complaints of ill treatment to local officials and especially to the newly cre-ated justices of the peace. Some, like Belletête of Trinité, attempted to provide free mixed-race individuals with the rights guaranteed them, but time and again ran up against the island's *colons* and the metropolitan royal prosecutor Champvallier. According to Belletête, Desgages, a wealthy Creole planter and head of the parish of Trinité, ordered an eighty-two-year-old *homme de cou-leur*, Laurant, to apologize to a white man for calling him by name when the man passed by Laurant's door. Although Laurant did as instructed, two days after he apologized the local police captain arrested his two children and, with Royal Prosecutor Champvallier's knowledge, held them for more than a year. Desgages also refused to bring charges against a white man, Rosier Seguin, a white proprietor in the parish of Trinité, who five witnesses confirmed had beaten a free mixed-race man, Ragot, close to death. When, due to his exten-sive injuries, Ragot failed to appear when summoned by Desgages, the parish commander had Ragot arrested and, again with Champvallier's knowledge, detained him in the local jail for over a year before he died.[78]

While Martinique's *gens de couleur* worked to gain the justice due them as French citizens, the island's enslaved population also took advantage of the new judicial organization to seek redress from a series of abuses that had long

existed despite laws against such behavior. The enslaved workers at the Bel-
fond plantation near Trinité also contacted Justice of the Peace Belletête to
complain about their ill treatment from their plantation manager, Vermeil.
According to a number of the plantation's inhabitants, for more than a month
he had denied them food and they implored the justice of the peace to intervene. When questioned by Desgages about his behavior, Vermeil insisted the
enslaved laborers on the plantation were in revolt; however, when a squadron of dragoons visited the plantation they found only enslaved field workers
and domestics "dying of hunger." Although Justice of the Peace Belletête had
relayed the information to Champvallier, who claimed to have told the *procureur général*, no charges ever came against Vermeil.[79] As a consequence, like
legally free people of African descent, the island's enslaved workers continued
to struggle to secure even the inadequate treatment promised them.

Although Martinique's Creoles and their supporters clearly hoped to, at
best, roll back the clock to earlier days or, at worst, continue the status quo,
the shift to Louis Philippe's reign and the July Monarchy in the summer of
1830 also brought significant changes to the continent and to the island's relationship with metropolitan France. The "Citizen King" Louis Philippe rose to
power as a compromise between the ultra-royalism that finally characterized
Charles X's reign and the volatile revolutionary republicanism that opposed
it. From the beginning, then, this new regime worked to create a balance between these two extremes, providing greater opportunities for a limited number of French citizens through a more consistent and equitable application of
the law, while safeguarding property and its owners.

This liberalizing zeal extended immediately to the colonies, too. On August 23, 1830, attempting to redefine the relationship between France and its
colonies, the July Monarchy created a "commission on colonial legislation"
to consider colonial reforms.[80] Inspired in part by the growing abolitionist
movement, the commission put forth a number of initiatives that would dramatically alter relationships between Martinique's varied inhabitants.[81] Most
specifically they signaled that the realm's *gens de couleur* could no longer be
treated differently than any other French citizens solely because of their racial
backgrounds. In a speech before the Chamber of Deputies the minister of
the marine argued, "France recognizes free men can not exist under different
[legal] conditions" and further insisted "all free men, whatever their color, are
equal before the law."[82] Creoles and their metropolitan supporters hoped once
again they could prevent such promises from becoming a reality.

* * *

In the fall of 1830, word of Charles X's abdication and the installation of the new Orleanist regime finally reached Martinique. Based on their concern that at least some of the island's elite Creoles would maintain their allegiance to the Bourbon monarchy as they waited for new colonial administrators to arrive, the Ministry of the Marine kept a close eye on the situation in Martinique and asked the head of police, Cardini, to continue his clandestine surveillance of the island and to determine whether or not colonial opinion favored "the new order."[83] If Creoles had any doubt about July Monarchy promises, within two weeks of his arrival in early November, the new governor, contre-amiral Jean-Henri-Joseph Dupotet, made it clear changes on the continent would extend to the colonies.

Motivated by his mission to create more uniformity in the opportunities afforded all of France's free citizens, regardless of race, Dupotet began his tenure on the island by prohibiting Martinique's overwhelmingly Creole notaries from using the phrase "*le nommé*," which had traditionally indicated a person of African descent, in any official documents and insisted they institute the September order to instead use "Sieur." The decree also contradictorily authorized officials to add "a certain *homme de couleur libre*," to designate the "Sieur" as a mixed-race person, however, thus in practice undermining the potential for true color blindness in official records.[84]

Creoles' initial response to such changes indicated disputes between them and colonial officials would only worsen with the regime's intention to expand rights for Martinique's *gens de couleur*. Many notaries, for example, still failed to employ the new language, indicating at least some continued to want official documents that clearly indicated racial boundaries and that they viewed any changes as an attack on their traditional powers and on the sanctity of white identity. Unlike under previous regimes, however, after Martinique's *gens de couleur* approached the governor and confirmed they found "a certain *homme de couleur libre*" humiliating, and in response to reports that those notaries who had made the change faced intense criticism, Dupotet ignored Creole desires and issued another decree ordering the offensive phrase excluded in the future. He also abrogated all other "unjust and vexatious" local laws, like those technically requiring free mixed-race individuals to wear a certain type of cloth, denying them the chance to hold public functions, or to hold the same name as a white inhabitant.[85]

Seeing Dupotet as an advocate of change, rather than an ally of Creole power like many previous governors, Martinique's *colons* thus turned to the guidance of Saint Pierre's royal prosecutor, Champvallier, who had just returned from his continental honeymoon with his Creole bride. In him they found a champion for Creole priorities in the courts. Shortly after his arrival back on the island in early December, Champvallier caused havoc in judicial matters by keeping four *gens de couleur* illegally imprisoned for forty hours at the request, rumor had it, of Martinique's elite whites. The metropolitan man's marriage to a Creole woman, Cardini indicated in a letter to the Ministry of the Marine, had not only left Champvallier a rich property owner but had also irrevocably allied him to the Creole population as evidenced by his inappropriate action.[86]

When the case came to the governor's attention through the protest of a local *juge d'instruction*, Adolphe Juston, the governor questioned Champvallier as to why he had imprisoned the four mixed-race men. Champvallier responded, "It is necessary, my general, when one imprisons four whites, to also imprison four *gens de couleur*, with or without reason. It sets a good example." According to Cardini, Governor Dupotet, greatly surprised by such action, immediately consulted the metropolitan *procureur général* who "severely reprimanded" Champvallier.[87] Despite these very different understandings of justice, however, Champvallier retained his position and through him Creoles continued their crusade to thwart metropolitan desires for racial fusion by specifically punishing poor white men who willingly involved themselves with *gens de couleur*. Such behavior now loomed even more dangerous, however, precisely because it reinforced metropolitan goals. Although such examples went directly against elite Creole desires to maintain racial separation, Martinique's white planters nonetheless still worked to keep *petits blancs* within the boundaries of whiteness by giving them lighter sentences than their accomplices.

On Christmas day in 1830 thirteen individuals—five whites, four free mixed-race men, and four enslaved men—appeared before Saint Pierre's court accused either of planning or complicity in the breaking and entering, armed theft, and attempted selling of contraband from a shipwrecked Spanish schooner, the *Constance*. As usual Royal Prosecutor Champvallier had the task of prosecuting the case and, according to Cardini, he once again "presented himself more as the defender rather than the prosecutor of these accused whites, against whom there existed overwhelming evidence."[88] After reviewing their answers to twenty-six questions posed during the proceedings, the Creole-controlled court acquitted two of the whites for lack of evidence. The remaining three received punishments ranging from a month to a year in prison. Most of the enslaved and free men of African descent did not fare as well, however. Although the court acquitted two of the enslaved Africans, it convicted two others of theft: one received twenty-nine whip lashes and attachment to a chain gang for two years; the other got one year on the chains. One *homme de couleur* received two years in jail; three others five days in prison. Although Cardini reported, mistakenly, to the minister of the marine that only "two whites, one a Creole and the other a European," were condemned, he noted correctly that the whites got "light sentences" for their transgressions and the "the iron hand of the tribunal was applied to the slaves."[89]

By February 1831 that "iron hand" would prove too much for Martinique's *gens de couleur* and enslaved populations and even for some *petits blancs*. Martinique had nearly equal white and free mixed-race populations in 1826. Within five years, however, those numbers had shifted to 9,362 whites, 14,055 *gens de couleur*, and 86,499 enslaved people.[90] This disparity made elite whites even more fearful the island's *gens de couleur* might violently demand more rights. And that they did after Dupotet transferred the *juge d'instruction* who had complained about Champvallier's inappropriate incarceration of four *gens de couleur*. Rumors swirled that Juston had informed on several Martinican Creoles who had tried to incite rebellion among their enslaved workers in order to intimidate Dupotet and slow the effects of the new policies for the island's free mixed-race inhabitants.[91] The island's Creoles, of course, denied any such actions but Juston's criticisms of Champvallier in December 1830 had made him odious among Martinique's elite planters.[92] Consequently it seemed likely the island's *colons* had maneuvered for his transfer to Guadeloupe—where the inhabitants greeted him as "*le mulâtre*,"—and that Dupotet had yielded to Creole displeasure with the judge.

On February 9, 1831, the trouble Creoles feared finally came when about 300 people attacked eleven plantations near Saint Pierre as well as three homes in the city. According to official reports and eyewitness accounts, the incident started in the cane fields of Perrinelle, a prominent Creole, and soon spread as the group made its way from plantation to plantation. Along their route, they invoked the revolutionary fervor that had swept France in 1830, singing to the tune of the *Parisienne*, "march forward against the planters" and "wash our furrows with the blood of whites."[93] Upon receiving news of the events, Dupotet called the colonial militias—both white and mixed-race—and the 45th regiment into action as approximately 300 women, children, and the infirm, nearly all of them white, fled for safety on ships anchored in Saint Pierre's port. As the militia and the troops moved on the bands of enslaved people in the nearby cane fields, the mixed-race fire brigade extinguished the flames within the city proper. By the middle of the following day, authorities had quelled the so-called "rebellion," but only after also implicating two whites, Bernard Xavier Bosc, the manager of the Dariste family plantation, and Théodore LeChevalier, a "wayward" member of a formerly important planter family.

Over the next six weeks authorities arrested more than 260 people in connection with the uprising and in early April the Royal Court officially accused forty-nine people, including Bosc and LeChevalier, for their actions.[94] *Patronés* or *libres de fait*, however, comprised the majority of those implicated and their complicated social and legal status would set off yet another extended debate on the island and in metropolitan France over the boundaries of French citizenship. At the end of April 1831, a royal ordinance granting complete civil liberties to the realm's *gens de couleur* was promulgated in Martinique. This ordinance, decreed in continental France at the end of February, allowed free mixed-race individuals to inherit from whites and abolished all previous decrees that prohibited mixed-race people from practicing medicine, surgery, or pharmacy; called for the verification of titles of liberty or birth or marriage notices; or forbade *gens de couleur* from retiring to or visiting continental France for extended periods. It also granted unlimited access to education.[95] The law deeply dismayed Martinique's Creole elite who believed it stripped the realm's white population of virtually every social, economic, and legal privilege they had held; only voting and the right to hold office remained bastions of white identity and they, too, appeared in jeopardy.

In response to their clearly diminishing influence and the growing political (although still theoretical) and numerical (literal) power of Martinique's *gens de couleur*, elite Creoles used their still considerable leverage on the Royal Court to try to reestablish control and thwart the now very public evidence of interracial cooperation on the island manifested in the Saint Pierre uprising. The Royal Court of Martinique, convoked in special session as an Assize Court by Governor Dupotet, began its deliberations in early May and after less than two weeks of testimony, it condemned twenty-six enslaved people to death for their participation in the uprising, sentenced one enslaved man to two years in prison and another enslaved woman to twenty-nines lashes of the whip, and acquitted the remaining enslaved Martinicans.[96] After some received stays of execution and the rest lost any right to appeal, the court hanged twenty-two enslaved individuals in Saint Pierre's public square.[97] As for Bosc and LeChevalier, the court acquitted Bosc.[98] LeChevalier never actually appeared before the court but rather fled the island for continental France before the trial; in his absence, the court fined him 2,000 francs and sentenced him to five years imprisonment for his failure to reveal the plot. By the end of the year, however, the king pardoned both his fine and sentence and eventually even authorized 2,000 francs for LeChevalier to return to Martinique.[99]

Martinique's Royal Court showed little mercy for those of African descent who had participated in the February incident in an attempt to rearrange the island's social hierarchy. Their handling of the two white Martinicans, how-ever, underscores how complicated upholding white hegemony had become in the early years of the July Monarchy. As the Royal Court's Act of Accusation reveals, the charges against Bosc, a *petit blanc*, and Théodore LeChevalier, a plantocrat, stemmed not simply from their actions on that evening but also from their previous relationships with the enslaved and free mixed-race com-munities. While elites had long worried about such transgressions of the racial code, in this new climate of opportunity for *gens de couleur* they viewed this very public alliance between whites and people of African descent with par-ticular horror and did all they could to mitigate its effect.[100]

The court charged the *petit blanc* Bosc based on his purported role in the planning and execution of the February 9 events and his attack against and violent resistance to members of the local militia during the commission of their duty that evening. Bosc's overt relationship with Pauline, his longtime enslaved partner with whom he had a daughter, appeared to confirm precisely the stereotype that some *colons* had constructed of poor white men. The Act of Accusation found that Bosc's efforts to move his material possessions and his daughter out of Saint Pierre before the uprising also made him a dubious character. So, too, did his reported failure to put out the flames of a neighbor-ing plantation on the night in question.[101] "If this criminal action was not determined by an irresistible force," it concluded, "it is the result of a man who has fallen into the most absolute insanity!"[102]

All of Bosc's efforts prior to the uprising could certainly seem circum-stantial evidence that he foresaw trouble. Likewise, reports that he stood with enslaved Africans on the Dariste plantation against government troops search-ing for participants in the rebellion suggest conscious interference with official duties. And, yet, in the end, the court cleared Bosc of all charges. Despite the fact that he explicitly confirmed elite white fears of interracial mixing and the stereotype of Martinique's *petits blancs*, perhaps the Royal Court ultimately thought it more prudent to cover up the reality that a poor white had sided with enslaved workers.[103] If word got out, especially in metropolitan France, presumably it might undermine Creole claims that impermeable racial bound-aries did still exist on the island.

As for Théodore LeChevalier, the Act of Accusation charged him, a for-mer merchant in Saint Pierre and member of a planter family, with "being an instigator of this plot and of having provoked it through suspect means." LeChevalier's previous behavior played just as important a role in the charges against him, however, as did his actions on the night in question. Accord-ing to the Act of Accusation, Saint Pierre's white "young men . . . had been irritated with him for a long time,"[104] due to his supposed role as the "chief" of the city's *gens de couleur*. LeChevalier's behavior in the days preceding the uprising—his address to a crowd of *gens de couleur* in the Saint Pierre public square—and also on February 9—his trip with his *patroné* to a ship in dock just hours before the uprising—also all seemed to confirm claims that he had allied with the island's free mixed-race inhabitants.

Bosc's *petit blanc* status could more easily explain if not excuse his actions; LeChevalier's background as a Creole from a plantocrat family, however, made his supposedly close relationships with Saint Pierre's *gens de couleur* even more worrisome for Martinique's *colons*. His family's position made it that much harder for elites to argue that only poor whites developed what they saw as inappropriate relationships with enslaved or free mixed-race Martinicans. It also made it more difficult not to grant him special consideration as a member of the island's elite. Perhaps this encouraged the Royal Court, following the sentence of a fine and twenty-three days imprisonment, to look the other way as he lingered in continental France. Just as likely, however, the rift between the island's Creole-controlled court and colonial officials provided an opening for LeChevalier to exploit. While his behavior may have rankled some elite Creoles, it may also have encouraged colonial administrators in France to help secure the pardon and indemnity he eventually obtained.

Fearing that *gens de couleur* would soon completely overthrow Martinique's racial and social hierarchy, following the Saint Pierre uprising and the subsequent trial, Martinique's elite whites fought back from their seats on the General and Private Councils, affirming their fragile, and now seemingly abandoned, position in the French Empire. In one General Council session, members insisted that the laws enacted under the new July Monarchy had made violence inevitable, if not from the *gens de couleur*, then from the enslaved population. By offering opportunities to some (*gens de couleur)* who still had such close, and seemingly inseparable, ties with others (enslaved individuals), they argued, the government had sent mixed signals that actually encouraged Martinique's enslaved community to take up arms.[105]

The potential for continued violence further distressed Creoles, the Council indicated, because despite their loyalty to metropolitan France, administrators now seemed to disregard their safety and ignore that they were also French citizens. Arguing "Martinique, always united with the mother country, followed the fortunes of France . . . and the *colons* rallied to a new order of things that promised prosperity for people and protection for property," members of the General Council asserted that this promise had not come to fruition because of Dupotet's measures. By enrolling even men from mixed-raced backgrounds in the militias, they asserted, Dupotet had given "these *proletariats*" a "military attitude" that could only "have a profound influence on the moral state of the colony, which worsens every day."[106] By helping integrate *gens de couleur* into the national family, the General Council not so subtly indicated, colonial administrators had simply created a number of agitators who, like their fellow *proletariats* on the continent, would now threaten the Orléanist regime in the colonies. By giving enslaved workers hopes for a change in the plantation system, administrators in metropolitan France had also ignored their promises to protect the property (enslaved people) of French (colonial) citizens.

In addition to taking issue with administrators in the colonies, the General Council also attacked the new minister of the marine, the Comte de Rigny, and further argued that as French citizens they too had a right to the July Monarchy's protections. When Dupotet first arrived, they asserted, the General Council had communicated to then-minister of the marine d'Argout that they understood the need for "wise modification [to the laws], gradually introduced and with circumspection." "These just and modest wishes," they continued, "these cries of distress *jétés* by French subjects in the heart of the Atlantic," had originally importuned the minister. Recent changes, however, indicated perhaps they could not trust "the rights of property would be as sacred in the colonies as . . . in the Metropole and . . . would receive just and necessary guarantees." At precisely the moment when France extended rights to the realm's *gens de couleur*, the Council asserted, they hoped she would not forget "her children," the white colonists, or the colonies "which are attached to her by so many sacred links and which are so necessary to her."[107]

Although they attacked colonial administrators on both sides of the Atlantic for recent events, the Saint Pierre uprising convinced Governor Dupotet that perhaps Creoles did know best how to manage the island and he increasingly supported their recommendations to create stability. This included removing yet another judge who the Creole-controlled Private Council believed too closely aligned with the island's *gens de couleur*. According to the Council Monsieur Duquesne of the Tribunal of First Instance frequently dined with mixed-race inhabitants to the detriment of the island. The planter Pierre Dessalles, then a member of the Council, strongly disapproved of Duquesne's behavior and told Dupotet "in a country where even though legal equality has been established in principle, the mores have not yet been modified by this principle, . . . such an act on the part of a magistrate could have disastrous results." Given the current climate, he asked Dupotet, did not such behavior "stir up exactly those passions which the wisdom of your administration tries daily to calm?"[108] Although Dupotet had instructions to facilitate precisely such exchanges between Martinique's whites and *gens de couleur*, he apparently agreed with Dessalles's assessment, for two days after the Private Council met to discuss Duquesne's case the governor dispatched the offending judge to continental France to explain his behavior to the minister of the marine.[109]

With Dupotet's help the Private Council also tried to further stymie Martinique's *gens de couleur* by thwarting their access to the island's educational institutions, now clearly assured by the February 1831 law. In particular they tried to prevent metropolitan efforts to create "racial fusion" in Martinique by opening public interracial schools for young free boys and girls in Saint Pierre and Fort Royal. Colonial administrators in metropolitan France had placed Madame Ballin, the wife of the inspector of public education in the colonies, in control of the schools of mutual instruction for girls, where older children would help to teach younger ones, and sent her to Martinique to oversee their creation.[110] Ballin encountered so much obstruction from the Private Council and Governor Dupotet, however, that within a year of her arrival on the island she returned to metropolitan France.

This fact was not lost on Martinique's *gens de couleur* or their supporters on the continent. Bissette and other Martinican *hommes de couleur* informed the minister of the marine that, despite what Governor Dupotet might claim, Ballin did not return to metropolitan France because of "family needs."[111] Rather, they asserted, she returned because she did not find "the zeal or protection for the establishments that she planned, or even obedience to the ministerial instructions . . . given to this effect." She tired of fighting, they argued, and thus hoped for the minister to act.[112] Within a month of receiving the letter from Bissette, the minister of the marine allocated money for Ballin's return passage to Martinique and also indicated Dupotet, rather than the Creole Private Council, would oversee her appointment and that of any future instructors.[113] Presumably by making Dupotet directly responsible for Ballin's financial needs, the ministry could accomplish two goals, forcing him to comply with metropolitan instructions and establishing the desired schools intended to bring about racial fusion on the island.

This strategy initially appeared successful when Martinique's director of the interior informed Ballin the island's Private Council would allocate 1,200 francs annually for her and Mademoiselle Garnerin, a white French metropolitan woman slated to provide assistance at the as yet nonexistent institution for young girls.[114] Ballin's response to the official, however, revealed Creoles' continued attempts to delay establishing the schools. Ballin refused the allocation, noting by offering both her and Garnerin 1,200 francs, Dupotet and the Private Council had misunderstood the minister's intentions; the minister, she insisted, had clearly charged her with organizing the girls' schools and appointed Garnerin to assist her. Because the Private Council had not yet located or begun construction on a school building, Ballin continued, she would wait until Dupotet moved to carry out the minister's intentions and then she would address her "proposals for its location and the material to build it."[115]

A shift in the Private Council's personnel perhaps accounts for their failure to actually establish a school. In July 1832, Pierre Dessalles served as Martinique's interim *procureur général* and as a member of the Private Council. When news reached Martinique that a July Monarchy law had banished Charles X and his family from French territory, however, Dessalles refused to countersign, not, he informed Governor Dupotet, because of disloyalty to King Louis-Philippe but rather because never before had a *procureur général* had to countersign a law for promulgation.[116] If he had complied, he continued, it would dishonor his family because they had always supported the Bourbon monarchy and still believed in the importance of "legitimacy."[117] After vainly trying to sway Dessalles, on August 4, Dupotet ordered him to appear before the Private Council and when Dessalles still refused to sign, Dupotet dismissed him as *procureur général* and from his place on the Private Council.[118] Not surprisingly, from this time forward, Dessalles saw only craven incompetence and compromise in those who held these positions.

Dessalles staunchly opposed any attempts to empower Martinique's *gens de couleur* and undoubtedly his absence from the Private Council eliminated at least one roadblock to Ballin's calls for a mutual school for free girls. After a long delay Martinique's administrators partially answered her requests in the fall of 1832 shortly after Dessalles's dismissal. Noting that the colony could not afford the approximately 17,500 francs estimated to build the school in Fort Royal, Director of the Interior Rosily suggested they go ahead with Dupotet's suggestion of holding classes in the same building as those intended for free boys. By varying the hours of instruction, Rosily concluded, the colony could economize and reach its goal of offering free mutual instruction for all free children.[119] The island's Private Council adopted the strategy, indicating the proposed facility in Fort Royal could accommodate the 150 students that metropolitan authorities hoped would attend the institution and certainly could handle the three students from the area and two from Saint Pierre who had actually enrolled to attend either establishment.[120] The Saint Pierre school of mutual instruction for free girls thus opened under the direct supervision of

Garnerin in November 1832, with a similar school to open in Fort Royal as soon as Dupotet deemed Mademoiselle Perronneau, a "Creole woman" presented as its director, adequately suited to the task.[121]

Although they had not blocked the creation of the public interracial mutual school for girls, Creoles had significantly delayed its opening and sent a clear signal to colonial administrators in metropolitan France that whenever possible they would wield whatever power they had to sustain white privilege. This included using the Private Council to support whites who actively resisted metropolitan efforts to create fusion between the island's white and mixed-race population. Duels between *petits blancs* and *gens de couleur* became increasingly common after the 1831 Saint Pierre uprising and this greatly disturbed Martinique's white plantocrats. Historically custom had reserved dueling for people of similar stations and therefore that whites now dueled with *gens de couleur* signaled to Creoles degradation in the social structure of the island and certainly of Creoles in the eyes of their metropolitan brethren. Pierre Dessalles informed his brother that because the "duels between the two classes [*gens de couleur* and whites] multiply infinitely," Creoles should expect violence from both the island's mixed-race and enslaved populations. "Our position is quite critical," he lamented, "and that of the government, by its own fault, will become increasingly critical."[122]

As the example of Baron Haugwitz demonstrates, while such duels prompted concern, they also provided elite Martinicans with yet another way to assert Creole privilege over Martinique's *gens de couleur* now that it was almost impossible to do so through the courts. Baron Haugwitz participated in many of the duels decried by Dessalles and as a result his appearance before the Private Council in April 1833 for insulting two *gens de couleur*, Messieurs Desfourneaux and D'Alboussières, gave Martinique's *colons* a chance to reenforce the island's racial hierarchy and defend Creole honor. Haugwitz, born in Saint Pierre to a poor white family, had returned to the island in early 1830 after trying (and failing) to make a living in Guadeloupe. Since that time, he had lived with his wife and child near the commercial center and during the February 1831 uprising had proved useful to authorities. According to Saint Pierre's new metropolitan police captain, Luminais, however, his "over exuberance," namely treating the individuals he arrested "with severity, as wild beasts," ultimately negated the good that could have come from his efforts. Among Creoles, however, his actions earned him a reputation for bravery and as a result, the captain noted, "an *affaire* [between whites and free mixed-race men] has not taken place where he did not appear as the witness, or the actor, or the troublemaker, or the impetus." Haugwitz was well known on the island as a *courtier marron* who made his living, in part, by participating in duels with free mixed-race men. He further supplemented his income by collecting debts others feared to handle, all in an attempt "to sustain, at whatever price, the precarious and licentious existence that he follows." In the six months before being summoned by the Private Council Haugwitz had not only insulted the *hommes de couleur* Desforneaux and D'Alboussières three times in one week, he had also participated in some way or another in at least eight different duels.[123]

Haugwitz's dealings and the Creole-controlled Private Council's response to them further attest to just how far at least some Creoles went to maintain white social privilege. Only after Luminais urged the director of the interior to investigate Haugwitz's behavior, and then Governor Dupotet threatened to deport Haugwitz for threatening public tranquility, did the council finally instruct him to prepare a document in his own defense and to appear before their next session to explain his behavior.[124] Prior to the meeting, Saint Pierre's police captain informed the Private Council that on March 19, 1833, Haugwitz had insulted D'Alboussières, an *homme de couleur* of considerable means, first when supposedly acting as a second in a proposed duel between D'Alboussières and a Creole, Durival, and then on his own account and in his own name. The following day Haugwitz, "along with a band of bad subjects," had again assaulted this same D'Alboussières with "hoots and threats," and then the next day confronted D'Alboussières and his mixed-race companion, Desfourneaux, and "pursued, injured, and threatened them in the middle of the street and in the presence of a crowd of individuals of both classes." "By these most outrageous remarks against the class of color," Luminais insisted, Haugwitz "very nearly started a riot." Although the accusations against Haugwitz did not qualify for prosecution before Martinique's Tribunal or Royal Court, the police captain concluded, the matter warranted close examination.[125]

As Luminais indicated to the director of the interior, Haugwitz's links to the island's elite Creoles made action against him, especially in places like the Royal Court, more complicated. "Despite his vices . . . he finds himself aligned with individuals who by their social position only admit among them irreproachable men," Luminais claimed and consequently Haugwitz's "party, or at least a *coterie*, entirely opposed to the government," likely would interfere with any dealings against him.[126] The Creole-controlled Private Council's response to Haugwitz's actions confirmed the police captain's fears. At the meeting, the director of the interior presented the accusations against Haugwitz and then read Haugwitz's responses. In the face of the first accusation, "being a habitual agent of discord" in the recent spate of duels between whites and *gens de couleur*, Haugwitz remained silent. He did, however, reply to the remaining four accusations and his responses illustrate not only the level of animosity between the island's whites and *gens de couleur* but also the depth of Creole concerns about white honor and privilege in the early years of the July Monarchy.

In response to the second accusation that he insulted D'Alboussières in the home of another free mixed-race man, Thomas, Haugwitz noted that Thomas admitted to inviting him into his home and had accepted Haugwitz's apology for any conflict. Haugwitz further contended, however, that D'Alboussières had provoked Haugwitz's comments when he claimed he did not "fight with riffraff," like Haugwitz or Durival, and then added that he would send for his valet "to measure swords with Durival." If Haugwitz had not responded to such assaults against his own honor and the Creole Durival's, Haugwitz continued, "where would I find my quality [as a gentleman]?"[127] Regarding the third accusation that he had publicly assaulted D'Alboussières with "hoots and threats," Haugwitz replied, "look at how fear distorts the facts. . . . Simple jokes are the hoots and threats." As for assertions that a "band of bad subjects" accompanied him, Haugwitz described them as simply men waiting outside the Assize Court. If they all laughed at the "contortions" that D'Alboussières underwent as he passed by "with his little flat hat, his arms crossed over his chest like a martyr," Haugwitz further contended, surely that did not merit the trouble he went through preparing his defense against deportation.[128]

In response to the fourth accusation that he "pursued, injured, and menaced" D'Alboussières and Desfourneaux, Haugwitz claimed he had in no way pursued the two *gens de couleur*. He further argued that even if he and Desfourneaux had exchanged words, by saying "these scoundrel whites despise *gens de couleur*, and those who have to suffer the scorn are worth one hundred times more than [the whites who deliver it]" Desfourneaux certainly presented a greater threat to public tranquility. He further expressed his surprise that he and not Desfourneaux found himself before a tribunal charged with judging offenses that fell outside of the law.[129] Regarding the most serious accusation, that Haugwitz had hurled insults at the island's mixed-race population in general, he responded that he certainly had said nothing more damaging than Desfourneaux had. Furthermore, Haugwitz retorted, no one had ever proven that he actually had said anything of a "grave and terrible character" that might warrant deportation.[130]

The Private Council found Haugwitz's actions had not compromised or troubled good order or public tranquility. They also declared that the conflicts lay between him and specific individuals and not Martinique's *gens de couleur* in general. "Due to the circumstances in which he found himself," namely his occupation as a debt collector, they further contended, Haugwitz's "discussions" with D'Aloussières and Desfourneaux constituted discussions among "people of the same class," and, as such, did not represent the "inciting of one class of the population against another," required to deport him. By defining Haugwitz, D'Aloussières and Desfourneaux as of the same "class," the elite Creoles on the Private Council used the government's rhetoric against the government itself, saving Haugwitz from deportation and reaffirming white social privilege over the island's *gens de couleur*. By specifically distancing themselves from men like Haugwitz, they also reaffirmed their social superiority over both *petits blancs* and *gens de couleur*. As the Saint Pierre police captain noted, and as the Private Council's finding against deportation indicated, although they may have felt Haugwitz's actions beneath them, the Creoles on the Private Council nonetheless wanted someone to carry them out. By calling on men like Haugwitz to do their dirty work, those same elite Creoles could save their own sense of self and of appropriate white behavior. But they also admitted a new social equivalency between Martinique's *petits blancs* and *gens de couleur* that would have far reaching consequences.

This was true in both the Caribbean and continental France where debates about slavery, the plantation system, and Martinique's place in the larger French Empire had found new energy under the July Monarchy. Another flurry of debates in the metropolitan press in late 1830 found colonists and their supporters claiming the entire plantation system would fail if *gens de couleur* gained legal equality and supporters of free-mixed race people indicating the colonial economy would fail if they did not. One planter from Guadeloupe, through a pamphlet published in Paris, decried characterizations of white planters as prejudiced "oppressors of the class of *affranchis*," and further claimed slavery had been established for the interest of the colonies, and therefore of France itself. As for the realm's *gens de couleur*, he argued they all, in some way, owed their freedom to those same masters who they now maligned.[131] Supporters of free mixed-race individuals retorted through their own press campaign. Bissette, for example, responded to the Guadeloupean planter's pamphlet in December 1830 with one of his own, and the unofficial representative for Guadeloupe's *homme de couleur*, Mondésir Richard, highlighted ongoing Creole abuses of free mixed-race individuals in yet another.[132]

In the immediate aftermath of the February 1831 uprising, Martinique's

Creoles stepped up their metropolitan press campaign to defend the colonial system, convinced that others would hold them responsible for the violence and that officials in metropolitan France would use the incident as more evidence that Creoles did not merit the full protections of French citizenship. Many, like the anonymous author of a pamphlet on the event published in Le Havre, blamed administrators on the continent for the uprising. The government, the author claimed, "turned all of their [*gens de couleur*] hopes towards liberty, and liberty for them is inseparable from fire and massacre; Saint Domingue has amply proven that."[133] Because of the *gens de couleur*'s "ties of color, bonds of family, ties of friendship,"[134] with the island's enslaved population, he concluded, enslaved workers involved in the February 1831 uprising understandably viewed the regime's overtures to the mixed-race population as personal opportunities and therefore the new regime necessarily bore responsibility for misleading the island's enslaved population. Another inhabitant of the island put it even more plainly in his letter to the pro-slavery *Journal du Havre*, noting the "carelessness" of the new governor and criticizing the "imprudent protection" that Dupotet offered to Martinique's *gens de couleur*.[135]

In their campaign to deflect responsibility from Martinican planters, some Creoles and their supporters tried again to claim any changes to the plantation system, and certainly the new regime's policies, placed white Martinican women, in particular, in danger. The details of the Saint Pierre uprising seemed to provide ample evidence for their argument. The Paris-based daily, *Le Temps*, specifically mentioned "the gloomy sound of the bells, the redoubled rings of the beating drums, the noise of the guns, the cries of the women and the infants who boarded the ships on the docks with fear."[136] Likewise, the *Gazette des Tribunaux* printed the general chronology of the event and what it called "the most important specific charges" against several of the accused, including how an enslaved man threatened to slit the throats of Dames Lesage and Delague when they refused to surrender their arms to him.[137] Another Creole wrote the *Journal du Havre* and insisted the recent gains made by the island's *gens de couleur* made them "greedy and unreasonable in their pretensions," and even compelled them to think they could "marry our daughters without obstacles, . . . sit at our tables, and . . . penetrate into our foyers, as if laws or violent conquest could give them these objects of inviolable reserve!"[138]In this Creole's view, white women, along with the inner sanctum of the home, had fallen vulnerable to free mixed-race men, if not through the laws then through violence. However the law might redefine their status, it did nothing to redefine their nature, he suggested, and therefore white women needed physical protection from both marauding enslaved men and seemingly civilized *gens de couleur.*[139]

Other Creoles and their metropolitan supporters further attempted to deflect blame for the violence by claiming metropolitan French who came to the island either fundamentally misunderstood the complexities of the plantation system, and thus the need for violence, or after their arrival became even crueler than the island's Creoles. In his *Memoirs of a Creole from Martinique*, one anonymous author argued regardless of whether the newly arrived "European" came from "the powerful" or from "the ordinary ranks of society . . . after a couple of stays in the colony, these newcomers surpass the Creoles themselves in vanity and prejudice."[140] Another metropolitan merchant from Saint Pierre told the editors of the *Journal du Havre* that before leaving metropolitan France, the "unceasing attacks" against white planters had encouraged him to view the island's *gens de couleur* more favorably than the white population. After arriving in Martinique, however, and in the wake of the 1831 uprising, he saw how the island's mixed-race population exercised free reign and even physically threatened local whites. If French metropolitan administrators failed to act to prevent such behavior, he indicated, what other choice did Creoles have? They mounted not the actions of barbarous Frenchmen, he suggested, but rather the only viable response available to a colonial French community maligned and then abandoned by its French brothers across the Atlantic.[141]

In response to Creole claims that the French Empire had abandoned its white French citizens in Martinique in the face of violence by people of African descent, some in metropolitan France again criticized colonial officials on the island for too closely aligning with Martinique's *colons* and chastised Dupotet for supposedly trying to maintain the respect that Creoles felt the "*gens de couleur* owe the whites."[142] Others directly denounced Dupotet as simply a dupe of Martinique's plantocrats, unable to effectively govern the island. The editors of the Parisian daily, *La Tribune*, contended that Dupotet "attacked outright by the General Council, booed by the Royal Court, surrounded by scheming Creoles, . . . no longer even dares to speak of his extraordinary powers. . . . [and] is incapable of administering a factious colony.[143] The editors of the *Gazette des Tribunaux* further argued that the transfer of the judge Duquesne offered "a new proof of the disastrous and too powerful influence," wielded by the colonists who "have been accustomed to see their needs met and their pretensions fulfilled."[144] The colonies, these editors argued, suffered not from metropolitan neglect but rather from continued Creole influence and exceptionalism.

The extensive metropolitan press coverage of the February 1831 uprising highlighted in a new and vivid way the complicated place the islands and their inhabitants held in the national realm. In addition to assigning blame for the event, increasingly Creoles and their supporters tried to communicate to a broader metropolitan audience concerns that Martinique's councils had relayed to the Ministry of the Marine. By emphasizing how the 1831 event influenced continental French, too, they undoubtedly hoped to exert more pressure on the government. For this reason, they specifically used rhetoric that highlighted not only the personal but also the economic links that existed between France's holdings on both sides of the Atlantic. By calling attention to the island's economic importance to Atlantic port cities and the French nation, they hoped to further integrate the colony and its inhabitants into metropolitan French conceptions of who and what constituted the French Empire. Bordeaux had deep ties to colonial trade and, because it lacked an industrial hinterland with which to trade, it felt particularly wary of disruptions in maritime trade.[145] For that reason business interests in the port could hardly have dismissed reports like one from a Saint Pierre merchant who told his commercial house "money is nowhere to be found . . . the metropole has given us nothing but hatred for our conservation . . . if they revoke [their commerce], they will bring such [economic] sluggishness that it might be beyond remedy."[146] The colony's financial troubles, the merchant explained, were Bordeaux's economic woes, too.

Other Saint Pierre merchants contacted the Le Havre Chamber of Commerce and blamed Dupotet and the new regime for the lack of commercial activity on the island.[147] Le Havre's dominance of the colonial trade by 1829 made its inhabitants concerned about Martinique's economic health as evidenced by an editorial in the *Journal du Havre* not long after news of the uprising reached continental France.[148] In this piece the editors of the pro-slavery newspaper condemned Minister of the Marine Saint-Hilaire, and the general populace of France, for not adequately concerning themselves about both the lot of the island's Creoles and France's port cities. "Speak to [the Minister of the Marine] about the *negroes* and he will listen to you," they claimed, "but speak to him about commercial interests and the future of the colonists, and it is evident that you are wasting his time!"[149] Just weeks later the members of Le Havre's Chamber of Commerce reiterated the *Journal du Havre*'s concern about the precariousness of commercial interests in the colonies and further argued Martinique had a right to assistance because it was part of France and its colonists Frenchmen. Several of France's maritime areas, they contended, depended on the health of places like Martinique and "their utility and their importance for France and its Navy can not be doubted. . . . They are an integral part of France, and, on this alone, they have a right to all of the state's interest, to all of its protection: the planters are our relatives, our friends, our brothers." On an unambiguously material note, the Chamber further urged the government to "take without hesitation all the necessary measures to guarantee the precious monies from our possessions."[150] For the chamber of commerce, the threads of trade and French blood, the colonies and the port city, intimately and intricately interwove and therefore a slight to Martinique also slighted port city commerce. In a moment of economic fragility for the nation, the abandonment of the sugar colonies could easily portend the abandonment of colonial trade more generally and potential disaster for the economies of places like Le Havre. Thus a month later the editors of the *Journal du Havre* repeated their earlier claims about the importance of the colonies and demanded an official response to the situation in Martinique. From their influential positions, Le Havre's elites urged the ministers to listen to the plight of "our poor *colons*" and "our chambers of commerce" and insisted, "this is not a question of political economy but French blood!"[151]

While the editors of the *Journal du Havre* and members of the Le Havre chamber of commerce focused on the plight of Martinique's white inhabitants, after news about the February 1831 incident reached the continent anticolonial forces also increasingly publicized their concern about the fate of enslaved and free mixed-race individuals around the French Atlantic. The case of Louizy Adzée simply fueled debate by once again touching on fundamental issues of French justice, both in the colonies and in metropolitan France, as well as French national identity. On June 18, 1831, the Court of Cassation in Paris heard the appeal of Louizy Adzée, a Martinican sentenced by the island's Court of Appeal to twenty-nine lashes of the whip, a sentence reserved solely for enslaved individuals. But like so many of those accused and executed in the February 1831 uprising, Adzée was a *patroné* who had gained de facto freedom from his master but had not yet obtained an official patent of manumission from the governor of the colony. According to Adolphe Gatine, Adzée's lawyer and a noted supporter of abolition and rights for *gens de couleur*, the "great question," before the court at his trial was simply "if the *patroné* is slave or free, because he must be one or the other."[152]

Although the Parisian Court of Cassation requested more information from the Martinican Court of Appeal and deferred immediate judgment in Adzée's case, the controversy mushroomed throughout the summer in both metropolitan France and Martinique because colonial authorities had denied the right to appeal to those sentenced to death for their role in the February uprising. As the Adzée case revealed, however, technically an 1828 criminal ordinance allowed enslaved individuals to seek appeal. Based on that fact, abolitionists argued, colonial authorities should have stayed the May executions of those *patronés* involved in the Saint Pierre uprising pending determination of the legal status of the *patroné*, and by association, other enslaved or free mixed-race individuals.[153] That they did not offered further evidence that Creoles continued to mete out their own version of justice, in the face of all efforts on the continent and in the colony to provide color-blind justice throughout the French Empire.

Such claims about continued Creole discrimination against Martinique's *gens de couleur* despite the new legal reality once again fed discussions about whether or not Martinique's Creole population was somehow less civilized, and therefore less French, than its continental counterpart. So did a November 1831 exchange between Gatine and Arsène Nogues, Martinique's *procureur général* during both the February 1831 uprising and the Adzée case.[154] In a letter to the *Journal du Havre*, Nogues argued strenuously that an enslaved individual, including the *patroné*, did not have a right to appeal. Gatine, however, described the court as still "very occupied . . . by the *patronés* or *libres de faits* . . . our co-citizens of the French Antilles." He further noted that Martinique's Royal Court continued to define the *patronés* as enslaved people, and Nogues continued to instruct the island's clerks to refuse any appeals by *patronés* or indisputably enslaved Africans, even though the Court of Cassation's preliminary decision distinguished *patronés* from enslaved individuals and despite the enslaved's right to an appeal.[155] Such blatant disregard for the standards of justice, many argued, suggested metropolitan France could no longer trust Creoles in judicial matters.

* * *

On July 12, 1832, King Louis Philippe once and for all decided the question of the *patroné* by decreeing that anyone who wanted to emancipate an enslaved person could do so without paying a manumission tax. Henceforth owners only had to declare their intention to the civil authority, which would then post the declaration on the local mayor's door and publish it three times in the paper so any objections to the manumission could be made within six months. As long as he or she had not fled an owner, a *patroné* also could apply for a permanent decree of liberty and the royal prosecutor could recommend freedom for any enslaved man who had completed eight years of service in the militia. Finally, and most directly linked to the Adzée case, the decree confirmed the right to appeal for the *patroné*.[156] Based on this decree the demographic balance of the island potentially shifted as a vast number of technically enslaved people could theoretically enter the ranks of the *gens de couleur* and take on the new rights granted them almost eighteen months before. When news of the measure reached the island later in 1832, Creoles and their supporters viewed it explicitly as an attack on private property. In fact, of course, this decree, together with the others preceding it, had gone a long way to define what it meant to be French, and in the process had technically eliminated most of the qualifications that Creoles cherished.

CHAPTER FIVE

"To Ensure Equality Before Those Laws to Free Men, Whatever Their Color": Changing Ideas of French Citizenship

THE BEGINNING OF 1833 brought even more conflict as Martinique's Creoles struggled on to defend white dominance, *gens de couleur* clamored ever more loudly for equal inclusion in the life of the colony, and enslaved workers continued their attempts to mitigate the brutality of the plantation system. An April 24, 1833, law that significantly restructured colonial and administrative practices, abolished "all restrictions or exclusions pronounced against the civil or political rights of the *hommes de couleur libres*," and moved even further toward eventual emancipation indicated soon the island's social and racial makeup would never be the same.[1] As word of the law made its way around Martinique in July 1833, the split between Martinique's plantocrats and colonial administrators solidified.[2] By creating a new colonial constitution, a Colonial Council (which replaced the General Council) to vote on local matters and allocate funds, and council-appointed Colonial Delegates to serve as representatives in France, the legislation again dramatically reorganized Martinique's administrative structure. By officially granting free mixed-race individuals full equality in civil and political affairs and making them equal to whites before French law, it also threatened to forever change the balance of power on the island.

This last measure theoretically meant Martinique's *gens de couleur*, roughly 20,000 people, now could vote and hold office. In practice, however, such participation lay well beyond the reach of most mixed-race Martinicans because eligibility for the new elective Colonial Council required one to pay taxes of 600 francs (roughly equal to owning 30,000 francs in property).³ As Bissette noted from his home in Paris, the tax restricted access to the island's wealthiest inhabitants and effectively blocked "the mass of workers—black, *mulâtre*, or even white—who form the majority of the population."⁴ None-theless Martinique's elite planters saw even the theoretical inclusion of *gens de couleur* in the political process as a betrayal and further resented that the metropolitan government, through the governor, continued to propose the budget, control legislative matters, and rule by ordinance on slavery, trade, education, and the press.

To thwart the metropolitan government's efforts to create equality for the realm's *gens de couleur* in practice, Creoles now looked primarily to social and cultural means to sustain white dominance. Maintaining racially segregated educational institutions stood, as ever, high on their list, but it became increasingly difficult in the shadow of both the April 1833 law and the Guizot law that required each commune in France (and thus in Martinique) to provide secular primary school education. While the institutions still required tuition, technically communes could waive it for poor families. The statute also distinguished explicitly between public and private education. Theoretically, anyone over the age of eighteen could petition the communal mayor to found a private school; the mayor and a surveillance committee then determined the individual's intellectual and moral fitness to run such a school. What exactly constituted a "poor family," and what counted as ability to teach, however, were complicated issues. In the case of ability, at least, Martinique's Creole Private Council apparently made the ultimate decision and, not surprisingly, gave preference to whites working to educate whites.

In the wake of the two laws whites-only institutions like the Sisters of Saint Joseph's Saint Pierre Royal School for Girls gained in popularity, despite ongoing concerns they might be forced to integrate. This institution continued to accept only Creole girls and that made it particularly attractive to those *colons* interested in maintaining de facto racial segregation in their daughters' educational environments. To expand the opportunities available for the island's white girls, in summer 1833 the Sisters of Saint Joseph announced they would create a new day school in Saint Pierre to prepare Creole girls for entrance into the Saint Pierre boarding school, which then taught 46 students.⁵ The school's launch could not have come at a worse time, however, for the announcement heralding the opening of the establishment coincided with publication of the April 1833 decree.⁶ Such news, the Sisters of Saint Joseph's headmistress argued, again made many Creoles reticent to enroll their daughters in either the day school or the boarding school for fear the nuns would have to accept free mixed-race girls at the establishments. But as of that moment the government had not yet informed the Order of any changes and headmistress Sister Marie-Thérèse Javouhey hoped that would continue to be the case. If not, she informed a member of her Order, "it would mean the end of the *pensionnat* in local [white] opinion."[7] Creoles wanted racial exclusivity at the Saint Pierre Royal School for Girls and would tolerate nothing else.

Abbé Pierre Paul Castelli's trip to Martinique shortly after the Sisters of Saint Joseph's announcement further convinced many Creoles the metropolitan government had abandoned them. To colonial officials on the continent, however, the planned opening of institutions like the Sisters of Saint Joseph's day school indicated the integration mandated by law had not occurred and consequently they instructed Castelli, Martinique's apostolic prefect, to tour the island's existing schools and suggest the best method to attain the metropole's goal of racial fusion.[8] Like others before him, Castelli believed education the key to this goal and found that, as currently arranged, Martinique's educational institutions actually prevented such fusion. For one thing, Saint Pierre and Fort Royal had too many schools relative to their populations, while the rest of the island suffered from a dearth of them. Furthermore, by 1833 nearly half of those requesting permission to open private primary schools looked to establish their institutions in either city where they could take advantage of the larger (in relation to the countryside) populations of both *gens de couleur* and *petits blancs*. Abandoning rural areas left the island's poorest whites and *gens de couleur* with few, and presumably, substandard educational choices, Castelli contended, thus consigning them to an ignorance that could only breed continued racial prejudice.[9]

Such racial prejudice increasingly played itself out in duels between Creoles and mixed-race people. While such contests of honor had concerned local officials since at least 1830, in an effort to quell the violence and create de facto boundaries that ceased to exist in law, local authorities now actively pursued *gens de couleur* they believed responsible for the fights. As a result they arrested a mixed-race man, Césaire, in late summer 1833 and charged him with ambushing members of the local white militia on their way to protect a white colonist, Lassèrre, who had refused to duel with another *homme de couleur*. At his trial in the early fall Césaire, represented by a recently arrived metropolitan lawyer, implicated two other mixed-race men in the ambush against the white militia, Rosemond and Louis Adolphe, both of whom vanished into the Martinican countryside near Grand'Anse after giving testimony against Césaire.[10]

After their flight the courts sentenced Césaire to death for having plotted to assassinate Lassèrre.[11]

While Césaire remained in prison, Creoles worked harder than ever to block the island's *gens de couleur* from exercising their newfound political right to vote and to hold office. They chose a faulty census as one mechanism and once again Governor Dupotet apparently collaborated. Rumors swirled among the island's inhabitants that Dupotet, swayed by Creoles, had certified the census even though it mysteriously identified only 305 eligible electors for the Colonial Council, 280 Creoles and only 25 *gens de couleur*.[12] In December 1833, authorities also began a series of house-to-house searches of free mixed-race individuals, purportedly as part of their larger investigation into the increased duels between *gens de couleur* and whites. Their endeavors took them to the lodgings of Rosemond, the now missing *homme de couleur* accused of ambushing the white militia in August, and during their search of his home officials reportedly found evidence also implicating Léonce, another free mixed-race Martinican, in the botched assassination of the Creole Lassère. On the night of December 24, 1833, local magistrates and *gendarmes* therefore went to Léonce's Saint Pierre abode, arrested him, and attempted to take him to prison. A crowd of *gens de couleur* soon confronted the magistrates, however, and tried to stop Léonce's transport. Only after the local justice of the peace arrived with a number of soldiers and restored order did the group of mixed-race inhabitants allow authorities to escort Léonce to Saint Pierre's jail.[13]

While these events played themselves out in Martinique's commercial center, Rosemond and Louis Adolphe purportedly led a band of between 150 and 200 armed *gens de couleur* whom they had convinced to join their ranks and to force authorities to grant them their rights as French citizens. The group traveled around the outskirts of Grand'Anse, calling on enslaved workers in the area to revolt and supposedly chanting, "massacre all whites." Fearing for their physical safety, Creoles in the region abandoned their property and late on Christmas Eve united at the Bonafon plantation strategically located at a high point overlooking the town. The local police captain, the Creole Desabaye, then issued a call for all proprietors in the area, regardless of racial background, to come to arms in defense of the commune.[14]

Over the course of the next three days, Rosemond, Louis Adolphe, and their followers succeeded in pillaging and damaging a number of plantations and burning those belonging to wealthy Creole planters known for upholding white superiority: Lasèrre (the white who escaped assassination in August), Duval, Dugué (who had conspired against the British), Assier, and Lessade. Although the band of *gens de couleur* had hoped for help from enslaved individuals on those properties, the workers on each plantation reportedly struggled to save whatever possessions they could from destruction and, consequently, the revolt lost momentum. When Captain Montigny, the head of the garrison in Saint Pierre, and 25 soldiers arrived on the scene on December 27, he called for the approximately 300 *gens de couleur* to disarm and when they did not he readied his men to fire. At that point many in the crowd fled, leaving only 83 who surrendered to authorities on condition that the government: (1) annul Césaire's death sentence; (2) free Léonce; (3) clear Rosemond and Louis Adolphe of all charges as Césaire's accomplices; (4) provide free passage for all *gens de couleur* on the enclosed property of white landholders, and; (5) offer complete amnesty for the insurrection.[15] In response to rumors that members of the *gens de couleur* militia (technically members of France's national guard) appeared in uniform among the rebellious crowd, Governor Dupotet temporarily suspended all of the island's militias to prevent further trouble.[16]

During the early months of 1834, authorities implicated 173 people—135 *gens de couleur* and 38 enslaved Martinicans—in the Grand'Anse Affair.[17] In metropolitan France, the minister of the marine responded to news of the uprising by first annulling the island's recent electoral lists and then delaying elections for the Colonial Council until February 1834 pending an accurate accounting.[18] While Dupotet's involvement remained uncertain, the suggestion that he had helped block Martinique's *gens de couleur* from voting for or acting as electors simply reinforced those in metropolitan France who claimed that the island's elite whites had too closely aligned for measures like the April 24, 1833, law to take effect. To rectify the situation, the minister of the marine thus replaced Governor Dupotet based on his close links to the island's Creoles. In his place the ministry named Vice Admiral Emmanuel Halgan, a military hero and eleven-year representative to the Chamber of Deputies, and he held the island's ultimate authority when 117 enslaved and free mixed-race Martinicans accused of a variety of offenses came before the island's Assize Court in June.[19] Over the next four weeks, the accused appeared daily for six hours before the court's president, de Périnelle (one of the Creole victims in the 1831 Saint Pierre uprising), two councilors, Messieurs Richard de Lucy (the former *procureur général*) and Lepelletier Duclary, and four *assesseurs* chosen by lot from the eligible pool of wealthy white plantocrats.[20]

These seven men, all members of the Creole plantocracy, asked questions of the accused, listened to the witnesses who testified for and against them, and sifted through the *procureur général*'s case. Nogues, the metropolitan-born lawyer who had presided over the trial for the Saint Pierre uprising and the

Adzée case that held metropolitan attention, once again acted on the government's behalf. His ties to other colonial officials (like his uncle, Governor Halgan) and rumors that he was "working with all of his power to win the hand of a young Creole, the daughter of a rich white colonist," during the course of the proceedings cast doubt on his loyalties to the judicial process, however, and led many to question his strong personal links to Martinique's white planters.[21]

As accounts of the violence of *gens de couleur* in December 1833 unfurled in the courtroom, the social situation elsewhere in Martinique also became increasingly chaotic. The new round of upheaval further exposed divisions between the island's Creoles and colonial administrators as well as the increased friction between the island's *gens de couleur* and white population in the aftermath of the Grand'Anse affair. Nogues's clearly compromised position highlighted Creole fears that Halgan had not committed himself to the island's *colons* and also the *gens de couleur* beliefs that the only way to gain justice was to claim it through force. The Creole planter LeClerc, who also served as police captain in François, noted that during the course of the trial several whites in his area had complained of harassment by free mixed-race individuals and further criticized Governor Halgan's unwillingness to take steps to prevent such behavior. According to his Creole constituents, a number of *hommes de couleur* had taken advantage of a new law that required two witnesses to alleged harassment for police to intervene and had confronted whites who were alone or with only one other person. The "silence of the authorities," namely Governor Halgan, the police captain continued, had strengthened these *gens de couleur* "troublemakers," to the point that "the whites, believing themselves without defense of their property, find themselves in the direst necessity not to bring about violence through self-defense." If "Justice" through colonial administrators did not curb such abuses, the police captain concluded, "it will necessarily result in grave troubles and maybe even collisions between whites and *gens de couleur*."[22] This time, the police captain suggested, Martinique's whites would initiate violence, and perhaps legitimately so.

News of the Grand'Anse affair, like that of the February 1831 uprising, quickly reached metropolitan France. The ongoing coverage of both the event and the trial, and the printing of editorials and the transcripts of the proceedings in metropolitan dailies like the *Gazette des Tribunaux*, provided ample opportunities for Creoles and their supporters, on the one hand, and *gens de couleur*, their supporters, and abolitionists, on the other, to once again debate the status of the colonies and its inhabitants vis-à-vis metropolitan France. After 1831 those discussions primarily had focused on whether those involved in the uprising were enslaved or free and how best to curtail any future violence. The spate of legislation between 1831 and 1833 that legally increased the number of *gens de couleur* in France and further made them full citizens, however, changed the nature of the debate. After 1833 the conversation shifted to whether the free individuals involved in the Grand'Anse affair had engaged in justifiable violence considering that Creoles had continually denied them their rights as French citizens. Not surprisingly Creoles and their continental supporters vehemently denied any responsibility for the Grand'Anse affair and described it as a violent event that exposed only too clearly the island's *gens de couleur* were unworthy of the freedoms already allotted them. They further warned metropolitan French that such violence did not contain itself to the colonies but rather had dire consequences for French on both sides of the Atlantic.

That hundreds of *gens de couleur* had taken matters into their own hands and retaliated against white oppression complicated their supporters' calls for equitable treatment for France's new citizens. Anticolonial advocates nonetheless defended the actions of those implicated in the Grand'Anse affair. The editors of *Le Constitutionnel*, for example, claimed, "the *hommes de couleur* were wrong in this case . . . [but] In the name of what morality will you tell them they are not right?" They also explicitly downplayed the violence of the event, noting, for example, that only one soldier perished in the uprising. Regrettable, they continued, but the blood that did *not* flow in the streets during the uprising, no doubt would drip "from the scaffolds" as Creoles took their revenge. Only ensuring Martinique's *gens de couleur* had access to the rights due them could prevent further bloodletting, they concluded, "because the scaffolds alone have never stopped a rebellion, only the rebels!"[23] By comparing the *gens de couleur* cause and those involved in the Grand'Anse affair with other French citizens who had fought against injustices in the Revolutions of 1789 and 1830 supporters of Martinique's mixed-race inhabitants hoped to further integrate the participants in the 1833 uprising into the pantheon of French citizens who had brought about monumental transformations in French society.

Other *gens de couleur* supporters downplayed the violence and disputed the details of the rebellion. In a letter to the editors of the *Gazette des Tribunaux*, the Martinican *mulâtre* Fabien argued Saint Pierre's mixed-race men did not arm themselves to burn and pillage plantations but rather took up weapons only after "the privileged" (whites) armed themselves and barricaded the Bonafon plantation. Fault for the rebellion, which he described as an effort to "repel by force the odious tyranny against which the *hommes de couleur* are fighting," therefore fell squarely on the shoulders of Martinique's Creoles he claimed.[24] Bissette also argued the *gens de couleur* of Grand'Anse did not burn the mentioned plantations nor did they set fire to the local police house, as widely rumored, rather they "spontaneously" took up arms at the same time as Creoles to engage in a "great duel."[25] With regard to claims that Léonce had joined Césaire in the failed assassination of the Creole Lassère, Bissette further noted the plantocratic "aristocrats of Martinique" had looked for any pretext to detain Léonce from the moment he had insisted that the tribunal's clerk of courts go to the prison to receive Césaire's request for an appeal.[26] By framing the Grand'Anse affair as a duel between whites and free mixed-race individuals, Bissette also placed *gens de couleur* and whites on equal footing and implied they had the same rights to defend their French honor as other male French citizens.

The language used to decry the ongoing injustices against the island's mixed-race inhabitants further revealed the complicated ways that race now factored into discussions about French national identity. Because race technically no longer served as a consideration among legally free people, those in metropolitan France who supported Martinique's *gens de couleur*, like the editors of *Le Constitutionnel*, took Governor Dupotet to task for referring to the island's "white population" in the text of one of his last proclamations. Such a reference, the editors argued, "is impossible not to deplore," and "appears imprinted with the fatal spirit which tends to perpetuate divisions and prejudices between two classes of inhabitants living on the same soil, and which the law has nonetheless placed in equal conditions."[27] They further noted while the new continental regime worked to "erase distinctions between the castes," by using the phrase "white population," Dupotet actually revived racial distinctions and ignored that Martinique had only "citizens or slaves."[28] Racial markers no longer mattered, the editors claimed, only the distinction between legal freedom and enslavement.

Other supporters explicitly reminded French around the Atlantic that thousands of *gens de couleur* in Martinique alone had joined the ranks of full French citizens and they had a right to all that entailed, despite the structure in place in the French West Indies. As the editors of *Le Constitutionnel* noted, "there will be even more prejudices to vanquish. . . . [to ensure] equality before those laws to free men, whatever their color."[29] A letter from a Martinican *homme de couleur* reprinted in the *Journal de Paris*, made the case even more plainly for mixed-race inhabitants' rights as fellow French citizens: "Now, having again become French after . . . not having the pleasure, we are so proud of this glorious title, which reunites us all in one great family."[30] Finally regaining the rights they had gained, and then lost, during the 1789

French Revolution, this mixed-race citizen argued, meant a long-awaited return to the French fold.

* * *

On June 30, 1834, Martinique's Assize Court reached a verdict in the Grand'Anse affair and acquitted 26 individuals, condemned 46 to death (26 *par contumace*), sentenced 10 to forced labor, and deported 25 to Senegal.[31] All those receiving punishment immediately appealed to the Parisian Court of Cassation. In anticipation of criticism Creoles and their supporters in the metropole thus renewed their campaign to highlight *gens de couleur* and enslaved violence and thus justify the trial's outcome. The *Gazette des Tribunaux* again chose to include excerpts from the trial that highlighted white Martinican women's fragile position. Unlike in 1831, however, the Grand'Anse proceedings illustrate that the island's mixed-race population knew of this Creole strategy and specifically worked to undermine the stereotype painting them as sexually violent individuals. This changed the nature of the debate about their role in the French national family and the island's relationship with metropolitan France.

Throughout the trial *procureur général* Nogues posited white female vulnerability in the face of black male hypersexuality. He recounted, for example, how the uprising played out at the plantation of Dame Elie Duval who had stayed alone on her land near Grand'Anse. During the course of events, several of those involved in the affair stole two guns, a sword, and, tellingly enough, seven pairs of shoes from her property. According to the editors of the *Gazette des Tribunaux*, despite the danger, this woman, "dominated by her firmness of character . . . opened the door and presented herself . . . without fear."[32] When Duval opened the door to her potential attackers, however, they reportedly told her that they "liked the brave and that they wanted nothing with women or children, only with men."[33]

Demoiselle Augustine Voisin also faced threats from the Grand'Anse insurgents. She initially had provided her brother, Julien d'Harcourt, refuge from the crowd, but shortly after his arrival at her home, a band of *gens de couleur* approached and d'Harcourt fled. When the group arrived, their leader reportedly "put his gun in the stomach of Demoiselle Augustine Voisin, announcing his intention to kill her" because d'Harcourt had evaded capture. One of his cohort stopped him, however, saying that they "had no business with women." In response, the leader apparently let Voisin go, but one in the band "took out his rage" by slashing Voisin's feather bed.[34]

The *Gazette des Tribunaux*'s coverage of events at the Dessalles de Boismarcel plantations near Grand'Anse also mentioned white women in harm's way during the Grand'Anse affair and suggests that rebellion hit the Pierre Dessalles family literally at home. Not only did the three plantations belong to Dessalles's uncle, one of Dessalles de Boismarcel's former enslaved domestics, Jean-Baptiste Agricole, had also served as a leader of the uprising.[35] In 1826, this same enslaved worker had accompanied Pierre Dessalles on a trip to metropolitan France and while there had spent extended time with Dessalles, his wife, his sons, and his daughters.[36] When Dessalles and his oldest son Adrien returned to Martinique the following year, Agricole had accompanied the two men and from that moment on Pierre Dessalles had worried the enslaved domestic might cause trouble. "Agricole is behaving badly," he noted in a letter to his mother, and further indicated he refused to see the enslaved man because "he speaks a lot about how people of color are treated in France."[37]

Despite all of this, immediately after the Grand'Anse affair Dessalles nonetheless assured his mother no harm had come to the family that night and further claimed his uncle conducted himself "in the most courageous manner. He did not leave his plantation and these villains did not dare to do him the slightest harm."[38] In its coverage of the trial, however, the *Gazette des Tribunaux* reported that during the Grand'Anse uprising a band of mixed-race men not only had stolen arms from one of the Dessalles de Boismarcel plantations and forced open the doors, "threatening to strike any who did not save themselves from their approach," one of the party (perhaps Agricole) had also threatened "a young Demoiselle Dessalles" with his rifle and followed her when she fled. Thankfully, the *Gazette* noted, a "*nègresse* saved her life" by throwing herself on top of Dessalles and reproaching the armed man who ultimately retreated, leaving the Dessalles woman shaken but physically unharmed.[39]

Because the Dessalles de Boismarcel of Grand'Anse did not have any children, the "young Demoiselle Dessalles" attacked was most probably one of Pierre Dessalles's own daughters and perhaps might have met the "armed man," at her family's home in metropolitan France. If that was the case, it would provide some reason as to why, in his public life, Dessalles consistently fought to block *gens de couleur* from any advancements and why, in his journal entries that begin again in 1837, Dessalles repeatedly worried about the safety of the island's Creole women.

In the end, none of the three white women highlighted in the proceedings suffered physical harm in their exchanges with *gens de couleur* during the Grand'Anse affair. Nonetheless the *Gazette des Tribunaux*'s inclusion of their experiences underscored the potential for, and Creole fears that, *gens de couleur* might subject white women to physical, *sexualized*, danger in moments of crisis. Nogues, and his metropolitan supporters who encouraged the printing of the proceedings, undoubtedly intended the stories of all three women to exemplify precisely this as well as white women's courage in the face of such danger. Ultimately, however, they revealed that *gens de couleur* well understood elite Creole stereotypes and knew that, if they hurt white women, Creoles would use those incidents as grounds for yet more repressive measures. Perhaps some *gens de couleur* used such fears to their own ends, demonstrating the potential to use such physical force but also the control, at least among leaders, not to.

Certainly the symbolic rape of Voisin's person—through the violent destruction of her bed—and the pursuit of Demoiselle Dessalles served as reminders that both women could have suffered harm if the band had not exercised restraint or a loyal *négresse* had not come to the aid of her mistress. Likewise, whether or not those who confronted the Creole women in question actually said at the time that they "wanted nothing with women or children," or "had no business with women," or whether they simply employed this strategy only at the trial matters less than the fact that accused *gens de couleur* turned the gender and racial ideals crafted by elites on their head.

To tap into fears that continental French had about a political rebellion in their midst, Creoles also tried to explicitly link the events on the island with violence that had recently threatened metropolitan France and indicate if *gens de couleur* were now French citizens, they were the wrong kind. During the trial Nogues likened the *gens de couleur* involved in the Grand'Anse affair to those involved in the 1830 Revolution on the continent and especially to recent troubles in Lyon, arguing "the proletariats imagine themselves to have gained everything in a reversal of the social order," and rather than "acquiring fortune (the object of their desire) by assiduous work" they found "it is easier to seize [liberty, equality, and fortune] by pillage and the assassination of those who possess them."[40] Nogues's further suggestion that Martinique's *gens de couleur* in Grand'Anse had worked "to abandon this important part of France overseas to the horrors of civil war" by participating in "an armed insurrection, prepared ahead of time and executed with an inconceivable *mélange* of cowardice and audacity" also incorporated Martinican territory into the French realm and reminded all that the island's white inhabitants belonged to the French citizenry, too.[41] By aligning the island's "new citizens" with "new citizens" in places like Paris and Lyon who caused unrest, Nogues no doubt hoped to gain support for the colonial cause.

While Creoles clamored loudly for sympathy, after the trial *gens de couleur* and their supporters made even bolder claims for their rights as law-abiding, rather than unruly, French citizens. In his newly established metropolitan newspaper, the *Revue des Colonies*, Bissette, like his Creole counterparts more than twenty years earlier, used familial language to integrate free mixed-race people into the French family, calling them "without restriction, part of the great French family. They are French citizens, or apt to become them," and further contended "France wanted all free men born in her bosom or in her colonies to be citizens . . . There are no longer *hommes de couleur*, for us, among the free, there are only Frenchmen."[42] In his treatise decrying the Grand'Anse ruling, Fabien also included *gens de couleur* in the French family, noting: "Grateful towards the metropole, towards this France which is also [its] *patrie*, [this class] would do nothing to trouble the peace that it is interested in maintaining."[43] The lawyer Gatine adopted the Creoles' own strategy of collapsing the distance between Martinique and the metropole when it suited their needs and blamed both Creoles and their supporters on the continent for what had happened in the French West Indies in December 1833. That *gens de couleur* stood " accused of exciting civil war" and cowardice simply invited chaos, he warned, and further chastised Nogues to consider "with what bitterness your reproaches of cowardice could here turn against you."[44]

Debates about the status of the colonies and its inhabitants vis-à-vis metropolitan France became even more charged after full emancipation finally went into effect in the British colonies after a six-month transitional period in early August 1834. For the next several weeks, both defenders and opponents of slavery awaited the outcome of the transition.[45] When it came without a violent uprising, French metropolitan debates about the possibility of emancipation resumed in earnest. The Société française pour l'abolition de l'esclavage (the French Society for the Abolition of Slavery) was formed in August 1834 under the direction of distinguished members of the Chamber of Deputies. Though never a mass movement, and never able to articulate a common approach to the question of slavery, many of the society's members held influential roles in the chambers and kept the society involved in state decision making throughout the July Monarchy.[46]

The appeals of Césaire, whose arrest had arguably immediately contributed to the Grand'Anse affair, and of those accused in the uprising also fueled metropolitan interest in the ongoing plight of Martinique's free mixed-race citizens. The Parisian Court of Cassation ultimately overturned Césaire's death sentence because, as the *Gazette des Tribunaux* noted in its coverage of the trial, the second session of Martinique's Assize Court had been illegally closed to the public.[47] The appeal for the Grand'Anse affair, on the other hand, erupted in what the *Gazette des Tribunaux* called the "improvisation" of Crémieux, one of the lawyers for the accused.[48] He took the floor during the final arguments of the appeal, the daily noted, not to offer new evidence but rather "to fulfill a duty of conscience and humanity."[49] Speaking of the original trial in Martinique, he noted "what justice is that of the colonies!.. But, good God! No mercy, no pity!"[50] Although he called on the court to show precisely those qualities, ultimately they refused to overturn the verdicts and the appeal failed.[51]

All was not lost for those condemned in the uprising, however. At the end of December 1834, King Louis Philippe commuted their sentences: those condemned to death would now serve either fifteen or twenty years of forced labor; those sentenced to a life of hard labor now faced ten years; those facing five years of labor now had to pay with five years in prison.[52] For Creoles this came as the final straw, dashing any hope of mending the rift between Martinique's white plantocracy and colonial administrators on both sides of the Atlantic. It also convinced them to shift their attentions away from preventing the realm's *gens de couleur* from exercising their rights and toward supporting the metropolitan proslavery lobby in emancipation debates. The proslavery lobby presented a remarkably well-coordinated effort to maintain the plantation economy, theoretically accepting emancipation while also trying to delay it through traditional (though by now less persuasive) arguments about the economic importance of the colonies.[53]

In an effort to portray emancipation as unwise, proslavery advocates undertook a multipronged approach. Letters to the editors, articles, and editorials emphasized three things: that legally enslaved workers constituted private property; that these enslaved workers needed civilizing before emancipation to avoid a replay of Saint-Domingue in Martinique and continental France, and; that continental France shared responsibility for the violence of the plantation system. In response to ongoing emancipation debates in the Chambers, the proslavery *Journal de Paris* argued, "the planters also have rights," and further warned, "when one recalls the terrible proof of Saint Domingue," one should act with prudence.[54] The journal also chastised antislavery forces in metropolitan France, and especially lawyers, for making what they saw as inflammatory remarks. It encouraged them to consider how their comments "might have as a result the massacre and ruin of the whites," as evidenced in "the bloody emancipation of Saint Domingue."[55] In a Chamber of Deputies session, Colonial Delegate Maugain also chided French in the metropole for their complicity in the plantation system and underscored the colonists' rights as French citizens under the July Monarchy: " if slavery is a crime, then the crime is yours [metropolitans] as well as theirs [colonists]. . . . The colonists . . . have only inherited the crimes . . . transmitted to them. . . . The colonists are French like you . . . they have a right to claim from her protection and security."[56] If colonists were wrong, Maugain chastised the Chamber's members and the metropolitan reading public, then so were all French citizens.

* * *

Two metropolitan measures in the spring of 1836, one that pushed ever closer to emancipation and another that further solidified the continental regime's commitment to free mixed-race inhabitants, provided yet another opportunity to reconsider who merited French citizenship and which rights went along with that status. Both measures had profound importance for the colonial system, in general, and certainly for Martinicans, shifting the demographic and social balance in ways never before seen. On April 26, 1836, the Chambers authorized the liberation of all enslaved individuals before their embarkation for France and freed any enslaved person who then found himself or herself on continental French territory.[57] Not surprisingly Creoles and their supporters in metropolitan France swiftly responded with outrage at what they viewed as a dangerous move toward emancipating the realm's enslaved inhabitants. To further their claims that general emancipation could only bring violence to the colonies, and thus unacceptably endanger France's colonial citizens, Creoles once again worked to highlight the threats white women, in particular, supposedly faced. This time, however, they focused the majority of their energies on the violence of enslaved, rather than free mixed-race, people. Cases like one where a male enslaved worker stood accused of killing his white mistress, widow Thoret, and her female servant provided just such an opportunity. In addition to serving as a warning to metropolitan French, however, the case also sent a message to any white women who considered embarking on the kinds of adventures that elite Creoles implied eventually brought about the widow's murder.

Thoret, a white woman born and raised in metropolitan France, had come to Martinique during the Restoration and "with the force of her work and industry," local authorities claimed, she had succeeded in earning "an independent existence." With only five enslaved laborers, she had established a small sugar processing station that thrived due to her "extraordinary activity." In her efforts to succeed, however, she demanded a great deal of her few workers and often "scolded and beat" them although, according to Fort Royal's royal prosecutor, Thoret had not been cruel.[58] Nonetheless her previous history of punishment, and threats of future punishments, apparently contributed to her undoing in late 1836.

The week before Christmas Thoret went to Fort Royal and left one of her enslaved workers, Laurent, in charge. Despite instructions to the contrary, during her absence, Laurent invited the *commandeur* (head enslaved worker) from a nearby plantation to dinner and when he arrived, accompanied by three other enslaved workers, Laurent decided to entertain them in his mistress's dining hall. Fearing his owner's reaction, however, Laurent swore the rest of Thoret's enslaved workers to secrecy. On the widow's return shortly after Christmas, Brigitte, a domestic servant and the widow's confidante, nevertheless told her mistress all that had transpired during her absence, supposedly out of fear from another beating from the widow if the secret emerged. Thoret, in anger, then informed Laurent and his accomplices Marie, Clothilde, and Edouard, that they must accompany her to the nearby plantation so they all could receive an appropriate punishment for their transgression. Marie, Clothilde, and Edouard obeyed but Laurent did not.[59]

From that moment on, the royal prosecutor noted, Laurent developed "sinister plans," and in two days he went through a transformation that turned him from being "inoffensive" into a "ferocious tiger, altered by blood and vengeance." On December 29, as Thoret returned from the nearby plantation, she encountered Laurent in the street and asked him if he had finished the work she had assigned him. According to his own testimony, upon meeting her Laurent moved toward Thoret with a large knife used for cutting cane and even though she commanded him to stop and put down his knife, he continued in her direction. At that point, Thoret threw down her parasol and picked up a nearby hoe, shouting, "If you advance, I will beat your skull!" Stunned by her bravery, the royal prosecutor claimed, Laurent then ran away.[60]

Two days later, however, knife in hand, he returned to the plantation at noon when he knew the other enslaved workers would be laboring in their gardens. Thoret was alone in the house with Laurent's six-year-old daughter who, upon seeing her father, called out, "There is papa." In response, Thoret reportedly came out of the house and asked Laurent, "Where have you been since you took your liberty?" At that point, Laurent closed on Thoret without speaking a word and struck her several times. She ran back into the house but Laurent followed her and there inflicted a "deep wound with large amounts of blood." According to the royal prosecutor, however, Thoret did not die there. Apparently she still had enough strength to drag herself out to the road, but Laurent once again pursued her, ultimately killing Thoret in a nearby manioc field. "There he wreaked his hatred and vengeance," the royal prosecutor claimed, leaving Thoret's body "riddled with wounds," and her head, "almost separated from her body . . . attached only by a small strand!"[61]

In addition to killing Thoret, Laurent also murdered her enslaved confidante. After leaving Thoret in the manioc field, Laurent returned to the plantation where he found Brigitte who, alerted by the cries of Laurent's daughter, had come from the garden and saw him following her mistress down the road. Upon seeing Laurent return, Brigitte ran to her own small cabin, gathered her one-month-old child in her arms and prepared to flee. "Drunk with blood and with his own fury," however, Laurent saw, pursued, and killed Brigitte. Like her mistress, she was found with her head nearly separated from her body. The infant apparently survived, for when authorities captured Laurent four days later, they charged him with only two murders, both of which he confessed to during his interview with the royal prosecutor.[62]

The violence of the crime deeply concerned the island's *colons*, especially because it appeared to confirm Creole fears about the kinds of dangers Martinique's white women might face in the aftermath of a general emancipation. As the royal prosecutor's remarks implied at Laurent's trial, however, the metropolitan-born Thoret differed from other white women on the island. She supervised her enslaved workers without any assistance, the royal prosecutor noted, and worked alongside them on a daily basis. She also personally disciplined them, both verbally and physically, and fear of this discipline supposedly encouraged Brigitte to tell of Laurent's actions and also drove Laurent to his "sinister plans." All of Thoret's actions, the royal prosecutor suggested, placed her well beyond the boundaries of appropriate behavior for the island's Creole women and the royal prosecutor's specific inclusion of her background as someone not native to the island undoubtedly meant to communicate her ignorance about the brutal dangers of the plantation system and its enslaved workers. Thoret's horrific and regrettable death, the royal prosecutor implied, perhaps might not have happened had she followed prescribed behavior and listened to the Creoles who had tried to warn her of her follies.

In addition to highlighting the dangers enslaved people like Laurent presented to the colonial community, Martinique's Creoles also tried to prevent the island's free mixed-race citizens from taking advantage of their rights as French citizens. Between 1831 and 1835, Martinique's white population declined from 9,362 to 9,000; due to recent legislation facilitating manumission, however, the *gens de couleur* population more than doubled from 14,055 to 29,955, and the enslaved population decreased from 86,499 to 78,076.[63] Although nearly 30,000 free mixed-race Martinicans now technically enjoyed full civil and political rights, approximately 20,000 of them had earned their freedom in the last ten years.[64] In practice this meant for the vast majority of the island's *gens de couleur* a lifetime of enslavement and no access to education left them without the common markers of civil identity. To help ease this transition from enslavement to freedom, a royal ordinance authorized free mixed-race inhabitants to adopt last names, deeming those held by whites off limits unless Creoles granted permission for their use.[65] Last names would allow all *gens de couleur* equality in official records, an important social consideration for those free mixed-race individuals who increasingly wielded economic power on the island and especially in Saint Pierre and Fort Royal. As records indicate, in 1838 *gens de couleur* owned approximately 11 percent of Martinique's land and nearly one-third of all urban property and these owners, in particular, wanted their social identifiers to match their economic clout.[66]

Although some mixed-race Martinicans had obviously found an economic niche, most of the nearly 20,000 mixed-race Martinicans who had recently gained their freedom had limited opportunities to make a living. As a result a great number turned to the island's charity bureaus for economic assistance, but those institutions found themselves woefully ill-equipped to help all of those in need and thus turned to the Colonial Council who determined their yearly allotment. The Creole-controlled Colonial Council, however, recommended against increasing funds to the island's charity bureaus simply to aid what some of the Council members described as "a mob of individuals." Instead they recommended the governor pass a new law on vagabondage to prevent abuses of charity bureau funds. Until such a law could be passed, to stop the soaring crime rate and protect society from the "ongoing danger due to the absence of any laws forcing these [*gens de couleur*] individuals to work," they also suggested the government require all free citizens between ages fourteen and seventy to carry an identity card indicating the bearer's name, sex, domicile, status, and means of existence.[67] Through such surveillance, the Colonial Council believed, authorities could ensure only worthy Martinicans received the benefits due them.

Although the Colonial Council hoped to prevent the island's *gens de couleur* from receiving aid through the charity bureaus, and thus to uphold the social and economic status of Martinique's white population, by early 1839 they lost that power, too. In an attempt to further curtail Creole power and ensure those inhabitants who needed government assistance got it, then governor Alphonse De Moges ordered a restructuring of the charity bureaus. Henceforth the rural outposts of the bureau would cease to exist leaving only those in Saint Pierre and Fort Royal to serve the entire island. Such consolidation, presumably, would help the administration more closely oversee charitable distribution, as would a new demand requiring "scrupulous discussion" of all Martinicans placed on the lists by the mayors, parish priests, treasurers, and four or five "notable inhabitants" assigned to each charity board. To make certain that inhabitants living in the island's other parishes received adequate aid, the administration also empowered a group of "charitable ladies" to deliver aid, whether money, food, or clothing, to homes around Martinique. These women also would be chosen by the island's mayors and priests and then confirmed in their positions by Governor De Moges himself. Although this stipulation helped guarantee that *femmes de couleur* would also be eligible for these positions, elite Creole women ultimately dominated the posts.[68]

By refusing to allow those who had participated in the Grand'Anse affair to return from continental France where they had been deported, Martinique's Creoles also hoped both to thwart *gens de couleur* efforts to exercise their freedoms and to maintain whites in a position of ever-diminishing social superiority. In June 1836 King Louis-Philippe pardoned twenty-three of those condemned in the 1833 uprising, and by November extended his grace to all individuals involved, with the stipulation that they remain under police surveillance for five years. By December, however, authorities dropped that requirement, too, and allowed the Grand'Anse participants complete freedom of movement throughout the French realm, reaffirming their status as full French citizens.[69] When a number requested passage to Martinique, however, the island's Creole-controlled Private Council vigorously argued against their return on the basis they would cause too much upheaval on the island. They also encouraged the new governor, Ange René Armand, Baron de Mackau, to utilize a provision of the February 1827 administrative restructuring that allowed him to prevent dangerous individuals from entering the colony. Mackau, a former military hero whose wife was a Creole, initially adhered to Creole requests and none of the pardoned returned during his tenure.[70]

The Ministry of the Marine later made it clear to Mackau, however, that allowing the return of those involved in the 1833 uprising best served everyone's interest. They encouraged the governor to use his discretionary powers to block admission to the island only in times of "absolute necessity," and pointed out it would be "regrettable" if those individuals convicted in the Grand'Anse affair who had stayed on the island received the benefits of the king's pardon, while those who had been deported to the continent were denied them. Such a discrepancy would be even more "regrettable," the minister noted, if it led the new governor's critics in metropolitan France, who worried about his close links to Martinique's white plantocrats, to attribute unequal application of justice to "the influence of the white population's hateful sentiments towards the population of color." To avoid such a conclusion, the minister of the marine warned the governor, "public opinion and the opinion of the Chambers," needed "some new evidence of [his] benevolence toward *hommes de couleur.*" By the time the governor left the island in 1838, however, that evidence was still forthcoming.[71]

In their efforts to uphold white social status, Martinique's Creoles renewed their efforts to maintain racial segregation in the island's schools. As of early 1837, with few exceptions, and then only in poor rural areas, whites attended schools founded by whites and *gens de couleur* attended those founded by free mixed-race men. "In no way is there a *mélange* between the two classes," the Minister of the Marine lamented, but continued to hope ultimately the new schools for "boys of the free class, which includes the white population as well as those of color" could "gradually bring about this fusion which ancient and powerful prejudices have been opposed to until now."[72] In this new environment Martinique's *colons* used their positions on the island's Private and Colonial Councils to thwart the continental regime's ever more explicit goal of racial fusion, sometimes by actively evading laws meant to create color blindness in matters involving free French citizens. Disagreements within the Private Council, however, indicated that even the island's elites were now divided over how best to move forward.

Nearly 40 percent of those asking the Private Council for permission to open private schools between 1835 and 1839 planned to establish them in the two major commercial centers of Saint Pierre and Fort Royal.[73] As a result, Martinique's rural areas still suffered from a dearth of schools, and while some of the island's poorest whites did attend school with *gens de couleur*, Creoles worried that such instruction could only bring havoc; therefore, they tried to block such racial mixing under the pretense of preventing another "uprising" like the Grand'Anse affair and to support racially segregated schools like the one proposed by the Creole Patin.[74] In his request to the Private Council for permission to open a private primary school, Patin indicated his intention to accept only white boys at the establishment. As the director of the interior indicated, however, to prevent such occurrences a ministerial dispatch required him to note Patin's segregationist intention when passing along his request for permission, making approval unlikely. Martinique's *procureur général* further added that, because the "actual state of the legislation" forbade any reference to a person's skin color and officially recognized only free or nonfree people, the Private Council could not allow "this sort of delimitation by class."[75]

Fort Royal's Creole royal prosecutor, however, believed that a technicality would allow the Private Council to support the request. Arguing that the recent ministerial dispatch technically did not require that the director of the interior mention Patin's intention, he suggested that they simply forward the request and give the director of the colonies demographic information at a later time, "after a certain number of students would have been received in the school," and "when it could be gathered by local authorities;" if the numbers indicated only white Martinicans had chosen to enroll in Patin's school, he implied, that was all the ministry needed to know. The Private Council unanimously approved the royal prosecutor's suggestion and then Governor Mackau himself signed the director of the interior's report regarding Patin's request, a report that in the end "did not contain mention of class or color."[76]

Feeling under siege because of their diminishing hold over markers of white social superiority, the island's plantocrats embraced the Private Council's efforts and pushed to open a number of private schools for the island's elite white children. In Saint Pierre, Cassius de Linval and his widowed mother, members of a well-established Creole family, had received permission to open a school for young white boys and one for young Creole girls in February 1833.[77] By early 1837, the planter Dessalles indicated both schools had succeeded beyond Cassius de Linval's greatest hopes and concluded "the general confidence in Monsieur and Madame Cassius's instruction was fully justified by the brilliant exercises" displayed by the students in both establishments.[78] A number of other Creole women also successfully applied to open or maintain private schools for white girls, despite the explicit rules against such racially segregated institutions.[79] Villeneuve and GuaryVeron asked to open a school for young girls in Trinité. Its location near the wealthiest one hundred plantations on the island, and Villeneuve's status on the island—her father was the French commander sent to the Caribbean in 1802 when the French reacquired Martinique from the British—made their school quite a success with Martinique's elite Creoles.[80] Yolande Marin, then living in Saint Pierre, also received permission to continue the work of her sister, Madame Mougenot, who in 1822 had established a boarding school for young Creole girls in Saint Pierre and, as of 1839, continued to accept whites only.[81]

In their quest to guarantee racially segregated education, Creoles also returned to the Sisters of Saint Joseph's Saint Pierre institutions. Through their positions on the Private and Colonial Councils, Creoles provided the orphanage and hospice funds for building maintenance. Although the local government's original agreement with the religious order had assigned them that expense, between 1835 and 1839, Creoles allocated nearly 11,800 francs to the Sisters of Saint Joseph for repairs to the building.[82] Private individuals, like Madame Blanc, "the fine mother" of a young Creole girl educated in the foundling home, also continued to give what they could to ensure their own children's education. Out of concern for the institution's "difficult position," she donated 370 francs to purchase books and supplies the Sisters had requested, but not yet received, from the Order in metropolitan France. Although Blanc also offered to acquire the supplies on her next trip to the continent, the Order's headmistress in Martinique felt in such desperate need of the materials that she risked sending the money along in a letter to Paris.[83]

By 1838, the foundling home housed forty white children and, despite economic hardships, the Sisters of Saint Joseph's other whites-only institutions had also managed to thrive. Although Creoles had initially worried the Saint Pierre day school would be required to integrate, in the aftermath of the Grand'Anse affair they flocked to the institution that opened in August 1834 with thirty Creole girls between the ages of four and eight.[84] By 1838 the school had done so well the Sisters of Saint Joseph spent nearly 25,000 francs for a new building to house the school, which had reached its capacity at forty students. They also spent nearly 10,000 francs making repairs to the Royal School for Girls that then taught fifty students.[85] Even though the school taught only about half the number of Creole girls as it had at its height during the Restoration, as the headmistress indicated, they all paid their fees despite the increasingly difficult financial conditions faced by local planters.[86] In fact Creoles of all financial backgrounds were so eager to give their children racially exclusive education that the Sisters of Saint Joseph in Martinique were able to send the head of the Order 10,004 francs in 1836, 8,862 francs in 1837, and 15,353 francs in 1838 to support the Order's efforts.[87]

As Martinique's Creoles again turned to whites who were willing to flout continental laws against whites-only institutions and to the Sisters of Saint Joseph who managed to avoid racial integration, the island's *gens de couleur* also took advantage of new educational opportunities to secure their rights as French citizens and looked to found even more schools to train the island's free mixed-race inhabitants. Although it is difficult to determine the racial background of those requesting permission for such schools from the Private Council, some *gens de couleur* petitioners were well known to local Creoles and Martinique's *gens de couleur*. Demoiselles Victorine and Amélie Aubert Armand, for example, received permission to open a *pensionnat* in Fort Royal for young girls as did the Demoiselles Bissette, relatives of Cyrille August Bissette.[88] According to the headmistress of the Saint Pierre Royal School for Girls, "there are many classes, even boarding schools, especially for *enfants de couleur*," and for that reason, unlike in Guadeloupe, she contended the government did not yet need to consider establishing free schools for free children.[89]

Although tuition-paying schools accepting free mixed-race children may have been succeeding, those like the schools of mutual instruction supported by the government struggled. The Saint Pierre school of mutual instruction for free girls closed shortly after its establishment. The school of mutual instruction in Fort Royal survived, however, and taught seventy free mixed-race girls in early 1837.[90] Ultimately Garnerin took over its supervision and like her superior, Ballin, encountered resistance from the island's elites. This was especially true when, after gaining control of the school, she requested new lodgings for the school on the first floor of the old Ministry of the Marine warehouse.[91] At that time, the mutual school for free girls still operated in the same room as the mutual school for free boys, simply at different hours, and Garnerin found the arrangement unacceptable. She voiced her concerns—that the school lay surrounded by Ministry of the Marine employees and that the girls had to meet in the heat of the afternoon—to the director of the interior but received little sympathy. In fact the Private Council concluded that Garnerin used her concerns simply as an additional excuse to ask for a new room. Such complaints did not merit the 2,200 francs required to remodel the room, they decided, and therefore, with Governor Mackau's approval, they refused Garnerin's request and determined she should continue teaching in her current location.[92]

In light of new metropolitan measures to emancipate enslaved people who touched metropolitan soil and their attempts to prevent Creoles from maintaining white social superiority through the courts and education, Martinique's elite white planters also increasingly closed ranks and tried to cement the personal links between them. Intermarriage had long served as an important strategy among the island's plantocrats and their decreasing hold over formal positions and increasing opportunities for France's *gens de couleur*, together with economic difficulties in sugar agriculture, made this power-sharing strategy more important in the late 1830s.

In the early years of the July Monarchy the government had tried to address the growing disparities between the continental sugar beet and colonial cane sugar interests. Although colonial cane sugar still dominated the French home market, beet sugar production increasingly drew a bigger margin and, in response, in 1832, 1834, and 1835 the metropolitan government levied a tax on beet sugar. By 1836, however, beet sugar had become such a presence in the French home market that colonists had to re-export as much as 30 percent of their sugar to foreign markets.[93] Because of their weak position in this re-export market, colonists called for officials in metropolitan France to seriously address the "sugar question" to ensure that colonial French had the same economic protections as metropolitan French.

All these factors combined made questions of family honor, in both financial and sexual matters, even more important to elite Creoles when considering marriage partners and further disrupted the intimately connected web of families who had historically controlled Martinique. Beginning in 1837 the diaries of the planter Pierre Dessalles offer an extensively detailed private reflection on the plight of finding a suitable mate. His daily logs contain references to local Martinican events and gossip and, because he was then searching for husbands for two of his daughters, he devotes part of many entries to the ideals of white male and female behavior. His reflections reveal how divisions—based on gender, economic position, and Creole or metropolitan status—among the island's *colons* influenced marriages for Martinique's plantocracy.

As anticolonial critics increasingly chastised Creoles for their support of the plantation system, a prospective male suitor's sexual relationships with mixed-race women more frequently had the potential to thwart otherwise suitable matches. Although the ideal of white womanhood called for wives to remain blissfully ignorant of their husband's extramarital and interracial affairs, such relationships appeared especially troubling for those elite Creole women who, because of their financial ease, could object to such behavior, and even scorn otherwise attractive suitors. One elite Creole woman, Madame Chauvigny did precisely this when she refused the overtures made to her daughters by Dessalles's nephews, Alexandre and Louis Le Vassor. The Le Vassors belonged to one of the wealthiest Creole families in Martinique and wielded tremendous social and political influence on the island. Despite such seeming virtues, however, Chauvigny voiced her concerns about Alexandre Le Vassor's conduct, in particular, and especially worried about "the influence of the *mulâtresses*" on the young man.[94]

Chauvigny also feared Alexandre Le Vassor sought to wed her daughter, Aline Chauvigny, for her money and would squander the family's considerable wealth. Money had been the deciding factor in her own reportedly unhappy marriage and Chauvigny knew the perils of such a match. So, too, did Pierre Dessalles, who reflected that when the marriage between the elder Chauvigny had taken place, "it was easy to predict that this union would be bad; when money alone decides the choice of a wife, happiness is very much compromised."[95] Ultimately Chauvigny's daughters faced no such melancholy choice. Noting, "my family, even the public, would blame me if I consented" to the Le Vassor proposals, Chauvigny informed Dessalles that no marriages would take place between her daughters and the Creole LeVassors.[96]

While the Chauvigny daughters apparently escaped their mother's fate, the newlywed Bonnet, daughter of an influential Creole planter and also a relative of Dessalles, met it. Bonnet "belonged to one of the best families of the country," and came from a Creole family with deep roots on the island. Her new husband, on the other hand, a freshly arrived metropolitan Frenchman, had no standing, Dessalles said, beyond "a petty magistrate whose conduct was far from exemplary."[97] Because the July Monarchy favored metropolitan magistrates, like Bonnet, over Creole magistrates, Dessalles argued, "one sees among those men sent from France only obscure and scheming individuals, enemies of the country for which they are responsible."[98] For Dessalles, the union between the newlywed Bonnets symbolized just how far Martinique's Creoles had fallen. Robbed of their traditional posts, Creole families like the Bonnets, out of economic necessity, now had to marry their daughters off to all sorts of questionable men.[99] In so doing the island's white plantocracy allowed into its ranks men who could not be trusted to maintain Martinique's Creoles in a superior social status, especially in the face of ongoing metropolitan measures intended to create parity for all free inhabitants in the colonies.

Dessalles's reflections on the unions of white Martinican women who had alliances with men of considerable political power under the new July Monarchy further reveals the complex intertwining of public and private issues in colonial politics. Although Dessalles himself hoped to contract a remunerative match for his own daughters, he disparaged a number of other local white women who had managed to make such matches by explicitly attacking their sexual honor. By casting such aspersions, however, he also questioned the private and public judgment of their husbands and confirmed metropolitan fears that the island's authorities were irretrievably linked to the Creole elite. Dessalles accused the wife of de La Bretonnière, then a candidate for governor, for example, of scandalous behavior. In 1806, when Dessalles had first arrived in Martinique, he claimed de La Bretonnière's wife already had the reputation of a "loose woman," and after the death of her first husband she had married de La Bretonnière, "a man with little education."[100] Gossip suggested "by her intrigues and the graces she accorded to the ministers and other men of power," she obtained advancement for de La Bretonnière and his career was founded on her sexual promiscuity. If named governor of Martinique, Dessalles noted, de La Bretonnière thus "would be prudent and wise" to come from the continent to Martinique alone; "the well-born ladies of the colony," Dessalles insisted, would not call on his wife and "his wife would be out of place here."[101]

Dessalles also attacked as sexually wayward Madame Cuvillier, the governor of Réunion's wife, as a way to further criticize that worthy for his recent political acts. In 1837, Governor Cuvillier had dissolved Réunion's Creole-controlled Colonial Council and Dessalles worried the metropolitan government would support the action and have precedent for interference in Martinique's Creole-controlled Private Council. In his diary, however, Dessalles explicitly linked the governor's public judgment on political issues with his personal judgment on sexual issues, noting the governor, "who married a Madame Alexandre—a white shop keeper in Saint Pierre, who had been the concubine of several merchants there—just dissolved the Colonial Council."[102] By placing Cuvillier's disbanding of Réunion's Colonial Council literally and metaphorically in the context of his wife's sexual relationships, he linked the governor's public and private choices. Whether or not any of the rumors Dessalles circulated about these white women had any basis in reality, clearly in the mind of Dessalles both of them had failed to maintain the sexual discipline required of "well born ladies" in Martinique and, as a result, they, and their husbands, laid themselves open to public criticism and threatened Creole solidarity and the plantation system.

Planters like Dessalles also worried about the government's creation of the Guizot-Rémusat Commission, named after its president, François Guizot, an opponent of slavery, and Charles de Rémusat, a member of the French Society for the Abolition of Slavery, and its mandate to thoroughly examine the issue of slavery and emancipation.[103] The Commission report to the Chamber in mid-1838 supported mass, rather than partial, emancipation, but only after 1840, when former British slaves had completed the transition from apprenticeship to full emancipation and when the French government would have had time to adequately institute and fund preparatory measures for the realm's enslaved Africans. Because the Chamber dissolved shortly after the report was issued, the measure technically had no legislative power. Nonetheless the Commission's recommendations served as another indication that antislavery advocates had gained significant political ground and they fueled increasingly virulent debates between the plantation system's opponents and proponents in the Chambers and the metropolitan press.[104]

Abolitionists, for their part, increasingly used Creole claims to both exceptionalism—a mandate for special privileges as inhabitants of the colonies—and to national belonging—a claim to the rights of every other Frenchman—to advance the antislavery cause. They particularly took issue with Creole supporters like a former delegate from Guadeloupe who wrote to the *Journal du Havre* and argued for colonial representation in the Chambers on the grounds that France's governing document, the *Charte,* was "government of the country by the country," and "in order for this to be completely true, it is necessary that . . . all parts of the country participate."[105] In response to such claims for "sameness," the antislavery Isambert argued in the Chambers that if the colonies called themselves part of France then they could not possibly have special privileges, and certainly not financial privileges denied other departments. As Isambert pointed out, Creoles from the French West Indies had long sent money to their metropolitan delegates to wage a press campaign against their opponents, a practice forbidden to continental departments. As a result, Isambert contended, if "the interest of the colonies is to move closer to the common law, to assimilate itself to our departments, to demand the same protection of the metropole," then certainly Martinicans had to abandon this practice.[106]

Such debates simply amplified the dichotomy between Creoles and French on the continent and rendered their exchanges even more difficult. When he returned to continental France in 1838 to find his daughter a husband and to right the family finances, Pierre Dessalles and his family encountered this charged environment. Dessalles himself had schismatic loyalties and, while he may have understood and felt a sense of kinship with his Creole counterparts because of their support of the plantation system and their efforts to maintain its accompanying social order, he always retained an important distinction between Creole and metropolitan Frenchman and considered himself, as technically was the case, a true European.[107] The realities of his trip, however, underscored how much he had come to resemble the Creoles who he believed to be his inferiors and further revealed how little his own family adhered to the ideals of appropriate white colonial behavior that he held so dear.

During his eighteen-month stay in metropolitan France, Dessalles missed Martinique a great deal. Shortly after returning to the family's home near Bordeaux, Dessalles lamented the comforts of his plantation back in Martinique: "Ah! poor Martinique! How I miss you!"[108] and, "I made a huge mistake in leaving Martinique."[109] The fact that his Creole wife, Anna Dessalles, chose to remain in metropolitan France for the majority of her adult life no doubt complicated Dessalles's desire to return to the island and made the increasingly derogatory characterizations of the island's white colonists even harder to bear.

The Dessalles family history illustrates the complex interplay between colony and metropole. In 1815, just seven years after their marriage in Martinique, Dessalles moved his wife and three children (Adrien born in 1809, Louise born in 1812, Calixte born in 1815) to metropolitan France, eventually settling at the family estate, Lespinassat, near Bordeaux. For the next ten years Anna Dessalles remained at the estate while Pierre Dessalles traveled between the family properties on both sides of the Atlantic, returning to the continent frequently enough to father three more children (Antoinette in 1817, Emilie in 1820, and Henri in 1821). During his visit in 1826, and concerned about the family's mounting debt, Dessalles sold Lespinassat, installed the family near his in-laws in Bordeaux, and then returned to Martinique with his oldest son Adrien. For the next four years, Anna Dessalles and the rest of the Dessalles children remained in metropolitan France until in 1830 she and her teenage daugthers, Calixte and Antoinette, returned to the island to join Pierre and Adrien, while Louise, Emilie, and Henri remained in continental France to pursue their educations. During that trip to the island, which overlapped with both the 1831 Saint Pierre uprising and the 1833 Grand'Anse affair, Calixte married her remote cousin George de Cacqueray-Valmenier and, despite her mother's disapproval, settled permanently at his family's sugar plantation near Fort Royal. The following year, in 1834, Anna and Antoinette returned to the family's metropolitan compound near Bordeaux just in time to attend the wedding of the Dessalles's oldest daughter, Louise, to Marie-Louis Cléret, a mortgage broker from the island's administrative capital. Although the couple returned to the island in 1836, they eventually settled permanently on the continent at Châtellerault, near Poitiers, and the entire family visited them on their trip from Martinique in 1838.[110]

Like many other white Martinican women, Anna Dessalles lived in metropolitan France, in part, to supervise her children's education on the continent; it was this task which originally took her to the metropole in 1815. In the increasingly difficult climate for France's Creole citizens, however, Dessalles felt it even more important to ensure Henri, his youngest son, the best education possible, calling it "a sacrifice," they owed the child.[111] In addition to supervising Henri's education, however, Anna Dessalles also represented the family in their negotiations with business associates in France's Atlantic port cities. She traveled to Bordeaux in 1824 to negotiate with the Durant brothers, then the Dessalles family's most important creditors, when they requested a lien on Lespinassat to cover Dessalles's debts; and in 1837 she negotiated with the Fontenau Company, which had representatives in Trinité, Martinique, and Nantes, France, personally delivering 12,000 francs to the port-city office to ensure the family ongoing credit.[112]

Emilie LeVassor (de Bonneterre), a cousin to Pierre Dessalles and mother to Alexandre and Louis LeVassor, also played a critical role in the Dessalles family sugar business. Like Anna Dessalles, LeVassor spent limited amounts of time in Martinique but continued her involvement in the family's island affairs from her home in Paris. She owned at least one quarter of the highly successful sugar plantation, Limbé, located near Saint-Marie and took an active role in increasing profit from that property. This included also negotiating with the Fontenau Company to sell the plantation's sugar harvests. As a series of letters indicate, however, although she welcomed Dessalles's advice, ultimately she made the final decisions to maximize her returns.

Well aware of the Pierre Dessalles family's recent negotiations with the Fontenau Company, in early January 1838, Le Vassor contacted Dessalles to help her and her sons settle their ongoing dispute with the sugar distributors.[113] Just a month later, however, she informed Dessalles that she had entered into legal proceedings against the Fontenau Company and further requested that no one in the extended family transact any future business with them.[114] Because he had finally reached a resolution with the firm, through Anna Dessalles, at the end of 1837, Pierre Dessalles was reticent to terminate the business relationship and tried to dissuade Le Vassor from going through with her case against the Fontenau Company.[115] Le Vassor had other plans, however, and, undoubtedly to prevent Pierre Dessalles from risking his own relationship with the Fontenau Company, she transferred the matter to a Creole lawyer, Massel, and informed Dessalles he would no longer have to negotiate on her behalf as she continued her lawsuit.[116]

Although he could do little about her decision, Dessalles resented LeVassor's choice to involve an outsider, rather than rely on her family in her business affairs. Her choice of another Creole, however, illustrates how Martinicans in the metropole, just like those in the colony, worked to solidify the colonial community's vast personal and professional network in the face of increased criticism from antislavery advocates. Dessalles's diary during his visit documents not only the extent of that colonial network living throughout continental France but also the particularly important role that personal ties, often facilitated by women, continued to play for this French Atlantic community. In 1838, there were at least one hundred prominent *colon* families from Martinique living in Bordeaux.[117] Consequently, in addition to their journeys around the region to visit immediate family on their trip to the continent, the Dessalles family met with Desrozeaux, a wealthy Martinican woman who had lived in Castillones for more than thirty years; with Vatable, a Creole from Martinique who had traveled to continental France to visit her fifteen-year-old son, a classmate of Henri Dessalles, and; with du Clary, the wife of Dessalles's former colleague and then president of Martinique's Royal Court, who was in Paris overseeing her children's education.[118]

While such visits to fellow Creoles apparently made for pleasant encounters, some with metropolitan Frenchmen, like one to the small village of Nasbinals near Bordeaux, clearly did not. One night when a dinner conversation with the village mayor turned to music, the mayor apparently remarked in

Martinique "the music of negroes is the whip!" In response Dessalles vigor-ously defended Martinique's plantocrats, retorting, "one uses the whip for horses and insolents; and the unhappiest negro in our colonies is still hap-pier than the happiest of your peasants."[119] Although he sometimes took issue with the behavior of his Creole neighbors, in the current climate Dessalles rose to defend them against what he saw as unflattering misperceptions, and lamented to his diary "what prejudices exist against our colonists!"[120]

The presence of Dessalles's mixed-race servant, Nicaise, undoubtedly only exacerbated Pierre Dessalles's relationships with his metropolitan brethren. The 1836 law that automatically emancipated any enslaved individual who touched French soil technically made Nicaise a free man. The exact nature of their relationship, however, is ambiguous. Based on the extensive intimacy Dessalles shared with Nicaise, they may have been father and son or even sexual companions.[121] Regardless, during their one-year trip to metropolitan France, Nicaise participated in virtually every aspect of the family's private and public life and underscored the intimate relationship between master and servant, regardless of Creole ideals.

Pierre Dessalles had once remarked that his *jeune nègre*, as he called Nica-ise, had "an elegance that captivates the world"[122] and while in metropolitan France that seemed so. Nicaise seemed to "amuse the society" at balls around the region and at the grand theater in Bordeaux.[123] Further away from the port city, however, Nicaise's skin color captivated the world, and not always for the better. During their visit to Nasbinals in August 1838, Pierre Dessalles noted, "Nicaise's skin color attracted the entire population."[124] Likewise, on a trip to the theater in Nîmes in early September, a young white man, "stunned by [Nicaise's] color," insulted him. In response, Nicaise exclaimed: "I am black, it is true. But understand that these black hands have as much power as your white hands."[125] Fortunately, Dessalles reported, no violence ensued between the two men. That Bordeaux, a major port in colonial commerce and former hub of the Atlantic slave trade, accepted Nicaise more readily than Nasbinals seemed logical. That said, Nicaise's trip to Nasbinals serves as an important reminder that French in even the most seemingly remote places of the interior encountered *gens de couleur* and sometimes felt compelled to lend their voice to ongoing discussions about the colony's inhabitants and its system of chattel slavery.

Heightened debates over the "sugar question," especially in and around France's port cities, also contributed to this increased general interest in the plight of France's free and enslaved mixed-race inhabitants, prompting propo-nents of slavery to again shift strategies to warn those in metropolitan France of the dangers of emancipation. Just as they used the press to show the supposed threats white colonial women faced in Martinique, the *Gazette des Tribunaux* also printed supposedly true stories highlighting how racial mixing *in metropolitan France* threatened the entire French realm. Shortly after the king pardoned all of those involved in the Grand'Anse affair, for example, the journal recounted the tale of Cesarine, the daughter of a *quateronne* and a respected ship captain from Bordeaux.[126] Cesarine, then an inhabitant of Bordeaux, had attended one of the best schools in Paris and had enjoyed all the luxuries that doting parents could shower on a young French woman, the editors claimed. Nonetheless the "fires of passion which brought about her birth," as well as "her own," the tale noted, had led her astray, bringing her to a life of prostitution in the port city at the age of fifteen. Her "four years of orgies," the story claimed, proved her depraved life that came to a climax when authorities arrested Cesarine for being part of a nighttime disturbance of the peace involving four men and three women near a Bordeaux brothel. De Lamarthonie, a member of the accused party, had tried to have Cesarine's arrest warrant suspended, presumably because of his own previous relationships with her, and in the course of his efforts, he had perpetrated the crime of "outraging a public functionary by word, gesture, and threat," and was sentenced to fifteen months in jail.[127]

The story of Cesarine, Creoles and their supporters undoubtedly hoped, served as a cautionary tale of what chaos would ensue in the metropole now that all people of African descent on continental French soil were free and theoretically enjoyed the privileges of French citizenship. It also underscored how concerns about racial purity increasingly influenced ideals of appropriate French behavior and particularly the actions of French women. The mixed-race Cesarine threatened the public order by disregarding the privileges of respectable (white) womanhood–education and economic security–and in so doing she corrupted de Lamarthonie and countless unnamed, presumably white, metropolitan Frenchmen. The mixed-race Cesarine caused disorder, the tale announced, and threatened families and the social order not only in the colonies but also in metropolitan France.

"The Devoted," also printed in the *Gazette des Tribunaux*, further illustrated how *gens de couleur*, and especially those who could pass undetected as whites in the metropole, threatened the honor and fortunes of white metropolitan families.[128] Because the story had created "an extraordinary sensation of surprise, enthusiasm, and admiration," in the colonies, the editors of the daily claimed, they felt compelled to share it with their metropolitan audience. In 1834, the tale went, a "most well-considered and esteemed" merchant from a French West Indian colony made a trip to Paris and there married a young woman from "an excellent family from Normandy." Shortly after the marriage, the young woman, who had an impeccable education and a considerable fortune, went to the French West Indies with her husband and her chambermaid and for two years the couple lived together happily and was blessed with a son.[129]

Once again, however, racial mixing threatened those involved for, the merchant "had African blood in his veins," which aroused "irrational jealousy" and he soon began to suspect his wife of having an affair with her cousin, recently arrived from Paris. One night, a fit of "fury and despair," overcame the merchant and he shot and killed his cuckolder. When brought before the colonial court, the merchant refused to declare his motive. Since he alone stood to inherit from the victim, many assumed that the merchant had killed to gain the cousin's considerable fortune. When the case came before the court, however, his "pale and thin" wife appeared before the magistrates and declared, "I alone am guilty, and it is to expiate my crime that I dare to present myself before you . . . I betrayed the confidence of my husband, . . . Miserable as I am, I have injected shame and despair into the heart of the man that I had vowed to respect and cherish all of my life." Based on his wife's statements, and the assumption that the wife and cousin had indeed been lovers, the court unanimously acquitted the merchant. When he returned home, he found that his wife had retreated to "a miserable abode outside the city: as the object of hatred and contempt of all, she had condemned herself to an eternal sequestration." Only her chambermaid had not abandoned her. Four years passed and still people would say as they passed her house: "It is there that the infamous tries to expiate her double crime: the death of her lover and the dishonor of her husband."[130]

After five years, the merchant fell deathly ill and called the magistrates, the governor, and the head clergy to his bed, and only then did he speak of the horrible crime years before. Thinking himself near death, the man claimed his wife "never ceases to be virtuous and pure" and explained that although he had shot his wife's cousin after seeing him exit his wife's chamber, he had since learned that the chambermaid, and not his wife, had been involved with the wife's cousin. His wife, "The Devoted," had begged him to let the lie stand, however, for the sake of the family's honor, and thus for five years, the merchant said, "this angel of abnegation has called the shame and contempt on her head to save mine." That very night, the tale proclaimed, after learning the truth, the entire town returned the "pious wife" to her husband's deathbed and all contempt for her dissolved into "enthusiasm and admiration" for her devotion to her husband. Undoubtedly as divine reward for "The Devoted's" purity, the merchant made a full recovery and the two lived the rest of their lives beyond reproach.[131]

Like the story of Cesarine, "The Devoted" served as a warning about *gens de couleur* who lived and worked in metropolitan France, sometimes without the knowledge of those around them, and the dishonor they could bring families on both sides of the Atlantic. Even though the "devoted" wife from Normandy, like Cesarine, embraced the ideals of education and economic security for elite white women, she twice fell victim to a mixed-race man passing as a white, once when marrying him and again when taking the blame for his violence. Unlike Cesarine, she did not corrupt any metropolitan Frenchman, but rather acted with appropriate honor and submission even to a husband who did not merit her devotion. The mixed-race merchant, whose lineage apparently had remained a secret during his time in continental France, not only killed his wife's wealthy metropolitan relative but also allowed his devoted wife to languish, ostracized, for five years. His deceit, the tale suggested, threatened both continental and colonial families and the social orders to which they adhered. If such mistakes occurred already, pro-slavery advocates implied, then emancipation could only cause more heartache.

Antislavery advocates, however, repeatedly highlighted the horrors of the plantation system and called for its abolition.[132] Some, like Bissette and the increasingly popular *Revue des Colonies*, called for an immediate end to chattel slavery while others, like the editors of the Parisian *Le Siècle*, called for gradual emancipation to ensure enslaved people would be appropriately prepared for entrance into civil life and ready to take on the responsibilities of French citizenship.[133] For France, they claimed, "the essential point [in abolishing slavery] is to atone for the crime of slavery through the moral and social regeneration of the *noirs*; it is to transform into citizens those whom the horrors of the [slave] Trade and of slavery have changed into beasts."[134] After 1839 discussions about emancipation increasingly included consideration of what would be required to turn enslaved individuals into French citizens.

"Amelioration of the White Race" and "The Sacred Rights of Property": The End of Slavery in the French Atlantic

BY SUMMER 1839 the colonial sugar industry had fallen into crisis and colonial interests increasingly called on the government for some kind of compromise on the "sugar question" in exchange for flexibility on the question of slavery. In some Creole minds, at least, the question of survival might trump the issue of slavery. For those pragmatists among the colonists, the utterly unthinkable had become possibly negotiable.

As debates in continental France over the "sugar question" and the terms (gradual versus immediate) of the abolition of slavery came to a head, Martinique's Creoles viewed a series of new laws regulating slave manumission and plantation management as further indication that colonial administrators saw them as less than full members of the French nation. A set of new operating instructions for Saint Jacques, Martinique's government-owned and operated sugar plantation, struck many Martinicans as a particularly dangerous infringement on their rights as property holders and their official positions. The instructions directed director of the interior Jean-Jacques Eyma to prepare the plantation's enslaved workers for emancipation by creating a school for enslaved children under the age of sixteen, offering material encouragements for enslaved people to marry, and limiting the use of the whip.[1] Planter Pierre Dessalles disparaged the instructions as the metropole's pernicious meddling in island affairs and decried "to touch the interior system that regulates the work and the discipline of plantations is to call down revolt and compromise the existence of the whites." He also chastised then Governor De Moges for misunderstanding that surveillance of Saint Jacques fell to Creole Director of the Interior Eyma, and not to the metropolitan governor, and that ultimately the Creole-controlled Colonial Council had authority over the plantation.[2] In Dessalles's opinion De Moges, like so many governors before him, had overstepped his authority and failed to appreciate *colon* expertise and Creole arenas of responsibility.

Creoles responded with similar outrage to an ordinance that greatly expanded enslaved people's eligibility for manumission, characterizing it as an attack against the property rights of French citizens and further evidence the metropolitan government did not see colonists as full French citizens. The ordinance freed any enslaved person who: married his or her master; married a free person with the consent of his master; was the result of such union; had been legally adopted by a free person under the Civil Code; had been named the tutor of his or her master's children; or was the mother, father, sister, or brother of a newly manumitted worker. To determine how many might meet the above criteria, and have a right to freedom, the measure also called for a census of the enslaved community.[3] The wealthy Creole Lepelletier Du Clary saw the government's efforts not just as an infringement on the colonists' right to protect their property, but as a "political plot against our new constitution," and evidence "the metropolitan legislature has concluded that it had the right to modify [the constitution] or to abridge it at its will."[4] One Colonial Council member went so far as to assert that the metropolitan government's recent actions justified Martinique's separation from the French Empire. Asking the Council members, "if you are not French, what are you?" he further argued if the colonists could not "like all other French, be in full possession of the sacred rights inherent in this title," then they should consider severing their ties with the French national family and "without crime, without fear of being accused of treason, renounce the protection that France formerly accorded you at the price of your submission to its monopoly, and your devotion to its commercial and maritime interest."[5] If France had turned its back on the colony, he not so subtly suggested, then the colony should feel free to go its separate way.

Another ordinance dictating extensive new rights for enslaved people and government oversight of private plantations evoked even more outrage for Creoles. This measure expanded the 1839 Saint Jacques instructions to the island's private plantations and added mechanisms to ensure Creoles followed them. The ordinance: ordered clergy to physically visit private plantations at least one a month to ensure masters instructed enslaved workers in the faith

(Articles 1, 2); required admission of enslaved Martinicans over the age of four into previously mandated free schools and authorized the teachers in charge of these schools to travel to nearby plantations to teach (Articles 3, 4); encouraged marriage among enslaved workers and ordered local magistrates to visit plantations to ensure masters followed the laws (Articles 5, 6); and stipulated any planters who did not accept the clergy on their plantations or send enslaved children to receive religious instruction would suffer a fine (Article 7).[6]

Dessalles, not surprisingly, called the ordinance "appalling!" and for a week after learning of it he and Jacques Lalanne, a close Creole friend and one-time mayor of Sainte-Marie, drafted a letter to the governor expressing their concerns.[7] While they noted, " the colonists, essentially French and attached to the mother country . . . hope that no attempt will be made against the sacred rights of property," they also indicated the recent measure so threatened their rights as Frenchmen that it, too, might jeopardize colonists' allegiance to France.[8] Ultimately Dessalles and Lalanne decided to hold the draft of their letter until they could gather signatures from other planters in the area.[9] The final sent draft nonetheless argued by diminishing "the authority of the master and [taking] the time of his slaves," the 1840 ordinance attacked "the most sacred right of property: a right that the ordinances and the edicts of our Kings have consecrated in the most formal manner." It also asserted "never has any property been more positively acquired or recognized by the colonists as that of the slave," and thus warned "the colonists will never understand that such a legitimate defense [of their property] could so upset the passions that the omission of justice could be the consequence!" The conclusion that the island's Creoles, who had "never contested the government's right to assure itself of the maintenance of regulations and of public peace in the plantation workshops," underscored just how vehemently Martinique's planters repudiated any infringement on their property rights and how much they believed themselves denied the justice due French citizens.[10]

Other colonists called on *colons* to confront those officials sent to private plantations to enforce the ordinance. When the royal prosecutor visited one Creole plantation, the owner "chased him shouting abuses." Likewise Desroseaux, a Creole from Robert, planned to hand the royal prosecutor a letter of protest when he arrived to enforce the ordinance. Huc, the Creole mayor of the commune of Prêcheur, told the governor "if [the royal prosecutor] stepped foot in his Quarter, [Huc] would arrest him as a disturber of the peace!"[11] In a letter to the ministers, colonial delegate for the French West Indies, Baron Charles Dupin, also deplored how the ordinance ignored the important familial links between the continent and the colonies and how metropolitan French treated Martinique's Creoles as less than full citizens. Contending "the white population has only French blood in its veins . . . they are the brothers of our fathers," he lamented "sectarian associations," as well as "the journal and the Tribunal," who denigrated the colonists and painted "the slaves as victims, the masters as beasts, the magistrates as tyrants, the impartial administrators as servants of the masters. . . ."[12] By characterizing *colons* as monsters, intervening in the internal operations of private plantations and alienating the colonists' (enslaved) property, Dupin intimated, metropolitan France had severely wronged their French brothers.

Although many Creoles agreed with Dupin's conclusions and remained convinced they could hold out against change, even as emancipation appeared a foregone conclusion, Martinique's white plantocracy increasingly disagreed about the future direction of the colony and the metropolitan government's role in regulating the plantation system. Although he blamed the Ministry of the Marine and the metropolitan governor for the series of new laws on plantation management, for example, Dessalles also damned Creole Director of the Interior Eyma for agreeing to implement the new orders at Saint Jacques, ridiculed him for letting Governor Moges impinge on his rights, and chastised Eyma for carrying out rather than "rejecting such illegal and baneful acts." "What infamy!" Dessalles concluded, lamenting that Eyma had "sold out to power."[13] By supporting what Dessalles saw as an infringement on Creole rights—not only planters' property rights but also the Colonial Council's administrative rights—he clearly believed Eyma had betrayed his fellow Creole Martinicans by casting his lot with metropolitan administrators.

As they complained about the effects of increased oversight of their property, Martinique's Creoles also worried about how increased access to manumission would practically influence sugar cane production and the island's racial and social hierarchy. In 1839, Martinique was home to 10,105 whites, 30,718 free mixed-race people, and 74,333 enslaved workers; within two years those numbers had changed to 10,362 whites, 32,319 *gens de couleur*, and 75,225 enslaved individuals.[14] That Martinique's *gens de couleur* now outnumbered whites nearly 3 to 1 deeply troubled Creoles. So too did the metropolitan government's continued efforts to ensure their education. As a result Martinique's *colons* worked even harder to maintain racial segregation in the island's tuition-based schools. Despite rigorous attempts by a host of administrators, by and large these schools had continued their racial exclusivity. As of 1839, approximately 36,517 Martinican children required instruction: 1,314 white boys and 1,356 white girls; 4,870 free mixed-race boys and 4,977 free mixed-race girls; and 11,900 enslaved boys and 12,100 enslaved girls under the age of fourteen.[15] Except for in a few rural areas, however, and among the poorest of the poor, the majority of Martinique's schools still taught only free mixed-race children.[16] Only 84 institutions offered instruction of any kind by 1840 and they had a combined enrollment of only 1,693 free children.[17] The fees for those schools also made it prohibitive for many of the island's poorest Martinicans to attend, regardless of their racial background, and, consequently, many of the schools failed.[18]

Creoles also tried to undermine government-supported schools for free children, like that run by Garnerin, in a further effort to thwart the government's goal of racial fusion. After 1839 Garnerin encountered renewed resistance from the Creole-controlled Private Council, which now chose to simply ignore, rather than to outright oppose, her school. An earthquake in early 1839 had virtually destroyed the Fort Royal building where the schools of mutual instruction for girls and boys continued to share space, forcing Garnerin to suspend classes. When, after "incessant solicitations," she finally did receive a new location, it lacked a yard, cabinets, lodgings, and even appropriate hygienic facilities. Furthermore, the building could house, at most, forty pupils and, by 1840, she had 124 enrolled.[19] If she had not spent her own money on other necessary supplies, the school would have gone completely without. After eight years of such struggles, Garnerin requested a one-year rest back in metropolitan France to "regain her health."[20] By the following year, however, she had renewed her campaign to establish interracial education for the island's free girls and she took her complaints about the Private Council's obstructionist tendencies directly to the minister of the marine in Paris. He, in turn, contacted Martinique's governor, Etienne Henri Mendi Duvaldailly, who assured the minister that local authorities would henceforth do everything possible to provide what Garnerin required.[21]

Because they had long viewed education as a marker of French citizenship, and the Sisters of Saint Joseph as their allies by providing whites-only education, Creoles resented that the Order finally had agreed to run the government's newly mandated free schools for the island's children. Sister Onésime, the Order's new headmistress, initially also expressed her displeasure that the Order would be required to offer such classes. Not because she disagreed with the goal, she informed her fellow nuns in continental France, but rather because the Order already had too much work for the twenty nuns then teaching in Martinique.[22] As soon as the government was able to provide appropriate buildings and supplies, she indicated, the Sisters of course would begin instruction.[23]

She nonetheless expressed her concern that the "new classes are going to bring us much trouble," especially if, as Governor De Moges had said would be the case, the Sisters were required to work alone in the schools established around the island. Sister Onésime indicated she believed such conditions violated the Orders' rules but, because she did not have any proof of such a rule, she asked Sister Marie-Thérèse Javouhey, a former headmistress in Martinique and Onésime's superior on the continent, to contact the governor and inform him how unacceptable it would be to have a nun "isolated in places without mores and without any resources to help her maintain her virtue." Such a letter, Sister Onésime felt confident, would certainly convince Governor De Moges to change his mind.[24] Apparently it did, for when the first two free schools opened in Fort Royal and the parish of Mouillage near Saint Pierre in January 1842, three nuns were assigned to each school.[25]

In response to the Sisters of Saint Joseph's agreement to run the new public schools, Martinique's Creoles also requested that the Order provide an *externat*, a day school, in Fort Royal to prepare the island's "virginal Creole girls" for admission to Saint Pierre's *pensionnat*. After arranging to rent space from a Creole woman, de Fleureuse, the Sisters operated a temporary school that taught nineteen "petites filles" within three months of its opening in August 1839.[26] The island's *colons* remained adamant that the island's white population receive an education superior to all others, however, and apparently saw the small space as inadequate to train young white women who required nurturing and tending to retain the freshness and innocence of youth integral to the ideal of white womanhood. They thus requested a much larger facility. Sister Onésime supported the idea, especially if it would bring in much needed funds to support the government-mandated free schools, but she refrained from making any commitments until the Order in continental France secured permission for such a school.[27]

Nearly a year after first seeking permission to create the school, Sister Onésime informed her superiors that the current climate made it "indispensable" to open such a school, further arguing that if the government opened free schools without authorizing this whites-only day school, Martinique's Creoles would "lose all confidence" in the Saint Pierre Royal School for Girls, much to the detriment of the entire Order. As further assurance that the institution would "be a great benefit to all," Onésime indicated that Creoles were so eager for the larger day school to open that the institution, before receiving official authorization, had already reached its enrollment capacity.[28] Such news, and the revenue a full school would generate for the benefit of the island's public schools, undoubtedly helped to convince the colonial administration in France to grant permission for the school, which opened with fifty students ranging from ages four to fifteen at the same time the Sisters of Saint Joseph finally opened the government-mandated free schools.[29]

Because of the increasingly difficult economic climate, the success of the tuition-based day school, and the money it could bring the Order, were quite important. Following an earthquake in 1839 and an outbreak of yellow fever, enrollment at the Saint Pierre Royal School for Girls had declined to only thirty students, bringing in just barely enough funds to meet general expenses.[30] With no more earthquakes, an end to the yellow fever epidemic, and the support of Governor De Moges and, especially, his wife who frequently visited the *pensionnat* in Saint Pierre and indicated "nothing was better" than a religious education, the school rebounded and nearly doubled its enrollment.[31] As a result the Sisters of Saint Joseph could once again send funds back to continental France to support the Orders' mission; although they managed to send only 2,050 francs in 1839, the following two years they sent 6,756 and 13,919 francs respectively.[32]

The metropolitan regime's increasingly successful attempts to level the playing field for all of Martinique's inhabitants made finding appropriate marriage partners who could maintain a Creole family's social and economic status even more important for families like the Dessalles. When it came to spouses for their children, however, both Pierre and Anna Dessalles continued to hold their Creole counterparts in lower esteem than metropolitan French. Dessalles—in effect echoing continental critics—lamented what he saw as the loose sexual morals that Creole women exhibited. Now, however, this had a new importance for him as he looked to find a wife for his oldest son, Adrien. For Dessalles, any evidence that a white woman had strayed from the ideal of having sexual relationships only with the appropriate white male partner inside the confines of legal marriage continued to disqualify her from the respect typically accorded white French women and most certainly made her an inappropriate marriage partner for his son. Dessalles's repeated attacks on the women of the Ballain family illustrate the consequences of even the rumor of such behavior. During his family's trip to continental France in 1838/9, Adrien Dessalles had remained in Martinique to oversee the family plantation and had involved himself with a young Creole woman, Lydie Ballain, growing quite attached to her. Pierre Dessalles viewed the possibility that his son might marry Ballain, however, as "a blow" and suggested he would "not survive such a shame." He derisively said of the Ballain women in general: "Madame Ballain is descended from *mulâtres* . . . her mother and her aunts had children by *nègres* and *mulâtres*, and several of these children are still alive. The young Ballain ladies have a horrible reputation, and the one whom Adrien wants to take as his wife has rotten morals."[33] For Dessalles, Lydie Ballain clearly was the wrong choice for his eldest son.

Despite his apparently strong attachment to the young woman, after his father's return from continental France, Adrien Dessalles renounced his plans to marry her and shortly thereafter, at his father's insistence, left the island to stay with family in the metropole.[34] Dessalles nonetheless continued his attacks against the Ballain women, accusing Lydie Ballain not only of an interracial affair but also of having her mother assist her in terminating the pregnancy that resulted from that relationship.[35] Dessalles also accused Adrien's former love interest of committing "a thousand naughty tricks," with his nephew, Alexandre Le Vassor, and the oldest daughter of living with "a câpre" (a mixed-race man) and planning to move to Puerto Rico with him.[36] Three years later, he further insisted that the oldest Ballain daughter and a Martinican Creole, Lagarigue de Survilliers, had abandoned their illegitimate twelve-day-old girl at the Lagarigue de Survilliers family plantation,[37]

For Dessalles such rumors served as positive proof that the island's Creole population no longer resembled the virtuous *colons* he had met and aligned with through marriage on his arrival in Martinique in 1808 and undoubtedly in his mind justified his efforts to interfere in his son's relationship with Lydie Ballain. It also encouraged him to disparage the sexual comportment of Madame Degorce, a Creole with whom he had an ongoing business dispute. Dessalles claimed some of her enslaved workers had stolen wooden planks from his plantation and to obtain satisfaction from Degorce, he had written Bonneville, then mayor of Sainte-Marie. The mayor's wife, however, a relative by marriage to Degorce, successfully interceded on the woman's behalf and Dessalles clearly resented both Degorce's ability to outmaneuver him as well as Madame Bonneville's interference in their dispute.[38] In his rants against Degorce, however, he questioned her sexual past, not her business acumen. As local Creoles looked for godparents for the twelve-day-old illegitimate girl supposedly abandoned by Ballain and Lagarigue de Survilliers, Dessalles admonished Degorce for forbidding her nephew from serving as a godfather. Because she "had had several bastards" before her marriage, Dessalles claimed, it seemed inappropriate for her now to "have no pity for the weaknesses of others."[39]

When Dessalles's own daughters, Emilie and Antoinette Dessalles, returned to the island with their mother the family faced the issue of finding them appropriate partners.[40] No matter how much the family needed money in the trying economic times, Dessalles could not stomach the prospect of a son-in-law beneath him in social standing, even if that man was metropolitan.

On his previous trip to the continent Dessalles had rejected the idea that his daughter, Antoinette, might marry a distant relative in Toulouse because he found the entire family lacking—in education, customs, and, it appeared, wealth earned through acceptable means. The Dessalles of Toulouse had earned a considerable fortune in salt mining, which had become more profitable under the July Monarchy, but Pierre Dessalles believed them "far too bourgeois," and concluded not only that his daughter "could never put up with it," but also remarked "by God! I do not think that I have fallen low enough to make this kind of an arrangement."[41] Even though the metropolitan family had money, it seems, for Dessalles everything else about them made them inferior to his own family and he could not stomach an alliance.

Dessalles demonstrated the same complicated distaste when certain suitors presented themselves for consideration in Martinique. Shortly after the Dessalles women's return to the island the family received a visit from Adolphe Hosten, who Dessalles disliked because "he has neither enough fortune, nor enough consideration in the colony to . . . aspire to one of my daughters." Anna Dessalles, for her part, apparently also found Hosten's "visits too frequent" and worried that the family would have to answer a marriage proposal.[42] His Creole status and lack of fortune, clearly, made such a possibility quite unwelcome to Pierre Dessalles. For the Dessalles women, so, too, did the possibility that Hosten, like so many other Creole men, participated in extramarital, interracial affairs.

Just as Madame Chauvigny had earlier raised concerns about the LeVassor's *mulâtresse* mistresses, other Creole Martinican women worried about the ramifications of white men's interracial encounters, in part because it raised the specter of having to contend with a husband's illegitimate mixed-race children. In Europe one could dispute the paternity of an illegitimate offspring; the plantation system, however, made it difficult to deny the mixed-race child of an enslaved female domestic, for example, as the child of the white plantation owner. Because the July Monarchy's recent manumission laws made such offspring free, rather than enslaved, and thus legitimate heirs (and potential rivals) for family property, undoubtedly Creole women found such relationships even more threatening.

Such was the case for Madame Lalanne, wife of Dessalles's good friend, Jacques, and mother of his seven legitimate children. Jacques Lalanne had long been involved in a sexual relationship with one of his enslaved domestics and, at precisely the moment the Dessalles were searching for husbands for their daughters, Madame Lalanne finally revealed "her chagrins" and informed the Dessalles that her domestic had recently given birth to Lalanne's child. For all practical purposes, Pierre Dessalles related in his diary, Lalanne had abandoned his white family, leaving them with nothing. Although he wondered how a fifty-five-year-old man "could provide his family with such an example," Dessalles nonetheless refused to discuss the situation with his friend and instead advised Madame Lalanne "to have patience and to keep silent," warning her she would only "deeply harm her husband if she made a scandal."[43]

Dessalles made no further references in his diary to Jacques Lalanne's indiscretions. After her revelation, however, Lalanne and her children called ever more frequently on the kindness of the Dessalles family, especially at dinner time, and for the next two years, Jacques Lalanne also spent a great deal of time at the Dessalles home.[44] While Dessalles continued his intimate friendship with Lalanne until the man's death, after helping settle Lalanne's estate, he could not refrain from noting what he viewed as the ruination of Lalanne's legacy. The estate appraisal came to 250,000 francs, no small sum. However, the description of the furnishings—six pairs of sheets, six tablecloths, twelve towels, five glasses, six platters, twelve plates—shocked Dessalles, leading him to conclude, "Any poor person would be outfitted better than that! Poor Lalanne is really blameworthy."[45] In the end, then, it was Lalanne's inattention to the material needs of his family, rather than his interracial affairs and illegitimate children that offended Pierre Dessalles.

While Dessalles heaped disdain on the Ballain women due to their rumored extramarital affairs, like other *colons* he obviously did not believe that such affairs fundamentally threatened elite white Martinican masculinity or automatically disqualified Creole men as acceptable marriage partners as long as, like Lalanne, they were discreet. Evidence indicates that Pierre Dessalles had not only engaged in interracial sexual affairs in the past, but that he also had at least one illegitimate mixed-race son, Saturnin.[46] Both Saturnin and his mother Trop were enslaved domestics for the Dessalles family and, as lifelong servants at La Nouvelle-Cité, became intimately involved in many family dealings. Throuhout his extensive correspondence and diary, Dessalles never mentions Saturnin as his son and Anna Dessalles appears not to have explicitly accused her husband of betrayal. Nonetheless, her actions suggest that she knew of Saturnin's parentage and found it troubling to deal with tangible reminders of Pierre Dessalles's own interracial sexual relationships.

The difficulty of daily facing their husband and father's interracial infidelities may well have contributed to the Dessalles women's preference for metropolitan France over Martinique. Spending time on the continent had long symbolized status for elite Creole women and, just as the director of the interior had warned during the Restoration, after being educated and spending their formative years in Bordeaux and Paris, the Dessalles family women found Martinique lacking. Less than a month after their return to Martinique, Emilie told her father "she detested the colony,"[47] and until their departure three years later all three women complained of what Anna Dessalles called the "boredom of the colony."[48]

Despite their discontent, Dessalles insisted economic necessity required the Dessalles women to remain in Martinique. While on the island, like many other elite Creole women they therefore tried to replicate the continent's supposedly superior standards by physically recreating metropolitan France in Martinique, most tangibly by importing costly material goods from Paris and France's Atlantic port cities. Such physical manifestations of attachment to continental France indicated not only a level of financial ease but also a level of sophistication cultivated by an extended stay in the metropole.[49] Even though the family finances were strained, because this attachment to metropolitan wares furnished an important marker of elite status, Dessalles tolerated such expenditures.

Anna Dessalles thus transported her piano and harp on her trips between Martinique and Bordeaux, no small feat logistically or financially.[50] She also dressed herself and her daughters in the latest metropolitan fashions. During their stay on the island the Dessalles women received two separate shipments from Bordeaux: a trunk that Dessalles thought contained some "very ugly dresses," and another trunk with hats and other fashions.[51] They also welcomed a shipment from Paris that included two silk dresses, two hats, two black mantillas, two sets of gloves, and some ribbon, in Pierre Dessalles's opinion all "of perfect taste and of an admirable freshness."[52] Although each individual item cost much less than luxury furniture, in some ways clothes were more important indicators of elite status precisely because a much broader public could see them explicitly attached to elite Creole women's bodies.

Metropolitan clothes also allowed white women to avoid forms of local dress that, at least in Pierre Dessalles's mind, illustrated the racial mixing endemic among the island's free mixed-race women. As metropolitan critics increasingly implied that all colonists, even the island's *colons*, bore the taint of racial mixing, Dessalles and others scorned those who voluntarily embraced African-influenced culture. He disparagingly called one Creole woman's madras kerchief, for example, "very ridiculous," and concluded that she resembled the unflattering mix of "a *mulâtresse* and a Chinaman."[53] Such distancing from the norms of metropolitan French culture, he and other Creoles worried, could only further degrade Martinique's white colonists in the eyes of other members of the French Empire.

In solidarity with the Creole opposition to metropolitan efforts at racial fusion, Dessalles also criticized elite white women who freely associated with mixed-race people. For men like him, concerns about the "stain of mixed blood," and his anger at shifts in the social hierarchy, ran so deep that white women risked their respectability, and thus their proper female identities, if they associated too closely with free mixed-race women, the ultimate symbols of both past and potentially future racial mixing and social disorder. As a result he looked askance at "Creole ladies" like Littée, a wealthy Creole friend, who "love to surround themselves with *mulâtresses*."[54] Littée frequently hosted dinner parties for both white and free mixed-race guests, something virtually unheard of in the British Caribbean and something Pierre Dessalles had found so disruptive in the early 1830s that, as previously noted, he personally helped remove a local magistrate for the offense.[55] He also damned Littée for telling her "intimate friend," the free mixed-race Saint-Rose, that "her son was in danger of being arrested for aiding runaway slaves."[56] Such closeness, Dessalles believed, went beyond poor taste and actually had significant social and political consequences, since aiding runaways threatened the safety of the plantation system, and eating together also blurred the supposedly clear boundaries between Martinique's different racial populations.[57] That some of the island's most influential families now hosted such events and considered free mixed-race Martinicans as close friends underscored how much things had changed during the July Monarchy and the depth of emerging divisions among Creoles.

As Martinican Creoles struggled to maintain the last vestiges of white social superiority on the island, in continental France antislavery forces hammered away at Creole intransigence and barbarism, repeatedly critiquing Creole exceptionalism and renewing debates about the status of all Martinicans within the French Empire. The *Gazette des Tribunaux*, for example, reported that even though the government had banned the use of the *cachot* Martinique's white planters continued to punish enslaved workers by confining them in the small enclosure and the island's Creole magistrates continued to allow the practice.[58] *Les français peints par eux-mêmes: encyclopédie morale du dix-neuvième siècle*, a nine-volume commentary on the residents of provincial France, complete with wood engravings and written descriptions of local dress, manner, and customs, also lamented the marked differences between colonial and metropolitan French. In volume eight the editor included three chapters on French West Indians, "Le Créole des Antilles," "Le Mulâtre," and "Le Nègre,"[59] each of which indicated how past and present Creole prejudice, and especially that of Creole women, distanced those in the islands from metropolitan mores. According to the Creole chapter's author, Roseval, "the inhabitants of these islands are French . . . in origin," and "although they submit to special rules that are the foundation of their slave society, and which are based in prejudices long banished from and currently unknown in Europe, the Antillean *colons* have a right to call themselves our brothers." Although he grudgingly admitted white French West Indians were indeed French, Roseval further indicated only "successive modifications in the political realm [and] frequent contact with European merchants has altered the primitive character of urban Creoles," and "isolation has allowed the rural Creole to retain his eccentric behavior, which he owes to Nature as well as his existence and his work."[60] Only contact with metropolitan French, and therefore continental mores, he contends, had saved Creoles in places like Saint Pierre and Fort Royal, a view that condemned isolated Creoles on their plantations to a primitive, uncivilized, state.

Roseval also disparaged Creole women, and in so doing, like many other critics of the colonial system, especially denounced their cruelty toward enslaved and free people of African descent. Although this criticism had first emerged in the 1820s, new legislation sparked metropolitan interest in colonial matters, and in particular the treatment of enslaved workers, making stories of female cruelty especially striking. Roseval claimed "this delicate and gracious" Creole woman was "likable" but also "quick-tempered," noting "when impatience shatters the woman's nerves, a madness that rapidly denatures her sometimes forces her to order atrocious punishments," of her enslaved workers.[61] He also blamed them for contributing to the "humiliation of this race" because of their "ever-increasing jealousy [of] their husbands' concubines, their rivals of color."[62] Feeling thwarted by "their rivals of color," and finding expression for the "burning ardor which inwardly consumes them," only at society balls, Roseval argued, Creole women made life much more difficult for "the citizens of the Antilles, emancipated by the 1833 law, who each day had to fight for the moral equality assured them in the political order."[63]

As for *le nègre*, Roseval argued, even though some might find his presence a "bizarre intrusion . . . in a gallery of popular types whose most salient traits combine to form the national face," he urged all doubters to reconsider their skepticism.[64] Recalling that in 1793 in Saint Domingue and in 1794 in Guadeloupe "*nègres* were declared French and that this quality admitted them to enjoy all rights as members of the nation," Roseval encouraged his metropolitan readers to give them their just dues and to keep in mind "no race, not even the Jews, have been so slandered."[65] As in the case of *gens de couleur*, Roseval blamed a portion of that on Creole women who, surrounded by enslaved domestics, forced them to specialize in such humiliating tasks as picking up a dropped handkerchief.[66]

The antislavery *Revue des Colonies* also took Creole women to task for their cruelty toward enslaved and free mixed-race Martinicans, including a particularly lurid example from "Memories of a Martinican Créole" by Gourard Fauvel, shortly after the new laws on plantation management appeared. That Fauvel, the same mixed-race man who had accused a number of the island's wealthiest white planters of conspiracy against the British government during their last occupation of the island, now referred to himself as a "Creole" further indicated just how much the world had changed.[67] In his memoirs, Fauvel told of la Marquise de Bellegarde, a wealthy Creole living near François, Martinique, who, despite her education and her eight volumes of Voltaire, delighted in watching others punish her enslaved workers. On one occasion, Fauvel claimed, she stood spellbound for nearly ten minutes watching six white men draw and quarter a young enslaved man suspected of poisoning other Bellegarde plantation workers.[68] The noted abolitionist Victor Schoelcher made similar claims about the cruelty of Martinique's Creole women, in *Des Colonies françaises*, arguing "Slavery is like a dissolvent of all sensibility, such that even women, who are so good, develop a special cruelty in the colonies . . . one can see them use their own hands, aided by a rope or a crop, to punish children who cry and let out screams that break the heart. Slavery makes women cruel."[69] Slavery itself had corrupted educated, innately good Creole women, both Fauvel and Schoelcher claimed, further implying that only abolition could remedy such ills.

Rumors that Creole women also used their privileged racial positions to participate in sexual relationships with free and enslaved mixed-race men further scandalized Creoles. When Bissette's *Revue des Colonies* published examples of white women bearing mixed race children from Martinique's civil records, *colons* and their metropolitan supporters mounted a vigorous counterattack in response to these perceived slurs against Creole women's sexual virtue.[70] Unlike their responses to similar claims in the 1820s, in this new environment, where claims of racial purity ranked among the last strongholds of white social superiority, Martinique's Creoles mounted a much more organized and better-supported campaign spearheaded, in part, by Bernarde-Adolphe Granier de Cassagnac, a pro-slavery metropolitan journalist in the pay of the Parisian colonial lobby.[71] Immediately after Bissette's story appeared in the *Revue des Colonies*, Granier de Cassagnac published a rejoinder in the pro-slavery *Revue de Paris* defining all *mulâtres* as the progeny of a white man and a black woman. Granier de Cassagnac asserted "the beautiful white [women] of the colonies were from too fine of families, too proud, too noble, too distinguished, too like princesses, to elevate a vile, stupid, dirty, and black *esclave* to their level."[72] If they were not, Creoles and their supporters worried, the plantation system could only fail.

* * *

In spring 1842 the climax of the controversy over the "sugar question" prompted many around the French Atlantic to trumpet the crucial link between commercial interests in the colonies and France's port cities.[73] Although the metropolitan government had attempted to deal with the growth of the beet sugar industry by enacting a number of complicated measures to grapple with the disparity between the continental beet and colonial cane sugar business, by 1842 French consumer demand for sugar hovered between 115,000 and 120,000 metric tons a year. By that time, however, more than 380 continental beet sugar factories produced between 27,000 and 50,000 metric tons, foreign sugar imports rose to 12,000 metric tons, while French colonial planters sent 80,000 metric tons of sugar for sale on the home market. As a result, sugar glutted the market and prices fell quickly. Some planters claimed that, after subtracting transportation costs, local and commercial charges in port cities, and the duty on colonial sugar, they only earned 6 francs per 50 kilograms sold.[74] The more efficient production of continental beet sugar vis-à-vis colonial cane sugar increasingly made protecting the colonial sugar cane market financially unwise and ignited even more heated discussion about the "sugar question."

So too did yet another significant shift in the island's demographics following delay on the issue. Between 1841 and 1843, the island's white population decreased by 1,475 (to 8,887), whereas the free mixed-race population increased by 3,387 (to 35,706), and the enslaved population by 511 (to 75,736).[75] This substantial outmigration of white inhabitants from the island, prompted in part by the financial crisis surrounding the future of the sugar cane industry, made Martinique's *colons* even more intent to cement personal and political alliances among Creole partners who embraced the prescribed ideals of white masculinity and femininity. The realities of the day, however, made such partners, and such alliances, harder and harder to find. Although *colons* continued to insist that Martinique's white women ideally live a life of luxury free from work, in the final years of the July Monarchy, necessity required elite white women to use their personal contacts to help facilitate family economic affairs. During her four-year stay in Martinique, for example, Anna Dessalles called on relatives and friends, and directly negotiated with sugar distributors in metropolitan France and Martinican creditors of all backgrounds, to ensure the family's economic security. By 1843 the family's debt to their sugar distributors in Bordeaux, the Durant Company, had reached dangerous new levels.[76] With the family in dire need of funds, Anna Dessalles thus urged her husband to request 40,000 francs from his relative Madame Emilie Le Vassor in Paris to cover the family's needs.[77] When that money did not materialize, she personally wrote Assier de Mont-Ferrier, another sugar distributor in Bordeaux, and, using her dowry as a guarantee, authorized a one-time payment of 7,000 francs to the Dessalles children living on the continent and also an annual payment of 2,500 francs.[78]

In addition to trying to stabilize affairs in continental France, Anna Dessalles also took the lead in making the most of the family's local relationships on the island. She encouraged her husband to ask Martinique's Governor Duvaldailly, for example, if he would recommend their oldest son Adrien for a government position in Cuba.[79] She also took issue with the way their plantation manager, de Gaalon, conducted himself and how he managed the family's enslaved workers, condemning the sexual liberties he took with the plantation's enslaved female laborers and the violence he used when he punished the enslaved work force.[80] Shortly before her departure for France in 1844, she also intervened with a free mixed-race creditor who came to La Nouvelle-Cité demanding payment, warning him "in view of his behavior," which she left unidentified, the family "would no longer deal with him and he could go to court if he wanted."[81] Given continued Creole control of the judicial system, despite years of attempted reform, and the Dessalles and Bence family connections, Anna Dessalles and the *mulâtre* creditor clearly understood he would find no help in collecting his debt through the tribunals.

Anna Dessalles's efforts to stabilize the family's finances undoubtedly rankled her husband even more than usual especially because she had recently objected to a union between her daughter, Antoinette, and the Creole Léopold Camouilly. Because white women outnumbered white men on the island in 1843, men like Dessalles found it even harder to find their Creole daughters acceptable matches, let alone a wealthy one like Camouilly, who stood to inherit nearly 500,000 francs.[82] In late 1843 Camouilly had approached the Dessalles family inquiring about a possible marriage with Antoinette. When asked her opinion about the match, however, Antoinette remarked she would "never consent" to a marriage with Camouilly and Anna Dessalles also felt "very displeased" about the prospect. As Dessalles's diary indicates, their objections to the union stemmed from rumors of the "misconduct" of Léopold Camouilly's father, namely, his reputation for keeping mixed-race mistresses, and Dessalles again lamented that such considerations stood in the way of such a lucrative match.[83] As he had repeatedly in the past, Pierre Dessalles refused to outright condemn Creole men who had interracial sexual relationships as long as they conducted them discreetly.

Clearly Anna and Antoinette Dessalles did not look favorably on a match with Léopold Camouilly, quite possibly because during their stay they both had been required to spend even more time than usual with Pierre Dessalles's illegitimate mixed-race son, Saturnin. Anna Dessalles's repeated criticisms of Dessalles for giving Saturnin liberties (like a day off to work on his own sugar cane), and her predictions that his freedoms would "make him proud and spoiled" suggest she remained acutely aware of the potential long-term effects of relationships like those that Camouilly *père* denied.[84] Based on their close relationship, it seems unlikely Anna Dessalles would have risked such a match for any of her daughters if she could prevent it.

Despite their troubled financial states at the height of the sugar question, Creoles' continued desire to assure the daughters of Martinique's *colons* had the best education available on the island sent them in even larger numbers to the Sisters of Saint Joseph. Despite all laws that ordered the contrary, the Order's Saint Pierre Royal School for Girls and its associated day school continued to accept only white students. By early March 1843 the boarding school taught 68 students and the *externat* 40, although the vast majority did not pay their tuitions.[85] Despite this fact, Sister Onésime was able to send nearly 16,000 francs back to continental France in mid-summer based on the income they earned from the *pensionnat*, the two external day schools for white girls, and their stipends for teaching in the government's free schools.[86] By the following spring the *pensionnat* taught 96 students and the Saint Pierre day school 45 girls, allowing Sister Onésime enough freedom to send nearly 24,000 francs, and potentially more if she had not chosen to keep some in reserve just in case "another earthquake or an anti-colonial law" shook the Order in the near future.[87]

Creole's also tried to make certain the Sisters of Saint Joseph's whites-only orphanage continued to flourish at the expense of Martinique's free and enslaved mixed-race inhabitants. Those same metropolitan laws that diminished elite Creole power on the island and threatened planters' financial stability also made it much harder for *colons* to support the racially exclusive institution. Through a variety of back-channel efforts, however, elites on the Private and Colonial Councils still found ways to give to the foundling home and keep Martinique's most vulnerable whites from a degrading poverty. To evade prohibitions against funding such entities, for example, the Private Council accepted a *rente perpetuelle* donation for the orphanage from former Director of the Interior Eyma. Although the Eyma in question may have been *Louis Eyma*, the director of the interior's brother, that man's deteriorating financial position makes his involvement unlikely. As Dessalles noted in a rant against Eyma shortly after the director agreed to new rules for the government-owned Saint Jacques plantation, Louis Eyma "had been bankrupt twice and had caused the ruin of many respectable families."[88] Consequently, it is probable that former Director of the Interior Eyma followed the letter, if not the spirit of the laws, and donated the money for the whites-only establishment, perhaps to appease Martinicans angry about his early "betrayals," as Dessalles called them.

The Private Council took an even bolder step at maintaining white social status by allowing the orphanage to accept free of charge, rather than for a fee, all poor white children with known relatives, or even with one surviving parent, if their relatives' "unfortunate position . . . did not permit them to offer an education."[89] The home still denied entrance to the island's free mixed-race children because, according to the nun in charge, "children of color, at any age, [could] always find positions as domestics."[90] To provide instruction for more whites, however, necessitated rearranging the institution's rules. In particular, the establishment changed the age students would enter and leave the institution and the duration of their stay. New admittance also now required nominations, made to the island's director of the interior, a copy of the death certificate of both parents, a birth certificate for the child, a vaccination record, and a certificate of indigence from the mayor of the child's commune.[91] Rather than force poor whites to choose between no education and interracial education in the island's free government schools, Martinique's *colons* believed it vital to provide whites-only educational opportunities for poor whites "to the greatest possible number of families."[92] To accommodate all the white girls who needed instruction, and continuing to see the Sisters of Saint Joseph as their allies, Creoles also looked to the nuns to open a day school for poor white girls in Saint Pierre. To that end the local mayor approached the Order's head and told her that the commune had already allocated 1,500 francs for precisely this purpose. As when previously approached to open a whites-only *externat* in Fort Royal, however, Sister Onésime refused to make a commitment without permission from metropolitan France.[93]

To further guarantee white boys would receive a racially exclusive education, Creoles and their supporters also introduced a plan to send Creole boys to metropolitan France for their education. The equality espoused by the government, some Creoles argued, demanded the government provide not just assistance to the island's *gens de couleur* and enslaved population but also opportunities for Martinique's *petits blancs*. Wealthy Creole boys went to America, or England, or metropolitan France to school, but the island's poor white boys had few available options. To rectify this untenable situation, in the French Chambers and press, Martinique's colonial delegate, Dupin, called on continental "philanthropists" to look beyond the plight of the island's enslaved community and work toward "amelioration of the white race in the colonies." In addition to establishing a secondary school in the principal town of each colony and sufficient primary schools with teachers from metropolitan France, Creoles called for "young *colons* without fortune" to attend primary and secondary schools in France. After "being formed in spirit and heart in the bosom of the metropole," Dupin argued, these young men could then return to their respective colonies and function as teachers in the newly established educational institutions.[94] Although he does not say so explicitly, Dupin and his Creole supporters undoubtedly hoped these *petits blancs* would join the ranks of white instructors who, after matriculating in metropolitan educational institutions, taught in whites-only schools that directly undermined the government's attempts at racial fusion through public interracial schools.

Thwarting that goal became even more important to Creoles as those schools taught an increasing number of free and enslaved children of African descent. In addition to the two government-mandated schools that opened in the parishes of Fort and Mouillage near Saint Pierre in 1842, another opened a year later at Trinité, in the heart of the most productive sugar growing land on the island, with two nuns available to teach up to one hundred students.[95] According to Sister Onésime, the government was particularly interested in reopening these schools in the aftermath of a small earthquake in February 1843 to ensure officials did not "abandon these unfortunates to their (sad) state."[96] By the following year all of the schools had nearly full enrollment and, by requiring eight nuns to oversee their instruction, brought the Order 9,600 francs annually.[97]

Despite continued Creole attempts to derail it, the school begun by Madame Ballin and continued by Mademoiselle Garnerin also continued on. Garnerin took particular issue with the Private Councils' support of the whites-only girls' day school that the Sisters of Saint Joseph opened in Fort Royal and bitterly complained that the Order, "to whom everything is given freely by the government," and their school would put an end to her establishment.[98] She also resented a new Creole tactic to shut down her establishment, noting Fort Royal's Creole "chiefs" had made her "advantageous offers," including promising to send their children to a whites-only school she might create, on the condition that she "abandon her school for colored girls."[99] She and the school nonetheless persevered and she even managed to convince the Private Council, under threats from the Ministry of the Marine, to allocate 200 francs for her to purchase prizes, rosaries, crosses, and other images for her students who made themselves known through their "intelligence and good conduct."[100]

The creation of an interracial social group further threatened Creoles who opposed the metropolitan government's goal of racial integration between white and free mixed-race Martinicans. In May 1843, a group of lawyers, wealthy merchants, and midranking civil servants of various racial backgrounds obtained authorization from Martinique's governor to form an elite private club in Fort Royal. According to its organizers, this club had the purpose of "discussing newspapers and events of the days," and would meet at the residence of Monsieur Labadie.[101] Theoretically open to all races, the group listed three mixed-race men (two lawyers and one Navy clerk) as members of the society.[102] According to the *Journal du Havre*, however, which reported the story for its metropolitan audience in an attempt to show continued *gens de couleur* violence in the colonies, after a short period of operation three unknown mixed-race individuals appeared at Labadie's home, demanded to play billiards, and then refused to leave after Labadie informed them the club was private.[103] A crowd of primarily free mixed-race Martinicans then formed outside Labadie's place and some eventually forced their way inside the residence and "broke up everything in sight."[104] Police reports claimed the crowd severely wounded seven people inside, including Dame Charvin, a local Creole woman, her daughter, and their enslaved female servant, before a riot among the police, local whites, and some free mixed-race inhabitants erupted outside.[105]

In his description of the incident to his superiors in Paris, Governor Duvaldailly attempted to downplay the racial character of the incident, instead highlighting the differences in economic station between the club members and those looking for admittance. The mixed-race members of the private club came from the better educated and economically more prosperous ranks of the island's former *gens de couleur*, he noted, unlike those who rioted outside— primarily artisans of all racial backgrounds. For this reason the governor defended the elite Creole members of the social club to the minister of the marine and supported their actions against their perceived economic inferiors. He asked, "[Must] honorable people be forced to admit among them masons, shoemakers, tailors, and even unskilled laborers, just because they are free, when white people who exercise these same professions would be excluded?"[106] While the club's Creole members may have denied the men admittance due to their economic rather than racial status, those local white artisans who rioted outside did so, in part, because at least some mixed-race men gained admittance denied to them. Although, technically, race had long ceased to matter legally, for many white Martinicans on the island, and for their supporters in metropolitan France, it clearly factored into the scuffle outside Labadie's home and continued to do so in many other aspects of daily life.

The return of a number of now free mixed-race inhabitants to the island from continental France and other places around the Caribbean also contributed to increased hostilities toward the government's goal of racial fusion. Three former enslaved workers belonging to the Dessalles family joined those free mixed-race Martinicans returning to the island and, as the planter's diaries make clear, he looked on their renewed presence with concern. Calixte, a male enslaved domestic, had accompanied Dessalles's oldest son, Adrien, to metropolitan France in the 1820s and had remained there with the Dessalles family until the family returned to the island in 1840. Since that time, Pierre Dessalles had become a troublemaker, going so far as to approach the planter and demand an act of liberty that Dessalles had refused. Although Calixte had been "well-behaved" during his time in metropolitan France, Dessalles noted, after returning to the island, "he believed that a [1836] royal ordinance that granted liberty to all slaves who touched French soil applied to him." Pierre Dessalles was quite relieved when Governor Duvaldailly refused to grant Calixte's liberty, however, on the grounds that another law was in effect when Calixte originally had arrived in France and confirming that Calixte had "never ceased to be a slave."[107] Dessalles nonetheless deeply resented the domestic's actions and scolded the man's enslaved family for welcoming Calixte back to the island when he had gone behind Dessalles's back to obtain his freedom.[108]

Dessalles also worried about the recent arrival of another domestic, Saint-Fort. Saint-Fort, along with his enslaved brother and mother, had accompanied Pierre Dessalles to continental France in 1816 and had been reprimanded by Dessalles at the time for writing his mother, Fortunée, back in Martinique. After Dessalles's mother granted Saint-Fort his freedom in continental France and the new *homme de couleur* returned to Martinique in the mid-1820s, Dessalles found his behavior "criminal" and lamented his visits to Fortunée on the Dessalles family plantation. At the time Dessalles asked his diary "how can I prevent" such reunions.[109] As his diary reveals in 1843, he apparently had managed to do so by making Saint-Fort's official liberty contingent on the domestic's agreement to leave the island for Guadeloupe and to never return to the family plantation. Times had clearly changed, however, as evidenced by the fact that by 1843 Saint-Fort and his family had returned to Martinique from their exile in Guadeloupe and, much to Dessalles's chagrin, were looking for a house in nearby Sainte-Marie.[110] At approximately the same time, Honoré, the enslaved domestic who had accompanied Dessalles to continental France in 1822 and gained his freedom and a return to the island in 1823, also made his way back to Martinique. Based on his diary entries it appears Dessalles also made good on his earlier threats to exile him from the island, for he noted in 1843 that Honoré and his wife recently had returned to the northeastern part of the island after finding "only misery" in Trinidad where they had gone to seek their fortune.[111] The arrival of these former enslaved workers from locations around the Atlantic, and especially other Caribbean islands where freedom for all had been the rule for almost a decade, further worried *colons* like Dessalles who viewed their return as a dangerous spreading of the contagion of liberty.

In the wake of the Ministry of the Marine's decision to table the "sugar question" Creoles and their supporters once again invoked their shared French nationality and denounced the government for failing to support its own (white) citizens. This time, however, heightened concerns about the potential collapse of the sugar cane industry, and its devastating effects on port city commerce, motivated the chambers of commerce in Bordeaux and Nantes to resign over the Chambers' delay. In their petition to the national Chamber of Deputies, Bordeaux's chamber explicitly linked the ports and the colonies in the Chamber's recent act, underlining "the long agony of the sea ports and the colonies" in the history of the controversy and contending "the last sugar law, which leaves a difference of 22 francs per 100 kilograms in favor of indigenous [beet] sugar, has brought disastrous results for maritime merchants and the colonies."[112] Marseille's chamber of commerce also lamented the Chamber of Deputies' decision and, although they did not offer their resignations, they noted that leaving the law unchanged after so many promises to revise it would mean a loss of at least 3 million francs for merchants in Marseille alone.[113]

In addition to these resignations and similar shows of support, supporters of the sugar cane industry from around the French Atlantic also took their case to the broader French populace. Citing the confidence that those in places like Le Havre and Martinique had placed in their government, and the abuses that had repaid that trust, the editors of the *Journal du Havre* hoped to shame officials into reexamining the matter and rectifying the injustices faced by the sugar cane interests. They asserted, "commerce feels itself shamefully used by a power to which it gave itself with confidence," and contended, "one question above all others particularly occupies the sea ports: it is that of sugar, on which depends the existence of our colonies and our shipping."[114] In a letter to those same editors, a Creole planter claimed that by refusing to establish equivalent taxes on beet and colonial sugar the government had "sacrificed the great interests of the country and left the colonies to the possibility of the most dreadful catastrophe."[115] Should all go awry in the French West Indies, or in France's Atlantic port cities, this letter writer indicated, the metropolitan government would bear the blame.

Others suggested even more forcefully that stasis on the "sugar question" combined with recent laws regulating enslaved workers in the colonies and pushing ever closer to emancipation could only result in violence. The *Journal du Havre*'s story about the murder of a white plantation manager, Lapeyronnie, provided just one more example of how violent the colonial world could turn for white colonists. In the paper's fifteen-paragraph story recounting the case of Lucien, an enslaved Martinican who stood before the Assize Court accused of murdering Lapeyronnie, the first ten featured a gruesome portrait of the plantation manager's body at the time of its discovery in a shallow grave: "his face was disfigured by ten knife cuts, his jaw was bruised, and his head was almost detached from his body by a profound blow that had severed the spinal column." The remaining five paragraphs dealt with the information provided at trial by two investigating magistrates, the royal prosecutor, the judge, twenty-two witnesses, and the defense attorney and concluded with the reading of the verdict, which condemned Lucien to forced labor for life and one hour in the public stocks in Saint Pierre's public square. The major space devoted to the violence of the act, and the minor space given to the rest of the proceedings, exhibited Creoles' determination to publicize the suffering of the Creole above all else.[116]

Supporters of the plantation system also worked to counter continued attacks against Creole women, which they viewed as yet another attempt to cast doubt on Creole claims, in general, and to distance white colonists from the French national family at a moment of crisis. They took great offense at accounts published in the Martinican *homme de couleur* Bissette's *Revue des Colonies* and in particular to those which cast doubt on the sexual virtue of Creole women and thus the racial purity of the entire Creole population. Using Martinique's civil registers as evidence, in 1842 Bissette identified different phrases Martinican officials had historically used when registering Creole newborns, phrases that he argued showed not only that elites had long understood "white" as a fluid, problematic category, but also their ongoing struggles to stabilize it. Prior to the July Monarchy, official records always noted the race of an individual, except in the case of whites. In those cases, the record gave no racial designation, thus creating "white" as the norm that did not need referencing. As a result, Bissette argued, when officials did make reference to "whiteness," they were working to denote the relative purity of blood for off-spring born to white women and mixed-race men, an interracial relationship that Creoles denied ever had or would take place.

Bissette identified six different categories. The first, and presumably purest, form of whiteness, a *"blanc pur sang,"* or pure-blood white, indicated the offspring of a white woman and a white man, and suggested recognition of this status by one of the royal physicians.[117] The second category, *"blanc, sang mêlé,"* or white with mixed blood, apparently denoted "the mixture of a male quarteroon with a 'beautiful princess' with pure white blood."[118] A third category *"estimés blancs,"* or estimated white, identified a child "from the union of a white woman with a *mulatto* or one of the other varied nuances of the great family of *negroes*."[119] The fourth category, *"mulâtre-blanc,"* or mulatto-white, denoted a child of a white woman and a *"negro"* man.[120] The category *"jugé blanc,"* or judged white, included a child of indeterminate color and a scenario where "the royal physician waited a bit of time to see if, through his contacts in the world, he could determine which 'beautiful princess' had recently given birth to a child, [with] skin . . . a little darker than expected."[121] Finally, came the child *"paru blanc,"* or appearing white, who the royal physician placed "in the social order of colors in the colonies."[122] Because the royal physicians had complete discretion to decide which children would benefit and which would suffer from these designations, the complicated nomenclature they used mattered a great deal, as did notaries' willingness to use such phrases. Such a vast white conspiracy to claim racial purity and uphold white social superiority, Bissette implied, further called into question repeated Creole claims that by extending rights to *gens de couleur* or freedom to enslaved workers the government endangered the sexual virtue of Martinique's Creole women.

In response to such affronts, Creoles and their supporters again enlisted the services of Granier de Cassagnac who reiterated his claims that white women of the French West Indies would never even contemplate interracial sexual relationships. Again he argued, "with great care," that a *mulâtre* could only be "the son of a white man and a black woman," further insisting "for a white woman of the colonies, a negro has only been a very lazy African, fairly crude, not particularly clean, and of a rather suffocating odor . . . he is ridiculous or frightening." For these reasons, he contended, "the alliance between a white woman and a negro in the Antilles, therefore, is not something that could be discussed, even if it could be imagined."[123] In his efforts to save the myth of the chaste Creole woman, for his French metropolitan audience Granier de Cassagnac invoked a series of sexist and racist stereotypes about both Creole women and African men that actively ignored longstanding evidence of such interracial sexual relationships.

In this tome Granier de Cassagnac also hoped to draw on the racist assumptions of white metropolitan French by arguing that Creoles' intimate involvement with interracial mixing could prevent those on the continent from being duped by free-mixed-race individuals passing as white. Because they had lived daily with "blacks, *mulâtres*, and whites," he claimed, Creoles could accurately distinguish between whites and even light-skinned mixed-race individuals, and thus Creoles could help their fellow (white) citizens on the continent from falling prey to "those beautiful *mestives* and fashionable women among the bourgeoisie of Paris, . . . who would like to be indiscreet and chagrin the world."[124] By passing as white and moving freely amid an unsuspecting white French population, Granier de Cassagnac indicated, mixed-race women, in particular, could trap unsuspecting metropolitan Frenchmen into marriage, an outcome, he hoped, most metropolitan French would find unacceptable.

* * *

By early 1845 debates in the Chambers about emancipation centered on a number of critical issues: some form of government oversight of the punishment, feeding, and clothing of enslaved Martinicans; the creation of government officials to ensure such efforts; the extension of educational and spiritual instruction to the enslaved population; and monies for the shipment of continental white agricultural workers to the islands and a "buy back" clause if those white workers proved unsatisfactory.[125] On July 18 and 19, 1845, the Mackau laws finally put these measures—many of which had previously been mandated but ignored—into effect and went a step further by also legalizing *rachat* (self-purchase), with the stipulation that the enslaved person continue working for five years for his or her master, and legitimating *pécule* (legalized savings toward manumission).[126]

Martinique's Creoles and other supporters of the plantation system saw the Mackau laws as the ultimate attack on their rights as French citizens and their passage opened the definitive chasm among the island's *colons* and the island's new governor, contre-amiral Aimé Mathieu, and colonial administrators in metropolitan France. The planter Dessalles decried that the "horrible Mackau laws had been passed with an unspeakable levity," and further resented that the laws, named after then Minister of the Marine and former

Martinican Governor Ange-René Armand Mackau, significantly restructured the plantation system by newly mandating the treatment of enslaved people and providing for the new modes of manumission described above.[127] They also offered an incentive for new white field laborers by allocating 360,000 francs to support model farms that would encourage whites and free mixed-race individuals to work side-by-side in the fields. The plan would transform plantations previously owned by the government into new agricultural establishments that would serve as the home base for any white metropolitan workers who had contracted directly with the Ministry of the Marine, as well as for those free mixed-race individuals who could not contract with their former masters for the mandatory five years following their emancipation.[128] By setting aside an additional 120,000 francs, both to defray the initial costs (transportation and food) planters would incur by contracting with white metropolitan agricultural workers and to serve as insurance against any workers who, for whatever reason, might have to return to the continent, the Mackau laws further encouraged the establishment of such farms. Contracts between colonists and white workers required approval first by the municipal authority and then by the local mayor who, if he agreed to the arrangement, would then transmit the agreement to the Minister of the Marine so he could examine the contracts before allocating any money for white workers to travel across the Atlantic.[129]

Immediately after the passage of the Mackau laws, Creoles particularly resented *rachat* and *pécule* as government efforts to expand the methods of emancipation. By December 1845, however, the continued high prices (set, on average, at around 1,200 francs)[130] involved in purchasing freedom—whether negotiated amicably or through force—and the continued stipulation that an enslaved person stay with his or her master for five years of service, in many ways had weakened those provisions.[131] Nonetheless, most planters resented that, in the words of one Creole who complained to the daily *Mémorial Bordelais*, "without our agreement, without our participation . . . the government precipitates the running of things and the destruction of the colonies."[132]

Disagreements as to whether or not Martinique's planters should contract with white metropolitan workers further demonstrated divergent Creole views on racial integration in Martinique and revealed their continued desperation to maintain white social hegemony in the face of emancipation. By allocating money to support racially integrated model farms in the Mackau laws, metropolitan colonial officials had come full circle. At the colony's founding in the mid-seventeenth century, *engagés* had performed the majority of agricultural work until replaced by enslaved African laborers with the introduction of labor-intensive sugar cultivation in the eighteenth century. Creoles saw the 1845 encouragement for white and free mixed-race Martinicans to work side-by-side on the plantations as a return to the seventeenth century and a degrading prospect that threatened the plantation system's very foundations. In the face of what they saw as the increasing erosion of white social and legal privilege, most elite Creoles thought keeping whites, even poor ones, from highly visible manual labor, like toiling in the sugar fields, essential to maintaining the integrity of white identity. As a result, initially most *colons* adamantly opposed any such effort to transport white metropolitan workers. Although undoubtedly many factors contributed to the colonists' unwillingness to hire such workers, even the minister of the marine indicated the principal cause for white planters' reluctance to hire such workers lay in "the repugnance that the *mélange* of workers of different origins, in principle, could inspire in them."[133]

In the increasingly fragile economic environment, however, some Creoles put aside their earlier arguments about white peoples' supposed physical unsuitability for working in the Caribbean sugar fields and looked once again to white metropolitan labor. Undoubtedly the uncertainty of a post-emancipation labor supply together with the ongoing numerical superiority of the island's free mixed-race population vis-à-vis the white population also contributed to their change of heart. In 1845, the white population had increased to 9,219; the free mixed-race population, however, had risen to 37,213 and outnumbered Martinique's whites more than four to one.[134] An influx of white workers could help to restore that balance, some believed, and potentially act as a buffer between the free populations and the nearly 76,042 enslaved Martinicans.[135] But contracting with white workers meant breaking with longstanding tradition about social distinctions and incurring the wrath of fellow Creoles. It also implied that, given the current situation, the colonies might just decay into a dumping ground for the metropole's surplus population, a status for the island that Creoles had fought against since long before the July Monarchy.

Even before the formal implementation of the Mackau laws, pehaps looking to benefit from any financial assistance they could find if emancipation came without indemnity, at least two Martinican planters acted on rumors that the government might provide monies to import white agricultural workers. One, St. Croix, proposed establishing a model farm run by metropolitan agriculturalists who would have a fixed contract for eighteen months and a guaranteed return to France if they could not make it in the colony. In his direct correspondence with the minister of the marine, St. Croix identified the ideal candidate as "a good agriculturalist [who] understands hard work and already has at least two years of practical experience."[136] Clearly he wanted metropolitan workers who knew how to farm, and not just continental whites who wanted free passage to the colony. DeHuc, a plantation owner from Case-Navire, also sought government help to secure and maintain between eighty and one hundred white metropolitan cultivators. In particular, he looked to obtain 225,000 francs (to build houses and to pay passage from continental France to Martinique), as well as an extra allotment for food to sustain the workers on arrival. These workers would take over complete cultivation of his plantation crops and serve as a private version of the proposed government-owned model farm.[137] Monsieur Titalin's request provided tangible evidence of the extent of the French Atlantic network and die-hard links to the French Empire. In his letter to the minister of the marine from his home in St. Louis, Missouri, Titalin espoused his support for abolition and his desire to "continue to be a French citizen," as his family had been since leaving the French Atlantic port city of La Rochelle. With the funds available for new model farms, he assured the ministry, he would establish "a rural farm based on the remunerated labor of free individuals."[138] Ultimately the ministry referred all of the men to Martinique's colonial administrators who would have to first approve any such plans. Their requests nonetheless indicate some white French colonists were willing to think the previously unthinkable.

The Ministry of the Marine hoped the monies allocated by the Mackau laws would help "the *colons* to successfully fight against the prejudice which made consideration of employing whites in rural work absolutely irreconcilable with the physical obstacles of the climate." Likewise they looked for the laws to "put an end to the hesitations that other proprietors might have . . . in taking on the expenses" necessary to contract with white metropolitan workers.[139] Although not many took advantage of the available funds, those who did provided further evidence that in the new economic and political climate even the most fervent proslavery supporters could reconsider their previous stances.[140] Cassius de Linval, a member of one of Martinique's wealthiest and most established planter families, a former municipal councilor, and head of a whites-only school extolled by Pierre Dessalles in the late 1830s, was one of those men. In the fall of 1845, he requested government permission and funds to recruit 25 to 30 white metropolitan laborers for his 146 hectare plantation near Macouba where he cultivated sugar, coffee, and foodstuffs.[141] While Governor Mathieu supported Cassius de Linval's efforts, securing the funds for such an endeavor involved sustained efforts from family members on both sides of the Atlantic. Nearly a year after his original request, Cassius de Linval's

son took time away from his law studies in Nantes to contact the minister of
the marine and secure a meeting to discuss his father's application.[142]

In addition to bureaucratic intransigence—extensive red tape lay between
the applicant and the money—the delay in this request undoubtedly also reflected the economic crisis that France, as a whole, faced in 1845 and 1846. As a
number of letters from white metropolitan men residing in continental France
reveal, the recent economic troubles had inspired many to consider making
the journey to Martinique to escape the financial troubles on the continent
and to find a new life for themselves and their families in the French West Indies. Despite an outpouring of interest in securing possible agricultural work
on the island, colonial administrators in metropolitan France apparently had
learned from their previous attempts in the early years of the Restoration to
send white workers to Martinique. In anticipation of elite Creoles' objections
to single white men, among the "fairly numerous" petitions for transport to
Martinique, the Ministry of the Marine only seriously considered those from
complete families.[143] Extolling the merits of sending white families to work in
the colonies, the ministry noted "the family is a guarantee of good conduct
and morality, and it is important that the emigrants are not obliged to separate
from one another."[144]

For this reason the ministry at least responded to Jean St. Nicosse's letter requesting passage for six to the French West Indies. St. Nicosse apparently had learned from "numerous people" of "lots of land to cultivate" in the
colonies and he wanted to travel there with his wife and four children to take
advantage of the opportunity.[145] Although the ministry informed St. Nicosse
that they could only note his request at that time, by early 1846 at least two
different transports of workers had sailed for Trinité, Martinique, destined to
work as mechanics in the sugar-processing foundry of Messieurs Gaste and
Cie. While officials originally intended the monies only for agricultural work,
because of the importance of the processing foundry to the sugar cane industry, and undoubtedly because enslaved laborers usually performed such work,
the ministry made an exception.[146] The minister of the marine also passed
along additional requests for transport to the colonies' metropolitan delegates
in Paris who could serve as "natural intermediaries" to make arrangements
between continental petitioners and French West Indian planters.[147]

The perceived danger that whites and people of African descent working
side-by-side in manual labor posed for the social hierarchy further inspired
Creoles to keep the island's private and public schools racially segregated in
practice. By 1845, only thirty private institutions, virtually all of them racially
segregated, operated with and without the consent of the government.[148] Fort

Royal boasted one private school for white boys and in Sainte-Marie the "fathers of families" created a whites-only school for their sons. Olivié also taught the white planters' boys in the southeastern commune of Saint-Esprit and in Gros-Morne Mouton taught twenty-three white boys.[149] White laywomen also operated three institutions for Creole girls. DeJean instructed fifteen white girls in one of the three private institutions in Gros-Morne and Demoiselle Touin ran a private school for white girls in Saint-Esprit.[150] In Trinité, Amélie Bellefontaine née Villeneuve instructed sixteen Creole girls at the only private institution in the area. In 1838, before her marriage, Villeneuve had opened a boarding school for young girls in Trinité, and three years later was best known for teaching music at her establishment. By 1845, however, she had married Bellefontaine, himself a music teacher who had once tuned the Dessalles family piano, and the two found much success in instructing Creole girls as evidenced by the permission they received from Martinique's Private Council to transfer their boarding school from Trinité to Saint Pierre.[151]

Although some Creole families contented themselves with private secular education for their daughters, most still looked to the Sisters of Saint Joseph to provide their daughters with traditional parochial instruction. The tumultuous economic climate on the island following rumor and then passage of the Mackau laws, however, seriously complicated instruction. As Sister Onésime told her superiors in continental France: "The Mackau Law has created dismay on the island and everyone fears disorder on the plantations and bankruptcy that will ruin commerce. Even if the damage is less than expected, everyone worries payments will be suspended and credit interrupted." As a result, even though the Saint Pierre Royal School for Girls had as many students as the previous year, none of them had paid their fees.[152] In response to the economic crisis, and "to assist those families who desire that their children be religiously educated," the *pensionnat* thus decided to once again lower their tuition for the more than one hundred students then attending the school.[153]

A ministerial dispatch in mid-1846 that enjoined the Order to accept free mixed-race girls at the *pensionnat* stunned the Sisters of Saint Joseph in Martinique and the Creoles who looked to the Order to maintain racially segregated schools. It set off internal fights within the Order over the nuns' responsibility to Martinique's inhabitants, to the Order, and to the colonial administration. When she learned of the news, just a year after passage of the Mackau laws, Sister Onésime informed the head of the Order in continental France that racial integration would mean the end of the institution "because white families will never permit their daughters to be in such close contact with *filles de couleur . . .* [and] on their admission not a single white girl will remain in the establishment."[154] By threatening to destroy not only the boarding school but also the other schools that depended on the success of the *pensionnat* for financial assistance, the directive endangered all of the Order's work, Sister Onésime lamented, just as they approached the "apogee of glory."[155] She further chastised the head of the Sisters of Saint Joseph, Sister Anne-Marie Javouhey, for ever agreeing to support such a plan (which a paragraph in the dispatch indicated she clearly had) and urged her to force the ministry to delay any changes in the boarding school's enrollment policy.[156]

Although she worried about how racial integration would affect the Order's finances in Martinique and their efforts on the continent, Sister Onésime also believed allowing *filles de couleur* into the Sisters of Saint Joseph's boarding school would incite conflict between Creoles and the mixed-race population and told Sister Anne-Marie Javouhey if the government wanted a fight, this measure was precisely what they needed.[157] She refrained from implicating Creoles in this potential violence, however, and her racist stereotypes of free mixed-race individuals further revealed how twenty years in the colony had aligned her with the *colons* who brought the Order success. According to Sister Onésime, racial integration would be particularly devastating for the *classe blanche*, especially at a moment when many of those families were experiencing financial calamity, whereas it would simply be another way for *gens de couleur* to flaunt another newly acquired right and further increase their pride.[158] "Once their pride is satisfied" by admitting even twenty students into the boarding school, she claimed, the rest would be more than happy "to return to the free schools run by the same teachers, allowing [those mixed-race families] to return to other luxuries" they displayed as evidence of their wealth. As for those Creoles who would no longer attend the school, she claimed, what were the nuns to do "when [they] saw [white] families with six, eight, or ten children on the verge of being deprived of an education?"[159]

In addition to complaining loudly to the Sisters of Saint Joseph and Governor Mathieu about the dispatch, as they had so many times before Creoles again sought a way around the newly proposed measure. Out of fear they might lose the Saint Pierre Royal School for Girls as one of the last institutions exclusively for whites, a number of Martinique's *colons* approached Sister Onésime to determine if the Order might provide a dozen or so nuns who, separate from the Order and free from government control, could open a private day school for white girls in Fort Royal. Because the Creoles agreed to pay for the nuns' passage and also provide a facility for instruction, Sister Onésime strongly encouraged the head of the Order to consider the request, at least temporarily, arguing "you know that time improves ideas [and] in making this concession to [Creole] families we would have the advantage of guiding them a little in their future paths."[160] With her knowledge of the Order's finances on the island, Sister Onésime undoubtedly also hoped to make certain any money these families spent to educate their daughters went to the Sisters of Saint Joseph.

Ultimately the Sisters of Saint Joseph and the Creole families who looked to them for instruction avoided making a decision about how to handle racial integration at the boarding school, when Sister Anne-Marie Javouhey managed to convince the Ministry of the Marine to delay such changes.[161] Although she averted any immediate crisis on the issue, in her correspondence with others, the head of the Order expressed her concern with Sister Onésime's close attachments with the island's Creole elite. Because the Sisters of Saint Joseph ultimately depended on the metropolitan government for support, both in the colony and on the continent, she worried Sister Onésime and the other nuns in Martinique "forget where they come from . . . and where they are going. . . . Dear Lord! It is difficult not to take on the spirit of the world that one lives in."[162]

Continued fears about racial integration, and the increasingly dire economic climate, brought only forty students to the boarding school when it opened its doors in 1847.[163] In February, however, the Order struck a deal with the government ensuring the Saint Pierre Royal School for Girls would remain a whites-only institution accepting only Creole pupils who could pay tuition or at least 800 francs. In return the nuns agreed to establish a new boarding school that would accept "without distinction of color, all young honest people, according to the intentions of the government."[164] After being assured the *pensionnat* would not accept free mixed-race girls in the near future, Martinique's elite Creole families returned their daughters to the school and by the end of February the boarding school had returned to its glory, teaching eighty-four Creole girls and helping the nuns send just more than 12,000 francs back to continental France despite the economic downturn.[165] Between their various institutions, the Sisters of Saint Joseph now would provide educational opportunities for all of the island's children, though certainly not the racial fusion that the metropolitan government had envisioned.

Although Martinique's Creoles managed to retain the Saint Pierre Royal School for Girls and its day schools for whites-only, other private schools for free mixed-race boys and girls flourished. Fort Royal, for example, had two private schools for free mixed-race children run by free mixed-race adults, and in Gros-Morne Edgard Clement taught twenty boys and girls of African descent[166] In Saint Pierre Miot taught the commune's free mixed-race girls and Testut taught young mixed-race boys.[167] An incident involving the white Testut nonetheless further demonstrates both the lengths to which Creoles would go to condemn any whites who supported Martinique's free mixed-race community and the ways Martinique's colonial administrators continued to support Creole goals for white social hegemony.

On December 10, 1845, a fight broke out in Saint Pierre's public square between one of Testut's mixed-race students and a student from the whites-only boys school in Sainte-Marie. The scuffle, which witnesses claimed began when one of Testut's students hit a Creole boy, attracted as many as four hundred people, including the *homme de couleur* Léonce who had once stood accused of assassination in the summer of 1833, and who in 1845 reportedly wanted to "strike a policeman with a club" for manhandling *gens de couleur*. Witnesses further described Testut, a white who had arrived on the island six years before from Guadeloupe, as "incensed" by the incident and "exasperated to have been isolated by the white population." Because Martinique's *colons* claimed Testut's students had repeatedly provoked Creole boys in the past, Governor Mathieu had no trouble believing the witnesses claims, he informed the Ministry of the Marine, and found Testut's actions, and especially his shouts at the police, inexcusable.[168]

Testut's private and public behavior, Creoles further complained to Governor Mathieu, placed him well beyond the boundaries of appropriate white male behavior and justified his removal as headmaster of Saint Pierre's secondary institution for free mixed-race boys. According to rumors Monsieur Testut had been born in continental France and had come to the French West Indies as a young man in 1828. For the next ten years, he spent his time in Guadeloupe, where for five years he headed a secondary institution for white boys. After arriving in Martinique in 1839, Testut had established a secondary institution in Saint Pierre for "children of all colors," but it had enrolled exclusively free mixed-race boys. Ongoing prejudices about the mixing of whites and free mixed-race Martinicans had produced the de facto segregation, Testut later informed the minister of the marine, and "only caste prejudices prevented me from having white children, fusion had not happened yet."[169] Concerns that Creoles voiced to Governor Mathieu suggest they had other worries, too, however.

Apparently elite Creoles had regarded Testut with suspicion from the moment he arrived on the island and viewed his instruction of free mixed-race boys as a betrayal of white identity. As a result, they did what they could to remove him from his position of authority and to exile him more generally from white Martinican society by accusing him of sexual immorality and link-ing him both to mixed-race women and to domestic violence. Since coming to Martinique with his wife, who many dismissed as nothing more than his "concubine," Testut had appeared twice before Saint Pierre's Tribunal charged with "immorality," the first time for supposedly beating Demoiselle Melanie, a free mixed-race woman, and the second time for a public fight with Dumores, who had accused Testut of having had "relations" with Dumores's wife.[170] "If rumors spoke the truth," Governor Mathieu informed the minister of the marine, Testut had continued his "scandalous conduct" by living publicly with a Dame Carbonne. If such evidence did not compel one to consider revoking Testut's right to teach, Governor Mathieu concluded, his response to the director of the interior's question about his conduct did; when questioned about his conduct, Testut told the official "his private life was no one's business."[171] Although Testut may have believed that to be the case, Creoles clearly had other opinions, and even Governor Mathieu felt his impertinence merited depriving him of his livelihood as a teacher on the island.

In addition to their denunciation of Testut's personal conduct, elite Creoles also viewed his education of Saint Pierre's free mixed-race boys as a threat to public tranquility and characterized it as such to the island's colonial administrators. They particularly worried that Testut's refusal to instruct his pupils in appropriate deference to the white population would further undermine eroding white status. Given the tenuous nature of their position, and the outright assault Creoles saw in the Mackau laws, Testut's behavior seemed particularly ill advised. It undermined Creoles' claims about the possibility of nonviolent racial integration and showed all too clearly that Testut, and no doubt more and more others, would not help police those racial boundaries that elites had perpetually viewed as crucial to white social status.

Ultimately Governor Mathieu, prompted in part by the Ministry of the Marine, did not remove Testut from his position as he desired and as elites demanded. Arguing that it would create "too much controversy" to revoke Testut's ability to teach, instead he decided to monitor the teacher's behavior and informed the minister of the marine if Testut did not change his "scandalous ways," the governor would take action against him. Such a removal did not happen. In fact, just two weeks after the scuffle, Governor Mathieu personally visited Testut's school and, undoubtedly in an effort to convince colonial administrators in metropolitan France that he did all he could to assure "racial fusion" in Martinique, he did so even though such a visit violated "the mores and prejudices then existing among the Creoles."[172]

Despite such continued prejudices, Martinique's *colons* ultimately lost their battle with Garnerin and her Fort Royal school of mutual instruction for free girls. She persevered in her efforts to provide interracial education in the face of repeated meddling and Creole pleas for her to teach only the island's Creole girls and, with the help of the Ministry of the Marine, finally forced the Private Council to grant her a 360 francs allocation for a second instructor for the school.[173] She also eventually opened a class for enslaved children and received a 3,700 francs increase for the school's annual budget and a one-time sum of 1,260 francs for materials. Although the class for enslaved children ultimately did not succeed as hoped, the interracial institution continued to flourish and Garnerin proceeded with her instruction there until her death "from a grave intestinal inflammation, the result of her assiduous work," in 1857.[174]

In the five years before the passage of the Mackau laws, Martinique alone had spent approximately 964,715 francs to facilitate the "moralization" of the enslaved population, increase the number of priests, erect rural churches and chapels, send Brothers and Sisters of religious orders to provide free education, and increase the number of government magistrates specifically working in the enslaved population's best interests; despite all of this the island had made little progress toward offering free education, in general, and had opened only three schools through the Sisters of Saint Joseph.[175] Consequently, beginning in early 1845, Governor Mathieu repeatedly asked the Sisters of Saint Joseph to supply an ever increasing number of nuns for public educational institutions around the island.[176] Because of the Order's dependence on the government, Sister Onésime noted, she believed it prudent to provide more teachers, if at all possible, or risk losing the opportunity, and revenue, to other religious orders.[177] Although such instruction was difficult—often the "children" were adults who did not even know their letters, Sister Onésime claimed—after much prompting the Sisters opened two new free schools in 1846, one in Marin with three teachers for 125 children, the other in Fort (a parish of Saint Pierre) with three teachers for 300 children.[178]

Although the free schools run by the Order technically admitted all Martinican children, as suggested above, in practice they taught almost exclusively enslaved people. After the schools opened in Marin and Fort, however, the Sisters confronted the question of whether or not free mixed-race individuals might also attend. In raising her concerns about the dangers of admitting *filles de couleur* into the Saint Pierre Royal School for Girls, Sister Onésime argued greed ultimately would drive free mixed-race parents to seek refuge in the free schools to avoid paying the boarding school's tuition. As of late 1846, however, she indicated the nuns remained uncertain whether or not *gens de couleur* would even request enrollment in the Order's free schools but assured her superiors in continental France that, unless the minister of the Marine reconsidered his directive, the nuns would be forced to accept them in the government-supported free academies.

Many of Martinique's mayors, on the other hand, claimed that *gens de couleur* absolutely refused to attend the free schools. Whereas Sister Onésime argued that free mixed-race individuals would opt to send their children to free rather than tuition-based schools, Creoles argued that because newly emancipated Martinicans did not want to associate with enslaved people, the island's free secular schools had failed and indicated the religious ones probably would, too. Martinique's *gens de couleur*, rather than Creoles, they claimed, actually provided the biggest obstacle to interracial education. Some, like the mayor of Rivière-Salée and Trois-Ilets, contended the free secular schools failed because "the newly emancipated . . . [who] generally consider laziness as the first benefit of liberty, do not see the need for labor, and have no desire to give any skills to their children," while the mayor of Trinité claimed, "these schools are frequented exclusively by children of color, who would desert the day that *une esclave* was admitted there." In Gros Morne, the mayor indicated, "the child of color does not come to sit at the same bench as the white and both [the mixed-race and white child] have a repugnance to have *un esclave* as a classmate. It is prejudice!" Likewise the mayor of Rivière-Pilote asserted, "the spirit and the mores of the population do not permit the hope for this fusion, not only because the white children are not joined with those of color, but because the *gens de couleur* feel even more revulsion in sending their children to a school where slaves are admitted."[179] Even Governor Mathieu claimed, "[while] the white class preserves unfortunate prejudices . . . people belonging to the ancient class of color [feel] the same . . . invincible repugnance to see their children mixed with slaves and sitting on the same bench with them."[180] Whether through the prejudice of Creoles or *gens de couleur*, free and enslaved Martinicans would not attend the same schools these officials contended.

Such disagreements over who could and would attend the island's government-supported public schools coincided with intensified debates in continental France about whether or not emancipation should be gradual—taking place over a series of years with a transitional period—or immediate—completely dismantled with one fatal blow. As it became clearer that the provisions of the Mackau laws, and especially those designed to facilitate manumission, remained poorly enforced, an extensive petitioning campaign developed on the continent and proved more organized and effective than previous efforts to mobilize public opinion.[181] Emancipation, sooner rather than later, now appeared a real possibility and with it Creole power seemed all but lost. Nonetheless in response French West Indian Creoles, especially those in Paris, once again tried to unify an increasingly divided Creole community.

This community included the Dessalles family, which had returned to continental France in August 1844, and their story provides a sustained look at how Creoles and their metropolitan supporters responded to the last days of slavery in the French Empire. After the family's arrival, they spent much of their time in Bordeaux and in Paris where at least seventy-five other French West Indian planters spent their days extolling their commitment to plantation slavery.[182] In light of the increasing hostility Creoles felt from metropolitan French, undoubtedly the Dessalles found comfort and safety with others who also publicly announced their commitment to the plantation system. Sporting mixed-race servants, all of whom were free after 1836, remained one of the most visible markers of Creole identity and the majority of colonists who the family visited employed at least one mixed-race domestic.[183] This included the Dessalles family for, even before departing Martinique, Dessalles lamented, "I will have difficulty letting whites wait on me" in the metropole "habituated as I am to the service of my domestics who care for me with such affection."[184] As a result, Nicaise, Pierre Dessalles's twenty-eight-year-old *mulatto* servant, once again accompanied the family on their trip.

Dessalles's extended stay in Martinique, and the very different racial sensibility that he had developed there, once again gave him a visceral longing for the island while in continental France, one that left him feeling even more alienated from his wife and children as the plantation system came under more heated attack. He undoubtedly believed that having Nicaise along would mitigate some of that anxiety and evoke if not a sense of "home," at least a sense of normalcy and comfort otherwise missing for the West Indian planter in metropolitan France. The markedly different way that servants on the continent functioned in comparison to enslaved or free mixed-race servants in Martinique, however, worried Dessalles. He fretted when Nicaise returned home inebriated and unrepentant and failed to believe Anna Dessalles when she accused Nicaise and a fifty-five-year-old female cook of having "carnal relations" even though Dessalles had warned his servant to behave with caution.[185] Such liberties undoubtedly reminded Dessalles of the immense changes that had taken place even since his 1838 visit and foreshadowed what abolition would bring to the colonies.

While Dessalles clearly approved of having mixed-race servants, because of the renewed attacks on Creole behavior, he openly criticized Creoles he viewed as too lenient or intimate with those servants. Increased questions about Creole women's sexuality and how the plantation system corrupted white women also prompted him to harshly rebuke Creole women who transgressed the ideal prescribed for them either by too freely associating with mixed-race individuals or suggesting racial mixing through their appearance. Even his relative Madame Le Vassor was not immune from his tirades. On one visit Dessalles complained because she insisted on being taken to the theater in Paris, "surrounded by three *negro* domestics!" and further despaired because her assistant, Monsieur Lescuyer, allowed her such behavior, offering proof, Dessalles believed, that the man wanted "to ruin her."[186] Dessalles also criticized widow Desbrosses and her daughter, distant Martinican relatives who visited with the family shortly after arriving on the continent. Dessalles called the widow "a good woman," but thought "her manners . . . too creole; she is heavy and brown."[187] Her weight seemed to mirror continental stereotypes of Creole women laying around in hammocks and, although his comments about her darkened skin may have referred to too much time in the Martinican sun, his near obsession with racial mixing suggests he also may have thought her "not quite white." If others thought the same, he feared, this would only confirm rumors then circulating about white Martinican women's sexual preferences.

Dessalles may have found his female relatives' association with mixed-race individuals particularly threatening at this moment because the women in his immediate family had also gone beyond prescribed ideals of appropriate behavior by taking over the family finances. Since arriving back on the continent, Dessalles decried the amount of money it required to maintain the family in metropolitan France and he blamed his wife and daughters for the financial hardship. Since selling the family estate, Lespinassat, nearly twenty years before, the Dessalles no longer owned property on the continent and he was dismayed, for it meant a series of expensive rents in Paris, in particular, where his wife and daughters insisted on staying. Although not long after their return to the continent Anna Dessalles declared she wanted to buy property in metropolitan France, Dessalles responded that he "wanted to die in Martinique."[188] Clearly at an impasse about their future plans, for the next two years the family lingered in Paris, despite its expense and despite Dessalles's increasing desperation to return to the French West Indies rather than "eat badly and suffer privations of every kind."[189] Although in the 1820s he believed Paris too dangerous for enslaved workers, by the 1840s he found it cold and expensive.

Dessalles did not enjoy Paris and increasingly lost significant sums of money that he did not have while gambling with other Creoles. Anna Dessalles and other female members of the family, on the other hand, busied themselves with business and domestic matters both in Martinique and on the continent through the Creole network facilitated by Creole women. From her permanent home in Poitiers, for example, Madame Le Vassor made plans to build a 150,000 francs sugar processing plant on her Martinican planta-tion.[190] Anna Dessalles tried to secure her youngest son, Henri's, future career by writing to an old friend, and the wife of a well-connected official in Caen, to request employment for the young man.[191]

By early 1846, however, life would change dramatically for the Dessalles. Their relative, Madame Le Vassor, died in April, leaving nearly 200,000 francs behind. Although they had experienced their differences, based on their long-standing relationship Dessalles expected to receive some kind of inheritance. At the reading of her will, however, he was shocked to learn that Le Vassor had left her assistant, Lescuyer, 60,000 francs, and that the man legally had claim to another 110,000 francs in property. As for the rest of the money, Le Vassor's two grandchildren received 20,000 francs, Dessalles received 6,000 francs, and each of the three mixed-race domestics who had shocked Dessalles by accompanying their mistress to the theater got 1,000 francs.[192] Dessalles was deeply disappointed and angry.

Then, just three days after the Ministry of the Marine yet again prescribed religious and elementary education for the enslaved workers in the West In-dies in response to increased criticism in the Chamber, Anna Dessalles died of consumption at age fifty-four.[193] Thus irony beset the Dessalles family: as Pierre Dessalles's disenchantment with life in continental France increased, Anna Dessalles, who loved France, died there, leaving behind nearly 200,000 francs in assets and Dessalles theoretically free to return to the Martinique for which he often yearned.[194] His children in Martinique and metropolitan France, however, had other ideas. They wanted his property on the island, but not him, which left him stuck in metropolitan France as the plantation system came under even harsher public scrutiny.

At the time of Anna Dessalles's death, Pierre Dessalles still owned the family's Martinican sugar and coffee plantations.[195] Within a month that had changed, however, and apparently because of his daughters' concern for the family fortune. Just six months before her death, Anna Dessalles received a letter from Jacques Languavant-Cléret, her son-in-law's brother, expressing the girls' opinion that Pierre Dessalles should surrender his property for the sake of his family. Languavant-Cléret also informed Anna Dessalles that he "would be happy to be able to contribute to [her] happiness" in any way possible.[196] Not surprisingly, Pierre Dessalles did not warm to this suggestion. After the death of his wife, however, he changed his mind. In June 1846, he sold La Nouvelle Cité to his children in exchange for an annuity of 6,000 francs and from that time forward his unmarried daughters, Antoinette and Emilie, took a keen interest in the details of the family's affairs around the Atlantic and most certainly right before their eyes.[197] Almost immediately after taking financial control, they encouraged their father to send Nicaise back to Martinique because of his behavior.[198] Although Dessalles refused—Nicaise, like Pierre Dessalles, stayed in metropolitan France until November 1847—the planter felt increasingly estranged from his daughters and troubled by the family finances.

Tensions between father and children increased as the revenues of the plantation plummeted in response to the economic crisis then gripping all of France and the especially dire colonial markets following the Mackau laws. By the end of the year the Dessalles, like many other Creole families, struggled to stave off bankruptcy. In response, it appears, Antoinette Dessalles looked to marry her brother-in-law's brother, Jacques Languavant-Cléret.[199] Dessalles opposed the marriage, in part because of Languavant-Cléret's suggestion regarding the Dessalles plantation, but also because the man clearly lacked enough money to save the family. Consequently Dessalles told Antoinette he would only grant permission after she "had taken the time to reflect on such foolishness."[200] But the Dessalles family lacked money, too, and therefore, Dessalles admitted, Antoinette had limited choices. After much delay, he finally consented to what he called this "most miserable marriage in the world," wondering if, without money, and "today, with her white hair and changed as she is, would [Antoinette] find a [truly] rich man?"[201]

When the Chamber of Peers, calling for more time for the Mackau laws to take effect, rejected thousands of petitions for immediate emancipation in early 1847, Dessalles and colonial planters savored a temporary victory.[202] Even the fearful prospect of emancipation only temporarily delayed could not induce unanimity among French West Indian Creoles, however, and this minor encouragement reinvigorated some Creoles' efforts to delay emancipation as long as possible. Following passage of the Mackau laws, French West Indians and their supporters had met more frequently in Paris to discuss not only what Dessalles referred to as the "atrocious Mackau laws" but also to create a coherent response to the evolving debates on emancipation.[203] Division, however, emerged between those who favored immediate abolition with a significant indemnity for planters and those who thought delaying the inevitable the best strategy. Because many, like Dessalles, believed that the Mackau laws had proven largely ineffective in practice, they suggested staying the course. The split, however, made it difficult for both groups to effectively make their case, leading Dessalles to lament after one contentious meeting with Guadeloupe's delegate to the Chambers, "the greatest misfortune of the colonists is that they do not speak with one voice."[204] Without a united front, he worried, Creoles stood to lose everything and would continue to be belittled by the metropolitan French who Dessalles held so dear.

After the death of his wife and his estrangement from his family, Dessalles found metropolitan French disdain of West Indian planters so worrisome that he even suggested he might accept the idea of association—providing enslaved workers their cabins, a portion of land, one day a week off, and a third of the plantation's net revenue—if this would appease the continental French: "one would quickly adopt this path, if it would give us peace and if, especially, the colonists would cease to be considered as pariahs," he confessed.[205] Even the suggestion of such a concession marked a significant shift for Dessalles. Previously he had steadfastly asserted the property rights of colonial planters and vehemently opposed any efforts by individuals or the government to modify the plantation system. That he would entertain such a change to avoid being considered a pariah suggests just how much his world had changed.

News that the Chamber of Deputies ran counter to the Chamber of Peers and overwhelmingly voted to have the abolition petitions referred to the cabinet and minister further changed Dessalles world. So did their criticism of colonial officials for failing to administer appropriate justice for enslaved people and their decision to allocate 400,000 francs to help enslaved workers in the French West Indies buy their own freedom.[206] In response, Dessalles and other Creoles met with Martinique's lobbyist to the Chambers, Jollivet, and like so many times in the past, decided to use the metropolitan press to respond to the "calumnies" voiced against them in the Chamber of Deputies. As Dessalles noted in his diary, at the meeting "we recognized the only way to defend the colonies was the press . . . it governs public opinion."[207] In the middle of gearing up the proslavery press, however, the sand beneath Creoles' feet shifted once again when Minister of the Marine Mackau resigned, supposedly in protest over what he saw as a betrayal by Prime Minister Guizot. Arguing that he could no longer assist the colonies in the current political situation, Mackau claimed, "he could not consent to be a part of and to cooperate in the destruction of our overseas possessions."[208] Clearly, for Mackau, the idea that emancipation might come, and without indemnity, distressed him as it did other Creoles and their supporters.

When the colonists gathered again in Paris less than two weeks later they decided to demand colonial representation in the Chambers, something long denied them because in practice the franchise in the French West Indies remained the exclusive preserve of a small number of the minority white population. At their meeting Creoles also decided to "spread throughout France" the results of an investigation, funded by the proslavery lobby, that refuted charges recently made against them in the Chambers. Before adjourning they also agreed to establish a club where all of the Creoles from the different colonies could meet. Such "reunions of Creoles," Dessalles concluded, "can only produce a good effect."[209]

*   *   *

By the summer of 1847, Pierre Dessalles, like many of the Creoles with whom he met in Paris, faced an increasingly dire financial situation. In June he noted, "my family's financial affairs are frightening . . . .The Martinican creditors are unhappy . . . the sugar has stopped . . . staples are horribly expensive and sugar is at a very low price."[210] Two months later, during a conversation with a recently arrived Martinican Creole, Dessalles learned the revenues from his family plantations had fallen so low that creditors threatened to stop all credit; he also came to understand his overseer at La Nouvelle-Cité had so antagonized his enslaved laborers that they refused to work and Dessalles risked losing all source of revenue.[211] Less than a week later, another Creole told him his daughter had written a family friend and claimed that Dessalles's creditors in Martinique opposed his return to the plantation.[212] To add insult to injury, she also indicated the 500 francs monthly income his family had promised in return for selling his sugar plantation to them would fall to 200 francs a month. Given this economic situation, it is perhaps not surprising that emancipation with indemnity increasingly appealed to him.

By the fall Dessalles's position became even more unbearable for him, and he felt "extremely humiliated" at accepting a 1,500 francs loan from a fellow Creole in Paris.[213] Undoubtedly to avoid a similar scene, Dessalles sold his furniture, including his clock, to a local merchant for 869 francs, but once again ended up at the same Creole friend's house where he "was forced to accept" 500 francs. Dessalles accepted the money, he claimed, with the intention of giving it to his son Adrien.[214] Shortly thereafter, he did in fact give Adrien 20 francs but failed to mention the other 480 francs.[215] Finally, after months of debate and despite the misgivings of his family, on November 6, 1847, Dessalles set out on a return journey to Martinique. After passing through Le Havre, he boarded a ship for the French West Indies and arrived in the colony five weeks later to a very different world from the one he had first encountered nearly forty years before.

CONCLUSION

THE WORLD PIERRE Dessalles found in Martinique in 1847 bore little resemblance to the one he had encountered in 1806. Just two months after his return, it changed yet again. On February 23/24, 1848, crowds erected barricades in Paris's poorer neighborhoods, bringing an end to the July Monarchy and the rule of kings in France. The following day, the provisional government declared a republic and also emancipation with indemnity. Before the details of the transition from enslaved to free labor got hammered out, however, on May 22 more than twenty thousand enslaved workers crowded the streets of Saint Pierre, Martinique demanding their freedom. Shortly afterward, the island's governor proclaimed emancipation and initiated a new chapter in the complex interplay of race, class, and gender in the French Atlantic.

Although chattel slavery no longer existed, Martinique hardly became a paradise of racial equality. Skin color continued to map closely to economic station immediately after abolition and some would argue still does. In mid-1848 a system of Association established contracts between newly freed workers (of African descent) and their former masters (primarily white) and usually provided enslaved workers use of cabins, a portion of land, Saturdays and Sundays off, and one third of the plantation's sugar before expenses. By 1849, many planters also implemented a system of sharecropping in response to declining sugar harvests and prices. With these new methods, Martinique's *békés*, former white elites, fought, as they had repeatedly in the past, to continue dominating the island's economy. Because they retained possession of the vast majority of capital (lands, tools, and buildings), they succeeded.

The island's former *gens de couleur* and former enslaved inhabitants gained a significant foothold in the political realm, however, for the 1848 Revolution brought not only abolition but also universal male suffrage. The April 27, 1848, decree extended the vote to all French men and suspended the Colonial Councils that had previously chosen the French West Indian delegates to the National Assembly. The Republican government named François-Auguste Perrinon, a mixed-race man, as the new republican commissioner in Martinique and he took over the functions of the island's former colonial council. Henceforth, all Martinican men, including those of African descent, could vote for the island's representatives in the new national and local representative bodies.

With their overwhelming majority—110,876 mixed-race Martinicans of a total population of 120,357 in 1848—they elected a number of mixed-race men as local mayors and municipal councilors. In April 1849, Bissette returned to the island after a twenty-five-year exile and, as a moderate politician devoted to law, order, and the metropolitan government's goal of "fusion," he gained the support of other wealthy mixed-race men and even some *békés*. Their backing helped elect him as representative to the new metropolitan Legislative Assembly in June 1849, where he served until his retirement in 1851.

For the Dessalles family, as for many of the old plantocracy, these changes permanently reconfigured family dynamics. In 1848, for example, Adrien Dessalles returned to the island and publicly recognized his fourteen-year-old mixed-race daughter, Palmire. She came to live at La Nouvelle Cité and even ate at the family dinner table. While Pierre Dessalles acknowledged Palmire as Adrien's daughter, he never accepted her as a family member and chastised his eldest son for so cavalierly including her as a Dessalles. In 1849 Adrien Dessalles began managing the family sugar estate, disbanded its unsuccessful association, and implemented a sharecropping system where tenants, though required to grow sugar, paid rent rather than produce in kind. In 1850 Pierre Dessalles finally sold La Nouvelle Cité to his children and moved to the family's coffee plantation, La Caféière. Until he left for metropolitan France in 1857, where he died months later, Pierre Dessalles lived at the coffee plantation with *his* mixed-race son, Saturnin, whom his daughter had convinced to care for their father. Saturnin's wife, children, and mistress also lived at the coffee plantation, although Pierre Dessalles never acknowledged Saturnin's paternity and maintained the fiction that Saturnin and his family simply served as his domestics.[1]

Although the specifics of the Dessalles family saga and Martinique's history are unique, in the nineteenth-century Atlantic countless other families and islands faced many of the same challenges and questions that had plagued the family during the final fifty years of slavery, each finding their own answers. As the story of Martinique indicates, however, often those families and islands connected through personal and professional bonds that not only linked the French West Indies with metropolitan France but also with other points around the Atlantic basin. Throughout the first half of the nineteenth century Martinique experienced a wave of in and out migrations that dramatically shifted island-wide demographics and shaped local events. Many of those who made the trans-Atlantic voyage between Martinique and metropolitan France, or the island and London, or even the mid-Atlantic American seaboard and port cities like Bordeaux, did so both voluntarily and involuntarily, as did those who traveled between the French, British, and Spanish islands in the Caribbean. Whether supervising children, serving as or escorting enslaved domestics, undertaking family business ventures or being deported because of them, Martinicans traveling around the Atlantic basin brought together people of all legal, economic, racial, and national backgrounds. In so doing they built extensive Atlantic world relationships that meant what happened in places like Saint Pierre not only mattered to those in Martinique or Bordeaux or Paris but also potentially to those in Wilmington, North Carolina, or Portsmouth, England or even Venezuela. As a consequence, their stories—whether of a white Creole elite employing increasingly futile strategies to maintain power, or a free mixed-race population struggling to take advantage of a shifting political environment, or an enslaved community hoping to capitalize on transitional moments, or a metropolitan populace struggling to come to terms with the realities of their colonial holdings—provide important reminders to those who study early nineteenth-century American or British or Latin American history of the myriad players shaping the Atlantic world during this period.

These in and out migrations, in addition to changing demographics around the Atlantic basin, also created an international trading zone that encourages scholars to reconsider how mercantilist policy actually worked in the nineteenth-century Atlantic.[2] During periods of French and British rule, and even in times of war, Martinique's inhabitants sent products of their own or of other's labor around the Caribbean and to the United States, Great Britain, and metropolitan France, and depended on return goods from each of these regions to make a profit or sometimes simply survive. Technically, as Martinique's *colons* so pointedly told the British king during that nation's occupation of the island, a colony existed for the profit of the mother country. Nonetheless time and again colonial administrators on both sides of the Atlantic adopted ad hoc policies, in response to war and even natural disasters, which flew in the face of that rule. During the last fifty years of slavery in the French Atlantic, Creole women and free mixed-race men and women played vital roles in the colony's economic affairs, despite ideals and stereotypes that suggested otherwise, whether by providing much needed goods and services or acting as intermediaries in the sugar trade, creditors to local wholesale merchants, or business partners in metropolitan France or Great Britain. Their work reminds us of the complexity of the local Martinican economy and its trans-Atlantic connections and suggests Creole women and free mixed-race individuals may well have played similar roles around the Atlantic basin.

In addition to carrying out business in this expanded trading zone, travelers around the Atlantic basin also carried with them new ideas that colonial administrators and *colons* often viewed with suspicion and others saw as a possible means to social mobility. French and British colonial administrators in Martinique and on the continent repeatedly worried not only about enemies in their midst but also about the dangerous ideas and people who might arrive on the next boat. Throughout the first half of the nineteenth century, colonial officials and elite colonists remained on the lookout for, and free mixed-race and enslaved Martinicans often hoped for, an Atlantic-wide conspiracy that might not simply overturn the plantation system, and thus bring the downfall of Caribbean islands like Martinique, but also disrupt life on the continent nearly 3,000 miles away. Moments of significant transition in the geopolitics of the Atlantic world—the founding of Haiti, the end of the Napoleonic Wars, the establishment of full emancipation in the British West Indies—piqued always present concerns that "another Saint Domingue" was just a heartbeat away. Although they could not be certain whether trouble would come this time from the United States, metropolitan France, Great Britain, or the nearby islands of Saint Domingue, Guadeloupe, or Cuba, the island's elite whites felt confident that it would come, and others indicated it was already underway. This fear, combined with their personal attachments to distant parts of the Atlantic world, prompted many of Martinique's inhabitants—enslaved or free, white, black, or mixed-race, male or female—to take a keen interest in the world around them and suggests scholars would be well served to place seemingly isolated incidents like a rebellion of enslaved workers in a broader Atlantic context.

The existence of these personal and professional links around the Atlantic basin further encourages scholars to reevaluate existing assumptions about how the reality of slave-holding colonies like those in the Caribbean shaped ideas about national identity and citizenship around the region during the first half of the nineteenth century. Martinique's history indicates that many variables influenced what it meant for different individuals in the islands or on the continent to be French or British or even Spanish during this volatile period. We gain a much richer understanding of national identity if we take into account how location and the marked differences between metropolitan and colonial contexts factored into such determinations. During the last fifty years of slavery in the French Atlantic, and often in the face of evidence that increasingly underscored how much the Creole project diverged from metropolitan norms, Martinique's elite whites repeatedly struggled to find a balance between affirming the colony's exceptional status within the French, or even the British, Empire, and arguing that colonists were every bit as French, or British, as those in Paris, or London, so they could enjoy all of the benefits due citizens. As the social and political terrain shifted on the continent, sometimes directly in response to events in the islands, Martinique's *gens de couleur* also grappled with the tangibly different rights, let alone opportunities, they could enjoy depending on whether they were in Paris or Fort Royal. The same held true for enslaved Martinicans, especially after the 1836 law that gave freedom to any enslaved person who touched French continental soil but denied it to those living on colonial soil. Such negotiations suggest scholars can learn a lot by seriously considering how location influenced common understandings of national identity in the first half of the nineteenth century.

Martinique's shift from French to British to French control during the Napoleonic period, and colonists' response to those changes, also illustrate how complicated it is to speak of national identity and citizenship during moments of international crisis like those that shook the Atlantic world of the nineteenth, and certainly the eighteenth century. As islands throughout the Caribbean repeatedly changed sovereignty at the turn of the nineteenth century, their inhabitants were forced to negotiate the costs and benefits of maintaining or dispensing with previous national attachments. Likewise colonial administrators, like the British in Martinique, had to find a way to secure the loyalty of a "foreign" population without making them feel foreign. Often this meant trying to strike an almost unachievable balance between respecting the status quo and ensuring compliance to a new set of rules. Because of the racial, economic, and legal differences among the colony's inhabitants, administrators found themselves constantly juggling constituents who had markedly different, and often diametrically opposed, interests. In response, they not only reworked official policy on the ground, giving it different inflections depending on whom it affected, but also recast the parameters of national citizenship in ways that force scholars to reevaluate the constantly constructed nature of such categories.

Due in part to their disparate positions in the island's social and racial hierarchy, Martinique's various groups also had different ideas about the meaning of French citizenship, and those variations provide an important reminder of how the economic and racial status of inhabitants around the Atlantic basin influenced broader debates about national identity during this period. By rejecting elite ideals of appropriate white behavior, for example, Martinique's *petits blancs* questioned the link *colons* and administrators made between public comportment and the privileges of French citizenship. The divisions not only between colonial administrators and Martinique's Creoles, but also among the island-born white population, suggests that scholars can gain a greater understanding of the complexities of the plantation system, and of the constructed nature of white identity in the nineteenth century more generally, by further exploring divisions within white communities on other Caribbean islands.

In much the same way, examining how enslaved and free mixed-race Martinicans understood and articulated their changing status in the French Empire allows us to see not only the variety of ways they found agency in a brutally repressive system but also how the actions and ideas of these groups influenced broader debates about citizenship and prompted legislation that eventually changed the legal and social status of hundreds of thousands of West Indians of African descent. As recent work demonstrates, increased interest in the eighteenth- and nineteenth-century French empire has given us a much better sense of the myriad ways that enslaved and free people of African descent contributed to and fought against the plantation system.[3] Building on this crucial work, future scholars now have the opportunity to demonstrate how, for example, an uprising of enslaved and free mixed race Martinicans illuminated the existence of the *patroné*, who existed in a liminal space between legal enslavement and freedom, and brought to the public's attention not only the horrible repression of enslaved individuals but also how race shaped access to the basic rights supposedly guaranteed all free French. The experiences of this group, and others like them, demonstrate how enslaved and free individuals influenced both their immediate environments and, in the case of Martinique, *la plus grande France.* They further underscore that change flowed both directions across the Atlantic, disrupting more conventional models that assume all progressive change originated in the metropole, be it British, French, or Spanish.[4]

In addition to revealing how differences among Martinicans shaped both colonial and metropolitan ideas about the boundaries of the French nation and qualifications for citizenship, the history of Martinique during this period also reveals the ways groups and individuals worked to create good citizens through educational, charitable, and judicial institutions and underscores the government's practical role in this process of social uplift. In Martinique, as elsewhere around the Atlantic basin, colonial administrators and free colonists of all racial backgrounds frequently identified education as not only a marker of social status but also an important prerequisite for citizenship. Consequently, Creoles pushed to retain racial exclusivity in formalized education while *gens de couleur* and eventually even enslaved individuals repeatedly pushed for increased access to organized learning. The same was true for access to government and religious charitable assistance and equitable justice through the island's courts. Through their repeated efforts to create stasis or change, stability or upheaval, depending on their position within the island's racial and social hierarchy, Martinicans who lived through the last fifty years of slavery in the French Empire provide an important reminder of the ad hoc nature of the colonial project. They also demonstrate that through their complex negotiations, shifting alliances, and perseverance in the face of seemingly constant change, individuals created and recreated the Atlantic world.

ABBREVIATIONS

AD-M   Archives départementales de la Martinique
           BOM   Bulletin officiel de la Martinique
           CG   Correspondance générale
           CM   Code de la Martinique

AD-G   Archives départementales de la Gironde

AD-H   Archives départementales de l'Hérault

AN   Archives nationales (Paris)
           ADXIX   Documents administratifs
           BB   Ministère de la Justice
           FD   Fonds divers
           FM-C   Fonds ministeriels: colonies

BA   Bibliothèque de l'Arsenal (Paris)

BNF   Bibliothèque nationale de France (Paris)

BS   Bibliothèque Schoelcher (Fort-de-France, Martinique)

CAOM   Centre d'archives d'outre-mer (Aix-en-Provence)
           BOM   Bulletin officiel de la Martinique
           CO   Colonial Office
           CM   Code de la Martinique
           FM   Fonds ministeriels
           SG-M   Series géographiques-Martinique

PRO   Public Records Office (Kew, UK)
           CO   Colonial Office
           WO   War Office

SSJ	Sisters of Saint Joseph Archives (Paris)
Dessalles	Pierre Dessalles, *La Vie d'un colon à la Martinique au XIXème siècle* Vol. 1, *Correspondance, 1808–1834*, présenté par H. Frémont (Courbevoie: Cauchard, 1980) Vol. 2, *Journal, 1837–1841*, présenté par H. Frémont et Léo Elisabeth (Courbevoie: Cauchard, 1984) Vol. 3, *Journal, 1842–1847*, présenté par H. Frémont et Léo Elisabeth (Mayenne: Manutention, 1985) Vol. 4, *Journal, 1848–1856*, présenté par H. Frémont et Léo Elisabeth (Mayenne: Manutention, 1986).
Isambert, *Receuil*	François André Isambert, *Recueil général des anciennes lois françaises depuis l'an 420 jusqu'à la révolution de 1789* (Paris: Belin-Leprieur, 1821–33)
Javouhey, *Lettres* III	Anne-Marie Javouhey, *Lettres*, texte établi et annoté par les soeurs Jan Hébert et Marie-Cécile de Segonzac, vol. III, *530 à 817, 4 août 1843–mai 1848* (Paris: Éditions du Cerf, 1994)

NOTES

INTRODUCTION: SWEET LIBERTY: THE END OF SLAVERY IN MARTINIQUE

1. This administrative center was known by its historic name, Fort Royal, from its founding in the seventeenth century until the end of the eighteenth century when it took the name Fort-de-France during the Revolution. It retained this name throughout the Napoleonic period and then reverted to Fort Royal after the Restoration of the Bourbon Monarchy in 1815. From that point forward, it was sometimes called Fort Royal, sometimes Fort-de-France, depending on the speaker. Only after the Revolution of 1848 was it consistently known as Fort-de-France. For the purposes of consistency, I have chosen to use the name Fort Royal throughout this work.

2. Dale W. Tomich, *Slavery in the Circuit of Sugar: Martinique and the World Economy, 1830–1848* (Baltimore: Johns Hopkins University Press, 1990), 91.

3. Arlette Gautier, *Les Soeurs de solitude: La condition féminine dans l'esclave aux Antilles du XVII au XIX siècle* (Paris: Éditions Caribéennes, 1985), 30.

4. Léo Elisabeth, "The French Antilles," in *Neither Slave Nor Free: The Freedman of African Descent in the Slave Societies of the New World*, ed. David W. Cohen and Jack P. Greene (Baltimore: Johns Hopkins University Press, 1972), 147.

5. Hilary McD. Beckles examines a similar phenomenon in the British West Indies in *Natural Rebels: A Social History of Enslaved Black Women in Barbados* (New Brunswick, N.J.: Rutgers University Press, 1989).

6. Unlike in the British or the Spanish Caribbean, throughout the eighteenth century and the first half of the nineteenth century, in the French West Indies the term "Creole" always designated a white individual born in the colonies.

7. The historiography on the Haitian revolution and its impact is extensive. For influential works written in the past decade see, among others noted below, John Garrigus, *Before Haiti: Race and Citizenship in French Saint-Domingue* (London: Palgrave, 2006); Laurent Dubois, *A Colony of Citizens: Revolution and Slave Emancipation in the French Caribbean, 1787–1804* (Chapel Hill: University of North Carolina Press, 2004); Dubois, *Avengers of the New World: The Story of the Haitian Revolution* (Cambridge, Mass.: Belknap Press of Harvard University Press, 2004); David Patrick Geggus, ed., *The Impact of the Haitian Revolution in the Atlantic World* (Columbia: University of South Carolina Press, 2002); and Geggus, *Haitian Revolutionary Studies* (Bloomington: Indiana University Press, 2002).

8. My work addresses questions that parallel and interweave with those raised in Dale Tomich, *Slavery in the Circuit of Sugar: Martinique and the World Economy, 1830–1848* (Baltimore: Johns Hopkins University Press, 1990); and Lawrence C. Jennings, *French Anti-Slavery: The Movement for the Abolition of Slavery in France, 1802–1848* (New York: Cambridge University Press, 2000). Tomich's book outlines the relationship between the growth of slave labor and plantation production in Martinique and world economic trends at this historical moment. As such, it primarily addresses "the question of how relations of production and exchange are socially constructed in history" (3). Jennings's work focuses on the abolitionist movement in metropolitan France during the same time frame, devoting the vast majority of his book to what he identifies as the development of a meaningful antislavery organization on the continent during the July Monarchy (chapters 2–9).

9. Scholarship on the Atlantic world has dramatically increased in the past ten years. For important theoretical discussions of the benefits and limitations of such an approach, see David Armitage, "Three Concepts of Atlantic History," in *The British Atlantic World, 1500–1800*, ed. David Armitage and Michael J. Braddick (New York: Palgrave, 2002), 11–27; and Bernard Bailyn, *Atlantic History: Concept and Contours* (Cambridge: Cambridge University Press, 2005).

10. Between slavery's overthrow in 1848 and early twentieth-century works like C. A. Banbuck, *Histoire politique, économique, et sociale de la Martinique sous l'ancien régime* (Paris: Rivière, 1935) and Henry Lémery, *La Révolution française à la Martinique* (Paris: Rivière, 1936) focused on the experiences of elite white men. Beginning in the 1960s, Antonie Gisler, *L'Esclavage aux Antilles françaises (XVIIe–XIX siècle): Contribution aux problème de l'esclavage* (Fribourg: Éditions Universitaires, 1965), Liliane Chauleau, *Histoire antillaise: La Martinique et la Guadeloupe du XVII siècle à la fin du XIX siècle* (Paris-Fort-de-France-Pointe-à-Pitre: Desormeaux, 1973), and Gabriel Debien, *Les Esclaves aux Antilles françaises, XVII et XVIII siècles* (Basse-Terre: Société d'histoire de la Guadeloupe, 1974), to name a few, examined the everyday experiences of enslaved Martinicans. More recently Georges B. Mauvois, *Un complot d'esclaves: Martinique, 1831* (Grenoble: Pluriels de Psyché, 1998), Gilbert Pago, *Les Femmes et la liquidation du système esclavagiste à la Martinique, 1848–1852* (Guadeloupe: Ibis Rouge, 1998), and Lucien René Abénon, "Les Résistances à l'oppression esclavagiste: Les révoltes servile à la Martinique de 1789 à 1831," in *Rétablissement de l'esclavage dans les colonies françaises, 1802: Ruptures et continuités de la politique coloniale française, 1800–1830*, ed. Yves Bénot and Marcel Dorigny (Paris: Maisonneuve et Larose, 2003), 241–50, have focused on specific moments of resistance. Françoise Thésée, *Le Général Donzelot à la Martinique, vers la fin de l'ancien régime colonial (1818–1826)* (Paris: Karthala, 1997) and Geneviève Léti, *Santé et société esclavagiste à la Martinique (1802–1848)* (Paris: L'Harmattan, 1998) further illustrate that we must pay attention to the interplay among Martinique's various populations.

11. The majority of recent studies on the early nineteenth-century West Indies concern almost exclusively the British Caribbean. See, for example, Kathleen Butler, *The Economics of Emancipation: Jamaica and Barbados, 1823–1843* (Chapel Hill: University of North Carolina Press, 1995); Cecily Forde Jones, "Mapping Racial Boundaries: Gender, Race, and Poor Relief in Barbadian Plantation Society," *Journal of Women's History* 10, 3 (1998):

9–31; David Lambert, *White Creole Culture, Politics and Identity During the Age of Abolition* (Cambridge: Cambridge University Press, 2005); and Christer Petley, "Slavery, Emancipation and the Creole World View of Jamaican Colonists, 1800–1834," *Slavery and Abolition* 26, 1 (April 2005): 93–114.

12. Until recently, scholarship on nineteenth-century French national identity has focused on life on the continent. See, for example, the classic Eugen Weber, *Peasants into Frenchmen: The Modernization of Rural France* (Stanford, Calif.: Stanford University Press, 1976); Rogers Brubaker, *Citizenship and Nationhood in France and Germany* (Cambridge: Cambridge University Press, 1992); Caroline Ford, *Creating the Nation in Provincial France: Religion and Political Identity in Brittany* (Princeton, N.J.: Princeton University Press, 1993); James Lehning, *Peasant and French: Cultural Contact in Rural France During the Nineteenth Century* (Cambridge: Cambridge University Press, 1995).

13. Recent scholarship on racial identities in France primarily has focused on racial others (nonwhites) in the eighteenth- and twentieth-century metropole. A good place to start for the eighteenth century is Sue Peabody, *There Are No Slaves in France: The Political Culture of Race and Slavery in the Ancien Régime* (New York: Oxford University Press, 1996); Carminella Biondi, "Le Problème des gens de couleur aux colonies et en France dans la seconde moitié du XVIII siècle," *Cromohs* 8 (2003): 1–12; Pierre H. Boulle, "Racial Purity or Legal Clarity? The Status of Black Residents in Eighteenth-Century France," *Journal of the Historical Society* 6, 1 (March 2006): 19–46; and Dwain Pruitt, "The Opposition of the Law to the Law: Race, Slavery and the Law in Nantes, 1715–1778," *French Historical Studies* 30, 2 (2007): 147–74. For the twentieth century, see, among others, Neil MacMaster, *Colonial Migrants and Racism: Algerians in France, 1900–62* (New York: St. Martin's, 1997); Sue Peabody and Tyler Stovall, eds., *The Color of Liberty: Histories of Race in France* (Durham, N.C.: Duke University Press, 2003); and David Beriss, *Black Skins, French Voices: Caribbean Ethnicity and Activism in Urban France* (Boulder, Colo.: Westview Press, 2004).

14. For recent scholarship on the historical construction of white identity in the United States see, for example, Kathleen M. Brown, *Good Wives, Nasty Wenches, and Anxious Patriarchs: Gender, Race, and Power in Colonial Virginia* (Chapel Hill: University of North Carolina Press, 1996); Neil Foley, *The White Scourge: Mexicans, Blacks, and Poor Whites in Texas Cotton Culture* (Berkeley: University of California Press, 1997); and Matthew Frye Jacobson, *Whiteness of a Different Color: European Immigrants and the Alchemy of Race* (Cambridge: Cambridge University Press, 1998). For works on whiteness outside the United States, see Richard M. Dyer, *White: Essays on Race and Culture* (London: Routledge, 1997); Jerry Davila, *Diploma of Whiteness: Race and Social Policy in Brazil, 1917–1945* (Durham, N.C.: Duke University Press, 2003); and David Lambert, *White Creole Culture: Politics and Identity During the Age of Abolition* (Cambridge: Cambridge University Press, 2005).

15. Scholars of empire have demonstrated the important connections between racial and gender identities for colonized and colonizers. For recent work, see contributions to Frederick Cooper and Ann Laura Stoler, eds., *Tensions of Empire: Colonial Cultures in a Bourgeois World* (Berkeley: University of California Press, 1997) and Catherine Hall, *Civilising Subjects: Colony and Metropole in the English Imagination, 1830–1867* (Chicago: University of Chicago Press, 2002). Although attention to these connections is important, feminist

scholars have warned against casting white women as either complicit agents or heroic opponents to imperial efforts. See, for example, Julia Clancy-Smith and Frances Gouda, eds., *Domesticating the Empire: Race, Gender, and Family Life in French and Dutch Colonialism* (Charlottesville: University Press of Virginia, 1998), and Ida Blom, Karen Hagemann, and Catherine Hall, eds., *Gendered Nations: Nationalisms and Gender Order in the Long Nineteenth Century* (Oxford: Berg, 2000).

16. I rely on Harry Magdoff's distinctions between imperialism and colonialism in my analysis. According to Magdoff, imperialism is a concept that signifies any relationship of dominance and subordination between nations whereas colonialism is a specific historical form of imperialism that involves direct military, economic, and political control. Harry Magdoff, *Imperialism: From the Colonial Age to the Present* (New York: Monthly Review Press, 1978), 117, 139.

17. For a discussion of the complex divisions within white colonial communities see, for example, Ann Laura Stoler, "Sexual Affronts and Racial Frontiers: European Identities and the Cultural Politics of Exclusion in Colonial Southeast Asia," in *Tensions of Empire: Colonial Cultures in a Bourgeois World*, ed. Frederick Cooper and Ann Laura Stoler (Berkeley: University of California Press, 1997); Shula Marks, "History, the Nation and Empire: Sniping from the Periphery," *History Workshop Journal* 29 (1990): 111–19; and Linda Colley, "Britishness and Others: An Argument," *Journal of British Studies* (October 1992): 309–29.

18. Laura F. Edwards, *Scarlett Doesn't Live Here Anymore: Southern Women in the Civil War Era* (Urbana: University of Illinois Press, 2000).

19. Catherine Clinton, *The Plantation Mistress: Women's World in the Old South* (New York: Pantheon, 1982), and Elizabeth Fox-Genovese, *Within the Plantation Household: Black and White Women of the Old South* (Chapel Hill: University of North Carolina Press, 1988) also examine white women as literal and figurative bearers of white identity in the context of the antebellum South.

20. Cooper and Stoler, eds., "Introduction," in *Tensions of Empire*, 27.

21. This system of racial classification is outlined in a number of places including Victor Schoelcher, *Des Colonies françaises: Abolition immédiate de l'esclavage*, reproduction of the 1842 edition (Basse-Terre: Société d'histoire de la Guadeloupe, 1976), 153, n1.

22. John Savage explores the complicated dynamics of Martinican colonial justice in the 1820s in "Between Colonial Fact and French Law: Slave Poisoners and the Provostial Court in Restoration-Era Martinique," *French Historical Studies* 29, 4 (2006): 565–94.

23. Elisabeth, "French Antilles," 162.

24. Ibid., 157.

25. As noted in P. F. R. Dessalles, *Les Annales du Conseil Souverain de la Martinique*, Tome II, vol. 1, notes and index Bernard Vonglis (Paris: L'Harmattan, 1995), 281.

26. As noted in Schoelcher, *Des Colonies françaises*, 177.

27. Elisabeth, "French Antilles," 162.

28. Dubois, *A Colony of Citizens* explores the consequences of this legislation in Guadeloupe.

29. Figures from Centre d'archives d'outre-mer (hereafter CAOM) Colonies, G1.470.

30. Elisabeth, "French Antilles," 151.

31. Archives départementales-Martinique (hereafter AD-M), 44648/v, Code de la Martinique (hereafter CM), 1805–1813, March 12, 1806, no. 1158—*Arrêt colonial qui autorise les donations en faveur des blancs, faites par des gens de couleur libres*, 134. Between 1789 and 1816, the number of free mixed-race Martinicans nearly doubled, from 5,235 to 9,364, and by the latter date the population basically equaled that of whites (9,289). For more information on manumission in Martinique see Elisabeth "French Antilles," 134–71.

32. See Elisabeth, "French Antilles," 145–52.

33. For more on the complicated relationships between white male slaveholders and their female slaves in the French Caribbean see, for example, Bernard Moitt, "Women and Manumission," in Moitt, *Women and Slavery in the French Antilles, 1635–1848* (Bloomington: Indiana University Press, 2001), 151–72; and "Freedom from Bondage at a Price: Women and Redemption from Slavery in the French Caribbean in the Nineteenth Century," *Slavery and Abolition* 26, 2 (August 2005): 247–56.

34. For more about the important networks of French West Indians in metropolitan France at this time, see R. Darrell Meadows, "Engineering Exile: Social Networks and the French Atlantic Community, 1789–1809," *French Historical Studies* 23, 1 (2000): 67–102.

35. Peabody, *There Are No Slaves in France*, 7. Boulle discusses the August 1777 law in "Racial Purity or Legal Clarity?"

36. AD-M, CM 1805–1813, July 20, 1807, no. 1220, *Circulaire ministérielle de M. Decrès, aux capitaines-généraux et préfets coloniaux, qui remet envigueur, avec quelques modifications, les anciennes mesures du gouvernement tendantes à empecher l'introduction et le séjour en france des noirs et gens de couleur des deux sexes*, 229.

37. François-André Isambert, *Recueil*, vol. 25, 1777–1778, April 5, 1778, "Arrêt de conseil portant défense de célébrer mariage entre les blancs, noirs, mulâtres, et autres gens de couleur, et à tous notaires de passer aucun contrat entre eux," 257–58. This ban appeared to suffer from a lack of enforcement, however, as no one ever faced prosecution for violating the decree in the Admiralty Court of France. Peabody, *There Are No Slaves in France*, 121–36.

38. Boulle estimates that in 1777/1778 approximately 5,000 individuals of African descent lived in metropolitan France, and Peabody agrees that no more than 4,000 to 5,000 people of African descent resided on the continent at any one time throughout the eighteenth century. Michael Sibalis estimates that number at between 1,600 and 1,700 in 1807. Boulle, "Racial Purity or Legal Clarity?"; Peabody, *There Are No Slaves in France*; Sibalis, "Les Noirs en France sous Napoléon: L'enquête de 1807," in *Rétablissement de l'esclavage dans les colonies françaises*, ed. Bénot and Dorigny.

CHAPTER 1. "THAT YOUR HEARTS WILL BLOSSOM AND AGAIN BECOME FRENCH": THE EARLY NAPOLEONIC PERIOD

1. For more on the duties of the three administrators see Liliane Chauleau, *Dans les îles du vent: la Martinique (XVIIe–XIXe siècle)*(Paris: L'Harmattan, 1993), 203–8.

2. AD-M, CG, C8A 105, 1802, fol. 149, November 21, 1802, Lefessier-Grandpré (Lefessier-Grandprey, Grand-Juge de la Martinique et de Sainte-Lucie), Observations sur l'état des esprits en Martinique, le conspirations tramées par les gens de couleur en liaison avec les révoltés de la Guadeloupe et les mesures de sécurité prises par Villaret-Joyeuse.

3. AN, F/5B/2 Colonies: État nominatif des passagers arrivés des colonies et partis pour les colonies pendant l'année 10ème (1802) quartier de Marseille. Transport of people and things between France's Atlantic holdings was always difficult. It could take anywhere from six to twelve weeks to make the trip around the Atlantic basin, depending on the time of year and local weather conditions. Wartime blockades only increased such difficulties. Kenneth J. Banks discusses difficulty in communication in the eighteenth-century French Atlantic in *Chasing Empire Across the Sea: Communications and the State in the French Atlantic, 1713–1763* (Montreal: McGill-Queen's University Press, 2002).

4. CAOM, C8B 25 (1790–1808), 1804: Aperçu général de la situation de la Martinique pendant l'administration de M. Bertin, conseiller d'état et préfet de cette colonie, sous le rapport de la population, de la culture, du commerce, des finances.

5. For more on Guadeloupe's struggles against the British in 1794 and against the reestablishment of slavery in 1802 see Jacques Adélaïde-Merlande, *Delgrès ou la Guadeloupe en 1802* (Paris: Karthala, 1986), 5–10; André Nègre, *La Rébellion de la Guadeloupe (1801–1802)* (Paris: Éditions Caribéennes, 1987), 12–13; Anne Pérotin-Dumon, *Être patriote sous les tropiques, 1789–1794* (Basse-Terre: Société d'histoire de la Guadeloupe, 1985), 216–31; Laurent Dubois, *A Colony of Citizens: Revolution and Slave Emancipation in the French Caribbean, 1787–1804* (Chapel Hill: University of North Carolina Press, 2004).

6. For a full account of General Richepance's efforts, see Oruno Lara, *La Guadeloupe dans l'histoire* (Paris: L'Harmatton, 1979).

7. AD-M, CG, C8A 105, 1802, fol. 149, November 21, 1802, Lefessier-Grandpré au ministre de la marine et des colonies.

8. AD-M, CG, C8A 105, 1802, fol. 9, October 9, 1802, Villaret-Joyeuse au citoyen ministre de la marine et des colonies.

9. AD-M, CG, C8A 105, 1802, fol. 77, September 14, 1802, Proclamation de l'amiral Villaret-Joyeuse, capitaine général de la Martinique, de Sainte-Lucie et dépendances.

10. AD-M, CG, C8A 105, 1802, fol. 90, October 3, 1802, Arrêté de Villaret-Joyeuse et Bertin qui autorise provisoirement l'admission des navires étrangers dans le port de Fort-de-France.

11. AD-M, CG, C8A 105, 1802, fol. 12, October 4, 1802, Pétition addressée à Villaret-Joyeuse par les négociants et habitants du Fort-de-France; AD-M, CG, C8A 108, 1803, fol. 49, July 4, 1803, Bertin au ministre de la marine et des colonies.

12. AD-M, CG, C8A 108, 1803, fol. 49, July 4, 1803, Bertin au ministre de la marine et des colonies.

13. AD-M, CG, C8A 107, 1803, fol. 108, October 5, 1803, Villaret-Joyeuse au ministre de la marine et des colonies; AD-M, CG, C8A 107, 1803, fol. 112, November 28, 1803, Villaret-Joyeuse au ministre de la marine et des colonies. By the end of December, Bertin lamented that no neutral vessels, and in particular no American vessels, had reached the island and captain-general Villaret-Joyeuse bemoaned the fact that he could not procure

much needed weapons for the island's national guard from the United States. AD-M, CG, C8A 108, 1803, fol. 88, December 20, 1803, Bertin au ministre de la marine et des colonies; AD-M, CG, C8A 107, 1803, fol. 116, December 20, 1803, Villaret-Joyeuse au ministre de la marine et des colonies.

14. AD-M, CG, C8A 105, 1802, fol. 26, November 14, 1802, Villaret-Joyeuse au ministre de la marine et des colonies.

15. AD-M, CG, C8A 105, 1802, fol. 149, November 21, 1802, Lefessier-Grandpré (Lefessier-Grandprey, Grand-Juge de la Martinique et de Sainte-Lucie), au ministre de la marine et des colonies.

16. Ibid.

17. AD-M, CG, C8A 105, 1802, fol. 28, October 25, 1802, Villaret-Joyeuse au ministre de la marine et des colonies; AD-M, CG, C8A 105, 1802, fol. 26, November 14, 1802, Villaret-Joyeuse au ministre de la marine et des colonies.

18. AD-M, CG, C8A 108, 1803, fol. 143, April 2, 1803, Lefessier-Granpré au ministre de la marine et des colonies.

19. Cecily Forde-Jones has found a similar dynamic in eighteenth-century Barbados. See "Mapping Racial Boundaries: Gender, Race, and Poor Relief in Barbadian Plantation Society," *Journal of Women's History* 10 (1998): 9–31.

20. AD-M, CG, C8A 105, 1802, fol. 99, November 16, 1802, Arrêté de Villaret-Joyeuse et Bertin accordantes rations de vivres jusqu'à leur embarquement pour la France aux veuves et enfants des officiers militaires et d'administration morts dans la colonie.

21. AD-M, CM, 1819–1823, October 20, 1819, no. 2103, Ordonnance du gouverneur administrateur relativement à l'établissement et à l'administration de l'hôspice des filles et femmes pauvres, orphelins, orphelines et enfants trouves [approuvée dans toutes ses dispositions par dépêche ministérielle du 24 decembre 1819]. Not all orphans went to the foundling home; local Martinicans adopted some. See, for example, *Revue des Colonies*, "Enfans trouvés," February 1842, 333 or AD-M, 1mi 389, Fort St. Pierre, François Landais, 25/2/1806–21/4/1808, March 1, 1806, notarial records of François Landais, Fort St. Pierre.

22. *Revue des Colonies*, "Enfans trouvés," April 1842, 427.

23. Ibid., 428.

24. CAOM, C8B 25 (1790–1808), Examen du budget de la Martinique, an 13 (September 1804–January 1805), joint à la lettre du préfet colonial, 27 nivoise an 13.

25. Ibid.

26. AD-M, CG, C8A 105, 1802, fol. 3, September 23, 1802, Villaret-Joyeuse au ministre de la marine et des colonies; AD-M, CG, C8A 105, 1802, fol. 87, September 27, 1802, Ordonnance de Villaret-Joyeuse et Bertin concernant la police générale des gens de couleur libres et des esclaves (imprimé).

27. AD-M, CG, C8A 105, 1802, fol. 26, November 14, 1802, Villaret-Joyeuse au ministre de la marine et des colonies.

28. AD-M, CG, C8A 105, 1802, fol. 24, November 10, 1802, Villaret Joyeuse au commissaire du gouvernement près le tribunal d'appel du Fort-de-France.

29. AD-M, CG, C8A 105, 1802, fol. 26, November 14, 1802, Villaret-Joyeuse au ministre de la marine et des colonies.

30. AD-M, CG, C8A 105, 1802, fol. 149, November 21, 1802, Lefessier-Grandpré (Lefessier-Grandprey, Grand-Juge de la Martinique et de Sainte-Lucie), au ministre de la marine et des colonies.

31. AD-M, CG, C8A 105, 1802, fol. 22, October 30, 1802, Villaret-Joyeuse au conseiller d'état Bertin, préfet colonial de la Martinique et de Sainte-Lucie; AD-M, CG, C8A 105, 1802, fol. 64, November 22, 1802, Villaret-Joyeuse au ministre de la marine et des colonies.

32. AD-M, CM, 1787–1804, March 15, 1803, no. 997, Arrêté des capitaine général et préfet colonial, qui ordonne la vérification des Titres dont se trouvent porteurs la gens de couleur se disant Libres; AD-M, CG, C8A 107, 1803, fol. 112, November 28, 1803, Villaret-Joyeuse au ministre de la marine et des colonies.

33. CAOM, C8B 25 (1790–1808), 1804, Aperçu général de la situation de la Martinique.

34. AN, F/15/2648, Secours, État des Colons retirés dans les départements au 1er vendémiaire de l'an 10 (1801).

35. Ibid.

36. Isambert, *Recueil*, vol. 25, 81, no. 1; Lucien Peytraud, *L'Esclavage aux Antilles françaises avant 1789, d'après les documents inédits des archives coloniales* (Paris: Hachette, 1897), 398–99, Isambert, *Recueil*, vol. 27, 268.

37. Isambert, *Recueil*, vol. 25, 81, no. 1; Peytraud, *L'Esclavage aux Antilles françaises*, 398–99.

38. For a fuller discussion of the importance of this ministerial decree to debates about interracial marriages in continental France during the Napoleonic period and the Restoration, see Jennifer Heuer, "The one drop rule in reverse? Interracial marriages in Napoleonic and Restoration France, *Law and History Review* 27, 3 (Fall 2009). The reintroduction of slavery, as well as the racial and travel restrictions discussed above coincided with the rise of a new, secularized pessimism about human nature that accompanied the Napoleonic consolidation. For more, see William M. Reddy, chap. 6, "Sentimentalism in the Making of the French Revolution (1789–1815)," in Reddy, *The Navigation of Feeling: A Framework for the History of Emotions* (Cambridge: Cambridge University Press, 2001). AD-H, Paris, le 18 nivose, an 11 de la République française, Le Grand-Juge, Ministre de la Justice, aux préfets de département.

39. Jon Kukla, ed., Angelita Rosal, comp., *A Guide to the Papers of Pierre Clément Laussat: Napoleon's Prefect for the Colony of Louisiana and of General Claude Perrin Victor at the Historic New Orleans Collection* (New Orleans: Historic New Orleans Collection, 1993), 6.

40. Ibid., 7–8.

41. AD-M, CG, C8A 109, 1804, fol. 134, September 17–20, 1803, Copie de lettres échangées entre Laussat et Villaret-Joyeuse.

42. Ibid.

43. AD-M, CG, C8A 111, 1805, fol. 15, January 5, 1805, Laussat au ministre de la marine et des colonies.

44. Stuart Woolf, "French Civilization and Ethnicity in the Napoleonic Empire," *Past and Present*. 124 (1989): 107, 109–10.

45. AD-M, CM, 1805–1813, November 9, 1805, no. 1137, Procès verbal de la séance de la cour d'appel de la Martinique, relativement à la promulgation du Code civil.

46. AD-M, CM, 1805–1813, November 7, 1805, no. 1133, Arrêté colonial, concernant la promulgation du Code civil, à la Martinique.

47. Ibid.

48. AD-M, CM, 1805–1813, November 9, 1805, no. 1137, Procès verbal de la séance de la cour d'appel.

49. Ibid.

50. Ibid.

51. Before 1789, and during British rule on the island from 1794 to 1802, the Sovereign Council had registered the acts of the king of France and of local administrators as well as titles of nobility, and also exercised a right of remonstrance. As such, it had civil and judicial functions. However, from 1802 to 1809 during the French First Empire, its name changed to the Court of Appeal and it took on a purely judiciary function. Chauleau, *Dans les îles du vent*.

52. CAOM, SG-M-Affaires judiciares, 29/244, Correspondance du capitaine G. Villaret et du préfet colonial de Laussat au sujet du projet de réorganisation judiciare (AN XIII-1806, 1824).

53. AD-M, CG, C8A 109, 1804, fol. 155, October 28, 1804, Laussat au ministre de la marine et des colonies.

54. Napoleon Bonaparte au contre-amiral Decrès, Saint-Cloud, May 25, 1804 (Napoleonic Correspondence: http://www. histoire-empire.org, accessed June 14, 2007). In July 1804, Napoleon ordered four more vessels to head to the French West Indies. Napoleon Bonaparte au contre-amiral Decrès, la Malmaison, July 3, 1804 (Napoleonic Correspondence: http://www.histoire-empire.org, accessed June 14, 2007).

55. AD-M, CG, C8A 109, 1804, fol. 147, October 13, 1804, Laussat au ministre de la marine et des colonies.; AD-M, CG, C8A 109, 1804, fol. 38, October 28, 1804, Villaret-Joyeuse au ministre de la marine et des colonies.

56. AD-M, CG, C8A 109, 1804, fol. 153, October 27, 1804, Laussat au ministre de la marine et des colonies.; AD-M, CG, C8A 109, 1804, fol. 40, December 16, 1804, Villaret-Joyeuse au ministre de la marine et des colonies.

57. AD-M, CG, C8A 111, 1805, fol. 57, January 31, 1805, Laussat au ministre de la marine et des colonies; AD-M, CG, C8A 111, 1805, fol. 31, June 7, 1805, Villaret-Joyeuse au ministre de la marine et des colonies; AD-M, CG, C8A 111, 1805, fol. 33, July 8, 1805, Villaret-Joyeuse au ministre de la marine et des colonies; AD-M, CG, C8A 111, 1805, fol. 39, July 16, 1805, Villaret-Joyeuse au ministre de la marine et des colonies; AD-M, CG, C8A 111, 1805, fol. 43, July 24, 1805, Villaret-Joyeuse au ministre de la marine et des colonies..

58. AD-M, CG, C8A 111, fol. 220 October 23, 1805: Laussat: nouvelles plaintes contre les vexations que lui a fait subir le capitaine général Villaret-Joyeuse à l'occasion de la réforme des directions de l'Artillerie et du Génie et de l'arrêté concernant le cours des monnaies d'or et d'argent dans la colonie; caricatures insultantes pour le préfet affichées à Saint-Pierre et à Fort-de France; reactions provoquées par la fermeture au commerce étranger des port autres que ceux de Saint Pierre, Fort-de France, la Trinité et le Marin; il

accuse formellement VJ d'avoir trop de complaisances pour certains membres éminents du parti anglophile.

59. Ibid.

60. Ibid.; AD-M, CG, C8A 112, 1806, fol. 28, January 8, 1806, Copie d'une lettre de Villaret-Joyeuse à Laussat.

61. AD-M, CG, C8A 111,1805, fol. 313, December 14, 1805, Laussat au ministre de la marine et des colonies.

62. AD-M, CG, C8A 112, 1806, fol. 28, January 8, 1806, Copie d'une lettre de Villaret-Joyeuse à Laussat.

63. AD-M, CG, C8A 111, 1805, fol. 313, December 14, 1805, Laussat au ministre de la marine et des colonies; AD-M, CG, C8A 111, 1805, fol. 157, December 9, 1805, Laussat au ministre de la marine et des colonies.

64. AD-M, CG, C8A 111, 1805, fol. 260, November 12, 1805, Laussat au ministre de la marine et des colonies.

65. Dessalles, vol. 1, Annèxe 4: Familles Alliées, 210–213.

66. AD-M, CG, C8A 111, 1805, fol. 244, November 12, 1805, Laussat au ministre de la marine et des colonies.

67. AD-M, CG, C8A 112, 1805, fol. 77, January 16, 1806, Extrait d'une lettre de Lebertre à Villaret-Joyeuse.

68. Ibid.

69. AD-M, CG, C8A 112, 1806, fol. 75, January 17, 1806, Villaret-Joyeuse au ministre de la marine et des colonies.

70. AD-M, CG, C8A 113, 1806, fol. 120, February 3, 1806, Laussat au ministre de la marine et des colonies.

71. AD-M, CG, C8A 111, 1805, fol. 111, June 9, 1805, Mouvement de la populations depuis 1788.

72. CAOM, C8B25 (1790–1808), July 13, 1807, Compte de Finance de la Martinique exercise an XIV depuis le 23 septembre 1805 jusqu'au 1 janvier 1807 (15 mois 10 jours).

73. CAOM, C8B25 (1790–1808), Examen détaillé du budget de la Martinique, an 13, joint à la lettre du préfet colonial, 27 nîvoise an 13.

74. Ibid.

75. AD-M, CG, C8A 109, 1804, fol. 20, February 15, 1804, Villaret-Joyeuse au ministre de la marine et des colonies. Studies on such a transatlantic network of free mixed-race men are part of a growing body of literature on the history of the Atlantic world. See, for example, Peggy K. Liss, *Atlantic Empires: The Network of Trade and Revolution, 1713–1826* (Baltimore: Johns Hopkins University Press 1983); Peggy K. Liss and Franklin W. Knight, eds., *Atlantic Port Cities: Economy, Culture, and Society in the Atlantic World, 1650–1850* (Knoxville: University of Tennessee Press, 1991); Julius S. Scott, "The Common Wind: Currents of Afro-American Communication in the Era of the Haitian Revoluiton" (Ph.D. dissertation, Duke University, 1986); Paul Gilroy, *The Black Atlantic: Modernity and Double Consciousness* (Cambridge, Mass.: Harvard University Press, 1993); David P. Geggus and David Barry Gaspar, eds., *A Turbulent Time: The French Revolution and the Greater Caribbean* (Bloomington: Indiana University Press, 1997). By 1805, the island's *gens de couleur*

population had increased by about 500 to 6,578 people. AD-M, CG, C8A 111, 1805, fol. 111, June 9, 1805, Mouvement de la populations depuis 1788.

76. AD-M, CG, C8A 110, 1805, fol. 194, June 20, 1805, Circulaire de Villaret-Joyeuse aux commissaires commandant les paroisses; AD-M, CG, C8A 111, 1805, fol. 186, July 8, 1805, Laussat au ministre de la marine et des colonies.

77. AD-M, CM, 1805–1813, March 12, 1806, no. 1158, Arrêté colonial qui autorise les donations en faveur des blancs, faites par des gens de couleur libres.

78. AD-M, CG, C8A 109, 1804, fol. 202, February 14, 1804, Arrêté de Villaret-Joyeuse donnant la liste des crimes commis par des esclaves qui seront passibles du tribunal spécial. As a number of scholars have demonstrated, it is difficult to distinguish between an actual increase in the crime of poisoning and an increase in the fear that unexplained deaths of animals or people are the result of poisoning. See, for example, John Savage, "Between Colonial Fact and French Law: Slave Poisoners and the Provostial Court in Restoration-Era Martinique," *French Historical Studies* 29, 4 (2006): 565–94; Yvan Debbasch, "Le Crime d'empoisonnement aux îles pendant la période esclavagiste," *Revue d'historie d'outre-mer* 51 (1963): 137–88; David P. Geggus, "The Causation of Slave Rebellions: An Overview," in Geggus, *Haitian Revolutionary Studies* (Bloomington: Indiana University Press, 2002), 59.

79. AD-M, CG, C8A 109, 1804, fol. 31, July 9, 1804, Villaret-Joyeuse au ministre de la marine et des colonies; AD-M, CG, C8A 112, 1806, fol. 36, January 16, 1806, Villaret-Joyeuse au ministre de la marine et des colonies.

80. AD-M, CG, C8A 111, 1805, fol. 111, June 9, 1805, Mouvement de la populations depuis 1788.

81. AD-M, CG, C8A 111, 1805, fol. 34, January 22, 1805, Laussat au ministre de la marine et des colonies.

82. AD-M, CG, C8A 114, 1806, fol. 32, May 6–10, 1806, Correspondance entre Madame de la Pagerie, mère de S.M. l'Imperatrice, et le préfet colonial, relativement à trois affranchissements accordés en mai 1806.

83. AD-M, CG, C8A 114, 1806, fol. 30, May 13, 1806, Laussat au ministre de la marine et des colonies.

84. AD-M, CG, C8A 114, 1806, fol. 32, May 6–10, 1806, Correspondance entre Madame de la Pagerie, mère de S.M. l'Impératrice, et le préfet colonial, relativement à trois affranchissements accordés en mai 1806.

85. AD-M, CG, C8A 114, 1806, fol. 32–33, May 10, 1806, Lettre de M. le préfet colonial à Madame de LaPagerie.

86. Napoleon au vice-amiral Decrès, La Malmaison, April 10, 1806, (http://www.histoire-empire.org, accessed June 14, 2007).

87. Ibid.

88. AD-M, CG, C8A 110, 1805, fol. 59, February 26, 1805, Lefessier-Grandprey au Ministre Decrès.

89. Napoleon au vice-amiral Decrès, Saint-Cloud, April 22, 1806, (http://www.histoire-empire.org, accessed June 14, 2007).

90. AD-M, CG, C8A 114, 1806, fol. 227, May 14, 1806, Minute d'une lettre du ministre a Villaret-Joyeuse.

91. In 1805 Bonaparte wrote some twenty-three letters concerning the island, its inhabitants, and its defense. See Napoleonic Correspondence, 1805 and January–March 1806, (http://www.histoire-empire.org).

92. See, for example, Madame de La Pagerie, mère de Joséphine, à Impératrice Joséphine, December 15, 1804, (#68); Madame de La Pagerie, mère de Joséphine, à Impératrice Joséphine, January 28, 1805 (#72); Rose Tascher de La Pagerie à Impératrice Joséphine, August 4, 1805 (#74); Rose Tascher de La Pagerie à Impératrice Joséphine, February 1, 1806 (#122); Madame de La Pagerie, mère de Joséphine, à Impératrice Joséphine, March 8,1806 (#257), http://www.tascher-de-la-pagerie.org.

93. AN, F/16/2648 Secours, minstère de l'intérieur à Monsieur Niot, conseiller d'état chargé du 2ème arrondissement de la police général de l'empire, Paris, le 14 vendemiaire, an 13.

94. AN, F/15/2648–Secours, Pierre François Delisle La Chasserie à la senateur ministre de la police général de l'empire français, à 5 vendemiaire an 13.

95. Ibid.

96. Ibid.

97. AN, F/15/2648 Secours, Secours aux colons propriétaires des isles du vent, le 24 fructidor, l'an 12.

98. Ibid.

99. AD-H, March 16, 1804, no. 1387, Le Grand-Juge, Ministre de la Justice, au préfet du département de l'Hérault, Paris, le 25 ventose l'an XII de la République.

100. AD-H, Paris, January 14, 1805, Le ministre de la guerre au préfet du département de l'Hérault.

101. Ibid.

102. Ibid.

103. Ibid.

104. AD-H, Paris, March 13, 1806, Le conseiller d'état chargé du 2ème arrondissment de la police générale.

105. AD-M, CG, C8A 114, 1806, fol. 160, May 20, 1806, Bence au ministre de la marine et des colonies. Pierre Nicolas François Bence de Sainte-Catherine was born in Lamentin, Martinique, on November 15, 1764. He was educated at the Collège du Juilly and served as a judge on Martinique's Superior Council, a judge on the island's Court of Appeal, interim general prosecutor in 1805, and interim chief judge from 1806 to 1809. He was named to the Legion of Honor in 1806 and died in Bordeaux on December 6, 1843. Dessalles, vol. 1, Annèxe 4: Familles Alliées, 210–213.

106. AD-M, CG, C8A 111,1805, fol. 103, May 25, 1805, Laussat au ministre de la marine; AD-M, CG, C8A 114, 1806, fol. 86, August 13, 1806, Laussat au ministre de la marine.

107. AD-M, CG, C8A 114, 1806, fol. 161, June 20, 1806, Bence au ministre de la marine et des colonies.

108. Statistics for 1805 from Léo Elisabeth, "The French Antilles," in *Neither Slave Nor Free: The Freedman of African Descent in the Slave Societies of the New World*, ed. David W. Cohen and Jack P. Greene (Baltimore: Johns Hopkins University Press, 1972); statistics for 1806 from CAOM, C8B25 (1790–1808), Compte de Finance de la Martinique exercise an

XIV depuis le 23 septembre 1805 jusqu'au 1 janvier 1807 (15 mois 10 jours) préfét colonial Laussat, 13 juillet 1807; statistics for 1807 from CAOM, C8B25 (1790–1808), Compte des finances pour l'année 1807.

109. AD-M, CG, C8A 112, 1806, fol. 210, June 9, 1806, Copie d'un jugement rendu par le tribunal spécial de la Martinique condamnant à être brûlée vive la négresse Émilie, accusée de tentative d'empoisonnment sur la personne de Mme de La Pagerie, mère de l'Impératrice; AD-M, CG, C8A 112, 1806, fol. 219, June 15, 1806, Villaret-Joyeuse au ministre de la marine et des colonies; AD-M, CG, C8A 114, 1806, fol. 163, July 10, 1806, Bence au ministre de la marine et des colonies; AD-M, CG, C8A 114, 1806, fol. 165, June 7, 1806, Interrogatoire de la métive Emile, accusée de tentative d'empoisonnment sur la personne de sa maitresse Madame de La Pagerie; AD-M, CG, C8A 112, 1806, fol. 174, June 9, 1806, Copie du jugement rendu contre la métive Émilie.

110. AD-M, CG, C8A 114, 1806, fol. 165, June 7, 1806, Interrogatoire de la métive Émile, accusée de tentative d'empoisonnment sur la personne de sa maitresse Madame de La Pagerie; AD-M, CG, C8A 112, 1806, fol. 174, June 9, 1806, Copie du jugement rendu contre la métive Émilie.

111. AD-M, CM, 1805–1813, March 16, 1807, no. 1200, Circulaire ministérielle de M. Decrès aux captaines-généraux et grand juges des colonies.

112. Ibid.

113. AD-M, CG, C8A 115, 1807, fol. 51, November 2, 1807, jugement rendu par le tribunal spécial contre des esclaves appartenant aux s. Eyma, de Leyritz, Pécoul, Chalvet, Fortier, Gradis, Lavener, Serrand, Ducoudray et Valmont accusés d'empoisonnements et de complot d'assassinat contre les économes du quartier.

114. AD-M, CG, C8A 117, 1808, fol. 116, August 31, 1808, Laussat au ministre de la marine et des colonies.

115. AD-M, CM, 1805–1813, October 24, 1808, no. 1281, Dépêche ministérielle de M. Decrès, aux capitaine-général et grand-juge de la Martinique, portant envoi du décret impérial, qui établit quatre juges assesseurs près la Cour d'appel de cette Colonie, et qui prescrit les mesures autorisées pour faciliter le passage en France des jeunes créoles destinés à étudier en Droit.

116. AD-M, CG, C8A 115, 1807, fol. 212, December 20, 1807, Laussat au ministre de la marine et des colonies.

117. AD-M, CG, C8A 117, 1808, fol. 117, September 5, 1808, Laussat au ministre de la marine et des colonies.

118. AD-M, CG, C8A 114, 1806, fol. 95, August 18, 1806, Laussat au ministre de la marine et des colonies; AD-M, CG, C8A 112, 1806, fol. 269, December 10, 1806, Villaret-Joyeuse au ministre de la marine et des colonies.

119. AD-M, CG, C8A 117, 1808, fol. 94, March 12, 1808, Traduction de l'Acte additionnel du Congrès des États-Unis; AD-M, CG, C8A 117, 1808, fol. 76, April 10, 1808, Laussat au ministre de la marine et des colonies; AD-M, CG, C8A 116, 1808, fol. 17, April 2, 1808, Villaret-Joyeuse au ministre de la marine et des colonies.

120. AD-M, CG, C8A 117, 1808, fol. 86, May 6, 1808, Laussat au ministre de la marine et des colonies; AD-M, CG, C8A 116, 1808, fol. 27, May 6, 1808, Villaret-Joyeuse au

ministre de la marine et des colonies; AD-M, CG, C8A 117,1808, fol. 88, May 11, 1808, Laussat au ministre de la marine et des colonies; AD-M, CG, C8A 116, 1808, fol. 64, September 10, 1808, Villaret-Joyeuse au ministre de la marine et des colonies; AD-M, CG, C8A 117, 1808, fol. 127, September 16, 1808, Laussat au ministre de la marine et des colonies.

121. AD-M, CG, C8A 117, 1808, fol. 104, August 18, 1808, Laussat au ministre de la marine et des colonies; AD-M, CG C8A 116, 1808, fol. 43, August 20, 1808, Villaret-Joyeuse au ministre de la marine et des colonies; AD-M, CG, C8A 117, 1808, fol. 133, October 5, 1808, Laussat au ministre de la marine et des colonies.

122. Statistics for 1805 from Élisabeth, "The French Antilles," 151; statistics for 1806 from CAOM, C8B25 (1790–1808), Compte de Finance de la Martinique exercise an XIV depuis le 23 septembre 1805 jusqu'au 1 janvier 1807 (15 mois 10 jours) préfét colonial Laussat, 13 juillet 1807; statistics for 1807 from CAOM, C8B25 (1790–1808), Compte de finances pour l'année 1807.

123. AD-M, CM, 1805–1813, February 12, 1807, no. 1194, Arrêté colonial, concernant les affranchissements obtenus hors de la Martinique.

124. AD-M, CM, 1805–1813, June 5, 1807, no. 1213, Lettre du préfet colonial à M. Legrand, officier spécial de l'Etat-civil, à Saint-Pierre.

125. Statistics for 1807 from AD-M, C8B25 (1790–1808), Compte de finances pour l'année 1807.

126. CAOM, C8B25 (1790–1808), Compte de Finance de la Martinique exercise an XIV depuis le 23 septembre 1805 jusqu'au 1 janvier 1807 (15 mois 10 jours) préfét colonial Laussat, July 13, 1807.

127. Statistics for 1805 from Élisabeth, "The French Antilles," 151; statistics for 1806 from CAOM, C8B25 (1790–1808), Compte de finance de la Martinique exercise an XIV depuis le 23 septembre 1805 jusqu'au 1 janvier 1807 (15 mois 10 jours) préfét colonial Laussat, 13 juillet 1807; statistics for 1807 from CAOM, C8B25 (1790–1808), Compte de finances pour l'année 1807.

128. AD-M, CG, C8B25 (1790–1808), Compte de Finance de la Martinique exercise An XIV depuis le 23 septembre 1805 jusqu'au 1 janvier 1807 (15 mois 10 jours), préfét colonial Laussat, le 13 juillet 1807; AD-M, C8B25 (1790–1808), Compte des finances pour l'année 1807.

129. AD-M, CM, 1805–1813, December 16, 1807, no. 1242, Circulaire du préfet colonial, relative aux contributions publiques, aux certificats d'indigence et aux non-valeurs.

130. PRO CO 166:1 1693–1814, de Curt, député de Martinique à Londres, le 31 mai 1794.

131. AD-M, CG, C8A 115, 1807, fol. 200, August 24, 1807, Laussat au ministre de la marine et des colonies.

132. Ibid.

133. Ibid.

134. This list was to include the name of any person of color, his port of origin, age, sex, and profession, his owner's name, and the place, date, and ship of departure. AD-M, CM, 1805–1813, July 20, 1807, no. 1220, Circulaire ministérielle de M. Decrès, aux capitaines généraux et préfets coloniaux, qui remet envigueur, avec quelques modifications, les

anciennes mesures du gouvernement tendantes à empecher l'introduction et le sejour en France des noirs et gens de couleur des deux sexes, 229.

135. AD-M, CG, C8A 114, 1806, fol. 60, July 11, 1806, Laussat au ministre de la marine et des colonies.

136. Susan Dwyer Amussen has explored similar dynamics in seventeenth-century Jamaica and Barbados in *Caribbean Exchanges: Slavery and the Transformation of English Society, 1640–1700* (Chapel Hill: University of North Carolina Press, 2007).

137. Rose Tascher de La Pagerie à l'Impératrice Joséphine, July 12, 1806, (#144), http://www.tascher-de-la-pagerie.org.

138. AD-M, CG, C8A 115, 1807, fol. 136, May 6, 1807, Laussat au ministre de la marine et des colonies.

139. Ibid.

140. AD-H, Paris, August 8, 1807, no. 5697, Conseiller d'état au préfets du départements maritimes.

141. Ibid.

142. AD-H, August 19, 1807, État des Hommes de couleur existant dans la ville de Montpellier, Hérault, Ville de Montpellier.

143. Archives départementales de la Gironde (hereafter AD-G) 2 MI 8433, October 5, 1807, État des noirs, mulâtres, et autres gens de couleur existant à Bordeaux,. For a close analysis of this population, see Michael Sibalis, "Les Noirs en France sous Napoléon: L'enquête de 1807," in *Rétablissement de l'esclavage dans les colonies françaises: Aux origines de Haïti*, ed. Yves Bénot and Marcel Dorigny (Paris: Maisonneuve et Larose, 2003).

144. See Sibalis, "Les Noirs en France sous Napoléon."

145. AD-M, CG, C8A 117,1808, fol. 140, November 13, 1808, Laussat au ministre de la marine et des colonies.

146. AD-M, CG, C8A 117, 1808, fol. 150, November 23, 1808, Laussat au ministre de la marine et des colonies.

CHAPTER 2. "HAPPY TO CONSIDER ITSELF AN ANCIENT BRITISH POSSES-
SION": THE BRITISH OCCUPATION OF MARTINIQUE

1. Adeline de Reynal, *"Le Mouillage": Port de Saint-Pierre de la Martinique, 3 siècles d'histoire* (Martinique: Caraib Ediprint, 1992), 95.

2. George Beckwith (1809), Lieutenant General John Brodrick (February 1810–June 1811), and Brigadier general Charles Wale (July 1811–1814). Beckwith technically served as governor from early 1809 until June 1809, when Brodrick was officially named to the post. However, Brodrick did not actually arrive in Martinique until the end of February 1810. See PRO, WO 1:40, 1810.

3. PRO, WO 1:42, 1811, part 2, December 19, 1811, Report upon the State of the Island of Martinique.

4. Dale W. Tomich, *Slavery in the Circuit of Sugar: Martinique and the World Economy, 1830–1848* (Baltimore: Johns Hopkins University Press, 1990), 100.

5. Pierre Dessalles, *Sugar and Slavery, Family and Race: The Letters and Diary of Pierre Dessalles, Planter in Martinique, 1808–1856*, ed. and trans. Elborg Forster and Robert Forster (Baltimore: Johns Hopkins University Press, 1996).

6. PRO, CO 166:5, August 10, 1809, Lord Castlereagh, Secretary of State for the Colonial Department, to Sir George Beckwith, Governor of Martinique.

7. PRO, WO 1:40, 1810, October 1, 1810, General John Brodrick to Secretary of State of the Colonial Office, Earl of Liverpool.

8. Ibid.

9. See the correspondence in PRO, CO 166:5 for 1809 and 1810.

10. For correspondence regarding repatriation of Martinicans stranded in Great Britain, see PRO, WO 1:39, 1809, November 11, 1809, Letter from Robert Thore Milnes to Honorable Cecil Jenkinson; PRO, WO 1:39, 1809, November 2, 1809, Statement of Joseph Maillet; PRO, WO 1:39, 1809, November 2, 1809, Daubas to Robert Thore Milnes; PRO, WO 1:39, 1809, November 6, 1809, Wilson and Company to Robert Thore Milnes; PRO, CO 166:5, December 27, 1809, H. E. Bunburg to General John Brodrick; PRO, CO 166:5, November 14, 1809, Letter from Honorable Cecil Jenkinson to Lieutenant general Beckwith; PRO, CO 166:5, November 14, 1809, Letter from Honorable Cecil Jenkinson to Lieutenant general Beckwith; PRO, WO 1:39, December 27, 1809, Letter from Robert Thore Milnes to Honorable Cecil Jenkinson; PRO, CO 166:5, December 28, 1809, Letter from Honorable Cecil Jenkinson to Officer commanding at Martinique; PRO, WO 1:39, n.d. Secret from Robert Thore Milnes to Honorable Cecil Jenkinson; PRO, WO 1:39, November 18, 1809, J. Beckett to Honorable Cecil Jenkinson; PRO, WO 1:39, 1809, November 24, 1809, Daubas to Robert Thore Milnes; PRO, WO 1:39, 1809, November 28, 1809, Robert Thore Milnes to Honorable Cecil Jenkinson; PRO, WO 1:39, 1809, December 22, 1809, Robert Thore Milnes to Honorable Cecil Jenkinson; PRO, CO 166:5, January 2, 1810, H. E. Bunburg to General John Brodrick.

11. PRO, WO 1:42, 1811 part 2, January 16, 1811, Robert Thore Milnes to Robert Peel.

12. PRO, WO 1:40 1810, April 10, 1810, General Brodrick to Secretary of State of the Colonial Office, Lord Castlereagh.

13. Ibid.

14. PRO, WO 1:42, 1811, part 2, January 16, 1811, Robert Thore Milnes to Robert Peel.

15. PRO, CO 166:5, January 19, 1811, Secretary of State of the Colonial Office, Lord Liverpool, to Governor John Brodrick.

16. PRO, WO 1:40, 1810, December 3, 1810, General John Brodrick to Secretary of State of the Colonial Office, Lord Liverpool.

17. PRO, WO 1:40, 1810, April 18, 1810, General John Brodrick to Secretary of State of the Colonial Office, Earl of Liverpool.

18. Ibid.

19. Ibid.

20. PRO, WO 1:40, 1810, August 6, 1810, General John Brodrick to Secretary of State of the Colonial Office, Earl of Liverpool.

21. PRO, WO 1:41, 1811, part 1, January 2, 1811, Statement of the procureur du roi at the Court of Appeal opening session.

22. PRO, WO 1:41, 1811, part 1, January 2, 1811, General John Brodrick to Secretary of State of the Colonial Office, Lord Liverpool.

23. PRO, WO 1:41, 1811, part 1, March 22, 1811, Governor John Brodrick to Secretary of State of the Colonial Office, Lord Liverpool.

24. PRO, WO 1:41, 1811, part 1, March 1, 1811, Au Roi.

25. Ibid.

26. Ibid.

27. PRO, WO 1:41, 1811, part 1, April 15, 1811, Governor John Brodrick to Secretary of State of the Colonial Office, Lord Liverpool.

28. PRO, WO 1:39, 1809, "Observations on the present state of Martinique, Guadeloupe, and of the British Isles" by DuBuc de Marintille (1809).

29. See Laurent Dubois, *A Colony of Citizens: Revolution and Slave Emancipation in the French Caribbean, 1787–1804* (Chapel Hill: University of North Carolina Press, 2004).

30. PRO, WO 1:39, 1809, "Observations on the present state of Martinique, Guadeloupe, and of the British Isles" by DuBuc de Marintille (1809).

31. CAOM, CM, 1805–1813, September 29, 1809, no. 1323, Proclamation de Son Excellence le Lieutenant-général George Beckwith, Commandant en Chef de la Martinique, concernant les Correspondances avec le Ministre Decrès.

32. PRO, WO 1:40, 1810, November 24, 1810, General John Brodrick to Secretary of State of the Colonial Office, Lord Liverpool; PRO, WO 1:42, 1811, part 2, February 12, 1811, J. Beckitt to Robert Peel.

33. PRO, WO 1:42, 1811, part 2, February 12, 1811, J. Beckitt to Robert Peel.

34. PRO, WO 1:42, 1811, part 2, le 11 9bre 1810, Monsieur Vernier à Monsieur Henri Petit.

35. CAOM, CM, 1805–1813, August 1, 1809, no. 1318, Ordonnance de S. Exe. le lieutenant-général George Beckwith, commandant en chef de la Martinique, concernant les déserteurs français et les marins prisonniers de guerre.

36. PRO, WO 1:40, 1810, February 13, 1810, Major general Carmichael to the earl of Liverpool.

37. CAOM, CM, 1805–1813, April 25, 1810, Lettre de son exellence le gouverneur de la Martinique, à M. le procureur du roi de St. Pierre.

38. CAOM, CM, 1805–1813, October 26, 1810, no. 1501, and December 5, 1810, no. 1371.

39. PRO, WO 1:40, 1810, December 10, 1810, General John Brodrick to Secretary of State of the Colonial Office, Lord Liverpool.

40. CAOM, CM, 1805–1813, January 23, 1811, no. 1379, Ordonnance de S. E le gouverneur de la Martinique, John Brodrick, portant creation de diverses retenues en faveur de bureaux de charité; CAOM, CM, 1805–1813, October 17, 1810, no. 1365, Règlement de son excellence le gouverneur de la Martinique, portant etablissement des bureaux de charité dans cette colonie.

41. PRO, WO 1:41, 1811, part 1, Article 6 of the *Ordonnance sur les impositions par son excellence l'honorable John Brodrick, major general, commandant en chef et gouverneur de la Martinique, vice amiral de ladite isle, etc, etc, etc.-, janvier 1811*; CAOM, CM, 1805–1813,

April 25, 1811, no. 1385, Règlement de S.E. le gouveneur de la Martinique, additionnel à celui du 17 octobre 1810 portant établissement des bureaux de charité à la Martinique.

42. The ordinance also required travelers to indicate their intended length of stay within five days of landing on the island. CAOM, CM, 1805–1813, July 19, 1809, Ordonnance de S.E. le lieutenant-général George Beckwith, commandant en chef de la Martinique, faisant suit à celle du 6 avril 1809, concernant le permis de résidence et les passe-ports.

43. CAOM, CM, 1805–1813, November 1, 1809, no. 1332, Règlement de S.E. le lieutenant-général George Beckwith, commandant en chef de la Martinique, concernant la police générale de la colonie.

44. Ibid.

45. PRO, WO 1:41, 1811, part 1, July 12, 1811, Lieutenant general Charles Wale to secretary of state of the Colonial Office, Lord Liverpool.

46. PRO, WO 1:42, 1811, part 2, December 19, 1811, Report upon the State of the Island of Martinique.

47. Dessalles, vol. 1, 26, October 4, 1811, Pierre Dessalles à beau-père Bence.

48. PRO, WO 1:42, 1811, part 2, September 18, 1811, Wale to Liverpool.

49. CAOM, CM, 1805–1813, September 20, 1811, no. 1400, Convocation de la cour d'appel, pour le jugement des auteurs et fauteurs de la conspiration découverte le 18 septembre 1811.

50. PRO, WO 1:42, 1811, part 2, October 12, 1811, Wale to Liverpool.

51. PRO, WO 1:42, 1811, part 2, October 11, 1811, Wale to Liverpool. Clearly the Colonial Office agreed, for on July 4, 1812 they granted Wale's request and pardoned Jean Pierre, dit nègre. PRO, WO 1:43, 1812, part 1, August 11, 1812, Governor Charles Wale to Secretary of State of the Colonial Office, Earl of Bathurst.

52. PRO, WO 1:42, 1811, part 2, October 11, 1811, Declaration of Edmond Thétis to the priest Gobel before being executed.

53. Dessalles, vol. 1, 31–32, October 12, 1811, Pierre Dessalles à beau-père Bence. Dessalles was named to the Court of Appeal in October 1808 under French rule and confirmed in this position in July 1809 by the British governor. For more details on Dessalles's tenure on the Court of Appeal, see Dessalles, vol. 1, 22–23.

54. PRO, WO 1:42, 1811, part 2, October 17, 1811, Wale to Liverpool.

55. PRO, WO 1:42, 1811, part 2, October 31, 1811, Ordinance on the Corps of Royal Martinicans.

56. PRO, WO 1:42, 1811, part 2, December 15, 1811, Wale to Liverpool.

57. PRO, WO 1:43, 1812, part 1, April 2, 1812, Wale to Liverpool.

58. PRO, WO 1:43, 1812, part 1, March 6, 1812, Wale to Liverpool.

59. Ibid.

60. Ibid.

61. PRO, WO 1:43, 1812, part 1, April 2, 1812, Wale to Liverpool.

62. Ibid.

63. PRO, WO 1:43, 1812, part 1, February 16, 1812, Examination of Monsieur Louis Michel de Luppé.

64. PRO, WO 1:43, 1812, part 1, April 2, 1812, Wale to Liverpool.

65. Ibid.

66. PRO, WO 1:43, 1812 part 2, n.d., Monsieur Du Buc St. Olympe to Lieutenant general Charles Wale.

67. PRO, WO 1:43, 1812, part 1, April 2, 1812, Wale to Liverpool.

68. Ibid.

69. PRO, WO 1:43, 1812, part 1, February 16, 1812, Examination of Monsieur Jean Baptiste Marie Chansel de Fonrose.

70. PRO, WO 1:43, 1812, part 2, n.d., Du Buc St. Olympe to Wale.

71. PRO, WO 1:43, 1812, part 1, February 17, 1812, Examination of Monsieur Jean Baptiste Marie Chansel de Fonrose.

72. PRO, WO 1:43, 1812, part 1, March 6, 1812, Wale to Liverpool.

73. PRO, WO 1:43, 1812, part 1, March 2, 1812, Examination of Monsieur Jean Baptiste Marie Chansel de Fonrose.

74. Ibid.

75. PRO, WO 1:43, 1812, part 1, April 2, 1812, Wale to Liverpool.

76. PRO, WO 1:44, part 2, June 10, 1812, Monsieur Plumer to Secretary of State of the Colonial Office, Lord Liverpool.

77. PRO, WO 1:43, 1812, part 1, April 2, 1812, Wale to Liverpool; PRO, CO 166:5, June 11, 1812, Colonial Office to Governor Charles Wale; PRO, CO 166:5, June 18, 1812, Secretary of State of the Colonial Office, Earl of Bathurst, to Governor Charles Wale.

78. PRO, CO 166:5, July 16, 1812, Bathurst to Wale.

79. PRO, WO 1:44, 1812, part 2, November 4, 1812, Wale to Bathurst.

80. PRO, CO 166:5, July 4, 1812, Bathurst to Wale.

81. PRO, CO 166:5, September 15, 1812, Bathurst to Wale.

82. PRO, WO 1:43, 1812, part 1, August 11, 1812, Wale to Bathurst.

83. PRO, WO 1:44, 1812, part 2, November 4, 1812, Wale to Bathurst.

84. Ibid.

85. AN, F/7/4237A, Jossie dossier, February 5, 1813, correspondance à Monsieur Doulert.

86. AN, F/7/4237A, Jossie dossier, January 26, 1813, correspondance à Fonrose Dariste.

87. In his work on the eighteenth-century French slave trade, Robert L. Stein argued for the primacy of familial relationships in cementing commercial links, noting "in a world dominated by uncertainty and change, only family ties could be trusted to endure." Robert L. Stein, *The French Slave Trade in the Eighteenth Century: An Old Regime Business* (Madison: University of Wisconsin Press, 1979), 61–62. Robert Forster makes a similar argument in *Merchants, Landlords, Magistrates: The Depont Family in Eighteenth-Century France* (Baltimore: Johns Hopkins University Press, 1980), as does Darrell Meadows in "Engineering Exile: Social Networks and the French Atlantic Community, 1789–1809," *French Historical Studies* 23, 1 (Winter 2000): 69.

88. AN, F/7/4237A, Jossie dossier, January 27, 1813, Monsieur Ranicille à Monsieur Gabrie; AN, F/7/4237A, Jossie dossier, November 3, 1812, Correspondence de Mézérenc.

89. AN, F/7/4237A, Jossie dossier, September 28, 1812, Monsieur Genty à Monsieur

Loubery; AN, F/7/4237A, Jossie dossier, January 29, 1813, Monsieur Genty à Madame Genty.

90. AN, F/7/4237A, Jossie dossier, February 4, 1813, Monsieur Genty à Madame Genty.

91. PRO, WO 1:42, 1811, part 2, September 12, 1811, Wale to Liverpool.

92. PRO, WO 1:44, 1812, part 2, January 26, 1812, Robert Thore Milnes to Secretary of State of the Colonial Office, Lord Liverpool.

93. Ibid.

94. PRO, WO 1:43, 1812, part 1, October 18, 1812, Privy Council petition.

95. Ibid.

96. PRO, WO 1:43, 1812, part 1, October 21, 1812, Wale to Bathurst.

97. Ibid.

98. Ibid.

99. In March 1813, fine sugar could sell for 75 to 80 livres rather than the 55 livres it had garnered at the beginning of the year. PRO, WO 1:45, 1813, part 1, March 19, 1813, Wale to Bathurst.

100. Ibid.

101. PRO, WO 1:45, 1813, part 1, May 10, 1813, Wale to Bathurst.

102. PRO, WO 1:46, 1813, part 2, February 25, 1813, Plumer and Garrow (King's Law Offices) to Secretary of State of the Colonial Office, Earl of Bathurst.

103. PRO, WO 1:46, 1813, part 2, October 24, 1812, John Reeves to the Lords of the Committee of Council for Trade and Foreign Plantations.

104. Ibid.

105. PRO, WO 1:45, part 1, July 23, 1812, Wale to Bathurst.

106. PRO, WO 1:45, part 1, July 30, 1813, Wale to Bathurst; PRO, WO 1:45, part 1, August 19, 1813, Wale to Bathurst.

107. PRO, WO 1:45, part 1, August 20, 1813, Proclamation.

108. PRO, WO 1:46, 1813, part 2, September 19, 1813, Robert Thore Milnes to Secretary of State of the Colonial Office, Earl of Bathurst.

109. Ibid.

110. PRO, WO 1:46, 1813, part 2, October 8, 1813, Office of the Committee of Privy Council Trade to Golbourn.

111. PRO, WO 1:43, 1812, part 1, February 15, 1812, Wale to Liverpool.

112. PRO, WO 1:43, 1812, part 1, January 13, 1812, Lieutenant general Charles Wale to Monsieur Valmenier, *procureur général du roi* at Fort Royal. On January 3, 1812, Governor general Charles Wale appointed Pierre Dessalles to Martinique's Court of Appeal. Dessalles, vol. 1, 32.

113. PRO, WO 1:43, 1812, part 1, January 13, 1812, Wale to Valmenier .

114. Ibid.

115. PRO, WO 1:47, March 31, 1814, Wale to Bathurst.

116. PRO, WO 1:46, part 2, August 30, 1813, *procureur général*, Monsieur Valmenier, to Governor Charles Wale.

117. PRO, WO 1:46, 1813, part 2, September 10, 1813, Monsieur Buffet, head of the

Bureau of *huissiers*, to Governor Charles Wale; PRO, WO 1:47, 1814, February 27, 1814, Valmenier to Wale.

118. PRO, WO 1:46, 1813, part 2, August 28, 1813, Governor Charles Wale to *procureur général*, Monsieur Valmenier; PRO, WO 1:46, 1813, part 2, August 30, 1813, Valmenier to Wale.

119. PRO, WO 1:47, 1814, March 31, 1814, Wale to Bathurst.

120. PRO, WO 1:47, 1814, May 16, 1814, Wale to Bathurst; PRO, WO 1:47, 1814, March 13, 1814, Governor Charles Wale to *procureur du roi* Regnaudin.

121. PRO, WO 1:47, 1814, May 16, 1814, Wale to Bathurst.

122. Ibid.

123. PRO, WO 1:47, 1814, March 17, 1814, Wale to Regnaudin.

124. PRO, WO 1:47, 1814, May 16, 1814, Wale to Bathurst.

125. PRO, WO 1:47, 1814, March 17, 1814, Wale to Regnaudin.

126. PRO, WO 1:47, 1814, May 16, 1814, Wale to Bathurst.

127. Ibid.

128. Ibid.

129. PRO, WO 1:47, 1814, July 3, 1814, Wale to Bathurst.

130. Ibid.

131. Ibid.

CHAPTER 3. "YOUR FRENCH AND LOYAL HEARTS": THE FIRST DECADE OF THE RESTORATION

1. CAOM, CM, 1814–1818, December 7, 1814, no. 1558, Proclamation des gouverneur et intendant, par interim, commissaires du roi de France pour la reprise de possession de la Martinique.

2. AD-M, CG, C8A 121, 1815, fol. 75, État nominatif des passagers arrives de France depuis le 8 octobre 1814; AN FM-C, F/5B/2, Liste des passagers, Quartier de Marseille, état nominatif des passagers d'arrivés du colonies et partis pour les colonies pendant l'année 1815, 1816, 1817.

3. AN, FM-C, F/5B/2, Liste des passagers, Quartier de Marseille.

4. This number includes only women who clearly would be counted among Martinique's *petits blancs* population on arrival; 100 women were listed. AN FM-C, F/5B/2, Liste des passagers, Quartier de Marseille; AD-M, C8A 121, 1815, fol. 75, État nominatif des passagers arrivés de France depuis le 8 octobre 1814.

5. Léo Elisabeth, "The French Antilles," in *Neither Slave Nor Free: The Freedman of African Descent in the Slave Societies of the New World*, ed. David W. Cohen and Jack P. Greene (Baltimore: Johns Hopkins University Press, 1972), 151.

6. AD-M, CG, C8A 120, 1815, fol. 203, December 2, 1815, Vaugiraud au ministre de la marine et des colonies.

7. Ibid.

8. Ibid.

9. CAOM, CM, 1814–1818, February 1, 1815, no. 1587, Avis officiel de l'intendant rélatif à la capture des deserteurs, gens sans aveu et vagabond.

10. Liliane Chauleau, *Guide des Archives de la Martinique* (Fort-de-France: Archives départementales, 1978), 41.

11. For the most part, the rules of the foundling home remained the same. However, under the new organization, the government now allocated 432 francs per girl and 324 francs per boy for children under the age of fifteen. CAOM, CM, 1814–1818, August 1, 1815, no. 1630, Ordonnance des administrateurs en chef portant réorganisation du service de l'hospice de Saint-Pierre affecté aux enfants trouvés ou orphelins et aux pauvres femmes et fille infirmées ou malades; CAOM, CM, 1819–1823, October 20, 1819, no. 2103, Ordonnance du gouverneur administrateur relativement à l'établissement et à l'administration de l'hospice des filles et femmes pauvres, orphelins, orphelines et enfants trouvés [approuvée dans toutes ses dispositions par dépêche ministérielle du 24 decembre 1819].

12. At this time, fees were paid in colonial livres, the local currency. One franc was equal to approximately 1.8 colonial livres; consequently the fees would be 2,700, 1,800 and 900 colonial livres. CAOM, CM, 1814–1818, no. 1652, Arrêté des administrateurs en chef portant rétablissement du college de Saint-Victor, autorisé par lettres patentes du 20 septembre 1768.

13. CAOM, SG-M-Instruction publique, 97/854, December 10, 1815, Rapport au lieutenant général gouverneur et administrateur pour le Roi, concernant la nouvelle organisation de la Maison Royale d'Éducation.

14. CAOM, CM, 1814–1818, March 20, 1816, no. 1668, ordonnance des administrateurs en chef portant établissement à Saint-Pierre d'une maison royale d'éducation pour les jeunes filles de la colonie. This training did not equal that offered in the pensions of metropolitan France. There one could receive religious and moral instruction, reading, writing, French grammar, arithmetic, French history, as well as modern geography, physics and natural history, art, music and foreign languages. For more about lay schooling during this period see, Isabelle Bricard, *Saintes ou pouliches: L'éducation des jeunes filles au XIX siècle*, especially "Le Pensionnat laïque" (Paris: Michel, 1985); and Sharif Gemie, *Women and Schooling in France, 1815–1914: Gender, Authority and Identity in the Female Schooling Sector* (Keele: Keele University Press, 1995).

15. CAOM, SG-M-Instruction publique, 97/854, December 10, 1815, Rapport au lieutenant général gouverneur et administrateur pour le Roi, concernant la nouvelle organisation de la Maison Royale d'Éducation.

16. CAOM, CM, 1814–1818, March 9, 1816, no. 1664, Instructions pour les familles qui demandent l'admission de leurs filles, soeurs, nieces, ou cousines dans la maison royale de Saint-Denis; CAOM, CM, 1814–1818, August 16, 1816, no. 1692, Dépêche ministérielle aux administrateurs en chef, annonçant la réserve faite au profit des familles creoles de places gratuites dans les maisons royales de Saint-Denis et de Paris.

17. CAOM, CM, 1814–1818, September 18, 1816, no. 1699, Ordonnance du roi qui réserve six bourses gratuites des colleges royaux aux sujets de l'île de la Martinique.

18. CAOM, CM, 1814–1818, October 4, 1816, no. 1701, Dépêche ministérielle portant

envoi de l'ordonnance royale du 18 septembre 1816, et diverses dispositions relatives au mode de présentation des élèves boursiers et au passage qui leur est accordé.

19. For more on the Pecoul family, see Dessalles, vol. 1, Annèxe 6, Personnalités diverses, #14 Pecoul, 220. Pecoul was a Martinican lawyer, son of a wealthy white planter, and brother of a future member of Martinique's Court of Appeal.

20. AN, FD, Papiers d'Origny et Pécoul, 376/ap/15, December 13, 1814, Veuve Soubiran à Monsieur Pecoul.

21. Ibid.

22. AN, FD, Papiers d'Origny et Pécoul, 376/ap/15, April 16, 1816, Veuve Soubiran à Monsieur Pecoul.

23. AN, FD, Papiers d'Origny et Pécoul, 376/ap/15, February 25, 1815, Veuve Soubiran à Monsieur Pecoul.

24. AN, FD, Papiers d'Origny et Pécoul, 376/ap/15, January 6, 1816, Veuve Soubiran à Monsieur Pecoul.

25. Ibid.

26. AN, FD, Papiers d'Origny et Pécoul, 376/ap/15, February 6, 1816, Veuve Soubiran à Monsieur Pecoul.

27. AN, FD, Papiers d'Origny et Pécoul, 376/ap/15, April 16, 1816, Veuve Soubiran à Monsieur Pecoul

28. AN, FD, Papiers d'Origny et Pécoul, 376/ap/15, March 13, 1820, Veuve Soubiran à Monsieur Pecoul.

29. AN, FM-C, F/5B/2, Liste des passagers, Quartier de Marseille, état nominatif des passagers d'arrivés du colonies et partis pour les colonies pendant l'année 1815, 1816, 1817.

30. Sue Peabody, *There Are No Slaves in France: The Political Culture of Race and Slavery in the Ancien Régime* (New York: Oxford University Press, 1996), 7; AD-M, CM, 1805–1813, July 20, 1807, no. 1220, Circulaire ministérielle de M. Decrès, aux capitaines-généraux et préfets coloniaux.

31. Excerpt from Baron de Montlezun de Labartète's *Souvenirs des Antilles: Voyage en 1815 et 1816* (Paris: Gide fils, 1818), reprinted in Dessalles, vol. 1, 39, 42; Dessalles, *Sugar and Slavery, Family and Race: The Letters and Diary of Pierre Dessalles, Planter in Martinique, 1808–1856*, ed. and trans. Elborg Forster and Robert Forster (Baltimore: Johns Hopkins University Press, 1996), 46n3.

32. AN, FM-C, F/5B/2 Liste des passagers, Quartier de Marseille, état nominatif des passagers d'arrivés du colonies et partis pour les colonies pendant l'année 1817.

33. CAOM, SG-M- Information, 2/10, Rapport au Conseil des ministres, ministre de la marine et des colonies, Monsieur St. Hilaire, 1817.

34. CAOM, CM, 1814–1818, October 17, 1817, no. 1816, Dépêche ministérielle qui remet en vigueur la déclaration du roi du 9 aout 1777 interdisant aux noirs et gens de couleur l'entrée du royaume.

35. Françoise Thésée, *Le Général Donzelot à la Martinique, vers la fin de l'ancien régime colonial (1818–1826)* (Paris: Karthala, 1997).

36. CAOM, Généralité-Immigration, 298/1985, March 12, 1818, Rapport sur des projets de colonisation de blancs aux Antilles et à Cayenne.

37. Ibid.

38. CAOM, Généralité-Immigration, 298/1985, August 1819, Rapport au conseil des ministres.

39. CAOM, Généralité-Immigration, 298/1986, February 16, 1820, Le ministre à Baron Donzelot; CAOM, Généralité-Immigration, 298/1985, August 1819, Rapport au conseil des ministres.

40. CAOM, Généralité-Immigration, 298/1986, February 16, 1820, Le ministre à Baron Donzelot.

41. CAOM, CM, 1819–1823, June 5, 1820, no. 2183, Dépêche ministérielle au gouverneur administrateur au sujet de l'envoi qui pourrait être fait dans la colonie d'une nombre d'enfants trouvés.

42. Ibid.

43. CAOM, SG-M-Information, 1/2, February 21, 1821, Fougainville à Donzelot.

44. CAOM, SG-M-Information, 1/2, February 18, 1821, Assier de Montrose à Donzelot.

45. CAOM, SG-M-Information, 1/2, Résumé des opinions de M. les habitans proprietaires à la Martinique, qui ont été consultés sur la question relative à l'envoi qui pourrait être fait dans la colonie, d'un certain nombre d'enfants trouvés. Count de Grenonville of François made a similar argument. CAOM, SG-M-Information, 1/2, February 11, 1821, Colonist de François à Donzelot. According to the editors of Dessalles, vol. 1, Jean-Marie Duval de Grenonville was a future president of the royal tribunal and gentleman of the king's bedchamber in 1819; he would later be a deputy of Martinique in 1830.

46. CAOM, SG-M-Information, 1/2, February 22, 1821, Monsieur Lagrange à Donzelot.

47. CAOM, SG-M-Information, 1/2, n.d., Resumé Année 1821 de Monsieur Duhaut, habitant à la Grand'Anse; CAOM SG-M-Information, 1/2, February 21, 1821, Monsieur de Perpignan de Saint-Pierre à Donzelot.

48. CAOM, SG-M-Information, 1/2, February 22, 1821, Monsieur Lagrange à Donzelot.

49. Ibid.

50. CAOM, SG-M-Information, 1/2, February 17, 1821, Projet d'envoyer aux colonies un certain nombre d'enfants trouves, Dugué.

51. CAOM, SG-M-Information, 1/2, March 29, 1821, Donzelot à Monseigneur le ministre de la marine.

52. CAOM, SG-M-Finance, 116/1037, Finances budgets communaux, Fort-de-France et St. Pierre, approbation par decrets coloniaux, 1823.

53. CAOM, CM, 1814–1818, October 14, 1818, no. 1962, Observations du gouverneur administrateur sur un état des indigents de la paroisse du Fort-Royal, présenté par le bureau de charité pour obtenir le dégrevement de ceux qui y sont denommés,.

54. CAOM, SG-M-Finance, 143/1282, n.d., Budget des récettes & depenses de la Martinique pour l'exercise 1819.

55. CAOM, SG-M-Correspondance générale, October 20, 1819, Extrait du registre de délibération du conseil de gouvernement & d'administration.

56. CAOM, CM, 1819–1823, October 20, 1819, Ordonnance du gouverneur administrateur relativement à l'établissement et à l'administration de l'hospice des filles et femmes pauvres, orphelins, orphelines et enfants trouves [approuvée dans toutes ses dispositions par dépêche ministérielle du 24 decembre 1819]. When the *dames dominicaines* had taken control of the foundling home and charity hospice in the mid-eighteenth century, they, too, could take on paying students. However, when these institutions transferred to lay control in 1815, that privilege expired.

57. CAOM, CM, 1819–1823, January 13, 1819, no. 2012, Règlement de gouverneur administrateur pour l'ordre, le service, la discipline intérieure de la maison d'éducation des jeunes demoiselles, à Saint-Pierre.

58. The daughter of Monsieur Fougainville, prominent enough to comment on the feasibility of Martinique accepting orphaned metropolitan boys in 1820, numbered among the pupils, as did the daughters of the Levassor and Litteé families, close friends of the Dessalles family. CAOM, SG-M-Instruction publique, 97/854, Comptabilité de la maison royale d'éducation pour les demoiselles, depuis son établissement a Saint Pierre, Martinique en aout 1816 jusqu'au 31 décembre 1818, inclusivement.

59. CAOM, SG-M-Instruction publique, 97/854, September 21, 1819, Lettre au ministre, secrétaire d'état de la marine et des colonies, par le lieutenant général governor et administrateur pour le roi, Donzelot.

60. CAOM, CM, 1819–1823, January 13, 1819, no. 2012, Règlement de gouverneur administrateur pour l'ordre, le service, la discipline intérieure de la maison d'éducation des jeunes demoiselles, à Saint-Pierre; CAOM, SG-M-Instruction publique, 97/854, February 13, 1819, Règlement au nom du roi.

61. CAOM, CM, 1819–1823, January 13, 1819, no. 2012, Règlement de gouverneur administrateur pour l'ordre, le service, la discipline intérieure de la maison d'éducation des jeunes demoiselles, à Saint-Pierre.

62. The Royal Court also henceforth served as a court of last resort for civil and commercial matters appealed from the Tribunal of First Instance and also as a last resort for criminal, correctional, and police matters. It constituted itself as a civil chamber to pronounce on civil and commercial matters and as a chamber of accusation for pronouncing on criminal, correctional, and police matters. The Tribunals of First Instance were first created under the empire. During the British occupation of 1809–1814, they were replaced by the Old Régime *sénéchaussés*. In 1819, however, they once again became the Tribunals of First Instance. Liliane Chauleau, *Guide des Archives de la Martinique* (Fort-de-France, Martinique, 1978), 55–56. For more on the changes in Martinique's judicial structure during the Restoration, see John Savage, "Between Colonial Fact and French Law: Slave Poisoners and the Provostial Court in Restoration-Era Martinique," *French Historical Studies* 29, 4 (2006): 565–94.

63. CAOM, SG-M-Police, 123/1101, Paris, December 26, 1822, Rapport.

64. CAOM, SG-M-Police, 123/1101, Fort Royal, September 9, 1822, Donzelot au ministre de la marine; CAOM, SG-M-Police, 123/1101, December 8, 1820, Donzelot au ministre de la marine.

65. CAOM, SG-M-Police, 123/1101, October 9, 1818, Deslandes à Monsieur Donzelot;

CAOM, SG-M- Police, 123/1101, November 15, 1819, Procès-verbal de la première séance du conseil spécial; CAOM, SG-M- Police, 123/1101, July 29, 1818, Regnaudin à Monsieur Donzelot.

66. CAOM, SG-M-Police, 123/1101, September 17, 1820, Procès-verbal de la seconde séance du conseil spécial.

67. CAOM, SG-M-Police, 123/1101, February 17, 1821, Procès-verbal de la trosième séance du conseil spécial.

68. CAOM, SG-M-Police, 123/1101, Fort Royal, September 9, 1822, Donzelot au ministre de la marine; CAOM, SG-M-Police, 123/1101, December 8, 1820, Donzelot au ministre de la marine.

69. CAOM, SG-M-Police, 123/1101, September 17, 1820, Procès-verbal de la seconde séance du conseil spécial; CAOM, SG-M-Police, 123/1101, May 4, 1821, Rapport concernant le Sr. Jean Philippe Egidius, tailleur, age de 36 ans, né a Rietberge en Westphalie, demeurant dans la paroisse du St. Esprit; CAOM, SG-M-Police, 123/1101, n.d., Rapport concernant le nommé Goubert (Jacques, fils de Jacques et Elizabeth Sauvage, age de 26 ans, né a Rouen, détenu à la geôle de St. Pierre, par ordre du procureur du roi du janvier 7, 1821; CAOM, SG-M-Police, 123/1101, September 28, 1821, Lieutenant-géneral gouverneur Donzelot à monsieur, le secrétaire d'état, ministre de la marine et des colonies. Most sentences banned the deported men from the colony for five years. However, since the special council operated in an extrajudicial capacity, it had no specific standards with which to judge the severity of an infraction or determine the appropriate sentence. Consequently, great discrepancy emerged among the sentences. Some, like Silvestre Mésire, received only five years banishment, despite raping a child, whereas Jacques Goubert found himself barred from Martinique for life for threatening his neighbors with a knife.

70. AN, FM-C, F/5B/114, Extrait d'état du navire du commerce la clementine, and extrait d'état du brick du commerce français, l'alexandrine , novembre 1820.

71. AN, FM-C, F/5B/115, Extrait de l'état nominatif de passagers embarqués aux Antilles sur la flute la Moselle, janvier 1821.

72. AN, FM-C, F/5B/114, November 15, 1818, Extrait du brick du commerce, *Les Deux Frères*.

73. AN, FM-C, F/5B/114, October 4, 1820, Extrait du navire de commerce, *Les Deux Amis*; AN, FM-C, F/5B/114, April 1821, Extrait du brick du commerce, *L'Angelique*.

74. Abbé Bernard David, "La Population d'un quartier de la Martinique au début du XIXème siècle d'après les registres paroissiaux: Rivière-Pilote, 1802–1829," *Revue française d'histoire d'outre-mer* 60, 220 (third trimester 1973): 330–63.

75. CAOM, SG-M-Police, 123/1101, Proces-verbal de la seconde séance du conseil spécial, September 17, 1820.

76. Ibid.

77. Ibid.; CAOM, SG-M-Police, 123/1101, December 8, 1820, Donzelot à la ministère de la marine.

78. CAOM, SG-M-Police, 123/1101, Proces-verbal de la seconde séance du conseil spécial, September 17, 1820.

79. CAOM, SG-M-Police, 123/1101, Proces-verbal de la troisième séance du conseil spécial, February 17, 1821.

80. Ibid.

81. Ibid.

82. Ibid.

83. Thésée, *Le Général Donzelot à la Martinique*, chap. 1, "Le droit colonial en question: La mission du Baron Delamardelle (mars–juillet 1820)," 17–39.

84. CAOM, SG-M-Police, 140/1265, January 9, 1821, Rapport sur la réorganization judiciaire.

85. CAOM, SG-M-Police, 123/1101, December 26, 1822, Note additionnelle au Rapport du M. le Baron Delamardelle.

86. For a more complete discussion of the complexities of identifying an actual increase in the use of poison by enslaved peoples, see especially John Savage, " 'Black Magic' and White Terror: Slave Poisonings and Colonial Society in Early 19th Century Martinique," *Journal of Social History* (Spring 2007): 636–62.

87. CAOM, SG-M-Affaires politiques, 52/430, September 28, 1822, Rapport du Général Donzelot.

88. Savage, "Between Colonial Fact and French Law," 573.

89. Savage, " 'Black Magic' and White Terror," 636. Joseph Elzéar Morénas estimated the court executed more than 600 and sentenced as many as 1,000 others before it was disbanded at the end of 1826. See Joseph Elzéar Morénas, *Précis historique de la traite des Noirs et de l'Esclavage colonial* (1828; rpt. Geneva: Slatkine, 1978), 323–24.

90. CAOM, SG-M-Police, 123/1101, September 9, 1822, Donzelot à Monsieur le Marquis de Clermont-Tonnerre, ministre secrétaire d'état de la marine et des colonies.

91. Ibid.

92. CAOM, SG-M-Police, 123/1101, December 26, 1822, Rapport du M. le Baron Delamardelle.

93. Ibid. Note additionnelle au Rapport du M. le Baron Delamardelle.

94. 172 in Nantes, 24 in Brest, 26 in Rochefort, 18 in Le Havre, 28 in Bordeaux, and 12 in Marseille. AN, FM-C, F/5B/36, État nominatif des passagers de toutes descriptions partis pour France, sur les bâtiments du commerce pendant le 2ème trimestre 1818.

95. CAOM, CM, 1814–1818, August 5, 1818, no. 1942, Circulaire ministérielle qui déclare que les gens de couleur libres peuvent librement et sans être assujettis à aucun cautionnement sortir des colonies pour se rendre soit en France, soit à l'étranger.

96. AN, FM-C, F/5B/36, État nominatif des passagers de toutes descriptions partis pour France, sur les batiments du commerce pendant le 2ème trimestre 1818.

97. Jennifer Heuer, "The One drop rule in reverse? Interracial Marriages in Napoleonic and Restoration France," *Law and History Review* 27, 3 (Fall 2009).

98. CAOM, SG-M-Justice, 29/251, Correspondance avec M. Richard de Lucy, procureur général par interim 1824–1825.

99. CAOM, SG-M-Information, 6/71, April 26, 1822, Donzelot à Monsieur le Marquis de Clermont-Tonnerre, ministre secrétaire d'état de la marine et des colonies.

100. Dessalles, vol. 1, 56, March 20, 1822, Pierre Dessalles à sa mère.

101. Dessalles, vol. 1, 57, April 20, 1822, Pierre Dessalles à sa mère.

102. CAOM, SG-M-Police, 18/157, October 28, 1822, Lieutenant général governor Donzelot au Ministre de la marine.

103. Françoise Thésée, "La Révolte des esclaves du Carbet à la Martinique (octobre–novembre 1822)," *Revue française d'histoire d'outre-mer* 80, 301 (1993): 551–84.

104. Dessalles, vol. 1, 73, October 21, 1822, Pierre Dessalles à sa mère.

105. Thésée, "La Révolte des esclaves du Carbet à la Martinique," 567.

106. CAOM, SG-M- Police, 18/157, November 24, 1822, Lieutenant général governor Donzelot au ministre de la marine.

107. Dessalles, vol. 1, 71, October 18, 1822, Pierre Dessalles à sa mère. According to Henri Frémont, editor of Dessalles's letters and diary, "Contrary to what the colonials thought—and Dessalles represents their view very well here—the government cared very much. The governors of Martinique and Guadeloupe had jointly hired an agent at Saint-Eustache, asking him to watch the activities of the rebels of Saint-Domingue and the insurgents of the Spanish colonies on the continent." Dessalles, vol. 1, 71n72. Elborg and Forster include the same information in *Sugar and Slavery, Family and Race* (50) and also cite David C. Geggus, "The Slaves and Coloreds of Martinique During the Age of the French and Haitian Revolutions: Three Moments of Resistance," in *The Lesser Antilles in the Age of European Expansion*, ed. Robert Paquette (Gainesville: University Press of Florida, 1996).

108. CAOM, SG-M-Police, 18/157, St. Pierre, Martinique, November 4, 1822, Monsieur Bellard.

109. *Journal de Paris*, December 14, 1822.

110. Ibid., January 12, 1823.

111. Bibliothèque nationale de France (hereafter BNF), *Moeurs des trois couleurs aux Antilles ou lettre de la Martinique sur les vices du système colonial dans les colonies françaises* (Paris, 1822).

112. Savage, "Between Colonial Fact and French Law."

113. For a similar interpretation of slavery's effects on white women in the southern United States see, for example, Catherine Clinton, *The Plantation Mistress: Women's World in the Old South* (New York: Pantheon, 1982); and Elizabeth Fox-Genovese, *Within the Plantation Household: Black and White Women of the Old South* (Chapel Hill: University of North Carolina Press 1988).

114. BNF, *Moeurs des trois couleurs aux Antilles.*

115. Ibid., 13–16.

116. CAOM, SG-M-Finance, 116/1037, Finances budgets communaux, Fort-de-France et St. Pierre, approbation par decrets coloniaux, 1823.

117. Dale W. Tomich, *Slavery in the Circuit of Sugar: Martinique and the World Economy, 1830–1848* (Baltimore: Johns Hopkins University Press, 1990), 43–46.

118. Ibid., 116–23.

119. Dessalles, vol. 1, Pierre Dessalles, 1822–1824. This was not an unusual practice. According to Robert Louis Stein, during the eighteenth century, widows in France's port cities "often replaced their dead husbands as active members of commercial companies including

sons, son(s)-in-law, or both." See Robert Louis Stein, *The French Slave Trade in the Eighteenth Century: An Old Regime Business* (Madison: University of Wisconsin Press, 1979), 62.

120. Tomich, *Slavery in the Circuit of Sugar*, 117.

121. Over the course of their business relationship, widow Dupuy handled nearly 125,000 pounds of Dessalles sugar and extended the family in Martinique and continental France nearly 68,000 francs in loans. See, for example, Dessalles, vol. 1, 62–63, July 15 and July 24, 1822, Pierre Dessalles à sa mère; Dessalles, vol. 1, 84, April 30, 1823, Pierre Dessalles à sa mère; Dessalles, vol. 1, 96, July 26, 1823, Pierre Dessalles à sa mère; Dessalles, vol. 1, 102–3, December 10, 1823, Pierre Dessalles à sa mère; and Dessalles, vol. 1, 132, November 6, 1824, Pierre Dessalles à sa mère.

122. Tomich, *Slavery in the Circuit of Sugar*, 116–23; Savage, "Between Colonial Fact and French Law," 582.

123. Dessalles, vol. 1, 91, July 4, 1823, Pierre Dessalles à sa mère.

124. CAOM, SG-M-Affaires politiques, 51/409, Copie de la lettre écrite à son excellence monsieur le gouverneur de la Martinique par les habitants commissaires commandants des paroisses de Macouba, du la Basse Pointe, et de la Grand'Anse. Melvin D. Kennedy also makes reference to an increased fear of mixed-race participation in the Carbet revolt. See Kennedy, "The Bissette Affair and the French Colonial Question," *Journal of Negro History* 45, 1 (January 1960): 1–10.

125. Dessalles, vol. 1, 87, April 30, 1823, Pierre Dessalles à sa mère; Dessalles, vol. 1, 92, july 4, 1823.

126. Dessalles, vol. 1, 77, January 6, 1823, Pierre Dessalles à sa mère.

127. Dessalles, vol. 1, 103, December 10, 1823, Pierre Dessalles à sa mère.

128. CAOM, SG-M-Affaires politiques, 51/428, Copie d'une lettre anonyme reçus par le procureur du roi de St. Pierre, le 30 novembre 1830.

129. CAOM, SG-M-Affaires politiques, 51/409, Copie de la lettre écrite à son excellence monsieur le gouverneur de la Martinique par les habitants commissaires commandants des paroisses de Macouba, du la Basse Pointe, et de la Grand'Anse.

130. For more on the Bissette affair see, for example, Kennedy, "The Bissette Affair and the French Colonial Question"; Robin Blackburn, *The Overthrow of Colonial Slavery, 1776–1848* (London: Verso, 1988), 477–78; Liliane Chauleau, *Dans les îles du vent: la Martinique (XVIIe-XIXe siècle)*(Paris: L'Harmattan, 1993), 226; Thésée, *Le Général Donzelot à Martinique*, 147–84; Stella Pâme, *Cyrille Bissette: Un Martyr de la liberté* (Fort-de-France: Désormeaux, 1999).

131. Savage, "Between Colonial Fact and French Law," 583.

132. Dessalles, vol. 1, 105–6, March 12, 1824, Pierre Dessalles à sa mere.

133. Pâme, *Cyrille Bissette*; Thésee, *Le Général Donzelot*; Chauleau, *Dans les îles du vent*, 226; Kennedy, "The Bissette Affair and the French Colonial Question," 3.

134. CAOM, SG-M-Justice, 29/251, December 21, 1823, Rapport addressé par M. de Champvallier, procureur du roi à St. Pierre, au gouverneur & administrateur pour le roi; CAOM, SG-M-Justice, 29/251, December 23, 1823, *Procureur général* Richard de Lucy au gouverneur Donzelot; CAOM, SG-M-Justice, 29/251, January 11, 1824, *Procureur général* Richard de Lucy au Marquis de Clermont-Tonnere, ministre de la marine et des colonies.

135. CAOM, SG-M-Justice, 29/251, December 23, 1823, De Lucy au Donzelot.

136. CAOM, SG-M-Justice, 29/251, March 7, 1824, *Procureur général* Richard de Lucy au Marquis de Clermont-Tonnere, ministre de la marine et des colonies. Because the government confiscated all their property on departure, and presumably absolved their debtors, many of them *colons*, of any financial commitments, this gesture was far less humanitarian than de Lucy described it in his explanation.

137. CAOM, SG-M-Justice, 29/251, March 7, 1824, De Lucy au Marquis de Clermont-Tonnere.

138. CAOM, SG-M-Justice, 29/251, January 11, 1824, *Procureur général* Richard de Lucy au Marquis de Clermont-Tonnere, ministre de la marine et des colonies.

139. Ibid.

140. CAOM, CM, 1824–1827, February 25, 1824, no. 4248, Dépêche ministérielle au gouverneur administrateur concernant les concessions d'affranchissements et l'accroissement anormal des gens de couleur.

141. CAOM, CM, 1824–1827, March 3, 1824, no. 4251, Dépêche ministérielle portant que la déclaration du roi de 9 aout 1777, en ce qui touche la faculté laissée aux habitants des colonies venant en France de se faire servir durant la traversée par des noirs esclaves, cessera d'avoir son execution; CAOM, CM, 1824–1827, June 8, 1824, no. 4269, Arrêté du gouverneur administrteur qui ameliore la solde et la nourriture des negres et negresses du roi employés dans les hopitaux maritimes.

142. See, for example, Dessalles, vol. 1, 1, July 12, 24, 28, August 12, 1824, Pierre Dessalles à sa mere; Savage, " 'Black Magic' and White Terror," 648–51.

143. Thésée, *Le Général Donzelot*, 107; Savage, "Between Colonial Fact and French Law," 583.

144. Dessalles, vol. 1, 143, February 18, 1825, Pierre Dessalles à sa mère.

145. In "Gender Ideologies in the Caribbean," Hilary McD. Beckles argues "the social needs of patriarchy [idealized] the white woman as a symbol of white supremacy, moral authority, and sexual purity. The patriarchal ideology of white supremacy required the social isolation of all white women, irrespective of class, from black men in order to minimize the dreaded possibility of mixing." "Gender Ideologies in the Caribbean," in *Identity in the Shadow of Slavery*, ed. Paul Lovejoy (London: Continuum, 2000), 168. He also argues, however, that emphasis should be shifted from white male efforts to "prevent the social access of black males to the white female in order to project her as a symbol of moral purity and ideal domesticity," to "the white male's principal concern was to limit the size of the free non-white group within society." Hilary McD. Beckles, "White Women and Freedom," in *Centering Woman: Gender Discourses in Caribbean Slave Society* (Princeton, N.J.: Markus Wiener, 1999), 69.

146. CAOM, SG-M-Information, 2/10, September 10, 1836, Notes sur la Martinique, soumises à Monsieur de St. Hilaire, conseiller d'état, directeur des colonies, par M. Gallard Montbrun, juge de paix de canton de la Trinité.

147. CAOM, SG-M-Cultes, 61/519, Paris, January 17, 1822, Lettre du ministre de la marine au gouverneur de la Martinique.

148. CAOM, CM, 1819–1823, December 24, 1823, no. 4234, Dépêche ministérielle

annoncant au gouverneur administrateur des dispositions prises en faveur de si soeurs de la congrégation de Saint-Joseph se rendant à la Martinique; CAOM, SG-M-Cultes, 61/518, November 9, 1822, Lettre du gouverneur de la Martinique au ministre de la marine. For more on the Sisters of Saint-Joseph in Martinique see chapter 4 in Philippe Delisle, *Renouveau missionnaire et société esclavagiste, La Martinique: 1815–1848* (Paris: Publisud, 1997).

149. As quoted in Delisle, *Renouveau missionnaire et société esclavagiste*, 83n25.

150. CAOM, CM, 1824–1827, January 14, 1824, no. 4241, Dépêche ministérielle demandant au gouverneur administrateur un prompt rapport sur les graves abus qui existeraient dans la maison royale d'éducation à Saint-Pierre.

151. CAOM, CM, 1819–1823, December 24, 1823, no. 4234, Dépêche ministérielle annoncant au gouverneur administrateur des dispositions prises en faveur de si soeurs de la congrégation de Saint-Joseph se rendant à la Martinique; CAOM, CM, 1824–1827, September 15, 1824, no. 4287, Décision du gouverneur administrateur portant que le pensionnat royal de jeunes demoiselles placé à Saint-Pierre sera regi, à l'avenir, par les dames religieuses de la congrégation de Saint-Joseph.

152. CAOM, CM, 1824–1827, September 15, 1824, no. 4287, Décision du gouverneur administrateur portant que le pensionnat royal de jeunes demoiselles placé à Saint-Pierre sera regi, à l'avenir, par les dames religieuses de la congrégation de Saint-Joseph.

153. CAOM, CM, 1824–1827, February 25, 1824, no. 4248, Dépêche ministérielle au gouverneur administrateur concernant les concessions d'afranchissements et l'accroissement anormal des gens de couleur.

154. CAOM, CM, 1824–1827, December 8, 1824, no. 4303, Arret du gouverneur administrateur portant creation d'une commission pour la revision des listes d'indigents rationnaires à la charge soit de la caisse municipale, soit de la caisse royale (extrait).

155. CAOM, SG-M-Affaires politiques, 51/418, Excerpt from April 22, 1824, *Le Pilote*.

156. John Savage has written extensively about the Lambert case in "Between Colonial Fact and French Law," and " 'Black Magic' and White Terror"; Kennedy, "The Bissette Affair and the French Colonial Question," 4.

157. *Mémoire pour les hommes de couleur de la Martinique* and *Mémoire à S.E. le ministre de la marine et des colonies sur la demande en communication des pièces relatives aux déportés de la Martinique et sur la legalité de la déportation 10 juillet 1824.*

158. Archives parlementaires, Series 2, volume 47, 365–70, July 1824, Constant in the Chamber of Deputies. Michael Kennedy has written about the importance of this debate in "The Bissette Affair and the French Colonial Question," 5–6.

159. CAOM, SG-M-Information, 1/6, December 1824, V. Gauvain, Cahier au régime colonial.

160. Ibid.

161. CAOM, SG-M-Affaires politiques, 51/418, August 15, 1824, Ministre de la marine à Donzelot.

162. CAOM, SG-M-Affaires politiques, 51/418, September 10, 1824, Vice amiral commandant de la marine, comte de Gourdoy au ministre de la marine; CAOM, SG-M-Affaires politiques, 51/418, September 29, 1824, Directeur de la police au ministre de la marine.

163. CAOM, SG-M-Affaires politiques, 51/413, September 21, 1824, Millet et Thébia au sous prefet du Havre, Cartier.

164. Ibid.

165. CAOM, SG-M-Affaires politiques, 51/413, n.d., Le sous préfet de Havre à monseigneur, ministre de l'intérieur.

166. CAOM, SG-M-Affaires politiques, 51/413, September 21, 1824, E. Petit au sous préfet de Havre.

167. CAOM, SG-M-Affaires politiques, 51/411, October 12, 1824, Henri Petit à Madame la duchesse de Reggio à Paris.

168. CAOM, SG-M-Affaires politiques, 51/413, n.d., Le sous préfet de Havre à monseigneur, ministre de l'interieur.

169. CAOM, SG-M-Affaires politiques, 51/411, October 25, 1824, Le sous préfet de Havre au ministre de la marine.

170. Ibid.

171. CAOM, SG-M-Affaires politiques, 51/411, November 4, 1824, Le sous préfet de Havre au ministre de la marine.

172. CAOM, SG-M-Affaires politiques, 51/413, August 2, 1826, Directeur de la police au ministre de la marine.

173. Dessalles, vol. 1, 169, August 22, 1825, Pierre Dessalles à sa mère.

174. Kennedy, "The Bissette Affair and the French Colonial Question," 7.

175. Thésée, *Le Général*, 185–89.

176. See, for example, Isambert, *À la chambre des pairs du royaume: Production nouvelle pour MM. Bissette, Fabien fils et Volny, déposé le 14 avril 1826* (Paris, 1826); Chauveau-Lagarde, *Plaidoyer . . . pour les sieurs Bissette, Fabien fils et Volny, condamnés à la marque et aux galères à perpetuité par la cour royale de la Martinique* (1826).

177. CAOM, SG-M-141/1270, October 18, 1826, letter. For more on the case, see Savage, "Between Colonial Fact and French Law," 588–89.

CHAPTER 4. "IN THE COLONIES, IT IS IMPOSSIBLE THAT A WHITE WOULD ALIGN HIMSELF WITH SLAVES": SHIFTS IN COLONIAL POLICY

1. Liliane Chauleau, *Dans les îles du vent: la Martinique (XVIIe–XIXe siècle)*(Paris: L'Harmattan, 1993), 223.

2. Ibid., 220–21.

3. SSJ, 2Ah3, État statistique des établissements depuis leur fondation jusqu'en 1852.

4. CAOM, CM, 1824–1827, July 17, 1827, no. 4593, Ordonnance du gouverneur qui confie la direction et l'administration de l'hospice des orphelines de Saint-Pierre aux dames religieuses de Saint-Joseph, 443.

5. SSJ, 3A, Lettres de Mère Marie-Thérèse Javouhey (juin 1818–août 1840), January 3, 1829, 68.

6. CAOM, CM, 1824–1827, July 17, 1827, no. 4593, Ordonnance du gouverneur qui

confie la direction et l'administration de l'hospice des orphelines de Saint-Pierre aux dames religieuses de Saint-Joseph, 443.

7. In 1830 alone, four different men applied to open private academies for Martinique's white boys. CAOM-SG-M-Instruction publique, 97/848, Extrait du registre des procès verbaux des délibérations du Conseil privé de la Martinique. For more on education in Martinique, see Joseph Rennard, "Les Écoles à la Martinique au XIXème siècle jusqu'à la IIIème République," *Annales des Antilles* 22 (1978): 46–53.

8. SSJ, 2Ah/8, December 20, 1827, Programme des exercices d'instruction soutenus par les élèves du Pensionnat Royal des Dames de Saint-Joseph; SSJ, 2Ah/3, Recettes des Soeurs St. Joseph de la Martinique, 1824–1827.

9. SSJ, 3A, Lettres de Mère Marie-Thérèse Javouhey (juin 1818–août 1840), no. 17, July 13, 1827, 25.

10. CAOM, SG-M-Information, 2/9, September 21, 1827, De Ricard, mémoire à Monseigneur de Clermont Tonnere, De l'Ordonnance de Bourbon définitivement appliquée à la Martinique par celle du 7 février 1827. Joseph-Barthélemy-Honoré-Louis-Amable de Ricard arrived in Martinique in 1818 as an assistant to Governor Donzelot's état-major. In 1826, he was named chief of the governor's état-major. For more on de Ricard see Françoise Thésée, *Le Général Donzelot à la Martinique, vers la fin de l'ancien régime colonial (1818–1826)* (Paris: Karthala, 1997).

11. CAOM, SG-M-Information, 2/9, September 21, 1827, De Ricard à Tonnere.

12. Ibid.

13. Ibid.

14. CAOM, SG-M-Travaux publiques, 166/1520, March 25, 1828, Vicomte Rosily au gouverneur de la Martinique; CAOM SG-M-Travaux publiques, 166/1520, April 28, 1828, Rapport à son excellence, l'aide de camp du roi, gouverneur de la Martinique.

15. For more on the standards of evidence used in court cases and efforts to maintain behavior see William M. Reddy, chap. 4, "The Ladder Up: Accumulating Honors in the Ministry of the Interior" in *The Invisible Code: Honor and Sentiment in Postrevolutionary France, 1814–1848* (Berkeley: University of California Press, 1997).

16. CAOM, FM-Greffes, 942, Tribunal de première instance, Fort-de-France, Affaires criminelles, May 28, 1828.

17. CAOM, FM-Greffes, 943, Tribunal de première instance, Fort-de-France, 3ème trimèstre, (juillet et septembre 1828), Affaires petits criminelles, August 27, 1828. Lamotte appealed the initial ruling, and this sentence represents a reduction based on his youth.

18. CAOM, FM-Greffes, 850, Cour royale, Fort-de-France, 1ère trimestre (janvier et mars 1828), matières criminelles, January 3, 1828.

19. CAOM, FM-Greffes, 942, Tribunal de première instance, Fort-de-France, Affaires criminelles, April 25, 1828.

20. John Savage has explored the increase in deportations of enslaved Martinicans after 1827 in "Between Colonial Fact and French Law," 590–92.

21. CAOM, FM-Greffes, 850, Cour royale, Fort-de-France, 1 ère trimestre (janvier et mars 1828), March 6, 1828.

22. CAOM, FM-Greffes, 943, Tribunal de première instance, Fort-de-France, 3ème trimestre, (juillet et septembre 1828), July 1, 1828.

23. Ibid.

24. *Revue des Colonies*, February 1836.

25. AN, FD, Papiers d'Origny et Pécoul, 376/ap/15, Sainte Pierre, Martinique, September 4, 1828, Monsieur Laval à Monsieur Pécoul.

26. In nineteenth-century Martinique, as in metropolitan France, the law restricted married women's property rights. A married woman was legally subservient to her husband and could not enter into binding contracts without his permission. Likewise, unless specifically noted otherwise, all property acquired or bought during marriage became the property of her husband. A married woman was also responsible for her husband's debts on his death and could lose all assets to his creditors.

27. Kathleen Mary Butler explores the importance of the laws of equity, which allowed married women to retain a "sole and separate estate" from their husbands, in the nineteenth-century British holdings of Jamaica and Barbados. See Kathleen Mary Butler, "White Women in the Plantation Economy," in Butler, *The Economics of Emancipation: Jamaica and Barbados, 1823–1843* (Chapel Hill: University of North Carolina Press, 1995), 92–94.

28. CAOM, FM-Greffes, 1093, Tribunal de première instance, Saint Pierre, 3ème trimestre (juillet et aout 1828), July 12, 1828, Sieur et Dame Beauvais vs. Dame Le Roy; CAOM, FM-Greffes, 1094, Tribunal de première instance, Saint Pierre, 4ème trimestre (septembre 1828), September 27, 1828, Dame Moulin Dusienne et Dame Labadie; CAOM, FM-Greffes, 850, Cour royale, première trimestre (janvier et mars 1828) March 3, 1828; CAOM, FM-Greffes, 943, Tribunal de première instance, Fort-de-France, 3ème trimestre (juillet et septembre 1828), July 12, 1828, Dame Chopard vs. Monsieur Belleroche.

29. A number of widows appeared in the Tribunal records, 4 representing their dead husbands' affairs, 4 representing their children, and 6 additional widows dealing with their own property. For Widow Schambourg's financial dealings, see CAOM, FM-Greffes, 1093, Tribunal de première instance, Saint Pierre, 3ème trimestre (juillet et aout 1828), July 12, 1828, Monsieur Garcin et Monsieur Théodore LeChevallier vs. Widow Schaumbourg; CAOM, FM-Greffes, 1093, Tribunal de première instance, Saint Pierre, 3ème trimestre (juillet et aout 1828), July 19, 1828, Sieur Bablot et Sieur Pinault vs. Widow Schaumbourg; CAOM, FM-Greffes, 1093, Tribunal de première instance, Saint Pierre, 3ème trimestre (juillet et aout 1828), August 1, 1828, vs. widow Schaumbourg; CAOM, FM-Greffes, 1093, Tribunal de première instance, Saint Pierre, 3ème trimestre (juillet et aout 1828), August 4, 1828, Sieur Niochet vs. Widow Schaumbourg; CAOM, FM-Greffes, 1093, Tribunal de première instance, Saint Pierre, 3ème trimestre (juillet et aout 1828), August 16, 1828, Sieur L. Deziles vs. Widow Schaumbourg. For more evidence of white widows acting as property owners, see CAOM, FM- Greffes 850, Cour royale, première trimestre (janvier et mars 1828) March 3, 1828 vs. Widow Anguetil de Briancourt; CAOM, FM-Greffes 944, Tribunal de première instance, Fort-de-France, 4 trimestre (octobre et décembre 1828), October 29, 1828 vs. Widow Gilmand; CAOM, FM: Greffes 944, Tribunal de première instance, Fort-de-France, 4ème trimestre (octobre et décembre 1828), December 28, 1828 vs. Widow

Gilmand; CAOM, FM-Greffes, 1093, Tribunal de première instance, Saint Pierre, 3ème trimestre (juillet et aout 1828), August 9, 1828 vs. Widow Issac; CAOM, FM-Greffes, 1094, Tribunal de première instance, Saint Pierre, 4ème trimestre (septembre 1828), September 27, 1828, Widow Morin vs. Widow Igout. Kathleen Mary Butler examines the importance of white widows as property owners in nineteenth-century Jamaica and Barbados. See Butler, "White Women in the Plantation Economy," 97–105.

30. In her work on the free women of color in eighteenth-century Cap Français, Saint Domingue, Susan Socolow has also found evidence of free women of color hawking and working as small merchants "alongside white middle-class women who ran small commercial establishments and shops." Nonetheless, she concludes that white women "were rarely visible acting on their own." See Socolow, "Economic Roles of the Free Women of Color of Cap Français," in *More Than Chattel: Black Women and Slavery in the Americas*," ed. David Barry Gaspar and Darlene Clark Hine (Bloomington: Indiana University Press 1996), 282. For more on the commercial links between poorer white women and free mixed-race women in the British West Indies, see Barbara Bush, *Slave Women in Caribbean Society, 1650–1838* (Bloomington: Indiana University Press, 1990); Bush, "White 'Ladies,' Coloured 'Favourites,' and Black 'Wenches'; Some Considerations on Sex, Race and Class Factors in Social Relations in White Creole Society in the British Caribbean," *Slavery & Abolition* 2, 3 (December 1981): 245–63; Hilary McD. Beckles, "White Women and Freedom," in Beckles, *Centering Woman: Gender Discourses in Caribbean Slave Society* (Kingston: I. Randle, 1999); and chap. 4, "Marketeers: The Right to Trade," in Beckles, *Natural Rebels: A Social History of Enslaved Black Women in Barbados* (New Brunswick, N.J.: Rutgers University Press, 1989).

31. CAOM, FM-Greffes, 1093, Tribunal de première instance, Saint Pierre, 3ème trimestre (juillet et aout 1828), July 13, 1828, Widow Pisant de la Rifaudière vs. Rosette; CAOM, FM-Greffes, 1093, Tribunal de première instance, Saint Pierre, 4 ème trimestre (septembre 1828),September 13, 1828, Widow Le Tavernier vs. Marguerite.

32. CAOM, FM-Greffes, 1094, Tribunal de première instance, Saint Pierre, 4ème trimestre (septembre 1828), September 20, 1828, Widow Puilhery vs. Anastasie.

33. Kennedy, "The Bissette Affair," 9; Stella Pâme, *Cyrille Bissette: Un martyr de la liberté* (Martinique: Désormeaux, 1999), 92–93.

34. *Cour de Cassation: Consultations et Mémoires à l'appui du recours en Cassations des hommes de couleur Bissette, Fabien, et Volny contre l'arrêt de la Cour royale de la Guadeloupe du 28 mars 1827* (Paris: Duverger, 1827).

35. Pâme, *Cyrille Bissette*, 92–93.

36. *Le Moniteur*, December 30, 1827; *Gazette des Tribunuax*, December 30, 1827.

37. BNF, *Pétition aux deux Chambres, des hommes de couleur de la Martinique, déportés aux colonies étrangères par le général Donzelot, en décembre 1823 et janvier 1824. (Signé : Bissette, Fabien fils.)* (Paris: Duverger, 1828).

38. Archives parlementaires, Serie 2, volume 54, 241–260, May 24, 1828, Chamber of Deputies.

39. AN, FM-C, F/5B/36, État nominatif des passagers embarqués pour les ports de France ou pour d'autres colonies, pendant l'année 1828.

40. BNF, Dame Sophie Mamy Doin, *Blanche et noir*, in *Nouvelles blanches et noires* (Paris: A. Desauges, 1828). Doris Y. Kadish has gathered these short stories and provided a literary and biographical context for Doin in *La famille noire suivie de trois nouvelles blanches et noirs* (Paris: L'Harmattan, 2002).

41. Doin, *Noire et blanc*, in *Nouvelles blanches et noires*.

42. Liliane Chauleau, *Guide des Archives de la Martinique* (Fort-de-France: Archives départmentales, 1978), 33, 54–56.

43. Josette Fallope, *Esclaves et citoyens: Les noirs à la Guadeloupe au XIXe siècle dans les processus de résistance et d'intégration: 1802–1910* (Basse-Terre: Société d'histoire de la Guadeloupe, 1992), 62–69, 233–35.

44. Dessalles, vol. 1, 182, November 22, 1828, Pierre Dessalles à sa mère.

45. Ibid., 182n7. This appointment allotted him 8,000 francs to pay for his lodging and furnishings in Fort-de-France. Dessalles participated in the judicial system until a controversy in the early years of the July Monarchy led to his dismissal.

46. Comte de Grenonville, *Mémoire*, non publiés, p. 81 as quoted in Pâme, *Cyrille Bissette*, 114.

47. Dessalles, vol. 1, 182n7, November 22, 1828, Pierre Dessalles à sa mère.

48. Louis Henri de Saulces de Freycinet had a long career in colonial administration, serving first as govenor of the Île de Bourbon (1821–1826), then French Guiana, (1826–1828), and finally as Martinique's governor in 1829–1830.

49. CAOM, SG-M-Police, 76/610, August 6, 1829, Monsieur Cardini, captain de gendarmerie à la Martinique au ministre de la marine.

50. CAOM, SG-M-Police, 76/610, September 28, 1829, Monsieur Cardini, captain de gendarmerie à la Martinique au ministre de la marine.

51. Robert A. Nye has discussed the important role that dueling played to maintain male honor in continental France during this same period. See Nye, *Masculinity and Male Codes of Honor in Modern France* (New York: Oxford University Press, 1993).

52. CAOM, SG-M-Police, 76/610, September 28, 1829, Monsieur Cardini, captain de gendarmerie à la Martinique au ministre de la marine. For more evidence on conflicts between Martinique's white metropolitan and Creole populations, see CAOM, SG-M-Police, 76/610, July 26, 1829, Monsieur Cardini, captain de gendarmerie à la Martinique au ministre de la marine.

53. SSJ, 3A, Lettres de Mère Marie-Thérèse Javouhey (juin 1818–août 1840), no. 40, January 3, 1829, 68.

54. SSJ, 2Ah/2, June 1829, Copie des conventions faites entre l'administration et la Congrégation lors de la remise du Pensionnat de St. Pierre, Martinique.

55. SSJ, 3A, Lettres de Mère Marie-Thérèse Javouhey, (juin 1818–août 1840), no. 47, August 18, 1829, 79–80.

56. CAOM, SG-M-Registre 125, Extrait de Registre de procès verbaux des délibérations du Conseil général, session ordinaire du mois de juin, 1830.

57. CAOM, SG-M-Cultes, 61/518, May 4, 1830, Extrait du Registre des procès verbaux des délibérations du Conseil privé de la Martinique, session ordinaire du mois de mai, séance du quatre, 1830.

58. CAOM, SG-M-Registre 125, Extrait de Registre de procès verbaux des délibérations du Conseil géneral, session ordinaire du mois de juin, 1830.

59. Letter 220, À Mère Marie-Thérèse Javouhey, à la Martinique, Cayenne, November 17, 1830, Anne-Marie Javouhey, Fondatrice de la Congrégation des Soeurs de Saint-Joseph de Cluny, *Lettres*, vol. 1, *Lettres 1 à 265, 1798–juin 1833*, texte présenté, établi et annoté par Les Soeurs Jean Hébert et Marie-Cécile de Segonzac, préface par Le Cardinal Gantin (Paris, 1994), 479.

60. CAOM, SG-M-Instruction publique, 97/850, July 18, 1830, Rapport sur l'éducation à la Martinique.

61. CAOM, SG-M-Instruction publique, 97/850, September 3, 1830, Extrait du registre des procès verbaux des délibérations du conseil privé de la Martinique.

62. Ibid.

63. *Pétition des hommes de couleur de la Martinique*, December 14, 1829 in Pâme, *Cyrille Bissette*, 122.

64. CAOM, SG-M-Police, 76/610, December 1, 1830, Rapport confidentiel du capitaine de la gendarmerie de la Martinique.

65. CAOM, SG-M-Police, 76/610, May 28, 1830, Cardini, confidentiel pour Monsieur de St. Hilaire, directeur des colonies.

66. For more on Richer's arrest, see Genevieve Léti, *Santé et Société esclavagiste à la Martinique—1802–1848* (Paris: L'Harmattan, 1998), 41; CAOM, FM-Greffes, 852, Cour royale, 3ème trimestre (juillet et aout 1830), August 9, 1830, Affaire du cirque.

67. Ibid.

68. Ibid.

69. *Bulletin des Lois: 1830 juillet–décembre, 2è partie, bulletin n 18*, September 7, 1830 ordinance, 381.

70. CAOM, FM-Greffes, 852, Cour royale, 2ème trimestre (avril et juin 1830), May 6, 1830, vs. Dancy.

71. CAOM, FM-Greffes, 852, Cour royale, 2ème trimestre (avril et juin 1830), May 6, 1830, vs. Auguetil.

72. CAOM, FM-Greffes, 852, Cour royale, 2ème trimestre (avril et juin 1830), May 6, 1830, vs. Guinel.

73. CAOM, FM-Greffes, 852, Cour royale, 2ème trimestre (avril et juin 1830), June 10, 1830, vs. Guinel.

74. CAOM, SG-M-Police, 76/610, May 28, 1830, Cardini, confidentiel pour Monsieur de St. Hilaire, directeur des colonies.

75. CAOM, FM-Greffes, 852, Cour royale, première trimestre, (janvier et mars 1830), February 5, 1830, vs. Lantibois, fils et Thiramène; CAOM, FM-Greffes, 852, Cour royale, 3ème trimestre, (juillet et aout 1830), July 14, 1830.

76. CAOM, FM-Greffes, 852, Cour royale, première trimestre, (janvier et mars 1830), February 5, 1830, vs. Thuret et Alfred.

77. CAOM, FM- Greffes, 852, Cour royale, première trimestre, (janvier et mars 1830), February 6, 1830, vs. Herman et Luther Ancinall, Delonge, et Thuret.

78. CAOM, SG-M-Justice, 29/253, August 31, 1830, Faits recueillis par M. Belletête,

juge de paix du canton de la Trinité, île Martinique, depuis le départ de Monsieur de Bour-dillon, procureur général.

79. Ibid.

80. For more on this commission and its role in colonial reform, see Lawrence C. Jennings, "The Revolution of 1830 and the Colonies," in Jennings, *French Anti-Slavery: The Movement for the Abolition of Slavery in France, 1802–1848* (Cambridge: Cambridge University Press, 2000), 30–32.

81. For more on the reforms of this period, and the abolitionist movement more generally, see Seymour Drescher, "British Way, French Way: Opinion Building and Revolution in the Second French Slave Emancipation," *American Historical Review* 96 (1991): 709–34; Jennings, "The Revolution of 1830 and the Colonies"; and Alyssa Goldstein Sepinwall, *The Abbé Grégoire and the French Revolution: The Making of Modern Universalism* (Berkeley: University of California Press, 2005).

82. Archives parlementaires, Series 2, volume 63, 664–684, September 25, 1830, Chamber of Deputies; *Courrier français*, September 26, 1830.

83. CAOM, SG-M-Police, 76/610, Fort-Royal, September 26, 1830, Rapport confidentiel du capitaine Cardini à M. de Saint-Hilaire, directeur des colonies.

84. CAOM, SG-M-Police, 18/159, March 12, 1831, Monsieur le gouverneur du procureur général du roi.

85. Ibid.

86. CAOM, SG-M-Police, 76/610, December 1, 1830, Rapport confidentiel du capitaine de la gendarmerie de la Martinique.

87. Ibid.

88. CAOM, SG-M-Police, 123/1103, Fort Royal, December 28, 1830, Le capitaine de la gendarmerie, Rapport confidentiel à Monsieur de St. Hilaire, directeur des colonies.

89. Ibid.

90. Léo Elisabeth, "The French Antilles," in *Neither Slave Nor Free: The Freedman of African Descent in the Slave Societies of the New World*, ed. David W. Cohen and Jack P. Greene (Baltimore: Johns Hopkins University Press, 1972).

91. *Gazette des Tribunaux*, "Colonies: Faits-observations," October 22, 1831.

92. CAOM, SG-M-Police, 76/610, December 1, 1830, Rapport confidentiel du capitaine de la gendarmerie de la Martinique.

93. CAOM, SG-M-Police, 18/161, May 19, 1831, Extrait du registre des procès verbaux des délibérations du conseil privé de la Martinique; CAOM, SG-M-Police, 18/161, April 16, 1831, Rapport de M. Dariste au ministre de la marine et des colonies; CAOM, SG-M-Police, 18/160, Rapport du capitaine Cazeneuve, commandant le navire Martinique, sur les événemens du février 1831 en Martinique; CAOM, SG-M- Police, 18/160, Lettre sur les derniers événemens de Saint Pierre, Martinique.

94. CAOM, SG-M-Police, 18/162, April 5, 1831, Acte d'accusation, Cour royale de la Martinique.

95. AD-M, BOM, no. 606, Arrêté qui préscrit la promulgation à la Martinique, de l'ordonnance royale ci-dessus (no. 605, Ordonnance du Roi accordant la jouissance entière

des droits civils aux gens de couleur libres, Donne à Paris, 24 février 1831), au Fort-Royal, 29 avril 1831.

96. Jacques Adélaïde Merlande, "Les reformes institutionnelles et la crise de fevrier 1831," in *L'Historial antillais*, vol. 3 (Pointe-à-Pitre, Guadeloupe: Dajani, 1981), 267.

97. CAOM, SG-M- Police, 18/162, May 21, 1831, Lettre du gouverneur Dupotet au ministre de la marine et des colonies. For a discussion of this event, see Geores B. Mauvois, "Nègres effrontés et rebelles," in *Un complot d'esclaves: Martinique, 1831* (Grenoble: Pluriels de Psyché, 1998), 87–89. Other primary sources note that twenty-three or twenty-four people were executed on May 19, and Merlande argues that twenty-six were originally sentenced to death, and three received a stay of execution. I have chosen to use Governor Dupotet's official account to the Ministry of the Marine that claims the government executed twenty-two individuals.

98. *Revue des colonies* 5, November 1834, 13.

99. CAOM, SG-M-Justice, 141/1272, November 15, 1831, Lettre du ministre de la marine et des colonies au LeChevalier; CAOM, SG-M-Justice, 141/1272, March 20, 1832, Lettre du ministre de la marine et des colonies au Monsieur Fleuriau, délégué de la Martinique.

100. For a full discussion of the Saint Pierre uprising, see Rebecca Hartkopf Schloss, "The February 1831 Slave Uprising in Martinique and the Policing of White Identity," *French Historical Studies* 30, 2 (Spring 2007): 203–36.

101. CAOM-SG-M-Police, 18/162, April 5, 1831, Acte d'accusation, Cour royale de la Martinique.

102. *Gazette des Tribunaux*, "Colonies françaises: Cour royale de la Martinique, 5 avril 1831," June 9, 1831.

103. Mauvois argues that, in fact, whites, *gens de couleur*, and enslaved blacks plotted to overcome the government in the 1831 uprising but that administrators worked to quickly squelch any evidence of the participation of the two whites or of unquestionably free people of color, all in a desire to move swiftly to a conclusion that could not be appealed. Mauvois, *Un complot d'esclaves*, 135–39.

104. CAOM, SG-M-Police, 18/162, Acte d'accusation, Cour royale de la Martinique, April 5, 1831.

105. CAOM-SG-M-Registre 125, Procès-verbal du Conseil général (1827–1835).

106. Ibid., July 12, 1831, Lettre du conseil général à la ministère de la marine.

107. Ibid.

108. *Gazette des Tribunaux*, "Colonies françaises,"October 20, 1831.

109. For a transcript of Juston's justicification to the minister of the marine, published and disseminated in Paris in 1832, see Xavier Tanc and Adolphe Juston, *Les Kalmanquious: Des magistrats indésireables aux Antilles en temps d'abolition*, ed. Jacqueline Picard (Gosier, Guadeloupe: Caret, 1998).

110. CAOM, SG-M-Instruction publique, 97/853, February 24, 1832, Le gouverneur de la Martinique au ministre de la marine. According to Delisle, the method of "enseignement mutuel" or mutal instruction "was very efficient because the more advanced students instructed their schoolmates." It also was very popular among the "liberal milieu" in power

in France during this period. Philippe Delisle, *Renouveau missionnaire et société esclavagiste: La Martinique, 1815–1848* (Paris: Publisud, 1997), 92.

111. CAOM, SG-M-Instruction publique, 97/853, February 24, 1832, Le gouverneur de la Martinique au ministre de la marine.

112. CAOM, SG-M-Instruction publique, 97/853, April 17, 1832, Fabien et Bissette au ministre de la marine.

113. CAOM, SG-M-Instruction publique, 97/853, May 1, 1832, Rapport du bureau administrative de la ministère de la marine.

114. CAOM, SG-M-Instruction publique, 97/853, August 8, 1832, Directeur général de l'Intérieur, le Vicomte de Rosily, à Madame Ballin, née d'Aine.

115. CAOM, SG-M-Instruction publique, 97/853, August 9, 1832, Madame Ballin au Vicomte Rosily, directeur général de la Martinique.

116. Dessalles, vol. 1, 189–190, July 28, 1832, Pierre Dessalles à son frère Charles Dessalles.

117. Ibid.

118. Dessalles, vol. 1, 192n22, August 11, 1832, Pierre Dessalles à son frère Charles Dessalles.

119. CAOM, SG-M-Instruction publique, 97/855, Fort Royal, Martinique, September 4, 1832, Le Directeur général de l'interieur, Le Vicomte de Rosily au gouverneur.

120. CAOM, SG-M-Instruction publique, 97/855, September 17, 1832, Procès verbaux des délibérations du conseil privé de la Martinique.

121. CAOM, SG-M-Instruction publique, 97/853, November 6, 1832, Bureau administrative de la gouverneur de la Martinique au Ministre.

122. Dessalles, vol. 1, 199, February 24, 1833, Pierre Dessalles à son frère Charles Dessalles.

123. CAOM, SG-M-Police, 76/621, March 25, 1833, A. Luminais, commissaire de police, au monsieur le directeur général, rapport no. 47.

124. CAOM, SG-M-Police, 76/621, March 25, 1833, Luminais, rapport no. 47; CAOM, SG-M-Police, 76/621, March 29, 1833, Gouverneur Dupotet au directeur général.

125. CAOM, SG-M-Police, 76/621, March 25, 1833, Luminais, rapport no. 47.

126. Ibid.

127. CAOM, SG-M-Police, 76/621, April 8, 1833, Défense devant le conseil privé de la Martinique pour le Sieur de Haugwitz.

128. Ibid.

129. Ibid.

130. Ibid.

131. *Des Hommes de couleur et de leur emancipation civile-et-politique par un habitant planteur de la Guadeloupe* (Paris: Mary, 1830), as quoted in Pâme, *Cyrille Bissette*, 124.

132. BNF, Bissette, *À un colon, sur l'emancipation civile et politique appliquée aux colonies* (Paris: Le Doyen, 1830); Mondésir Richard, *Des hommes de couleur (5 septembre 1830)* (Paris: A. Mies, 1831).

133. CAOM, SG-M-Police, 18/160, Lettre sur les dernier événemens à Saint-Pierre, Martinique. For more on the legacy of Saint Domingue and the way that it was repre-

sented both rhetorically and through its refugees see, for example, Meadows, "Engineering Exile," and Meadows, "The Planters of Saint-Domingue, 1750–1804: Migration and Exile in the French Revolutionary Atlantic" (Ph.D. dissertation, Carnegie Mellon University, 2004); Jennifer Pierce, "Discourse of the Dispossessed: Saint-Domingue Colonists on the Revolution, Race, and Empire, 1789–1825" (Ph.D. dissertation, Binghamton University, 2005).

134. CAOM, SG-M-Police, 18/160, Lettre sur le derniers événemens à Saint-Pierre, Martinique.

135. *Journal du Havre*, April 12, 1831. For similar letters blaming the February uprising on the new government and its concessions to Martinique's *gens de couleur*, see also the letter from the commander of the Brave, *Journal du Havre*, May 7, 1831 and the letter from a French colonist, *Journal du Havre*, May 10, 1831.

136. CAOM, SG-M-Police, 18/160, *Le Temps, Journal des progres*, "Colonies," April 13, 1831.

137. *Gazette des Tribunaux*, "Colonies françaises: Cour royale de la Martinique," June 9, 1831.

138. *Journal du Havre*, "À Monsieur le Rédacteur du Journal du Havre," November 23, 1831.

139. David Lambert found a similar dynamic in Barbados following the 1816 Bussa Rebellion. David Lambert, "Locating Blame for the 1816 Rebellion," in *White Creole Culture: Politics and Identity During the Age of Abolition* (New York: Cambridge University Press, 2005), 105–39. In her analysis of marriage petitons from interracial couples residing in continental France during the early Restoration, Jennifer Heuer notes that, unlike in the 1830s, French authorities did not articulate concerns that white womanhood would be endangered by marriage between whites and *gens de couleur*. See Jennifer Heuer "The One drop rule in reverse?" Interracial Marriages in Napoleonic and Restoration France," *Laws and History Review* 27, 3 (Fall 2009).

140. *Revue des Colonies*, "Extrait des mémoires d'une créole de la Martinique," April 1835.

141. *Journal du Havre*, "Lettre de Saint Pierre, Martinique, 2 octobre 1831," November 21, 1831.

142. CAOM, SG-M-Police, 18/160, March 12, 1831, Dupotet à la ministère de la marine.

143. CAOM, SG-M-Police, 18/161, *La Tribune*, "Colonies," October 4, 1831.

144. *Gazette des Tribunaux*, "Colonies Françaises: Faits-Observations," October 22, 1831.

145. Dale W. Tomich, *Slavery in the Circuit of Sugar: Martinique and the World Economy, 1830–1848* (Baltimore: Johns Hopkins University Press, 1990), 36.

146. CAOM, SG-M-Police, 18/160, March 15, 1831, Lettre de St. Pierre, Martinique au Messieur Balguerie et compagnie à Bordeaux.

147. CAOM, SG-M-Police 18/160, Fort Royal, March 25, 1831, Dupotet à la ministère de la marine.

148. Tomich, *Slavery in the Circuit of Sugar*, 36.

149. *Journal du Havre*, April 9, 1831.

150. CAOM, SG-M-Police, 18/161, Le Havre, April 25, 1831, Les membres composant la chambre de commerce du Havre, à son excellence monsieur le ministre secretaire d'état de la marine et des colonies à Paris.

151. *Journal du Havre*, May 6, 1831.

152. *Gazette des Tribunaux*, "Justice criminelle: Cour de cassation," June 20, 1831.

153. *Gazette des Tribunaux*, "Execution de 24 condamnés à St. Pierre," July 6, 1831.

154. *Journal du Havre*, November 5, 1831.

155. *Gazette des Tribunaux*, "Urgence d'une législation coloniale," November 5, 1831.

156. *Gazette des Tribunaux*, "L'ordonnance sur l'affranchissement des esclaves," reprinted August 6, 1832.

CHAPTER 5. "TO ENSURE EQUALITY BEFORE THOSE LAWS TO FREE MEN, WHATEVER THEIR COLOR": CHANGING IDEAS OF FRENCH CITIZENSHIP

1. The law of April 24, 1833 as reprinted in *Revue des Colonies*, August 1834, 11.

2. Lawrence C. Jennings, *French Anti-Slavery: The Movement for the Abolition of Slavery in France, 1802–1848* (New York: Cambridge University Press, 2000), 34–36.

3. *Revue des Colonies*, "Des délégues de l'artistocratie colonial et des mandataires des hommes de couleur," August 1834, 12.

4. The law of April 24, 1833 as reprinted in *Revue des Colonies*, August 1834, 11. For a similar interpretation see Jennings, *French Anti-Slavery*, 36.

5. Philippe Delisle, *Renouveau missionnaire et société esclavagiste: La Martinique 1815–1848* (Paris: Publisud, 1997), 125.

6. SSJ, Classeur 3A, Lettres de Mère Marie-Thérèse Javouhey, no. 81, July 12, 1833, Marie-Thérèse Javouhey à Madame Rosalie.

7. Ibid.

8. For more on the concept of fusion through education in Martinique, see chap. 4 of Delisle, *Renouveau missionnaire*.

9. For more on Castelli's visit, see Delisle, *Renouveau missionnaire*, 89. CAOM, SG-M— Instruction publique, 97/848, Extrait du registre des procès verbaux des délibérations du Conseil privé de la Martinique.

10. *Gazette des Tribunaux*, "Colonies françaises: Événemens de la Martinique," March 12, 1834. A recently arrived metropolitan lawyer represented Césaire at trial.

11. *Gazette des Tribunaux*, "Chronique," March 20, 1834.

12. *Le Constitutionnel*, "Antilles françaises," February 18, 1834, no. 49.

13. *Gazette des Tribunaux*, "Colonies françaises: Événements de la Martinique."

14. Ibid.

15. Ibid.

16. Ibid.

17. *Gazette des Tribunaux*, "Colonies françaises: Cour d'assises de Saint-Pierre, Martinique," August 3, 1834.

18. *Le Constitutionnel*, "Antilles françaises," February 18, 1834, no. 49.

19. Ibid. On January 7, 1834, Emmanuel Halgan officially replaced governor Dupotet. Halgan took office on March 25, 1834. *Guide des sources de l'histoire de l'amérique latine et des Antilles dans les archives françaises* (Paris: Archives nationales, 1984), 645.

20. *Gazette des Tribunaux*, "Colonies françaises: Cour d'assises de Saint Pierre," August 20, 1834.

21. *Revue des Colonies*, September 1834, no. 3, 38; *Revue des Colonies*, September 1834, no. 3, 12, "Insurrections et leur cause a la Martinique."

22. CAOM, SG-M-Police, 84/686, June 14, 1834, La commissaire commandant Le Clerc au monsieur le directeur de l'interieur.

23. *Le Constitutionnel*, "Antilles françaises," February 18, 1834.

24. *Gazette des Tribunaux*, "Chronique," March 14, 1834.

25. *Gazette des Tribunaux*, "Chronique," March 20, 1834.

26. Ibid.

27. *Le Constitutionnel*, "Affaire de la Martinique," February 19, 1834, no. 50.

28. *Le Constitutionnel*, February 22, 1834, no. 53.

29. *Le Constitutionnel*, "Antilles françaises," February 18, 1834, no. 49.

30. *Journal de Paris*, February 20, 1834.

31. *Gazette des Tribunaux*, "Colonies françaises: Cour d'asises de Saint Pierre," August 20, 1834.

32. *Gazette des Tribunaux*, "Colonies françaises: Cour d'assises de Saint Pierre, Martinique," August 6, 1834.

33. Ibid.

34. *Gazette des Tribunaux*, "Colonies françaises: Cour d'assises de Saint Pierre, Martinique," August 3, 1834.

35. Dessalles, vol. 1, 200n30.

36. Dessalles, vol. 2, 86n2.

37. Dessalles, vol. 1, 178, December 27, 1827, Pierre Dessalles à sa mère.

38. Dessalles, vol. 1, 200, March 9, 1834, Pierre Dessalles à sa mère.

39. *Gazette des Tribunaux*, "Colonies françaises: Cour d'assises de Saint Pierre, Martinique," August 3, 1834.

40. Fabien, *Appel aux amis de l'humanité contre un épouvantable arrêt* (Paris, Imprimerie de Dezauch, Montmartre, no. 11, August 1834), 12.

41. *Gazette des Tribunaux*, "Colonies françaises: Cour d'assises de Saint Pierre, Martinique," August 3, 1834.

42. *Revue des Colonies*, July 1834; *Revue des Colonies*, August 1834.

43. Fabien, *Appel aux amis de l'humanité*, 14. For further examples of explicit reference to free mixed-race people's rightful inclusion in the French national family, see *Gazette des Tribunaux*, July 3, 1834.

44. *Revue des Colonies*, "Affaire de la Grand'Anse," Monsieur Gatine, August 1834, 15–16.

45. For more on the French reaction to British slave emancipation see especially Jennings, *French Anti-Slavery*, 48–49 and *French Reaction to British Slave Emancipation* (Baton Rouge: University of Louisiana Press, 1988).

46. For more on the society, see Seymour Drescher, "British Way, French Way: Opinion Building and Revolution in the Second French Slave Emancipation," *American Historical Review* 96, 3 (June 1991): 714; Jennings, *French Anti-Slavery*, 48–75; Nelly Schmidt, *Victor Schoelcher et l'abolition de l'esclavage* (Paris: Fayard, 1994); Patricia Motylewski, *La Société française pour l'abolition de l'esclavage, 1834–1850* (Paris: L'Harmattan, 2000).

47. *Gazette des Tribunaux*, "Justice Criminelle: Cour de Cassation," September 14, 1834.

48. *Gazette des Tribunaux*, "Justice Criminelle: Cour de Cassation," November 24, 1834.

49. Ibid.

50. Ibid.

51. *Gazette des Tribunaux,* "Justice Criminelle: Cour de Cassation," November 28, 1834.

52. *Gazette des Tribunaux*, "Chronique," January 1, 1835.

53. These efforts are thoroughly documented in chapter 4 of Jennings, *French Anti-Slavery*. See as well Drescher, "British Way, French Way," 716.

54. *Journal de Paris*, "Intérieur," April 23, 1835.

55. *Journal de Paris*, "Revue de la Semaine," April 27, 1835.

56. *Revue des Colonies*, May 1835, 28.

57. Léo Elisabeth, "The French Antilles," in *Neither Slave Nor Free: The Freedman of African Descent in the Slave Societies of the New World*, ed. David W. Cohen and Jack P. Greene (Baltimore: Johns Hopkins University Press, 1972), 138–39.

58. CAOM, SG-M-Police, 84/687, Parquet du Tribunal de 1 ère instance, no. 47, Fort Royal, January 16, 1837, Procureur du roi, Le Royer Dubisson au procureur général Arsène Nogues.

59. Ibid.

60. Ibid.

61. Ibid.

62. Ibid.

63. Elisabeth, "The French Antilles," 151.

64. Frédéric Régent, *La France et ses esclaves: de la colonization aux abolitions (1620–1848)* (Paris: Grasset & Fasquelle, 2007), 283.

65. Ibid.

66. Robin Blackburn, *The Overthrow of Colonial Slavery (1776–1848)* (London:Verso, 1988), 487.

67. AN, FD- AD XIX, L Analyse des votes des conseils coloniaux, Quatrième session, ouverte le 23 mai, close le 4 août 1836, 249.

68. CAOM, BOM, March 15, 1839, no. 354, Arrêté qui constitue de nouveau les bureaux de charité de Fort Royal, Saint Pierre, du Marin et de la Trinité, 92.

69. *Revue des Colonies*, January 1837, 273.

70. For more on Mackau's time in Martinique see, for example, Jennings, *French Anti-Slavery*, 190–91.

71. CAOM, SG-M-Affaires politiques, 46/376, Copie d'une dépêche adressée par le Ministre de la marine au gouverneur de la Martinique en date du 11 juillet 1837.

72. CAOM, SG-M-Instruction publique, 97/850, February 15, 1837, Extrait d'une lettre du gouverneur de la Martinique au ministre; Note en réponse aux questions de l'abbé de la Mennais, October 1836, as quoted in Delisle, *Renouveau missionnaire*, 92.

73. CAOM, SG-M-Instruction publique, 97/848, Extrait du registre des procès verbaux des délibérations du Conseil privé de la Martinique.

74. CAOM, SG-M-Information, 2/10, September 10, 1836, Notes sur la Martinique soumises à Monsieur de St. Hilaire, conseiller d'état, directeur des colonies, par M. Gallaird Montbrun, juge de paix du canton de la Trinité.

75. CAOM, SG-M-Instruction publique, 97/848, October 3, 1836, Extrait du registre des procès verbaux.

76. Ibid.

77. CAOM, SG-M-Instruction publique, 97/861, February 13, 1833, Extrait du registre des procès verbaux des délibérations du Conseil privé de la Martinique.

78. Dessalles, vol. 2, 3, January 7, 1837.

79. For other women who looked to open private schools for Martinican girls during this period, see CAOM, SG-M-Instruction publique, 97/861, April 1, 1845, Extrait du registre des procès verbaux délibérations du conseil privé; AD-M, BOM, March 1837, no. 780, 50; AD-M, BOM, July 1837, no. 822, 138; CAOM, SG-M-Instruction publique, 97/861, July 23, 1838, Extrait du registre des procès verbaux délibérations du conseil privé.

80. CAOM, SG-M-Instruction publique, 97/861, January 23, 1838, Extrait du registre des procès verbaux délibérations du conseil privé . For more on Villeneuve, see AD-M, CG, C8A105, 1802, fol. 9, September 1802, Devrigny au Décrès, ministre de la marine.

81. AD-M, BOM, July 1839, Mlle Marin est autorisée à se livrer à l'instruction publique, 1839, 322; Bibliothèque Schoelcher, [hereafter BS], *Le Courrier de la Martinique*, February 15, 1842.

82. AN, FD, Analyse des votes des conseils coloniaux, May 18, 1835, Conseils coloniaux, Troisième session, 37; AD-M, Conseil privé, December 4, 1837, crédit supplémentaire de 4657.90 centimes pour l'hospice des orphelins de Saint Pierre.

83. SSJ, 3A, Lettres de Mère Marie-Thérèse Javouhey, no. 94, April 21, 1836, 153.

84. SSJ, 2Ah3, État statistique des établissments depuis leur fondation jusqu'en 1852.

85. Ibid.; SSJ, 3A, Lettres de Mère Marie-Thérèse Javouhey, no. 100, April 2, 1838, 162.

86. Ibid., no. 103, September 6, 1838, 168.

87. SSJ, 2Ah3, État statistique des établissments.

88. CAOM, BOM, Décision pour l'ouverture d'un Pensionnat de jeunes filles a Fort-Royal, July 1837, no. 822, 138; Décision pour l'ouverture d'un Pensionnat de jeunes filles a Fort-Royal, November 1837, no. 825, 233.

89. SSJ, 3A, Lettres de Mère Marie-Thérèse Javouhey, no. 100, April 2, 1838, 162.

90. CAOM, SG-M-Instruction publique, 97/850, February 15, 1837, Extrait d'une lettre du gouverneur de la Martinique à la ministère de la marine.

91. CAOM, SG-M-Instruction publique, 97/855, n.d., Mademoiselle Garnerin au governeur de la Martinique; CAOM, SG-M-Instruction publique, 97/855, October 9, 1837, Procès verbaux des délibérations du conseil privé de la Martinique.

92. Ibid.

93. Dale W. Tomich, *Slavery in the Circuit of Sugar: Martinique and the World Economy, 1830–1848* (Baltimore: Johns Hopkins University Press, 1990), 66–67.

94. Dessalles, vol. 2, 28, March 9, 1837.

95. Ibid.

96. Ibid.; vol. 2, 92, January 23, 1838.

97. Ibid., vol. 2, 30, March 16, 1837.

98. Ibid., vol. 2, 67, October 17, 1837.

99. Ibid., vol. 2, 30, March 16, 1837.

100. Ibid., vol. 2, 59, August 30, 1837.

101. Ibid.

102. Ibid., vol. 2, 77, December 1, 1837.

103. The commission consisted of nine members, seven of whom in some way supported the antislavery cause.

104. Jennings, *French Anti-Slavery*, 109–12.

105. *Revue des Colonies*, February 1839, 274.

106. These efforts are thoroughly documented in chap. 4 of Jennings, *French Anti-Slavery*.

107. Although he uses it to describe the situation of mixed-race people traveling throughout the Atlantic world, Paul Gilroy's notion of "double consciousness" is also a useful way to conceptualize the tensions between metropolitan/European identity and colonial/Creole identity for elite whites like Dessalles. See, for example, chapter 1, "The Black Atlantic as a Counterculture of Modernity," in Paul Gilroy, *The Black Atlantic: Modernity and Double Consciousness* (Cambridge, Mass.: Harvard University Press, 1993).

108. Dessalles, vol. 2, 124–25, July 18, 1838.

109. Ibid., 126–27, July 23, 1838.

110. See the editors' introduction to Dessalles, vol. 2, 9; Dessalles, vol. 1, February 1833; as well as Robert Forster's editorial notes in Pierre Dessalles, *Sugar and Slavery, Family and Race: The Letters and Diary of Pierre Dessalles, Planter in Martinique, 1808–1856*, ed. and trans. Elborg Forster and Robert Forster (Baltimore: Johns Hopkins University Press, 1996), 43, 44, 78, 81, 90.

111. Dessalles, vol. 2, 121–22, July 9, 1838.

112. Dessalles, vol. 1, 108–10, April 29, 1824, Pierre Dessalles à sa mère.

113. See, for example, Dessalles, vol. 2, 87, diary entry for January 4, 1838.

114. Dessalles, vol. 2, 98, diary entry for February 8, 1838.

115. Ibid., vol. 2, 103, diary entry for March 5, 1838.

116. Ibid., vol. 2, 108, diary entry for March 30, 1838.

117. Dessalles, vol. 2, 152, November 19, 1838.

118. Dessalles, vol. 2, 144, September 24, 1838; Dessalles, vol. 2, 158, December 13, 1838.

119. Ibid., 131, August 10, 1838.

120. Ibid.

121. For a fuller discussion of these two possibilities, see Dessalles, *Sugar and Slavery*, 19.

122. Dessalles, vol. 2, 24–25, February 17, 1837.

123. Ibid., 154–55, November 25 and 26, 1838; 160, December 27, 1838; 166, February 9, 1839.

124. Ibid., 131, August 13, 1838.

125. Ibid., 137, September 8, 1838.

126. According to colonial taxonomies, the offspring of a supposedly white person and someone who was considered seven-eighths white was called a *quateron(ne)*. *Gazette des Tribunaux*, "Police correctionelle de Bordeaux," December 31, 1836.

127. Ibid.

128. *Gazette des Tribunaux*, "The Devoted," June 2, 1839.

129. Ibid.

130. Ibid.

131. Ibid.

132. For an extensive analysis of the antislavery movement during this period, see Jennings, *French Anti-Slavery*, especially chap. 5, "Abolitionist Proposals and Parliamentary Commissions," 103–34.

133. See, for example, *Revue des Colonies*, July 1836; *Revue des Colonies*, December 1836.

134. Bibliothèque de l'Arsenal, [hereafter BA] *Collection de Journaux*, Paris, *Le Siècle*, Monday January 21, 1839.

CHAPTER 6. "AMELIORATION OF THE WHITE RACE" AND "THE SACRED RIGHTS OF PROPERTY": THE END OF SLAVERY IN THE FRENCH ATLANTIC

1. Dessalles, vol. 2, 190n15, July 5, 1839.

2. Ibid.

3. AD-BOM, July 1839, June 11, 1839, ordinance, 288.

4. *Revue des Colonies*, September 1840, 87.

5. AN, AD XIX L 248, Martinican Colonial Council, November 1, 1839, session, 82.

6. *Exécution de l'ordonnance royale du 5 janvier 1840 . . .* (Paris: Imprimerie Royale, April 1842), 8.

7. Dessalles, vol. 2, 248–49, May 8, 9, 11, 14, 15, 1840.

8. Ibid., 349, *Annexe, Documents 1 A, Lettre rédigée le 15 mai 1840*.

9. Ibid., 249, Pierre Dessalles, May 15, 1840.

10. Ibid., 351–52, *Annexe, Documents 1B, Lettre rédigée le 6 juin 1840*.

11. Ibid., 258, July 9, 1840.

12. AN, BB 17A 136, Paris, February 10, 1844, À Monsieur le Garde des Sceaux de Conseil des délégues des colonies françaises, Baron Charles Dupin.

13. Dessalles, vol. 2, 190, July 4, 1839.

14. *Tableaux et relevés de population, de culture, de commerce, de navigation, etc. formant, pour l'année 1839, la suite des tableaux et relevés insérés dans les notices statistiques sur les colonies françaises* (Paris: Imprimerie Royale, 1842); *Tableaux de population, de culture, de*

commerce, et de navigation, formant, pour l'année 1841, la suite des tableaux et relevés insérés dans les notices statistiques sur les colonies françaises (Paris: Imprimerie Royale, July 1847).

15. CAOM, SG-M-Instruction publique, 97/855, July 30, 1840, Extrait du mémoire laissé par M. à son successeur dans le gouvernement de la Martinique.

16. CAOM, SG-M-Instruction publique, 97/850, Extrait du compte moral & raisonné du directeur de l'intérieure a la Martinique pour l'exercice 1839.

17. CAOM, SG-M-Instruction publique, 97/855, July 30, 1840, Extrait du mémoire laissé par M.

18. Ibid.

19. CAOM, SG-M-Instruction publique, 97/855, 1840, n.d., Mlle. Garnerin au gouverneur.

20. Ibid.

21. CAOM, SG-M-Instruction publique, 97/855, August 24, 1841, Amiral gouverneur du Valdailly au ministre de la marine.

22. SSJ, 2Ah5, Lettres de Mère Onésime, July 4, 1839.

23. Ibid., August 1, 1839.

24. Ibid., December 12, 1839.

25. SSJ, 2Ah3, État statistique des établissements depuis leur fondation depuis 1852. For more on the role of the Sisters of Saint Joseph in teaching free mixed-race girls, see Liliane Chauleau, *La Vie quotidienne aux antilles françaises au temps de Victor Schoelcher: XIXe siècle* (Paris: Hachette, 1979), chap. 12, "L'Enseignement source de promotion," 277–310.

26. SSJ, 2Ah5, Lettres de Mère Onésime, August 1, 1839.

27. Ibid., June 17, 1840.

28. Ibid., April 27, 1841.

29. Ibid., August 1, 1839; 2Ah3, État statistique des établissements.

30. SSJ, 2Ah5, Lettres de Mère Onésime, July 4, 1839; SSJ, 2Ah5, Lettres de Mère Onésime, November 23, 1839; SSJ, 2Ah5, Lettres de Mère Onésime, March 16, 1840.

31. Ibid., November 20, 1839; SSJ, 2Ah5, Lettres de Mère Onésime, March 16, 1840.

32. SSJ, 2Ah3, État statistique des établissements.

33. Dessalles, vol. 2, 197, July 27, 1839.

34. See, for example, ibid., 208–9, September 9, 1839; ibid., 214, October 7, 1839.

35. Ibid., 217, November 10, 1839.

36. Ibid., 210, September 17, 1839.

37. Dessalles, vol. 3, 33, July 14, 1842; Dessalles, vol. 3, 35, August 3, 1842.

38. Ibid., 10–11, January 17–21, 1842.

39. Ibid., 33, July 14, 1842.

40. Upon their arrival, the three women joined two of the other Dessalles children, Calixte and Adrien Dessalles. The remaining two children, Louise and Henri, remained on the continent to complete their educations.

41. Dessalles, vol. 2, 123, July 14, 1838.

42. Ibid., 289, January 3, 1841.

43. Ibid., 223, December 10, 1839.

44. Ibid., 222, December 13, 1839; 232, January 13, 1840; 248, May 9, 1840; 249, May 11, 14, 15, 18, 1840; 250, May 25, 1840; 274, October 29, 1840; 302, March 30, 1841.

45. Ibid., 323, June 14, 1841.

46. According to the editors of Dessalles's journal, his daughter, Calixte Dessalles Valmenier, believed "no one will take better care of her father than a half-brother of color." They give no other evidence to confirm that Saturnin was Pierre Dessalles's son. However, because these journals were published by Dessalles's descendants, who appear to have exercised some form of editorial control in other parts of the diary, such an admission is striking. Dessalles, vol. 4, 193n52. For more on the role of Saturnin in the Dessalles family, see Pierre Dessalles, *Sugar and Slavery, Family and Race: The Letters and Diary of Pierre Dessalles, Planter in Martinique, 1808–1856*, ed. and trans. Elborg Forster and Robert Forster (Baltimore: Johns Hopkins University Press, 1996), 20.

47. Dessalles, vol. 2, 279, November 16, 1840.

48. Ibid., 330, August 2, 1841.

49. In her studies of the colonial period in South East Asia, Ann Stoler has found similar evidence of colonial society's efforts to reproduce the metropole in the colony. See, for example, Stoler, "Sexual Affronts and Racial Frontiers—European Identities and the Cultural Politics of Exclusion in Colonial Southeast-Asia," *Comparative Studies in Society and History* 34, 3 (July 1992); and "Carnal Knowledge and Imperial Power: Gender, Race, and Morality in Colonial Asia," in *Gender at the Crossroads of Knowledge: Feminist Anthropology in the Postmodern Era*, ed. Micaela di Leonardo (Berkeley: University of California Press, 1991).

50. Dessalles, vol. 2, 280, November 24, 1840.

51. Ibid., 293, February 1, 1841; 334, August 28, 1841.

52. Dessalles, vol. 3, 99, December 22, 1843.

53. Dessalles, vol. 2, 308, April 17, 1841.

54. Dessalles, vol. 3, 13, January 31, 1842.

55. See Chapter 4.

56. Dessalles, vol. 3, 30, June 25, 1842.

57. For a fuller discussion of the complicated relationships between Martinique's female inhabitants, see Rebecca Hartkopf Schloss, "'Superb Ladies,' 'Uncultivated Creoles,' and 'Intimate Friends': Female Identity in Nineteenth-Century Martinique," in *Pouvoirs dans la Caraïbe*, special issue, Série Université de juillet, Session 1998 (September 2000): 15–32.

58. *Gazette des Tribunaux*, "Colonies françaises," January 22, 1841. In October 1841, a decree finally stipulated that masters could only confine their slaves to solitary confinement for fifteen consecutive days, and then only in police facilities. *Gazette des Tribunaux*, "Chronique," October 2, 1841.

59. *Les Français peints par eux-mêmes: Encyclopédie morale du dix-neuvième siècle*, tôme 8, (Paris: Curmer, 1841–1842), Duke University, Rare Book, Manuscript, and Special Collections Library.

60. Ibid., vol. 8, 285–86.

61. Ibid., 292.

62. Ibid., 295.

63. Ibid., 293, 295.

64. Ibid., 307.

65. Ibid., 307, 308.

66. Ibid., 293.

67. *Revue des Colonies*, July 1840, Gourard Fauvel, "Memoirs d'un Créole de la Martinique," 18–20.

68. Ibid.

69. Victor Schoelcher, *Des Colonies françaises: Abolition immédiate de l'esclavage*, reproduction of the 1842 edition (Basse-Terre: Société d'histoire de la Guadeloupe, 1976) 88–89, 242n.

70. *Revue des Colonies*, September 1840, "Portefeuille colonial: Les beautés princières des antilles," 97–103.

71. Jennings argues that as early as 1835 the colonial lobby in Paris had paid Granier de Cassagnac, "one of the leading defenders of servitude," to defend them in local journals sympathetic to slavery. Granier de Cassagnac also appears to have been in the pay of Guadeloupean delegates between 1835 and 1837. Apparently, he was so close to the colonial lobby that in September of 1841, the colonial representative Jollivet authorized him to receive 7,500 francs to serve as "second editor" for the pro-slavery *Le Globe* (previously known as *L'Outre-Mer* and run by Granier de Cassagnac in 1837) as well as additional amounts for his other writings. While Granier de Cassagnac served the colonial lobby, Pierre Dessalles personally felt he was a "confidence man" who would write anything if the price was right. See Lawrence C. Jennings, "Slavery and the Venality of the July Monarchy Press," *French Historical Studies* 17, 4 (1992): 957–978 and *French Anti-Slavery: The Movement for the Abolition of Slavery in France, 1802–1848* (New York: Cambridge University Press, 2000), 80–81; Dessalles, vol. 2, 336, September 10, 1841. For more on other aspects of Granier de Cassagnac's career, see William M. Reddy, chap. 5, "Condottieri of the Pen: The Political Honor of Journalists," in Reddy, *The Invisible Code: Honor and Sentiment in Postrevolutionary France, 1814–1848* (Berkeley: University of California Press, 1997), 217–20; and Karen Offen, *Paul de Cassagnac and the Authoritarian Tradition in the Nineteenth Century* (New York, Garland, 1991).

72. *Revue des Colonies*, September 1840, "Portefeuille colonial: Les beautés princières des antilles," 96.

73. Seymour Drescher also has noted the close relationship between colonials and their "allies" among merchants in Atlantic port cities. See "British Way, French Way: Opinion Building and Revolution in the Second French Slave Emancipation," *American Historical Review* 96, 3 (June 1991): 716.

74. Dale W. Tomich, *Slavery in the Circuit of Sugar: Martinique and the World Economy, 1830–1848* (Baltimore: Johns Hopkins University Press, 1990), 67–71.

75. *Tableaux de population, de culture, de commerce, et de navigation* (1847).

76. Dessalles, vol. 3, 69, April 21, 1843.

77. Ibid., 69, April 25, 1843.

78. Ibid., 78, July 13, 1843.

79. Ibd., 85, September 14, 1843.

80. Ibid., 112, April 28, 1844.

81. Ibid.

82. *Tableaux de population, de culture, de commerce, et de navigation* (1847).

83. Dessalles, vol. 3, 94, November 25, 1843.

84. Ibid., 76, June 22, 1843.

85. SSJ, 2Ah5, Lettres de Mère Onésime, March 4, 1843.

86. SSJ, 2Ah3, État statistique des établissements.

87. SSJ, 2Ah5, Lettres de Mère Onésime, May 8, 1844; July 26, 1844; SSJ, 2Ah3, État statistique des établissements.

88. AD-M, 5K12, Conseil privé, September 26, 1839, Donation faite par Monsieur EYMA à l'hospice des orphelins; Dessalles, vol. 2, 190, July 5, 1839.

89. AD-M, BOM, 1842, no. 1309, Arrêté réglant les conditions d'admission et de sortie des enfants entretenus à l'hospice des orphelines, 191–93.

90. Schoelcher, *Des Colonies françaises*, 200.

91. AD-M, BOM, 1842, no. 1309, Arrêté réglant les conditions d'admission et de sortie, 191–93.

92. Ibid.

93. SJS, 2Ah5, January 29, 1844, Lettre de la Mère Onésime à la supérieure générale, Saint Pierre.

94. AN, BB 17A 136/5, February 10, 1844, À Monsieur le Garde des Sceaux du Conseil des délégues des colonies françaises, Baron Charles Dupin.

95. SSJ, 2Ah3, État statistiques des établissements.

96. SSJ, 2Ah5, Lettres de Mère Onésime, March 4, 1843.

97. Ibid., May 8, 1844; SSJ, 2Ah3, État statistiques des établissements.

98. CAOM, SG-M-Instruction publique, 97/855, October 1842, Mademoiselle Garnerin au conseil privé.

99. Ibid.

100. CAOM, SG-M-Instruction publique, 97/855, November 2, 1843, Extrait du registre de procès-verbaux des délibérations du conseil privé de la Martinique.

101. CAOM, SG-M-Police, 84/685, June 6, 1843, À M. le gouverneur par M. le procureur général.

102. CAOM, SG-M-Police, 84/685, June 8, 1843, C. Amiral Gouverneur Du Valdailly au Ministre de la Marine.

103. *Journal du Havre*, July 23/24, 1843.

104. Ibid.

105. CAOM, SG-M-Police, 84/685, June 6, 1843, À M. le gouverneur par M. le procureur général.

106. CAOM, SG-M-Police, 84/685, June 8, 1843, C. Amiral Gouverneur Du Valdailly au Ministre de la Marine.

107. Dessalles, vol. 3, 240, March 16, 1840.

108. Ibid., 288, December 30/31, 1840.

109. Dessalles, vol. 1, 157, May 26, 1825.

110. Dessalles, vol., 3, 95, November 27, 1843.

111. Ibid., 81, August 11, 1843.

112. *Journal du Havre*, "Pétitions à la chambre des députés," March 27/28, 1842.

113. *Le Sud*, March 23, 1842.

114. *Journal du Havre*, "Effets de la décision ministérielle relative à la question des sucres," March 18, 1842.

115. *Journal du Havre*, "Au rédacteur, question des sucres," March 19, 1842.

116. *Journal du Havre*, "Colonies: Cour d'Assises de la Martinique," February 9, 1844.

117. *Revue des Colonies*, April 1842, "Enfans trouvés," 430.

118. Ibid.

119. Ibid., 431.

120. *Revue des Colonies*, March 1842, "Mulâtres-Blancs," 383–84.

121. *Revue des Colonies*, April 1842, "Enfans trouvé," 432.

122. Ibid.

123. Bernard-Adolphe Granier de Cassagnac, *Voyage aux Antilles françaises, anglaises, danoises, espagnoles* (Paris: Dauvin et Fontaine Libraires, 1842), 227–29.

124. Ibid., 227.

125. AN, AD XIX L 241, Emploi des fonds alloués pour l'enseignement religieux des noirs et l'introduction des travailleurs libres, 1846, March 31, 1846. Compte rendu au roi de l'emploi des fond alloués, depuis 1839, pour l'enseignement religieux et élémentaire des noirs, et de l'execution des lois des 18 et 19 juillet 1845 relatives au régime des esclaves, etc., du Ministre de la Marine.

126. Jennings disscusses the Mackau laws in *French Anti-Slavery*, 214–28.

127. Dessalles, vol. 4, 174, June 6, 1845.

128. AN, AD XIX L 241, Emploi des fonds alloués pour l'enseignement religieux des noirs et l'introduction des travailleurs libres, 1846, March 31, 1846; SS2, Formation d'établissements agricoles, compte rendu au roi de l'emploi des fonds alloués, depuis 1839, pour l'enseignement religieux et élémentaire des noirs, et de l'execution des lois des 18 et 19 juillet 1845 relatives au régime des esclaves, etc., du ministre de la marine.

129. AN, AD XIX L 241, Emploi des fonds alloués pour l'enseignement religieux des noirs et l'introduction des travailleurs libre, 1846, August 29, 1845, Extrait d'une dépêche du ministère de la marine à messieurs les gouverneurs de la Martinique et de la Guadeloupe, annexe no. 17, 116.

130. Bernard Moitt, *Women and Slavery in the French Antilles*, 1635–1848 (Bloomington: Indiana University Press, 2001), 167.

131. For a broader discussion of the difficulties of *rachat*, see Jennings, *French Anti-Slavery*, 220 and Moitt, *Women and Slavery in the French Antilles*, 167–72.

132. *Mémorial Bordelais*, "Conseil colonial de la Martinique," June 26, 1846.

133. AN, AD XIX L 241, Emploi des fonds alloués pour l'enseignement religieux des noirs et l'introduction des travailleurs libre, 1846, August 29, 1845, Extrait d'une dépêche.

134. *Tableaux de population, de culture, de commerce et de navigation, formant, pour l'année 1845 insérés dans les notices statistiques sur les colonies françaises* (Paris: Imprimerie Nationale, January 1849), 10–11.

135. Ibid.

136. CAOM, Généralités-Immigration, 147/1238, May 4, 1845, Monsieur St. Croix au ministre de la marine.

137. Ibid. The ministry finally responded in September 1845 and informed DeHuc that his request was not likely to be accepted and that, according to the new regulations outlined in the July 18 and 19 Mackau laws, he should address his plan to the local Martinican administration. CAOM, Généralités-Immigration, 147/1238, September 12, 1845, Ministère de la Marine au Monsieur DeHuc.

138. CAOM, Généralités-Immigration, 147/1238, July 2, 1845, Monsieur Titalin, St. Louis, Missouri à la ministère de la marine.

139. AN, AD XIX L 241, Emploi des fonds alloués pour l'enseignement religieux des noirs et l'introduction des travailleurs libres, 1846, August 29, 1845, Extrait d'une dépêche.

140. One creative planter, Durhemin, even attempted to use the Mackau laws not to request money for workers, but rather to sell the government his seven-hectare plantation by the sea for use as a model farm. AN, AD XIX L 241, Emploi des fonds alloués pour l'enseignement religieux des noirs et l'introduction des travailleurs libre, 1846, March 31, 1846, SS2. Formation d'établissements agricoles, Compte rendu au roi de l'emploi des fond alloués, depuis 1839, pour l'enseignement religieux et élémentaire des noirs, et de l'execution des lois des 18 et 19 juillet 1845 relatives au régime des esclaves, etc., du ministre de la marine.

141. CAOM, Généralités-Immigration, 147/1238, November 10, 1845, M. Cassius de Linval au ministre de la marine; September 1, 1846, Gouverneur de la Martinique au ministre de la marine.

142. CAOM, Généralités-Immigration, 147/1238, September 13, October 8, 1846, Linval fils au ministre de la marine.

143. AN, AD XIX L 241, Emploi des fonds alloués pour l'enseignement religieux des noirs et l'introduction des travailleurs libres, 1846, March 31, 1846, Compte rendu au roi de l'emploi des fonds alloués.

144. AN, AD XIX L 241, Emploi des fonds alloués pour l'enseignement religieux des noirs et l'introduction des travailleurs libres, 1846, August 29, 1845, Extrait d'une dépêche, 115.

145. CAOM, Généralités-Immigration, 147/1236, July 27, 1845, Monsieur Jean St. Nicosse au ministre de la marine.

146. AN, AD XIX L 241, Emploi des fonds alloués pour l'enseignement religieux des noirs et l'introduction des travailleurs libres, 1846, March 31, 1846, SS2, Formation d'établissements agricoles.

147. Ibid.

148. AN, AD XIX L 241 Emploi des fonds alloués pour l'enseignement religieux des noirs et l'introduction des travailleurs libres, 1846, Tableau des établissements d'instruction élémentaire existant à la Martinique en décembre 1845, 62–63.

149. Ibid.

150. Ibid.

151. Ibid.; Dessalles, vol. 2, 285, December 25, 1840; 291, January 17, 1841; CAOM,

SG-M-Instruction publique, 97/861, January 4, 1847, Extrait du registre des procès verbaux délibérations du conseil privé.

152. SSJ, 2Ah5, Lettres de Mère Onésime, July 26, 1845.

153. Ibid., February 3, 1846.

154. Ibid., July 3, 1846.

155. Ibid., August 25, 1846.

156. Ibid., July 3, August 25, 1846

157. Ibid., July 3, 1846.

158. Ibid.

159. Ibid., September 23, 1846.

160. Ibid.

161. Ibid., October 19, 1846.

162. Javouhey, *Lettres III*, Lettre 708, À mère Rosalie Javouhey, à Cluny, August 21, 1846, 273.

163. SSJ, 2Ah5, Lettres de Mère Onésime, February 10, 1847.

164. Javouhey, *Lettres III*, Lettre 732, À mère Onésime Lefèvre, à la Martinique, 304.

165. SSJ, 2Ah5, Lettres de Mère Onésime, February 25, 1847; SSJ, 2Ah3, État statistiques des établissements.

166. AN, AD XIX L 241, Emploi des fonds alloués pour l'enseignement religieux des noirs et l'introduction des travailleurs libres, 1846, Tableau des établissements d'instruction élémentaire existant à la Martinique en décembre 1845, 62–63; CAOM, SG-M-Instruction publique, 97/861, January 4, 1847, Extrait du registre des procès verbaux délibérations du conseil privé.

167. SJS, 2Ah5, January 29, 1844, Lettre de la Mère Onésime à la supérieure générale.

168. CAOM, SG-M-Instruction publique, 97/860, December 11, 1845, Gouverneur de la Martinique au ministre de la marine, confidentielle.

169. CAOM, SG-M-Instruction publique, 97/860, September 27, 1848, Testut au ministre de la marine.

170. CAOM, SG-M,-Instruction publique, 97/860, December 11, 1845, Gouverneur au ministre de la marine.

171. Ibid.

172. CAOM-SG-M, Instruction publique, 97/860, January 8, 1846, Gouverneur de la Martinique au ministre de la marine.

173. CAOM, SG-M-Instruction publique, 97/855, August 3, 1846, Extrait du registre des procès verbaux délibérations du conseil privé.

174. CAOM, SG-M-Instruction publique, 97/855, February 3, 1847, Extrait d'un rapport du directeur de l'intérieur à la Martinique; CAOM, SG-M-Instruction publique, 97/855, December 10, 1847, Extrait d'un rapport du ministre de la marine; CAOM, SG-M-Instruction publique, November 22, 1857, Gouverneur au ministre de la marine.

175. AN, AD XIX L 241, Dépenses acquittés pour l'augmentation du clergé, la construction des chapelles, et le service de l'enseignement gratuit pendant les années, emploi des fonds alloués pour l'enseignement religieux des noirs et l'introduction des travailleurs libres, 1846, 19.

176. SSJ, 2Ah5, Lettres de Mère Onésime, March 10, 1845, November 19, 1845

177. Ibid., March 10, 1845.

178. SSJ, 2Ah3, État statistiques des établissements; SSJ, 2Ah5, Lettres de Mère Oné-sime, November 19, 1845.

179. AN, AD XIX L 241, Tableau des établissements d'instruction élémentaire existant à la Martinique en décembre 1845, Emploi des fonds alloués pour l'enseignement religieux des noirs et l'introduction des travailleurs libres, 1846.

180. AN, AD XIX, L 241, Annexe no. 11, observations générales des gouverneurs sur l'enseignement religieux et élémentaire des noirs, extrait d'une lettre du gouverneur de la Martinique au ministre de la marine, en date décembre 25, 1845, 92.

181. Jennings, *French Anti-Slavery*, 238–39.

182. At least 53 Martinican and 24 Guadeloupean Creole planters lived in Paris in 1847. See Jennings, *French Anti-Slavery*, 258.

183. Dessalles, vol. 3, 137, September 12, 1844; 140, October 6, 1844; 177, July 10, 1845; 179, August 9, 1845; 188, November 19, 1845.

184. Ibid., 122, June 21, 1844.

185. Ibid., 154, January 12, 1845; Ibid., 210, May 9, 1846.

186. Ibid., 189, November 19, 1845.

187. Ibid., 208, April 19, 1846.

188. Ibid., 187, October 22, 1845.

189. Ibid., 199, February 19, 1846.

190. Ibid., 142, October 11, 1844.

191. Ibid., 161, February 25, 1845.

192. Ibid., 208, April 18, 1846.

193. Jennings, *French Anti-Slavery*, 235; Dessalles, vol. 3, 213, May 21, 1846.

194. Dessalles, vol. 3, 217, May 30, 1846; 208, April 18, 1846.

195. Ibid., 217, May 30, 1846.

196. Ibid., 188, November 16, 1845.

197. Ibid., 218, June 6, 1846.

198. Ibid., 219, June 13, 1846.

199. Ibid., 229, September 6, 1846.

200. Ibid.

201. Ibid. Dessalles encouraged his youngest son, Henri, to attend the nuptials. When they came to pass however, neither Henri nor Dessalles's oldest son, Adrien, attended; 234–35n35, November 12, 1846, Pierre Dessalles to Henri Dessalles.

202. Jennings, *French Anti-Slavery*, 246.

203. Dessalles, vol. 3, 172, May 31, 1845; June 4, 1845; 173, June 5, 1845; 202, March 11, 1846.

204. Ibid., 246, April 3, 1847.

205. Ibid.

206. Jennings, *French Anti-Slavery*, 247; *Journal officiel de la Martinique*, May 26, 1847.

207. Dessalles, vol. 3, 249, April 28, 1847.

208. CAOM-Généralités, 173/1388, May 30, 1847, Reizet and Jabrun to president of the Colonial Council of Guadeloupe.

209. Dessalles, vol. 3, 250, May 10, 1847.

210. Ibid., 252, June 11, 1847.

211. Ibid., 259–60, August 28, 1847.

212. Ibid., 260, August 30, 1847.

213. Ibid., 262, September 25, 1847.

214. Ibid., 264, October 16, 1847.

215. Ibid., 265, October 21, 1847.

CONCLUSION

1. In early 1857, at the urging of his children, Pierre Dessalles returned to the continent, where he took ill and died in March 1857. He was buried in Paris's Père Lachaise cemetery next to his wife, Anna Dessalles. His family, however, lived on. All the children spent the remainder of their days in continental France, and by 1886 they no longer owned any property in their father's beloved Martinique. For more on the Dessalles family, see "Conclusion," in Dessalles, vol. 4.

2. For a detailed look at this phenomenon in a previous period see Alison Games, *Migrations and the Origins of the English Atlantic World* (Cambridge, Mass.: Harvard University Press), 1999.

3. See, for example, Bernard Moitt, *Women and Slavery in the French Antilles, 1635–1848* (Bloomington: Indiana University Press, 2001) and Frédéric Régent, *La France et ses esclaves: De la colonisation aux abolitions, 1635–1848* (Paris: Grasset, 2007).

4. For a recent example of such work see Catherine A. Reinhardt, *Claims to Memory: Beyond Slavery and Emancipation in the French Caribbean* (New York: Berghahn, 2006).

INDEX

ACKNOWLEDGMENTS

THIS BOOK HAS been a long time in the making, and I could not have completed it without the support of numerous individuals and institutions.

My early graduate seminars with Nancy Hewitt, Bill Reddy, and Susan Thorne at Duke University opened my eyes to pressing questions in comparative women's history, the history of nineteenth-century France, and the study of empire, and planted the seeds for this book. Each helped me think through different aspects of the project, as did my colleagues in these classes, and I thank them all for their support. Summer research grants from the Ford Foundation's "Oceans Connect" program, administered in part by Duke University's Center for International Studies, and a Katherine Stern Dissertation Year Fellowship from Duke University's Graduate School supported the research for this project at critical moments.

At the departmental archives in Martinique, Liliane Chauleau offered me her expertise and encouragement during the early stages of my research. Myriam Cottias and Nancy Green did the same at the Université de juillet, a week-long seminar that brought together scholars working on the Caribbean at the University of the Antilles-Guyane's Schoelcher campus. I thank the seminar participants for their engaging intellectual exchange and for introducing me to *zouk* and dookoonu. At the French colonial archives in Aix-en-Provence, a number of staff members provided invaluable assistance, and I especially thank my fellow scholars Tanisha Fazal and Jennifer Sessions for their personal support and fun-filled companionship on outings to Mont Sainte-Victoire, Arles, and Cannes during my time in southern France. I could not have completed important research at the Archives nationales, Bibliothèque de l'Arsenal, and Bibliothèque nationale de France, without Nat Godley and Steven Rowe, who allowed me to sleep on their couch in Paris for four weeks and listened to me ramble on about Martinique in the evenings. I thank them for their generosity and their good cheer. The very helpful staff at the Public Records Office/National Archives in Kew, UK also gave freely of their time to help a French historian navigate the sometimes confusing records of the nineteenth-century British Empire.

At Texas A & M University, generous support from the College of Liberal Arts, the Department of History and the Melbern G. Glasscock Center for Humanities Research allowed me the time and financial support to turn my dissertation into a publishable manuscript. Members of the Queer Studies Working Group of the Melbern G. Glasscock Center for Humanities Research and the Department of History's Junior Faculty Reading Group provided feedback on part of Chapter 3, and Cyndy Bouton, Laurent Dubois, Katherine Carté Engel, April Hatfield, Sylvia Hoffert, and Harold Livesay read the complete manuscript at one time or another. I thank all of them for their critical input, their professional collegiality, and their friendship. At the University of Pennsylvania Press, Bob Lockhart and Kathleen Brown read the manuscript and provided invaluable feedback that dramatically improved this book, and Alison Anderson and the editorial staff helped shepherd me through the production process. I thank them for their time and generous spirit.

I also thank my family, near and far, for their constant love and support during this long process. My parents, Mary and David Hartkopf, have repeatedly expressed their pride in my accomplishments, and my brothers, Scott and Eric, remind me it is important to laugh a little, too. I thank my in-laws, Stina and Kurt Schloss, for generously sharing their house in the Colorado Rockies so I could finally finish my dissertation, and I am grateful to my Texas cousins, Peter, Hadass, and Meravie Schloss, for providing a slice of home when we were far away from other family. Last, but never least, I thank my husband, Steven George Schloss, who was here before the project began and will remain after it is finished, and my daughter, Hazel Kallio Schloss, whose boundless energy and excitement keep me grounded in the here and now.